P9-CET-270

THE STORM
and Other Russian Plays

THE STORM

and Other Russian Plays

Translated and Introduced by

DAVID MAGARSHACK

A MERMAID DRAMABOOK

HILL AND WANG – NEW YORK

Manufactured in the United States of America
by the Colonial Press

CONTENTS

INTRODUCTION

THE SIXTY-ODD YEARS that separate Gogol from Gorky have witnessed a remarkable growth of Russian dramatic writing of the most varied type and character. The best illustration of this is provided by the five famous plays in this volume, of which three, *The Government Inspector*, *The Storm* and *Uncle Vanya*, were written by dramatists of genius and two, *The Power of Darkness* and *The Lower Depths*, by writers of genius who, though not dramatists *par excellence*, were able to make a considerable contribution to the Russian theatre.

Gogol wrote *The Government Inspector*, one of the greatest masterpieces of Russian drama, at the age of twenty-six. It took him two months to write it: from October to the beginning of December, 1835. The subject of the comedy was suggested to him by Alexander Pushkin, who two years earlier had been mistaken for a secret government agent during his travels through some of the remoter parts of the Russian Empire. The play was first performed at the Alexandrinsky Theatre on April 19, 1836, in the presence of Nikolai I, who seemed to have greatly enjoyed it and is reported to have remarked: "Everyone has caught it, but I have caught it more than anyone." But in spite of the royal patronage, the play aroused a storm of protests from high-placed Russian officials who quite rightly saw themselves displayed in a far from flattering light on the stage. The result was a violent campaign of abuse against Gogol. "Everyone is against me," Gogol wrote to a friend. "Elderly and respectable civil servants are declaring that I hold nothing sacred. Policemen are against me, shopkeepers are against me, the literary clique is against me . . . And these are the people who are already trying to get my play banned. Now I realize what it means to be a comic writer. The least sign of truth and all classes of the population rise up against you." Indeed, the attacks on Gogol became so vicious that he left Russia and, but for two short visits to Moscow, spent the next thirteen years abroad, mostly in Rome.

Gogol was present at the rehearsals of his play in Petersburg and, like many another playwright, was appalled at the way it was mangled by the producer and the actors. He therefore left a number of valuable notes on the way in which he wanted certain characters in his play acted. One of these deals with Khlestakov, the play's chief character. It was important to keep in mind, Gogol insisted, that Khlestakov was not a "professional liar," that, in fact, he was not aware that he was telling lies and was almost convinced of the truth of what he said. "He lets himself go," Gogol wrote. "He is in high spirits. He sees that everything is going well, that he is listened to, and for that reason he speaks smoothly and unconstrainedly, and while telling his lies, reveals himself for what he really is. Khlestakov," Gogol continues, "does not lie at all wildly or in a boastfully theatrical way; he lies with feeling, and the spectator ought to be able to see in his eyes the pleasure he derives from it. To all appearances, he does not differ from any other young man. Indeed, he carries himself well, even speaks with authority sometimes, and only where presence of mind and character are required does his mean and trivial nature come to light. . . . What in the last analysis is Khlestakov?" Gogol asks. "A worthless young man, but one who has many qualities possessed by people whom the world would not call worthless. To show these qualities would be unjust, for by doing so the author would hold them up to ridicule. Rather let everyone find a part of himself in that role . . . In short, this character must be the type of many things one finds in different people, but which, as often happens in real life, have been concentrated in one character. Everyone becomes a Khlestakov for a moment or for several moments. . . ." Gogol, indeed, might have said the same about the other characters of his comedy. Each of them possesses an individuality of his own and yet at the same time something that makes him a

universal character, a character that can be found everywhere in the world in conditions quite different from
those prevailing in Russia in the reign of Nikolai I.

In another note Gogol deals at length with the last
scene of the play, undoubtedly one of the most difficult
scenes to be produced satisfactorily. Gogol maintains that
this scene can never be successful until it is clearly understood that "it ought to represent a group turned to stone,
that here drama comes to an end and is replaced by dumb-
show, that the curtain must not come down for two or
three minutes, that all this ought to resemble the so-called
tableaux vivants." And in reply to the objection that such
a scene might cramp the actors' style, he declares that a
man of talent can never be confined within prescribed
limits. "A sensitive actor," he writes, "can express everything in a given pose. His face is free to express any
emotion; it is only the grouping that is composed. In this
dumb show there is infinite variety. The panic of each
character is as different as his nature. The extent of his
fear depends on the extent of his transgressions. The
Mayor is struck dumb in a different way from his wife
and daughter; the Judge is scared in a different way, and
so are the Postmaster, the Inspector of Schools, etc. Bobchinsky and Dobchinsky are struck dumb in a special way
and turn to each other with a question frozen on their
lips. Only the guests are struck dumb in the same way,
but they form the background of the scene which must
be painted with one stroke of the brush and in one and
the same color. In short, everyone has to carry on with
his part in mime. . . ."

Gogol revised the text of *The Government Inspector*
in 1842 preparatory for its publication in the fourth volume of his collected works. It was in this edition that he
added the famous words the Mayor addresses to the audience: "What are you laughing at? You are laughing at
yourselves!"—a line that emphasized the play's tremendous
social implications.

The Storm, Alexander Ostrovsky's great tragedy, is also,
according to Russian critics, not so much a personal
tragedy of a young girl caught between the upper millstone
of a great love for a man too pitifully inadequate to be

worthy of it and the nether millstone of a ruthless and tyrannical mother-in-law and a weak-willed husband, as a protest against what one brilliant Russian critic called "the dark realm" of ignorance, brutality and acquisitiveness that were so characteristic of the Moscow merchant class in the fifties and sixties of the last century. The more radical Russian critics even went so far as to see in the heroine's suicide not only a condemnation of the intolerable social and economic conditions of those days, but also a prophecy that the Russian people would no longer tolerate the police state of the Tsars. It is very doubtful, however, whether Ostrovsky, whose sixteenth play it was, had any other intention than to write a tragedy of a young woman whose religious scruples were in violent conflict with her personal feelings and whose fundamental purity and innocence were crushed by the ignoble instincts of the people among whom she was forced to live.

Ostrovsky began writing his famous tragedy on July 1, 1859, finishing it on October 9. The play was first performed on November 16 of the same year at the Maly Theatre in Moscow, where most of Ostrovsky's plays were performed under his personal direction. It was published in January, 1860, and in September of the same year the Russian Academy awarded Ostrovsky the Uvarov Prize for it. Tchaikovsky wrote an overture for it (he gave up the idea of writing an opera), and later on Ostrovsky wrote a libretto based on his play for the Russian composer V. Kashperov, whose opera *The Storm* was first performed in Petersburg and Moscow at the end of October, 1867. More recently the Czech composer Janacek wrote his now famous opera *Katya Kabanova*, which follows closely upon the text of Ostrovsky's tragedy.

Unlike *The Storm*, Tolstoy's realistic tragedy of peasant life cannot by any stretch of the imagination be said to have any social and political implications. Its sole moral purpose becomes apparent from Tolstoy's epigraph from St. Matthew (5:28-29): "But I say unto you, that whosoever looketh on a woman to lust after her hath committed adultery with her already in his heart. And if thy right eye offend thee, pluck it out, and cast it from thee: for it is profitable for thee that one of thy members should perish, and not that thy whole body should be cast into hell."

Tolstoy wrote *The Power of Darkness* while recovering from a serious illness in the autumn of 1886. "What am I doing?" he wrote to his chief disciple, V. G. Chertkov, on November 14, 1886. "I have just written a drama on the subject of adultery. I think," he added rather gruesomely, "it is good."

About ten years later Tolstoy revealed to a newspaper correspondent that he had got the plot of the play from an account of a murder trial held at the Tula district court. "The trial," Tolstoy declared, "dealt with the same facts as in *The Power of Darkness*, the murder of a child the accused had had by his stepdaughter and his public confession at his stepdaughter's wedding. The poisoning of the husband is my own invention, but all the chief characters of the play were suggested by an actual occurrence." Tolstoy, in fact, was given the particulars of the trial by the public prosecutor of the Tula district court as far back as 1880. Six years later his friend A. A. Stakhovich visited him in Yasnaya Polyana and, at his request, read him the plays of Gogol and Ostrovsky. When Stakhovich visited Tolstoy three weeks later, Tolstoy said to him: "Your reading shook me up. After you had gone, I wrote a play. Either I've forgotten what a play ought to be like or it really has turned out something marvelous."

Tolstoy revised the play seven times. It was first published in the twelfth volume of his collected works in 1886. In a letter to a correspondent, written on March 5, 1887, Tolstoy gave the following additional particulars about Akim: "According to my idea, Akim is fair-haired and not at all gray or bald; his hair even curls a little and his beard is scant. He talks with a slight stammer. Words burst from him suddenly, but every now and then he falters and all he can bring out is: 'I mean, er-er. . . .' I don't think he mumbles. He walks with firm steps; splayed feet in bast shoes. His movements and gestures are full of animation and it is only fluency of speech that God has denied him. He is very observant. He listens carefully to what people say and is particularly attentive to the person whose opinions he approves of, but if he hears anything that is against his moral convictions, he immediately shows his disapproval and looks uneasy. At the sight of his son's shocking behavior in Act Three he must be seen to suffer physically. Use should be made," Tolstoy emphasized, "of the contrast between his comic and incoherent blabbering and the fervent and sometimes solemn enunciation of the words he does succeed in uttering properly. In Act Five he must at first resist his son's invitation to enter the house, being loath to be present at such a wedding, but soon he begins to realize his son's intention and is beside himself with delight at his son's action, and at the end of the act he even uses physical force in order to prevent those who are trying to interfere with his son's solemn confession."

The Power of Darkness was not performed on the professional stage in Russia till 1895. Alexander III was at first greatly impressed by the play which he had read to him and was in favor of its being staged, but he changed his mind at the intervention of Tolstoy's bitter enemy, the Procurator of the Holy Synod, K. P. Pobedonostsev, who maintained that the play represented "a negation of ideas," "a debasing of moral values" and "an offense against good taste." The play was thereupon banned by the censor. When Tolstoy met the young Konstantin Stanislavsky (at the time an amateur actor and producer) in Tula in 1893, he said to him: "Please, do all you can to gladden the heart of an old man. Remove the ban from *The Power of Darkness* and get it performed." But it took another two years before the play was licensed for public performances. It was performed by the Moscow Art Theatre for the first time in 1902.

Chekhov, who first saw *The Power of Darkness* performed in Moscow by an amateur company on January 12, 1890, was present at the Moscow Art Theatre production of the play but was not particularly impressed by the acting. "The actors," he wrote to a correspondent, "are nothing to write home about, but there is a great deal of conscientiousness and love of the theatre in the production." Chekhov only knew the Moscow Art Theatre when Stanislavsky and his company were still young and inexperienced. He never agreed with Stanislavsky's interpreta-

tion of his plays, though *Uncle Vanya* was the only play
of his whose production by the Moscow Art Theatre did
not actually provoke him to violent criticism. Chekhov
himself regarded the play as "old-fashioned." What he
meant was that as a revised version of an old unsuccessful
play of his (*The Wood Demon*), it did not possess the
consummate technical skill of his three other great indirect-
action plays. It was for that reason that he subtitled the
play: "Country Scenes in Four Acts."

Chekhov completed *Uncle Vanya* before the end of
1896, and it was first published in 1897. The play was
first performed by the Moscow Art Theatre on October
26, 1899, and was only moderately successful. It had
previously appeared on the provincial stage where it was
a much greater success. "My *Uncle Vanya*," Chekhov
wrote to his elder brother, Alexander, "is being performed
all over the provinces and is a great success everywhere.
You never know, do you? I never had any great hopes
for it."

Although a free adaptation of *The Wood Demon*,
Chekhov always insisted that *Uncle Vanya* was quite a
new play. And so, indeed, it is. It is completely shorn of
the melodramatic inconsistencies of its parent play and,
in fact, is both structurally and psychologically the most
marvelously well knit of all Chekhov's plays. It is not only
compact, but also highly expressive dramatically. Its main
theme, contrary to what is generally assumed, is not frus-
tration but courage and hope. In no other of Chekhov's
great plays is the contrast between two of his female
characters so subtly drawn, Sonia (Sophia) representing
spiritual beauty and Yelena (Helen) physical beauty. The
same symbolism is evident in the names of Astrov, the
doctor, who, in spite of his down-to-earth realism, is a
true idealist, whereas Voynitsky, who at the age of forty-
seven is still spoken of by everybody by his pet name of
Uncle Vanya, is the false idealist who comes to realize
too late that he has sacrificed his life to a phantom, a
"soap bubble," a "learned minnow." (Chekhov character-
ized the difference between the two characters in this
cryptic fashion: "Uncle Vanya," he told Stanislavsky,
"cries, but Astrov whistles. Understand? He whistles.")

The most common mistake in the production of *Uncle Vanya* is to treat Professor Serebryakov as a humbug, for such treatment necessarily reduces Uncle Vanya himself to the stature of an ineffectual fool, which he most certainly is not. Serebryakov is, of course, a most distinguished scholar whose "fame" easily deceives the romantic Uncle Vanya. It was only after the professor had retired from the university and had descended upon his first wife's estate that Uncle Vanya became disillusioned with him and as a result of this disillusionment realized for the first time that his life had been wasted.

If *Uncle Vanya* presented the Russian playgoing public as well as the producers and the actors of the Moscow Art Theatre with a new kind of highly charged dramatic experience, Maxim Gorky's *The Lower Depths* presented them with an entirely new set of human types, the down-and-outs, the tramps, who for the first time in the history of the Russian stage became the heroes of a dramatic work.

Gorky's first idea of the play differed greatly from its final version. This is how Gorky described it to Stanislavsky in Yalta at the beginning of 1900:

"A doss house, a huge, stuffy room, a long, boring winter. Their horrible life turns the inmates into beasts. They lose patience, they give up hope, they get on each other's nerves and spend all their time philosophizing. Everyone does his best to show that he is still a human being. An ex-waiter is particularly fond of his paper shirt front, the only thing that remains of the evening dress he once wore. To annoy the ex-waiter someone steals his shirt front and tears it in two. When the ex-waiter discovers his torn shirt front, he is in despair, for with its destruction the last link with his former life is snapped, and the whole place is suddenly turned into a bear garden. The fighting and quarreling go on till late at night, peace at last being restored by the news that a police raid is expected. After secreting everything of a compromising nature, they all lie down on their bunks and pretend to be asleep. The police arrive. Someone is led away to the police station. The tramps fall asleep on their bunks. Only one man climbs slowly down from the stove, takes out a candle end, lights it and starts praying. Then the head of a Tartar appears from some bunk. 'Pray for me,' the Tartar murmurs."

It will be seen that with the exception of the doss house, the praying pilgrim and the Tartar, nothing of this original sketch remains in the final version of the play. A further rough sketch of the play which Gorky sent to a friend in October, 1901, gives a much fuller account of the characters: "Tramps, a Tartar, a Jew, an actor, the woman doss-house keeper, thieves, a detective, prostitutes. It will be terrific. I have the plans ready and I can visualize the characters, their speeches, the motives of their actions are clear to me—everything is clear!"

Gorky began writing *The Lower Depths* at the end of 1901 in the Crimea where he read some scenes to Tolstoy. In the spring of 1902 he read two acts of the play to Nemirovich-Danchenko, one of the directors of the Moscow Art Theatre. Exiled in Arzamas, he completed the play on June 15, 1902. The title of the play underwent several changes in the course of the writing. At first it was called "Without Sun," then "The Doss House," "The Bottom" and, finally, it appeared on the playbills of the Moscow Art Theatre as "At the Bottom" (its title literally translated). It was first performed on December 31, 1902, and its success was instantaneous.

Gorky himself was not altogether satisfied with the play. Apart from the fact that he had always had serious misgivings about his dramatic talents ("I have written twenty plays," he was to declare a few years before his death, "but all of them are just a series of badly strung together scenes"), he was worried about Satin's final speech, which he realized was completely out of character. "Satin's speech about man and truth," he wrote to a friend on July 15, 1902, "is very unconvincing. Unfortunately, there was no one else who could deliver it, and Satin himself could not possibly have put it more vividly. As it is, the speech does not sound natural in his mouth."

Challenged to justify the absence of "a signal to revolt" in *The Lower Depths* twenty years later, Gorky declared that the "signal" could be heard in Satin's last speech. In 1933, however, he dismissed the play as "old-fashioned," although, he added, it was still being performed after thirty years. "It was," he wrote, "the result of my observation of the world of 'has-beens.' I realized quite early in life that these people were incurable. When I created Bubnov, I saw before me not only the familiar tramp, but also a member of the intelligentsia, a former teacher of mine. Satin, a nobleman, a post-office official, a dipsomaniac and a rowdy who had served a four-year sentence for murder, also had his 'double'—the brother of one of our great revolutionaries who committed suicide in prison."

Weak though it is dramatically (it was Chekhov who pointed out to Gorky that no real dramatist would get rid of his leading characters before the last act), *The Lower Depths* is certainly Gorky's greatest play, and it has exerted a tremendous influence not only on Russian but also on European drama.

D. M.

THE GOVERNMENT INSPECTOR

A Comedy in Five Acts by

NIKOLAI GOGOL

It is no use blaming the looking glass if your face is crooked.
—A proverb

CHARACTERS

ANTON ANTONOVICH SKVOZNIK-DMUKHANOVSKY, *the Mayor*
ANNA ANDREYEVNA, *his wife*
MARIA ANTONOVNA, *his daughter*
LUKA LUKICH KHLOPOV, *Inspector of Schools*
MRS. KHLOPOV, *his wife*
AMOS FYODOROVICH LYAPKIN-TYAPKIN, *Judge*
ARTEMY FILIPPOVICH ZEMLYANIKA, *Superintendent of Infirmaries*
IVAN KUZMICH SHPEKIN, *the Postmaster*
PETER IVANOVICH DOBCHINSKY ⎫ *town landowners*
PETER IVANOVICH BOBCHINSKY ⎭
IVAN ALEXANDROVICH KHLESTAKOV, *a Petersburg civil servant*
OSIP, *his servant*
CHRISTIAN IVANOVICH HÜBNER, *district doctor*
FYODOR ANDREYEVICH LYULYUKOV ⎱
IVAN LAZAREVICH RASTAKOVSKY ⎱ *retired civil servants, dis-*
STEPAN IVANOVICH KOROBKIN ⎰ *tinguished town personages*
MRS. KOROBKIN ⎰
STEPAN ILYICH UKHOVERTOV, *the Police Superintendent*
SVISTUNOV ⎱ *constables*
DERZHIMORDA ⎰
ABDULIN, *a shopkeeper*
FEVRONYA PETROVA POSHLYOPKINA, *a locksmith's wife*
A SERGEANT'S WIDOW
MISHKA, *the Mayor's servant*
A WAITER AT THE INN
A GENDARME
GUESTS, SHOPKEEPERS, TRADESPEOPLE, PETITIONERS

CHARACTERS AND COSTUMES—
NOTES FOR THE ACTORS

The Mayor, grown old in the service and in his own opinion far from stupid. Though he takes bribes, he carries himself with the air of a conscientious public servant. He is serious, even somewhat sententious; talks neither too much nor too little, neither too loud nor too soft. His every word is significant. His features are hard and rough, as is usual with men who have started on the lowest rung of the civil service ladder. His transition from fear to rejoicing, from obsequiousness to haughtiness is rapid, as is usual with a person of coarsely developed instincts. He dresses, as a rule, in his uniform with facings and top boots with spurs. He wears his graying hair short.

Anna Andreyevna, his wife, a provincial coquette, in early middle age, brought up partly on novels and albums and partly by the bustle of household duties and by the supervision of girl serfs. She is very curious and at times very vain. Sometimes overrides her husband, but only because he is at a loss for an answer; but this is only true of trifles and finds expression in scoldings and sarcastic remarks. She changes her clothes four times in the course of the play.

Khlestakov, a young man of twenty-three, thin and slender; rather stupid or, as they say, not too bright, one of those who are known as brainless ninnies in government circles. He talks and acts without any reflection. He is incapable of concentrating for a moment on any idea. His speech is abrupt, and the words come out of his mouth quite unpredictably. The more the performer of this part displays frankness and ingenuousness, the more successful it will be. He is dressed fashionably.

Osip, Khlestakov's servant, is like most elderly servants. He is always in a serious frame of mind, tends to look on the ground when talking, likes to argue and repeat moral maxims to himself and to his master. His voice is almost always smooth, and when talking to his master he assumes a severe and even somewhat churlish expression. He is more intelligent than his master and hence much quicker to see which way the wind is blowing, but he dislikes talking a great deal and is a taciturn rascal. He wears a shabby gray or blue coat.

Bobchinsky and Dobchinsky are both shortish little men, very inquisitive; they are very much alike, both with small paunches;

3

they talk very rapidly and gesticulate a great deal. Dobchinsky is a little taller and more serious-minded than Bobchinsky, but Bobchinsky is more lively and free and easy.

Lyapkin-Tyapkin, the Judge, is a man who has read five or six books in his life and is, therefore, somewhat of a freethinker. He is rather keen on propounding his own theories and, consequently, gives his words great weight. The actor who performs this part must always look self-important. He speaks in a bass voice with a drawl, wheezing like an old-fashioned clock before it strikes.

Zemlyanika, the superintendent of the town infirmary, is a fat man, slow and clumsy, but for all that a rogue and intriguer. Very officious and bustling.

The Postmaster is simplehearted to the point of naïveté.

The other parts do not need any special explanation. Their prototypes are to be found everywhere.

The actors must pay particular attention to the last scene. The last word uttered on the stage must have the effect of an electric shock on all the characters of the play. Its effect must be instantaneous. The whole group must change its attitude in the twinkling of an eye. All the women must utter a cry of astonishment simultaneously, just as though it escaped them at one and the same moment. The whole effect of the scene can be ruined if these instructions are not faithfully observed.

THE GOVERNMENT INSPECTOR

ACT ONE

A room in THE MAYOR's *house.*

THE MAYOR. I've asked you to come and see me, gentlemen, because I have a very unpleasant piece of news to
communicate to you: we're going to have a visit from a
Government Inspector.

Lyapkin-Tyapkin. A Government Inspector!

Zemlyanika. A Government Inspector!

The Mayor. A Government Inspector from Petersburg.
Incognito. And with secret orders.

Lyapkin-Tyapkin. Good Lord!

Zemlyanika. We've had no worries, and now. . . .

Khlopov. Dear me, and with secret orders!

The Mayor. I had a premonition, you know: last night
I kept dreaming about two enormous rats. I've never seen
anything like them before: black, of quite an unnatural
size. They came, they sniffed and they went away again.
But let me read you the letter I've received from Andrey
Ivanovich Chmykhov. You know him, Zemlyanika. This
is what he writes: "Dear friend and benefactor [*mutters
under his breath, running through the letter quickly*] . . .
and to inform you. . . ." Oh, yes! "I hasten incidentally
to inform you that an official has arrived with instructions
to inspect the whole province and especially our district.
[*Raises his finger significantly.*] I've learned this from most
trustworthy people, though he passes himself off as a private person. I know that, like the rest of us, you have your
little foibles, for you are a sensible fellow and you don't

5

like to let things slip through your fingers. . . ." [*Pausing.*]
Well, we're all friends here. . . . "So I advise you to
take precautions, for he may arrive any moment, if indeed he hasn't already arrived and is living somewhere
incognito. . . . The other day I . . ." Well, this is just
family affairs. . . . "My sister Anna Kirilovna and her
husband are staying with us; Ivan Kyrilovich has put on
weight and does nothing but play the fiddle . . . Et
cetera, et cetera. So that's the position!

Lyapkin-Tyapkin. Yes, it's, er—an extraordinary position.
Yes, quite extraordinary. There's something behind it.

Khlopov. But why, Mr. Mayor? Why? Why send a
Government Inspector to us?

The Mayor. Why? I expect it's just fate! [*With a sigh.*]
Till now, thank God, they've been taking other towns by
surprise, and now it's our turn, I suppose.

Lyapkin-Tyapkin. I can't help thinking, Mr. Mayor, that
there's a deep and more of a political reason here. What
I mean is, that Russia, you see, is about to, er—er—go
to war, and the ministry, you see, has sent this official to
find out if there is treason anywhere.

The Mayor. Good heavens, the things you think of!
And you an intelligent man, too! Treason in a district
town! We're not a frontier town, are we? Why, you could
gallop from here for three years and not reach a foreign
country.

Lyapkin-Tyapkin. No, sir, let me tell you you're wrong.
You don't—er— You see, the authorities have all sorts of
deep-laid plans: our town may be far away, but it has to
take everything into account.

The Mayor. Whether it does or does not take everything into account, I've warned you, gentlemen. You see,
I've already taken some measures in my own department
and I advise you to do the same. Especially you, Zemlyanika. I have no doubt the official will first of all want
to inspect the infirmary under your supervision. So you'd
better see that everything is in decent order: see that the
nightcaps are clean and that the patients don't look like
blacksmiths as they usually do in their everyday clothes.

Zemlyanika. Oh, well, that's nothing much. I daresay
we could let them have clean nightcaps.

The Mayor. Yes, and see that over every bed there's an inscription in Latin or some other foreign language. . . . That's something that concerns you, doctor. I mean, what illness, and when each patient was taken ill, the day, the date. . . . And I don't think your patients ought to smoke such strong tobacco. Makes me sneeze every time I enter a ward. And it would be much better if there were fewer of them. He'll think it's due to bad management or the incompetence of the doctor.

Zemlyanika. Oh, the doctor here and I have taken all the necessary measures for the treatment of our patients: the nearer to nature, the better. We don't use expensive medicines. After all, they are only peasants. If they die, they die. If they get better, they'd get better anyhow. Besides, the doctor would find it difficult to explain himself. He doesn't know a word of Russian.

DR. HÜBNER *emits a sound partly like the letter "i" and partly like the letter "e."*

The Mayor. And as for you, my dear judge, I'd advise you to do something about your courtroom. Your porter keeps geese and goslings in the antechamber, and the birds keep darting under the applicants' feet. Now, of course, it's a very good thing to keep poultry and there is no reason in the world why a porter should not keep them, except that, you see, it doesn't look nice in a place like that. I meant to mention it before, but I kept forgetting.

Lyapkin-Tyapkin. I'll order them to be taken to my kitchen today. Would you like to come to dinner tonight?

The Mayor. And, besides, I don't think it's nice at all that all sorts of rubbish is hanging out to dry in your courtroom and a hunting crop over the cupboard with the official documents. I know, of course, that you're very fond of hunting, but I should tidy it up for the time being at any rate. When the inspector's gone, you could put it back again. Then there is that clerk of yours. I mean he may be a mine of information, but he smells as though he had just come out of a distillery. That isn't very nice, is it? I meant to tell you about it a long time ago, but something happened at the time to put it out of my mind. Can't remember what it was. If it really is, as he says, his natural body odor, there must be a remedy for it: you could tell him to eat onions or garlic or something, or perhaps the doctor could prescribe something for it.

DR. HÜBNER *emits the same kind of sound.*

Lyapkin-Tyapkin. No, I'm afraid it's impossible to get rid of it. He says his nurse dropped him when he was a child and he has smelt a little of vodka ever since.

The Mayor. Oh, well, I thought I'd mention it. As for the way you conduct the business in the court and what Chmykhov in his letter calls little foibles, I simply don't know what to say. And, indeed, what is there to say? What man is without sin? The good Lord has arranged it that way, and it's no use freethinkers protesting against it.

Lyapkin-Tyapkin. But what do you mean by little foibles? There are sins and sins. I freely admit I take bribes. But what sort of bribes? Borzoi puppies. That's quite a different matter.

The Mayor. Well, puppies or something else—it's bribes just the same.

Lyapkin-Tyapkin. No, sir, it is not. Now, if, for instance, a man takes a fur coat worth five hundred rubles, or a shawl for his wife. . . .

The Mayor. Well, what does it matter if you do take Borzoi puppies as bribes? The trouble is, my dear sir, that you do not believe in God! You never go to church! I, at any rate, am firm in my faith and I go to church every Sunday. But you. . . . Oh, I know you. When you start talking about the creation of the world, it makes my hair stand on end.

Lyapkin-Tyapkin. Well, at least I've thought it all out for myself—it's my own views.

The Mayor. Well, in some cases, a lot of brains is worse than none at all. However, I've only mentioned the district court. To tell the truth, hardly anyone is likely to look into it: a place like that is to be envied—God himself must be protecting it. It is you, my dear Khlopov, who, as Inspector of Schools, must keep an eye on the teachers. They are, of course, great scholars, educated in all sorts of colleges, but their behavior is certainly very peculiar, though it may be part of their learned profession. One of them, for instance, I mean the fellow with a fat face—can't remember his name—always makes faces when he goes to his desk. Something like that [*makes a face*], and then he starts ironing out his beard from under his cravat. Now, of course, if he makes faces like that at one of the boys, it doesn't matter. It may be necessary, I'm afraid I don't know anything about that. But what if he should do the same thing to a visitor? It might lead to all sorts of very unfortunate consequences. The Government Inspector or some other official might think it was meant for him. Goodness only knows what might come of it.

Khlopov. What can I do with him? I've spoken to him about it several times. Only the other day when our marshal of nobility came into the classroom he made a face the like of which I never saw before! He did it with the best intentions, but I was reprimanded: why do I permit the boys' minds to be corrupted by godless ideas?

The Mayor. And there's the history master—I mean to say, a man of great erudition, one can see that. Must have a vast amount of knowledge. But he talks with so much heat that he quite forgets himself. I happened to hear him speak once. Well, I mean, while he was talking about the Assyrians and Babylonians he was all right, but when he came to Alexander the Great, I simply can't tell you what happened to him. I thought the house was on fire! He jumped down from the desk, got hold of a chair and banged it on the floor. Now, of course, Alexander the Great was a great general, but why break the chairs? After all, they are government property, and a broken chair is a loss to the treasury.

Khlopov. Yes, he certainly is a hothead. I've spoken to him several times about it, but he says: "Say what you like, but I'm ready to give my life in the cause of learning!"

The Mayor. Yes, such, I suppose, are the mysterious ways of Providence! Clever men are either drunkards or they make faces as if there's nothing sacred to them.

Khlopov. Well, I suppose there can't be anything worse than to serve in the department of education! You're afraid of everything: everyone interferes, everyone wants to show what a clever fellow he is.

The Mayor. All this wouldn't matter so much—it's this

damned incognito! He may look in any moment and say: "Ah, so that's where you are, my dear fellows. And who is judge here?" "Lyapkin-Tyapkin." "Let's have Lyapkin-Tyapkin here! And who is the Superintendent of Infirmaries?" "Zemlyanika." "Let's have Zemlyanika here!" That's what's so awful!

THE POSTMASTER *comes in.*

The Postmaster. Tell me, Gentlemen, what's all this about an official?

The Mayor. Why, haven't you heard?

The Postmaster. I heard something from Bobchinsky. He's just been to see me at the post office.

The Mayor. Well, what do you think about it?

The Postmaster. What do I think? Why, there's going to be a war with the Turks.

Lyapkin-Tyapkin. Just what I said! I thought the same myself.

The Mayor. And both wide of the mark.

The Postmaster. I'm sure it means war with the Turks. It's the Frenchmen up to their usual dirty tricks.

The Mayor. War with the Turks indeed! It's we who're going to catch it, not the Turks. That's clear enough. I've a letter.

The Postmaster. Ah, well, in that case, there won't be war with the Turks.

The Mayor. Well, and what do you think about it?

The Postmaster. Me? What about you?

The Mayor. What about me? I'm not frightened, I'm just perhaps a little bit uneasy. I'm worried about the shopkeepers and the tradesmen. I'm told they hate me like poison, but God knows, if I have taken anything from any of them, it has been without any ill feeling. You see, my dear sir [*takes him by the arm and leads him aside*], you see, I wonder whether there hasn't been some secret denunciation of me. Why else should they send a Government Inspector here? Now, look here, my dear fellow, couldn't you—er—open and read every letter which comes to the post office for the benefit of all of us? I mean, just unseal it a little bit and, well, read it through to see if there is any denunciation of any one of us, or simply anything about us. If not, you could seal it up again, or, indeed, deliver the letter unsealed.

The Postmaster. I know, I know. You can't teach me anything about that. I do it already, not as a precaution, but simply out of curiosity. You see, I like to know what goes on in the world. And let me tell you it makes most interesting reading. Some letters you read with real pleasure, all sorts of curious incidents are so excellently described and . . . it's so edifying! Much better than *The Moscow News*.

The Mayor. Well, tell me, have you found anything about an official from Petersburg?

The Postmaster. No, sir, nothing about a Petersburg official, but quite a lot about officials in Kostroma and Saratov. It's a pity you don't read those letters. There are beautiful passages in them. The other day, for instance, a lieutenant wrote to a friend describing a ball in a most playful way—very, very beautifully: "My life, dear friend," he wrote, "is spent in the empyrean: lots of girls, bands playing, banners flying. . . ." He described it all with great feeling. I have kept it on purpose. Would you like me to read it to you?

The Mayor. Afraid I've other things on my mind now. So please, my dear fellow, do me the favor: if you happen to come across any complaint or denunciation, keep it without any compunction.

The Postmaster. Glad to do so.

Lyapkin-Tyapkin. Take care, you'll get into trouble for that one day.

The Postmaster. Oh, dear, do you think so?

The Mayor. Nonsense, nonsense. It would be different if you made any of it public, but this is just among friends.

Lyapkin-Tyapkin. Yes, I'm afraid there's going to be trouble! And I, Mr. Mayor, was coming to offer you a present of a puppy—a sister of the hound you know. I suppose you must have heard that Cheptovich has started a lawsuit against Varkhovinsky and I'm in clover now: I'm coursing hares on the lands of both.

The Mayor. My dear sir, I don't care a rap about your hares now: it's that damned incognito that's worrying me. Any minute now the door might open and in will come—

Bobchinsky *and* Dobchinsky *come in breathless with running.*

Bobchinsky. A most extraordinary thing!

Dobchinsky. An unexpected piece of news!

All. What's happened? What's the matter?

Dobchinsky. A most amazing thing: we went into the inn—

Bobchinsky [*interrupting*]. Dobchinsky and I went into the inn—

Dobchinsky [*interrupting*]. Now please, please, Bobchinsky, let me tell it.

Bobchinsky. No, please let me! Please, please. You haven't got the right style. . . .

Dobchinsky. And you'll get confused. You won't remember everything.

Bobchinsky. I shall, I shall remember. Please, don't interrupt. Let me tell it. Please don't interrupt! Please, gentlemen, tell Dobchinsky not to interfere.

The Mayor. For goodness' sake, tell us what it is all about. My heart is in my mouth. Sit down, gentlemen. Find yourselves chairs. Here's a chair for you, Bobchinsky. [*They all sit down around* Bobchinsky *and* Dobchinsky.] Well, what is it?

Bobchinsky. Please, please let me tell you everything as it happened. As soon as I had taken leave of you, after you were so upset by that letter—yes, sir, I ran along—please, please don't interrupt, Dobchinsky. I know everything, everything! So, you see, I ran in to see Korobkin and as he wasn't at home, I went to see Rastakovsky and as he wasn't at home, I went to see the Postmaster here to tell him about the news you had received. But on the way from the post office I ran across Dobchinsky—

Dobchinsky [*interrupting*]. Near the stall where they sell pies.

Bobchinsky. Near the stall where they sell pies. Well, sir, so I met Dobchinsky and I said to him: "Have you heard the news the Mayor has received in a letter from a most reliable person?" And Dobchinsky had heard all about it from your housekeeper Avdotya, who was sent for something to Phillip Antonovich Pochechuyev—

Dobchinsky [*interrupting*]. To get a keg for the French brandy.

Bobchinsky [*waving him aside*]. To get a keg for the French brandy. So Dobchinsky and I went to Poche-chuyev's. . . . Now please, please, Dobchinsky, don't interrupt. Please, don't interrupt. So off we went to Poche-chuyev's, and on the way Dobchinsky said to me: "Let's go into the inn, there's something wrong with my stomach—I have had nothing since morning so there is a sort of upheaval there. . . ." Yes, sir, in Dobchinsky's stomach, that is. "And," he says, "they've just got some fresh salmon in so we could just have a snack." But no sooner had we walked into the inn than a young man suddenly—

Dobchinsky [*interrupting*]. Quite good-looking, but in civilian clothes. . . .

Bobchinsky. Qute good-looking and in civilian clothes. . . . He was walking about the room and there was a sort of thoughtful expression on his face—I mean, a—a physiognomy and—and gestures—and here [*twirling his hand about his forehead*], a great, great deal. I had a kind of presentiment and I said to Dobchinsky: "There's some-thing behind it all." Yes, sir, and Dobchinsky had already beckoned to the innkeeper, the innkeeper Vlas whose wife gave birth to a son three weeks ago, and such a lively little fellow, too! Keep an inn like his father, he will. Well, so we called Vlas, and Dobchinsky asked him quietly, "Who is that young man?" to which Vlas replied: "That," he says. . . . Now please don't interrupt, Dobchinsky, please don't interrupt. You won't tell it properly, I know you won't. You've got a lisp. You've got a tooth in your head that whistles. . . . "That," Vlas says, "is a young official, an official—yes, sir—from Petersburg, and his name," he says, "is Ivan Alexandrovich Khlestakov, and he is on the way to the province of Saratov and, he says, he behaves in a most peculiar way: he's been here two weeks, never thinks of leaving, takes everything on credit and doesn't pay a penny!" As soon as he told me this, a light dawned on me. "Ah," I said to Dobchinsky. . . .

Dobchinsky. No, Bobchinsky, it was I who said "Ah!"

Bobchinsky. You said it first and then I said it. "Ah!"

Dobchinsky and I said, "Why is he staying here when he's bound for Saratov?" Yes, sir. Well, you see, he is that official.

The Mayor. Who? Which official?

Bobchinsky. The official, sir, you've been notified about in your letter—the Government Inspector.

The Mayor [*in dismay*]. What are you talking about? Good heavens! I'm sure it's not him.

Dobchinsky. It is. You see, he pays no money and he doesn't go away. Who else could it be? And he has an order for post horses to Saratov.

Bobchinsky. It's him, I'm sure it's him. So observant. Looked at everything. Saw that Dobchinsky and I were eating salmon—chiefly on account of Dobchinsky's stomach—yes, so he peered into our plates. It gave me quite a turn.

The Mayor. Lord have mercy upon us, miserable sinners! What's the number of his room?

Dobchinsky. Room number five, under the staircase.

Bobchinsky. The same room where some army officers had a fight last year.

The Mayor. And how long has he been here?

Dobchinsky. Two weeks. He came on St. Vassily the Egyptian's Day.

The Mayor. Two weeks! [*Aside.*] Dear, oh dear! Help me, holy saints! Within these two weeks the sergeant's wife has been flogged. No rations have been issued to the convicts! Drunkards, filth in the streets! Disgrace! Dishonor! [*Clutches his head.*]

Zemlyanika. Well, Mr. Mayor, hadn't we better wait on him in a body?

Lyapkin-Tyapkin. No, no, let the clergy and the representatives of the merchants' guild go first. You see, in the book *The Acts of John the Mason.* . . .

The Mayor. No, no, let me go first. I've had difficult cases to deal with before in my life and everything went off all right. Why, I've even been thanked for it. Perhaps God will make it all come right now. [*Addressing* BOB-CHINSKY.] You say he's a young man?

Bobchinsky. Yes, sir. Twenty-three or -four at most.

The Mayor. So much the better. It's easier to see

through a young man. An old devil is a damned nuisance, but a young man is all on the surface. Now, gentlemen, you get everything ready in your departments, and I will go round alone or with Dobchinsky here, privately, just for a stroll, to see whether the travelers are treated properly. Hey, there, Svistunov.

Svistunov. Yes, sir?

The Mayor. Go at once and fetch the Police Superintendent. Or, no, I'll want you. Tell someone to fetch the Police Superintendent immediately and you come back here.

The CONSTABLE *runs off.*

Zemlyanika. Come along, come along, Lyapkin-Tyapkin. There really may be serious trouble.

Lyapkin-Tyapkin. What have you to be afraid of? Put clean nightcaps on your patients and none will be the wiser.

Zemlyanika. Nightcaps! We were ordered to give the patients oatmeal gruel, and there's such a stink of sour cabbage in all the corridors that you have to hold your nose.

Lyapkin-Tyapkin. I'm not worried. Who wants to look in at the district court? Why, even if he does come and look into some of the papers, he won't be able to make head or tail of it. I've been sitting on the bench for the last fifteen years and every time I glance into the court records—I just give it up. King Solomon himself could not decide what was true and what was false in them.

LYAPKIN-TYAPKIN, ZEMLYANIKA, KHLOPOV *and* THE POSTMASTER *go out. In the doorway they run across the* CONSTABLE, *coming back.*

The Mayor. Well, is the carriage at the door?

Constable. Yes, sir.

The Mayor. Go into the street, but no, wait. Where are the others? You haven't come back alone, have you? Didn't I tell Prokhorov to be here, too? Where is he?

Constable. Prokhorov is at the police station, sir. But he can't be used for anything.

The Mayor. Why not?

Constable. He can't, sir. You see, sir, he was brought in

this morning dead drunk. We've poured two buckets of water over him, but he hasn't got sober yet.

The Mayor [clutching his head]. Oh, dear, oh, dear! Go quickly into the street. No, first run into the other room and fetch me my sword and new hat. Well, Dobchinsky, let's go.

Bobchinsky. Me, too, me, too! Please let me come, too, sir.

The Mayor. No, no, you can't come with us, you can't. It wouldn't look nice. Besides, there's no room for you in my carriage.

Bobchinsky. Never mind that, sir. I'll run behind all the way. Behind your carriage. All I want is to peep through a crack in the door just to see what he will do.

The Mayor [takes the sword to the CONSTABLE]. Run at once and get some more men and let every one of them take— Look at that sword! Scratched all over! That damned shopkeeper Abdulin sees his mayor hasn't got a new sword and never thinks of sending him a new one. Oh, they're a crafty lot! I expect the rogues are already composing petitions on the sly against me. Let every one of you take a street in his hands—damn it—a broom and sweep the street all the way to the inn, and sweep it clean, too—do you hear! And you'd better take care! I know you—making friends here and there with shopkeepers and slipping silver spoons into your boots. You'd better look out! I know you! What have you been up to with Chermyayev, eh? He offered you two yards of cloth for a uniform, and you walked off with the whole roll! See that it never happens again! You're not taking according to your rank! Go now!

The POLICE SUPERINTENDENT *comes in.*

The Mayor. Ah, my dear fellow, where on earth have you been? It's really too bad!

Police Superintendent. I was just around the corner.

The Mayor. Now, listen, my dear fellow. The official from Petersburg has arrived. What arrangements have you made?

Police Superintendent. Why, sir, I've carried out your orders. I've sent Police Constable Pugovitsyn with the others to sweep the pavements.

The Mayor. And where is Derzhimorda?

Police Superintendent. Derzhimorda has gone out with the fire pump.

The Mayor. And Prokhorov's drunk?

Police Superintendent. Yes, sir.

The Mayor. How could you allow it?

Police Superintendent. Afraid I couldn't do anything about it, sir. There was a fight outside the town yesterday. He went there to restore order and came back drunk.

The Mayor. Now, listen carefully. Better do this: put Constable Pugovitsyn—he's such a tall fellow—on the bridge to put up a good appearance. Then pull down the old fence beside the cobbler's as quickly as possible and put poles with markers as if new streets were being laid out. You see, the more things we pull down, the more it shows that the Mayor is active. Oh, dear, I quite forgot that there are about forty cartloads of rubbish heaped up beside that fence. What a nasty, rotten town this is! As soon as you put up a monument or even a fence, people come along and shoot all sorts of rubbish. Goodness only knows where they get it from. [*Sighs.*] Now, if the Petersburg official asks any of the police whether they are satisfied or not, make sure they all reply: "We're perfectly satisfied, sir!" And if any of them isn't perfectly satisfied, I'll give him something to be dissatisfied about! Oh, dear, oh, dear, I can see I'm to blame, much to blame in many things. [*Picks up hatbox instead of the hat.*] God grant everything turns out satisfactorily as soon as possible, and I'll put up the biggest candle that ever was put up in church: I'll get every rascal of a shopkeeper to contribute a hundredweight of wax. Oh, dear, oh, dear. Come along, Dobchinsky, let's go. [*Puts on the box instead of the hat.*]

Police Superintendent. That's the box, not the hat, sir.

The Mayor [*flinging down the box*]. Well, if it's the box, it's the box, damn it! Oh, and if he asks why the hospital chapel, for which a sum of money was assigned five years ago, has not been built, don't forget to say that the building was begun, but it got burned down. I sent in a report about it. But I expect someone might forget and blurt out like a fool that it was never begun. And tell Derzhimorda not to be too free with his fists. He gives

black eyes both to the guilty and the innocent for the
sake of preserving law and order. Come along, Dobchinsky,
come along. [*Goes out and comes back.*] And don't let the
soldiers out of the barracks half naked: these disgusting
garrison soldiers put on their uniforms over their shirts and
forget all about their trousers. [*They all go out.*]

ANNA ANDREYEVNA *and* MARIA ANTONOVNA *run in.*

Anna. Where are they? Where are they? Oh, dear!
[*Opening door.*] Husband! Anton! Anton, darling! [*Speaks
rapidly.*] And it's all your doing, all your fault! You would
be rummaging and dawdling about: "Must get another pin,
must get a fichu!" [*Runs up to the window and shouts.*]
Anton! Where are you off to? What? Has he come, the
Government Inspector? Has he a mustache? What sort of
mustache?

The Mayor's Voice. Later, later, my love.

Anna. Later? How do you like that! Later, indeed! I
don't want to be later. All I want to know is—what is he?
A colonel? [*Scornfully.*] He's gone! You'll pay for that!
And it's all because of you! "Mummy! Mummy! Wait!
Let me pin my fichu behind! I won't be a minute!" That's
what comes of your minute! Haven't found out anything,
and all because of your confounded flirtatiousness! You
heard the Postmaster was here and you had to start minc-
ing before the looking glass, turning this way and that! She
imagines he's in love with her, but all the time he's making
faces at you when your back is turned.

Maria. But it can't be helped, Mummy, can it? We
shall know all about it in an hour or two.

Anna. In an hour or two! Thank you very much! I'm
obliged to you for your clever answer, I'm sure! I wonder
you didn't think of saying we shall know better still in a
month! [*Leaning out of window.*] Hey, there, Avdotya!
What? Have you heard if anyone has come? You haven't?
Oh, what a fool! He waved you away? Let him wave! You
should have found out everything all the same. You
couldn't find out? Her head's full of all sorts of rubbish—
all she cares about are men. What? They drove off too
quickly? Why didn't you run off after the carriage? Go on,
run after them! Do you hear? Run and find out where

they've gone to. Find out everything. What kind of a man he is, what he looks like—do you hear? Peep through the keyhole and find out everything. What color eyes he's got, are they black or not, and come back at once, do you hear? Hurry, hurry! [*Shouts till the curtain falls. The curtain hides them both from the view of the audience as they stand at the window.*]

ACT TWO

A small room at the inn. A bed, a table, a trunk, an empty bottle, a pair of top boots, a clothesbrush, etc.

OSIP is lying on his master's bed.

OSIP. Damn it all, I'm so hungry my belly's rumbling as if a whole regiment was blowing their trumpets there. I don't suppose we shall ever get home at this rate. What's to be done? It's two months since we left Petersburg. He's gambled away his money on the road and now he's sitting here with his tail between his legs and doesn't care a hang. He'd have had enough, more than enough, for the fares. But no! He has, you see, to show off in every town! [*Mimicking him.*] "I say, Osip, go and book me a room, the best room you can find, and order me the best dinner they have. I can't eat an ordinary dinner! I must have the very best!" It would have been all right if he had really been someone, but he is just a copying clerk! Makes friends with other travelers and then sits down to a game of cards, and now he's gone and lost everything! Oh, I'm sick and tired of this kind of life. I'd much rather live in the country. It's true there's no public life there, but there's less trouble there, too. Get yourself a woman and spend your time lying on the stove as long as you like and eating pies. But of course, life in Petersburg can't be beaten. So long as you have money to spend, your life there is elegant and refined. Theatres, shows, dancing dogs and anything you like. Everyone speaks nice and polite-like, almost as good as the nobility. You go to the Shchukin Arcade, and the shopkeepers call you "sir." In the ferryboat you sit next to a civil servant. If you want company, all you have to do is to go into the first shop. There an old soldier will tell you about life in camp, explain the meaning of every star in the sky, so that it's all as plain as plain can be. An old lady, an officer's widow, will drop in, and sometimes a pretty lady's maid will come in looking like— Whew! Whew! [*Laughs and shakes his head.*] Real civility, damn it! You never hear a rude word. Everyone treats you as if you was a gentleman! If you're tired of walking, you hail a cab and sit like a lord. And if you don't want to pay, you don't! For, you see, every house has a gate at the back, and all you have to do is to dart through it and no devil will be able to catch you. One thing is not so good, though: one day you gorge yourself, and another you nearly die of hunger, just as now, for instance. And it's all his fault! What's one to do with him? No sooner does his dad send him money than it's all gone! Instead of keeping it, he starts gambling and having a merry time, driving about in cabs. Get him a ticket for the theatre every day and a week later he sends me to the flea market to sell his new dress coat. Sometimes he loses everything down to his last shirt so that all he's got left is a shabby tail coat and a tattered overcoat. . . . Yes, indeed! And all fine English cloth, too! Pays a hundred and fifty rubles for the dress coat alone and then lets it go for twenty in the flea market. As for the trousers, they fetch next to nothing. And why's that? It's all because he won't work. Instead of going to the office, he goes for a walk on the avenue, or plays cards. Oh, if the old master only knew! He wouldn't care a damn whether you're a civil servant or not. He'd lift up your shirt and give you such a thrashing that you'd be rubbing yourself for the next four days. If you've got a job, then do it, I say! Take the innkeeper here. He says he won't give us anything till we've paid up for what we've had. But what if you don't pay? [*Sighs.*] Oh, dear, if only I could have some cabbage soup! I feel I could eat the whole world. I can hear footsteps. I expect it's him. [*Gets off the bed quickly.*]

Enter KHLESTAKOV.

Khlestakov. Here, take these. [*Gives him his cap and cane.*] Been sprawling about on my bed again, have you?

Osip. Why should I sprawl on your bed? Haven't I seen a bed before?

Khlestakov. That's a lie. I can see you've been sprawling on it. It's all rumpled.

Osip. What do I want it for? Don't I know what a bed is? I've got legs, I can stand. What do I want your bed for?

Khlestakov [*pacing the room*]. See if there's any tobacco left in the pouch.

Osip. How should there be any, sir? You smoked the last four days ago.

Khlestakov [*pacing the room, pursing his lips in all sorts of ways. At last says in a loud and determined voice*]. I say, Osip!

Osip. Yes, sir?

Khlestakov [*in a loud, but not so determined voice*]. Go down there.

Osip. Where?

Khlestakov [*in a voice not at all determined or loud, but almost imploring*]. Downstairs, to the dining room. . . . Tell them to—to send me some dinner.

Osip. I'm sorry, sir, but I'd rather not.

Khlestakov. How dare you! You fool!

Osip. It won't make no difference, sir. Even if I go, nothing will come of it. The landlord says he won't serve you any more meals.

Khlestakov. How dare he refuse! What nonsense!

Osip. Well, he says he'll go to the Mayor and tell him you've paid him nothing for three weeks. "You and your master," he says, "are swindlers. Your master is a rogue," he says. "We've seen such scroungers and scoundrels before," he says.

Khlestakov. And you enjoy telling me all this, you brute!

Osip. "This way," he says, "anyone might come along, make himself at home, run up a bill, and I shouldn't be able to throw him out afterwards. I'm not going to be trifled with," he says, "I'll go straight to the Mayor with a complaint and have you taken to the police station and thrown into jail."

Khlestakov. All right, all right, that's enough, you fool. Go, tell him. What a coarse animal!

Osip. I think I'd better ask the landlord to come and have a talk with you himself.

Khlestakov. What do I want the landlord for? You go and tell him yourself.

Osip. But really, sir—

Khlestakov. Go on, damn you, fetch the landlord. [*Osip goes out.*] I'm ravenous. I went for a walk thinking my appetite would wear off, but damn it, it won't. If I hadn't gambled away all my money in Penza, I'd have enough left to get home on. That infantry captain got me into a proper fix. The brute won every game; it only took him a quarter of an hour to clean me out. I do wish I could have another game with him, but there seems to be no chance. What a beastly little town! Won't let me have anything on credit in their lousy shops. It's really mean. [*Whistles first from "Robert le Diable" and then a Russian folk song and at last some unrecognizable tune.*] There's somebody coming.

Enter OSIP *and* WAITER.

Waiter. The landlord, sir, has sent me to ask you what he can do for you.

Khlestakov. Ah, good morning, my dear fellow. Well, how are you?

Waiter. Thank you, sir, I'm all right.

Khlestakov. Well, how are things at your inn? Is everything going well?

Waiter. Yes, thank you, sir, everything's all right.

Khlestakov. Many travelers?

Waiter. Yes, sir, quite a few.

Khlestakov. Look here, my dear fellow, they haven't brought me dinner yet. Will you please hurry them up? You see, I have something to do after dinner.

Waiter. I'm afraid, sir, the landlord said he wouldn't serve you any more meals. I believe, sir, he was going to complain about you to the Mayor today.

Khlestakov. What about? Now, really, my dear fellow, just think, I have to eat, haven't I? Or else I might starve to death. You see, I'm very hungry. I'm not joking.

Waiter. No, sir. But he said, sir, "I'm not going to serve him any more dinners until he pays me for what he's had." That was what he said, sir.

Khlestakov. But you must make him see reason, my dear fellow. Try to persuade him.

Waiter. But what am I to say to him, sir?

Khlestakov. You must talk to him seriously. Explain that I have to eat. Money's quite a different matter. He thinks that if a peasant like himself can go without food for a day, other people can do the same. What an idea!

Waiter. All right, I'll tell him. [WAITER *and* OSIP *go out.*]

Khlestakov [*alone*]. It'll be awful, though, if he doesn't give me anything to eat. I don't think I've ever been so hungry. Shall I sell some of my clothes for ready cash? My trousers? No! I'd rather starve than not arrive home in my Petersburg suit. Pity Joachim the coachbuilder would not let me hire a carriage. Oh, it would have been wonderful to arrive home in a carriage, drive up to the house of some neighboring landlord with the lanterns burning and Osip in livery perched up behind. Damned wonderful! I can imagine how excited everybody would be: "Who's that? What is it?" And my footman would go in [*draws himself up, representing the footman*]: "Ivan Alexandrovich Khlestakov, from Petersburg! Are they at home?" The damned clodhoppers don't even know what "at home" means. If some fool of a landowner goes to see them, he barges straight into the drawing room like a bear. You go up to a pretty daughter: "Madam, may I. . . ." [*Rubs his hands and scrapes his foot.*] Damn! [*Spits.*] I'm so hungry I feel quite sick.

Enter OSIP, *followed by the* WAITER.

Khlestakov. Well?

Osip. They're bringing your dinner.

Khlestakov [*clapping his hands and bobbing up and down on his chair*]. They're bringing it, bringing it, bringing it!

Waiter [*with plates and napkins*]. The landlord is letting you have dinner for the last time, sir.

Khlestakov. The landlord, the landlord. . . . I don't

care a damn for the landlord! What have you got there?

Waiter. Soup and roast meat, sir.

Khlestakov. Only two courses?

Waiter. Yes, sir.

Khlestakov. What nonsense! I won't have that. Go and ask him what he means by it. That's not enough.

Waiter. Well, sir, the landlord says it's too much.

Khlestakov. And why is there no sauce?

Waiter. There's no sauce, sir.

Khlestakov. Why not? I saw them making a lot when I passed by the kitchen. And there were two shortish gentlemen in the dining room this morning eating salmon and lots of other things.

Waiter. Well, sir, there is, and again there isn't.

Khlestakov. What do you mean?

Waiter. Well, sir, there isn't.

Khlestakov. And what about the salmon, the fish, the cutlets?

Waiter. That's for the better class customers, sir.

Khlestakov. Oh, you fool!

Waiter. Yes, sir.

Khlestakov. You disgusting pig. How is it they can eat and not me? Damn it all, why can't I have it? Aren't they travelers the same as me?

Waiter. Of course they're not the same, sir.

Khlestakov. What sort are they, then?

Waiter. The usual sort, sir. You see, sir, they pay!

Khlestakov. I won't even argue with a fool like you. [*Pours out the soup and begins eating.*] What sort of soup is this? You've simply poured some water in the cup. No flavor. It just stinks. I won't have this soup. Give me another kind.

Waiter. I'll take it away, sir. The landlord said if you don't like it, you needn't have it.

Khlestakov [*protecting the soup with his hand*]. All right, all right! Leave it, you fool. You're used to treating other people like that, but let me tell you I'm not that kind. No, sir. I don't advise you to treat me like that. . . . [*Eats.*] Good Lord, what soup! [*Goes on eating.*] I don't think there's anyone else in the world who'd swallow such soup: look at the feathers floating in it instead of fat. [*Carves the chicken.*] Dear me, what a tough chicken.

Let's have the roast meat. Osip, there's a little soup left over. You can have it. [*Carving the meat.*] What sort of meat is it? It's not meat.

Waiter. What then is it, sir?

Khlestakov. Goodness only knows what it is. All I know is that it isn't meat. You've roasted the chopper instead of the beef. [*Eats.*] Swindlers! Swine! The things they give one to eat! Your jaws ache from eating a mouthful of it. [*Picking his teeth.*] The blackguards! Like a piece of bark, can't even get it out. I shouldn't be surprised if my teeth turned black after such courses! Rogues! [*Wipes his mouth with his napkin.*] Isn't there anything else?

Waiter. No, sir.

Khlestakov. The swine! The blackguards! No sauce or pudding? The good-for-nothing scoundrels! Just fleecing travelers.

The WAITER *clears the table and carries off the plates with the help of* OSIP.

Khlestakov [*alone*]. I feel as if I hadn't had anything at all. Just enough to whet my appetite. If I had a few coppers, I'd send Osip to the market for a bun at least.

OSIP *comes in.*

Osip. The Mayor has arrived, sir. He's making inquiries and asking about you.

Khlestakov [*scared*]. Good Lord, that beast of a landlord must have sent in a complaint already! What if they really do drag me to prison! Well, if they treat me like a gentleman, I might. . . . No, no! I won't go. All sorts of army officers and crowds of people stroll about the streets and, besides, I've been setting the fashion and exchanging glances with a shopkeeper's pretty daughter. . . . No, I won't go. And how dare he, anyway! Who does he think I am? A shopkeeper or a workman? [*Tries to keep up his spirits and draws himself up.*] Why, I shall tell him, I shall say, "How dare you, sir, how dare you. . . ."

The door handle turns, KHLESTAKOV *turns pale and shrinks within himself.* THE MAYOR *and* DOBCHINSKY *come in.* THE MAYOR *and* KHLESTAKOV *stare in alarm at one another for a few minutes.*

The Mayor [collecting himself a little, with his hands stiffly against the seams of his trousers]. How do you do, sir?

Khlestakov [bows]. How do you do?

The Mayor. I'm sorry.

Khlestakov. Don't mention it.

The Mayor. It's my duty as mayor of this town to see that travelers and persons of rank are not in anyway inconvenienced. . . .

Khlestakov [at first stuttering a little, but almost shouting at the end of his speech]. But what am I to do? It's not my fault. I—I'll pay. . . . I'm expecting money from the country. [BOBCHINSKY *peeps around the door.*] It's his fault really. He gives me beef as hard as a board, and the soup—goodness only knows what he puts into it. I've had to throw it out of the window. He's been starving me for days. The tea is very peculiar: it tastes of fish and not of tea. Why then should I? I mean—really!

The Mayor [quailing]. I'm terribly sorry, sir, but it isn't my fault. The beef in our market is always excellent. It's brought by Kholmogorsk merchants, sober fellows all of them, and of excellent character. I don't know where he gets such stuff. But, of course, if anything—er—is not to your liking. . . . Permit me, sir, to suggest that you accompany me to other quarters.

Khlestakov. No, sir, I won't go. I know what you mean by other quarters. You mean prison, don't you? What right have you? How dare you, sir! Why, I—I—I'm in government service, sir. In Petersburg, sir! [*Plucking up courage.*] I, I, I. . . .

The Mayor [aside]. Oh, dear, what a violent temper he has! He knows everything, those damned shopkeepers must have told him everything.

Khlestakov [summoning up courage]. Why, if you came here with a whole regiment of soldiers, I wouldn't go! I'll go straight to the minister! [*Bangs fist on the table.*] How dare you, sir! What do you mean?

The Mayor [drawing himself up and trembling all over]. Please, sir, don't ruin me! I've a wife and little children. Don't make a man unhappy.

Khlestakov. No, I won't. . . . Fancy that! What do I

care? Just because you have a wife and children I must go to prison! How do you like that! [BOBCHINSKY *peers through the door and draws quickly back in alarm*.] No, sir, thank you very much! I won't go.

The Mayor [*trembling*]. It was all because of my inexperience, sir. I assure you, sir, it was all because of my inexperience. Insufficient salary. . . . Judge for yourself, sir. My salary doesn't pay for the tea and sugar. If I have taken bribes, sir, they did not amount to much. Something for the table and a bit of cloth for a couple of suits. As for the sergeant's widow who keeps a shop, sir, and whom I'm supposed to have flogged, it's slander, sir. Pure slander. An invention of my enemies. They're terrible people! They'd murder me if they could!

Khlestakov. Would they? Well, that's nothing to do with me. [*Thinking it over*.] Still, I don't understand why you are telling me all this about your enemies and a sergeant's widow. . . . A sergeant's widow is one thing, but you won't dare to flog me, not on your life. What an idea! Who do you think you are! I'll pay, I'll pay my bill, but I haven't the money now. The only reason I'm staying here is that I haven't a penny.

The Mayor [*aside*]. Oh, what a clever rogue! See what he's driving at. Got me all confused. Can't make head or tail of it. Don't even know how to get at him. Well, I'll try. Perhaps that's what he wants. I'll risk it. It may come off. [*Aloud*.] If you are really in need of money, sir, or anything else, I'm quite ready to be of service to you this very minute. It is my duty to aid travelers.

Khlestakov. Yes, do lend me some money. I'll pay the landlord at once. All I want is two hundred rubles or even less.

The Mayor [*offering him the money*]. Exactly two hundred rubles, sir. Pray, do not trouble to count it.

Khlestakov [*accepting the money*]. Thank you very much, sir. I'll send it back as soon as I reach my country estate. I can see that you're a gentleman, sir. Now, it's quite—er—different.

The Mayor [*aside*]. Thank God! He has taken it! I think things will go much better now. I managed to slip him four hundred instead of two hundred.

Khlestakov. Hey, Osip! [Osip *comes in.*] Call the waiter, will you? [*To* The Mayor *and* Dobchinsky.] Why are you standing? Do sit down, please. [*To* Dobchinsky.] Sit down, sir.

The Mayor. It's quite all right. We don't mind standing.

Khlestakov. Do sit down, sir. I can see now how straightforward, generous and hospitable you are. You see, sir, I thought that you had come to. . . . [*To* Dobchinsky.] Do sit down, sir.

The Mayor *and* Dobchinsky *sit down.* Bobchinsky *peeps in at the door and listens.*

The Mayor [*aside*]. I must be bolder. He wants to be considered incognito. Very well. Let's see what we can do by promising all sorts of things. Let's pretend that we don't know who he is. [*Aloud.*] You see, sir, as I was walking along on official business with Mr. Dobchinsky here, who is a local landowner, I called at the inn to find out whether travelers were being properly treated, for you see, sir, I'm not like some mayors who care nothing about such things. Quite apart from my official duties, as a good Christian and as a lover of humanity I'd like every mortal to be given a good reception, and, as though as a reward, sir, chance has presented me with such a pleasant acquaintance.

Khlestakov. I, too, am very glad, sir. But for you, I don't know how long I'd have had to stop here. You see, sir, I simply did not know where to get the money to pay the bill.

The Mayor [*aside*]. A fine story! Didn't know how to pay his bill! [*Aloud.*] May I ask you, sir, where you're bound for?

Khlestakov. I'm on my way to my own estate in the province of Saratov.

The Mayor [*aside with an ironical expression*]. In the province of Saratov! And not a blush! Oh, you have to be on your guard with him. [*Aloud.*] An excellent idea, sir. Though, mind you, people say that traveling has its drawbacks: for instance, delays occasioned by the shortage of horses, though, on the other hand, of course, it provides a great deal of mental distraction. I expect, sir, you are traveling chiefly for your own pleasure.

Khlestakov. No, sir, my father has sent for me. The old man is very angry with me because I have not yet succeeded in obtaining a high position in Petersburg. He thinks that as soon as you get to Petersburg, they stick the order of Vladimir in your buttonhole. I wish I could send him to jostle about in a government office.

The Mayor [aside]. Just listen to his tales! Even dragged in his old father! [*Aloud.*] And how long do you propose to stay on your estate?

Khlestakov. I really don't know, sir. You see, my father is as stupid and obstinate as a block of wood, the silly old fool! I shall tell him straight: "Say what you like, but I can't live away from Petersburg." And why indeed should I ruin my life living among some stupid peasants? A gentleman needs other things now. My soul, sir, is athirst for enlightenment.

The Mayor [aside]. A likely story! He's lying, he's lying and yet he speaks so glibly. And what a plain-looking, puny fellow! One push and he'd be out for the count. Ah, you wait, my dear fellow! I'll make you talk. I'll make you tell me a little more about yourself. [*Aloud.*] You put it very nicely, sir. What can one do in some Godforsaken hole in the country? Take this town, for instance. You spend sleepless nights trying to think what to do for your country. You don't spare yourself, but you never know when you will be rewarded for your pains. [*Glancing around the room.*] This room seems a little damp, doesn't it?

Khlestakov. It's a disgusting room, and there are bugs as big as I've ever seen anywhere: they bite like dogs.

The Mayor. You don't say! And such a cultured visitor like yourself to suffer from what? From a lot of good-for-nothing bugs that ought never to have been born. It's rather dark in this room, isn't it?

Khlestakov. Yes, very dark. The landlord refuses to let me have a candle. Sometimes you feel like doing something, reading or writing, but you can't do it! It's dark, dark.

The Mayor. May I take the liberty of asking you, sir— but no, I am unworthy.

Khlestakov. What is it?

The Mayor. No, no, I'm unworthy, I'm unworthy.

Khlestakov. But what is it?

The Mayor. I'd have taken the liberty, sir, to—er—you see, I have a beautiful room for you in my house—a quiet, sunny room. . . . But no, I realize it would be too great an honor. . . . Do not be angry, sir. . . . I assure you, it was out of the simplicity of my heart that I offered it.

Khlestakov. On the contrary, sir, I accept your offer with pleasure. I'd feel happier in a private house than in this pothouse.

The Mayor. I'll be very glad, indeed, sir. And my wife, too, will be very happy to have you. You see, sir, it has always been my rule even as a child: hospitality above everything, especially if the person is a man of culture. Please do not think I'm saying this because I want to flatter you. No, sir, that is not a vice of mine. I speak from the fullness of my heart.

Khlestakov. Thank you very much, sir. I, too, detest two-faced people. I must say I like your frankness and your cordiality. And so far as I'm concerned, sir, all I ask from people is respect and loyalty, respect and loyalty.

Enter the WAITER *accompanied by* OSIP. BOBCHINSKY *peers through the door.*

Waiter. You sent for me, sir?

Khlestakov. Yes, let me have my bill.

Waiter. But I gave it to you again a short while ago, sir.

Khlestakov. I don't remember your stupid bills. Tell me, how much is it?

Waiter. The first day, sir, you were so good as to order dinner, and on the second you only had some salmon, and after that you had everything on credit.

Khlestakov. Imbecile! You'll be trying to add it up next. How much do I owe you?

The Mayor. Don't you trouble about it, sir. He can wait. [*To the* WAITER.] Get out. The money will be sent to you.

Khlestakov. Well, yes, that's quite true. [*Puts away the money.*]

The WAITER *goes out.* BOBCHINSKY *peers through the door.*

The Mayor. Would you like to inspect some of the institutions in our town, sir? The public infirmary and others?

Khlestakov. Why, what's there to see?

The Mayor. Why not have a look around, sir? Just to see how things are done here. I mean the way we manage everything.

Khlestakov. I'd be delighted, sir. I'm at your service.

BOBCHINSKY *pokes head through the door.*

The Mayor. Also if you like, sir, we could go from there to the district school, to see the way our schools are run.

Khlestakov. Yes, by all means, by all means.

The Mayor. And then, if you like, we could pay a visit to the police station and the prison to see how we deal with our prisoners.

Khlestakov. Why go to the prison? We'd better have a look at the infirmary.

The Mayor. As you please, sir. How do you wish to go? In your own carriage or with me in my light carriage?

Khlestakov. I'd rather go with you in your carriage.

The Mayor [*to* DOBCHINSKY]. Well, my dear fellow, there will be no room for you, I'm afraid.

Dobchinsky. It doesn't matter, I shall walk.

The Mayor [*quietly to* DOBCHINSKY]. Listen, you run along as fast as you can and take two notes. One to Zemlyanika at the infirmary and the other to my wife. [*To* KHLESTAKOV.] May I ask your permission, sir, to write a few lines in your presence to my wife, to tell her to get ready to welcome such a distinguished guest?

Khlestakov. But why bother? However, here's the pen and ink, but I'm afraid I haven't got any paper. Could you write it on this bill?

The Mayor. Yes, I'll write it on the bill. [*Writes and at the same time talks to himself.*] Well, we shall see how things will go after a good lunch and a good bottle of wine. We've some local Madeira—it's not much to look at, but it would knock an elephant off its feet. All I want is to find out what sort of person he is and how much I have to be afraid of him. [*Having written the note, gives it to* DOBCHINSKY *who walks up to the door, but at that moment the door comes off its hinges, and*

BOBCHINSKY, *who has been eavesdropping, is precipitated onto the stage. All utter cries of surprise.* BOBCHINSKY *picks himself up.*]

Khlestakov. You haven't hurt yourself, sir?

Bobchinsky. It's nothing, sir, nothing. Nothing to worry about. Only a little bruise on my nose. I'll run to our doctor. He has a plaster which will put it right in no time.

The Mayor [*gestures reproachfully to* BOBCHINSKY. *To* KHLESTAKOV]. It's nothing, sir. After you, sir. I'll tell your servant to bring your trunk to my place. [*To* OSIP.] Bring everything around to my house, my good man, to the Mayor's. Anyone will show you where it is. After you, sir! [*Shows* KHLESTAKOV *out and follows him, but turning around, says reproachfully to* BOBCHINSKY.] You would! Couldn't you find another place to fall down in? Sprawling on the floor, too, like the devil knows what. [*Goes out, followed by* BOBCHINSKY.]

Curtain.

ACT THREE

Same as Act One.

ANNA ANDREYEVNA *and* MARIA ANTONOVNA *stand at the window in the same attitudes.*

ANNA. We've been waiting here for hours and it's all because of you with your stupid affectation. You were dressed, but no! You must still go rummaging about. I wish I hadn't listened to her at all. What a nuisance! Not a soul in sight. Just as though everything was dead.

Maria. But really, Mother, we shall know all about it in two minutes. Avdotya is sure to come back any moment now. [*Looks out of the window and shrieks.*] Look, Mother! Mother, somebody is coming! There, at the end of the street.

Anna. Where? Who's coming? You're always imagining things. Oh, yes, I see now. Somebody is coming. Who is it? A little man in a frock coat. Who could it be? Oh, what a nuisance! Who can it be, do you think?

Maria. It's Dobchinsky, Mother.

Anna. Dobchinsky! What are you talking about? It isn't Dobchinsky at all. [*Waving her handkerchief.*] You there! Come here! Quick!

Maria. Really, Mother, it is Dobchinsky.

Anna. I can see you're saying that on purpose to contradict me. I tell you it isn't Dobchinsky.

Maria. Well, Mother, what did I tell you? You see it is Dobchinsky.

Anna. All right, so it is Dobchinsky. I can see now. What are you arguing about? [*Shouts out of the window.*] Quick, quick! You walk so slowly. Well, where are they? What? Tell me from where you are. It's all right. What? Very stern, is he? And my husband, my husband? [*Withdrawing from the window a little, with annoyance.*] What a silly man! Won't tell me anything till he gets into the house.

Enter DOBCHINSKY.

Anna. Well, tell me, aren't you ashamed of yourself? I counted on you being a decent sort: everyone rushed out of the house and you after them, and I can't get a word of sense from anyone. Aren't you ashamed? I stood godmother to your Vanya and Liza and this is how you treat me.

Dobchinsky. But, my dear lady, I've run so fast to pay my respects to you that I'm quite out of breath. How do you do, Maria Antonovna?

Maria. Good afternoon, sir.

Anna. Well, what happened? Tell us, how are things there?

Dobchinsky. Your husband has sent you this note.

Anna. Well, who is he? A general?

Dobchinsky. No, not a general, but he's as good as any general. Such an educated man and such grand manners!

Anna. Oh, so it is the same man my husband had a letter about?

Dobchinsky. Yes. The very same. Bobchinsky and I were the first to discover it.

Anna. Well, tell us all about it!

Dobchinsky. Well, thank God, everything went off satis-factorily. At first he did receive the Mayor a little sternly. Yes, ma'am, he was very angry and said that things were not as they should be at the inn, that he wouldn't come and stay with him, and that he didn't want to go to prison because of him. But afterwards, as soon as he saw that the Mayor was not to blame and after he had talked a little more to him, he changed his mind, and then, thank God, all went well. They've gone to inspect the infirmary now. At first, I confess, your husband did think that there might have been a secret report about him, and I was a little afraid myself.

Anna. What have you got to be afraid of? You're not in the service.

Dobchinsky. Well, you see, when an important man like him speaks, one can't help feeling nervous.

Anna. Well, this is a lot of nonsense, anyway. Tell me, what is he like? Old or young?

Dobchinsky. Oh, he's young. Quite a young man. About twenty-three at most. But he speaks like an old man. "Why, certainly," he says, "I don't mind, I'll go there, and there." [*Waving his arms.*] It was all so nice. "I like to write and read a little," he says, "but," he says, "I can't do it because it's so dark in the room."

Anna. And what does he look like? Is he dark or fair?

Dobchinsky. No, more auburn, and his eyes are as quick as little animals. They throw you into confusion.

Anna. Let's see what he has written to me in his note. [*Reads.*] "I hasten to inform you, my love, that my posi-tion was truly dreadful, but trusting in God's mercy for two pickled cucumbers specially and half a portion of caviar, one ruble and twenty-five kopecks." [*Stops.*] I don't understand. What have pickled cucumbers and caviar to do with it?

Dobchinsky. Oh, well, you see, your husband wrote it on some bill because he was in a hurry.

Anna. Oh, yes, I see. [*Continues to read.*] "But, trusting in God's mercy, I believe that it will all end well. Get a room ready quickly for our distinguished visitor, the one with the yellow wallpaper. Don't trouble to have any-thing extra for dinner, because we are going to have lunch

at the infirmary with Zemlyanika, but get more wine.
Tell Abdulin to send his best or else I shall ransack
his cellar myself. Kissing your little hand, my love, I
remain your Anton Skvoznik-Dmukhanovsky." Oh, my
goodness, this has to be done quickly. Hey, who's there?
Mishka!

   Dobchinsky [*runs and shouts through the door*]. Mishka!
Mishka! Mishka!

Enter MISHKA.

   Anna. Listen, run to Abdulin's. Wait, I'll give you a
note. [*Sits down at table, writing and goes on talking.*]
Give this note to Sidor the coachman and see that he
runs with it to Abdulin's and comes back with the wine.
And go yourself at once and put the room in order for
our visitor. Put in a bedstead, a washbasin and everything.

   Dobchinsky. Well, my dear lady, I think I'd better run
along now to see how he's carrying out his inspection
there.

   Anna. Go, go, I'm not stopping you. [*DOBCHINSKY goes
out.*] Well, my dear Maria, we'll have to think carefully
what we are going to wear. Don't forget he's a Petersburg
dandy and God forbid he should find anything in us to
laugh at. You'd better put on your pale blue dress with
the flounces.

   Maria. Heavens, Mother, not the pale blue! I don't like
it a bit, and Mrs. Lyapkin-Tyapkin wears a blue dress,
and the Zemlyanika girls, too, wear blue. No, I think I'd
much rather wear my flowered dress.

   Anna. Your flowered dress! Really! You'd say anything
to spite me. The blue dress will look much nicer on you
because I'm going to wear my primrose. I'm very fond of
my primrose dress.

   Maria. Really, Mother, primrose doesn't suit you at all.

   Anna. Primrose does not suit me?

   Maria. It doesn't, Mother. I bet you anything it doesn't.
For a primrose dress you must have dark eyes.

   Anna. How do you like that! Aren't my eyes dark?
They're very dark. What nonsense you talk! They must
be dark since I always tell my fortune by the queen of
clubs.

Maria. Really, Mother, you're more like the queen of hearts.

Anna. Nonsense, absolute nonsense! I never was like the queen of hearts. [*Goes out hurriedly with* MARIA, *speaking behind the scenes.*] What do you say to that? Queen of hearts! My goodness!

After their departure, the double door opens, and MISHKA *sweeps out some dirt from one of the rooms.* OSIP *comes out of another door with a trunk on his back.*

Osip. Where am I to put this?

Mishka. This way, please.

Osip. Wait. Let me get my breath. Oh, dear, what an awful life! On an empty belly every load seems heavy.

Mishka. Tell me, is the general coming here soon?

Osip. What general?

Mishka. Why, your master.

Osip. My master? What sort of general is he?

Mishka. Why, isn't he a general?

Osip. Yes, he is a general, only the other way around.

Mishka. Is that more or less than a real general?

Osip. More.

Mishka. Well. I never! So that's why there's all the fuss in the house.

Osip. Look here, I can see you're a clever fellow. Get something for me to eat, will you?

Mishka. There's nothing ready for you yet. I don't expect you'd eat plain food. When your master sits down at table, you'll get the same as he does.

Osip. Well, and haven't you got any plain food?

Mishka. Cabbage soup, oatmeal pudding and meat pies.

Osip. Let's have it—cabbage soup, oatmeal pudding and pies. Don't worry, I can eat it all. Come, help me with this trunk. Is there another way out there?

Mishka. Yes. [*Both carry the trunk into the side room.*]
Two CONSTABLES *open the double door. Enter* KHLESTAKOV *followed by* THE MAYOR, ZEMLYANIKA, KHLOPOV, *then* DOBCHINSKY *and* BOBCHINSKY *with a plaster on his nose.* THE MAYOR *points out to the* CONSTABLES *a piece of paper on the floor, and they rush to pick it up, jostling each other in their haste.*

Khlestakov. Excellent institutions. I like your custom of showing visitors everything in your town. In other towns I wasn't shown anything.

The Mayor. In other towns, sir, if I may make so bold as to point it out to you, the mayors and officials are more concerned with feathering their own nests. In this town, however, we think of nothing else except of how to earn the good opinion of the authorities by constant vigilance and decorum.

Khlestakov. The lunch was very good. I've never had so much to eat in my life. Do you have such meals every day?

The Mayor. No, sir. It was prepared specially for such a distinguished guest as yourself.

Khlestakov. I like a good meal. But, then, what is life for if not to pick the flowers of pleasure? What was the name of that fish we had?

Zemlyanika [*running up to him*]. Labberdaan,* sir.

Khlestakov. It was very tasty. Where was it we had lunch? At the hospital, wasn't it?

Zemlyanika. Yes, sir, at the infirmary.

Khlestakov. Yes, yes, I remember. Where all those beds were. And had most of your patients recovered? There were only a few of them, I believe.

Zemlyanika. There are only about a dozen left, sir. The rest have all recovered. That's the way we do things here, sir. Ever since I took over the supervision of the infirmary —this, sir, may appear quite incredible to you—all the patients get well like flies. As soon as a patient is admitted to the hospital, he gets better. And it's not so much a question of medicines as of honesty and good management.

The Mayor. But, sir, if I may make bold to point out to you, the duties of a mayor are simply nerve-racking. So many things to worry about. Cleanliness, repairs, improvements. In fact, the most intelligent man might find himself in difficulties, but thanks be to God, all goes well. Another mayor, of course, would be putting his own interests first, but, believe me, sir, that even in bed I keep thinking, "Dear Lord, what can I do to prove my zeal to the authorities and earn their approval?" Whether they

---

* Salt codfish from Aberdeen imported from Holland.

reward me or not is of course for them to decide, but at least my mind is set at rest. So long as law and order are preserved in the town, the streets swept, the convicts looked after, not many drunkards about—what more could I want? I assure you, sir, I want no honors. Mind you, I won't deny that the prospect of receiving an honor is a tempting one, but what does it amount to compared with virtue? Dust and ashes! Vanity of vanities!

Zemlyanika [*aside*]. What a good-for-nothing rogue! How he lays it on! Fancy God bestowing such a gift on a man like him!

Khlestakov. That's true. I must admit I like airing my views myself, sometimes in prose and another time in verse.

Bobchinsky [*to* DOBCHINSKY]. Perfectly true, perfectly true! Such clever remarks! One can see at once he's a highly educated man.

Khlestakov. Tell me, please, haven't you any diversions here—clubs, where one could have a game of cards, for instance?

The Mayor [*aside*]. Aha! We know, my dear fellow, what you're driving at! [*Aloud.*] God forbid! No such clubs have ever been heard of here. I've never held a card in my hand. I don't even know how to play cards. Can't even look at a card. Indeed, if I happen to see a king of diamonds or something of the kind it simply makes me sick! Once to amuse some children I built them a house of cards, and I dreamt of those damned things all night. No, I don't want to have anything to do with them. How people waste so much precious time on them is something I shall never understand.

Khlopov [*aside*]. And he won a hundred rubles from me last night, the blackguard!

The Mayor. I prefer to devote my time to the welfare of our country.

Khlestakov. No, sir, you go too far, surely. It all depends on how you look at it. If, for instance, you fail to double the stakes when you really should have trebled them— well, then, of course. . . . No, no, don't say that. It's very nice to have a game of cards sometimes.

Enter MARIA *and* ANNA.

The Mayor. May I introduce my wife and daughter, sir?

Khlestakov [*bowing*]. I'm so happy, ma'am, to have the pleasure of meeting you.

Anna. It gives us even greater pleasure, sir, to meet such a distinguished personage.

Khlestakov [*showing off*]. Why, ma'am, quite the contrary. It is I who am more greatly pleased.

Anna. How can you say that, sir? I'm sure you're merely saying it as a compliment. Do sit down, sir.

Khlestakov. To stand beside you is enough to make me happy, ma'am. However, if you insist, I will sit down. I am so happy, ma'am, to be sitting beside you at last.

Anna. Why, sir, I can't possibly believe you're in earnest. I expect after Petersburg your journey must have seemed extremely disagreeable to you.

Khlestakov. Extremely disagreeable. Accustomed as I am to live, *comprenez-vous*, in high society, suddenly to find oneself on the road, dirty inns, rank ignorance. But the chance that brought me to—er—I—I confess [*gazes at* ANNA *and shows off before her*] . . . makes up for everything. . . .

Anna. Indeed, sir, you must have found it very unpleasant.

Khlestakov. Still, ma'am, at this moment I find it very pleasant indeed.

Anna. How can you say a thing like that, sir? You do me too much honor. I don't deserve it I'm sure.

Khlestakov. Not deserve it? You do deserve it, ma'am.

Anna. I live in the country. . . .

Khlestakov. Well, ma'am, the country, too, has its little hills and its brooks. . . . But, of course, you can't compare it to Petersburg. Ah, Petersburg! You can't imagine what life is like there. I expect you must think that I'm just a copying clerk. No, ma'am. The chief of my department is on most friendly terms with me. He slaps me on the back and says, "Come and have dinner with me, my dear fellow!" You see, I look into the office for only two minutes and that, too, just to say: "Do this like that and do that like this!" There's an official there, a poor blighter, who does nothing but scratch with his pen: Trrr—Trrr. . . . They wanted to raise me to the rank of Collegiate Assessor, but I thought to myself, what the heck for? And the porter, you know, runs after me up the stairs with a brush: "Let me clean your boots sir," he says. [*To* THE MAYOR.] Why are you standing, gentlemen? Please sit down.

The Mayor. A person of my rank, sir, can stand.

Zemlyanika. We don't mind standing, sir.

Khlopov. Don't worry, sir.

Khlestakov. Don't stand on ceremony, gentlemen. Do sit down. [THE MAYOR *and all the rest sit down.*] I don't like standing on ceremony. On the contrary, I always like to try and slip in unobserved. But I just can't imagine it! I just can't make myself inconspicuous however much I try! As soon as I come in anywhere, people say: "Look, there goes Khlestakov!" On one occasion I was even taken for the commander-in-chief himself. The soldiers all rushed out of the guardroom and presented arms. An officer, a great friend of mine, told me afterwards: "Well, my dear fellow, we were quite sure you were the commander-in-chief."

Anna. Fancy that!

Khlestakov. I know all the pretty actresses. You see, I've written a few amusing comedies myself. . . . I meet all sorts of writers. Pushkin and I are great friends. . . . I used often to say to him: "Well, Pushkin, old man, how goes it?" "Why," he used to answer, "my dear fellow, so-so. . . ." He's a great character.

Anna. So you write! It must be wonderful to be an author. I expect you publish things in the journals too?

Khlestakov. Yes, I publish things in the journals. I've published lots of things: *The Marriage of Figaro, Robert le Diable, Norma.* Can't remember all the titles. And, you know, it was all by chance. I never thought of writing anything, but the theatre managers kept saying to me: "Please, my dear fellow, write us another play." Well, I thought, why not? And I wrote the whole thing in an evening. Surprised them all. You see, thoughts and ideas simply came pouring out of my head. In fact, everything that has appeared under the name of Baron Brambeus—*The Frigate Hope,* and the *Moscow Telegraph*—I wrote them all.

Anna. Goodness, so you are Brambeus!

Khlestakov. Why, of course. I correct all their articles. Smirdin, the publisher, pays me forty thousand a year for that.

Anna. Then I expect *Yury Miloslavsky* is also your work?

Khlestakov. Yes, it's also my work.

Maria. But, Mother, it says on the book that Mr. Zagoskin wrote it.

Anna. I knew you'd start arguing about that.

Khlestakov. Oh, yes, it's quite true. That novel is by Zagoskin. But there is another *Yury Miloslavsky* and that was written by me.

Anna. Well, I expect it was yours I read. It's so beautifully written.

Khlestakov. You see, I simply live for literature. I have the finest house in Petersburg. Everybody knows it as Ivan Alexandrovich Khlestakov's house. [*Addressing all of them.*] Pray, gentlemen, if you are ever in Petersburg, please come and see me. I give balls, too.

Anna. I can just imagine the fine taste and magnificence of a Petersburg ball.

Khlestakov. Oh, it's beyond all description. Now, on the table, for instance, there will be a watermelon that costs seven hundred rubles. The soup in the saucepan has come straight from Paris by steamer. They remove the lid, and the aroma! There's nothing like it on earth. I go to balls every day. We make up a whist party of our own: the Foreign Minister, the French ambassador, the English ambassador, the German ambassador and I. You can't imagine how tired I get playing cards! I've never felt anything like it. Well, after the ball I rush back home, run up the stairs to my room on the fourth floor and say to my cook, "Here, take my coat, Mavrushka!" But what am I talking about? I forgot that I live on the first floor. Why, my staircase alone is worth . . . You really ought to look into my entrance hall in the morning while I'm still asleep. Princes and counts jostling each other and buzzing like bumblebees. All you can hear is: Bzzz-zz, bzzz-zz. . . . Sometimes, even a cabinet minister. . . . [THE MAYOR *and the others get up nervously from their chairs.*] My letters are addressed to "Your Excellency. . . ." Once I was in charge of a department. It was a queer business altogether. The director went away and disappeared no one knew where. Well, of course, people began wondering who was going to take his place. Many generals volunteered to take over the department, but as soon as they began tackling the job, they realized it was too much for them. It seems easy at first, but when you look more closely, it's the very devil of a job. When they realized that, they had to come to me in the end. Well, all at once the streets were swarming with government messengers. Messengers, messengers, messengers—thirty-five thousand messengers! "What's the position?" I asked. "Ivan Alexandrovich," they said, "you must take charge of the department." I must confess I felt a little uneasy. I came out in my dressing gown and was about to turn it down, but then I thought to myself it might come to the ears of the Emperor and, besides, there's one's official service record to consider. "Very well, gentlemen," I said, "I accept it. So be it. But," I said, "you'd better look out. No nonsense, you understand. I won't stand for any—er—any—you understand. I—I—I. . . ." And so it was. Every time I walked through the department it was like an earthquake. Everything was trembling and shaking like a leaf. [THE MAYOR *and the others shake with fear.* KHLESTAKOV *grows more and more worked up.*] Oh, I'm not one to be trifled with. I gave them all the sharp edge of my tongue. The State Council itself is terrified of me. And well they may be. I'm like that. I don't consider anyone. I tell 'em all: "I know everything myself!" I go everywhere. Absolutely everywhere. I am at the palace every day. Tomorrow I'm going to be made a field marshal. [*Slips and almost sprawls full-length on the floor but is caught and supported respectfully by the officials.*]

The Mayor [*walks up to him, trembling all over and unable to enunciate a word*]. Y-y-your—y-y-your. . . .

Khlestakov [*in a sharp and abrupt tone*]. What is it?

The Mayor. Y-y-y-your. . . .

Khlestakov [*in the same tone*]. Can't make out a thing. It's all nonsense.

The Mayor. Your-your-your-your—ex-ex-excellency, w-wouldn't you like to lie down? There's your room and everything you need.

Khlestakov. Lie down? Nonsense. However, I don't mind lying down. The lunch was excellent, gentlemen. Excellent. I'm pleased, very pleased. [*Declaims.*] Labberdaan, Labberdaan! [*Goes into side room, followed by* THE MAYOR.]

Bobchinsky. Now this, sir, is a man! That's what one means by a man. Never in my life have I been in the presence of so important a personage. I nearly died of fright. What do you think, sir, his rank can be?

Dobchinsky. I think he must be almost a general.

Bobchinsky. And I, sir, think a general isn't fit to tie his bootlaces! If he is a general, then he must be a generalissimo. Did you hear how he wiped the floor with the State Council? Come, let's tell it quickly to Lyapkin-Tyapkin and Korobkin. Good-by, Anna Andreyevna.

Dobchinsky. Good-by, ma'am. [*Both go out.*]

Zemlyanika [*to* KHLOPOV]. I'm terrified, you know. But what of, I don't know myself. And we're not even in uniform. What happens if he walked off and dashed off a report to Petersburg? [*Goes out thoughtfully, together with* KHLOPOV, *saying.*] Good-by, ma'am!

Anna. Oh, what an agreeable man!

Maria. Oh, what a darling!

Anna. And what refined manners! You can see at once he's a Petersburg dandy. The way he carries himself and everything. . . . Oh, how wonderful! I'm awfully fond of young men like that. I'm simply entranced! He liked me very much, I think. I noticed that he kept looking at me.

Maria. Really, Mother, he was looking at me.

Anna. Don't talk such nonsense, child. It's quite out of place here.

Maria. But, Mother, he really was!

Anna. There! You can't help arguing, can you? You just can't help it. Why should he look at you? For what reason should he be looking at you?

Maria. But really, Mother, he did keep looking at me all the time. When he began talking about literature, he glanced at me and when he told us how he played whist with the ambassadors he also looked at me.

Anna. Oh, he may have looked at you once, and that, too, only because he thought to himself, "Oh, well, let's have a look at her."

Enter THE MAYOR.

The Mayor [*on tiptoe*]. Sh-sh!

Anna. Well?

The Mayor. I'm sorry I made him drunk. I mean, what if no more than half of what he said is true? [*Ponders.*] But why shouldn't it be true? A man who is drunk usually tells you everything: what's in his heart is on his tongue. Of course he did embroider a little, but then nothing is ever said without exaggerating a little. Plays cards with Cabinet ministers, is at the palace every day. The more you think of it, the more you don't know what to make of it, damn it. It's as if you were standing on top of a belfry or were going to be hanged.

Anna. And I didn't feel a bit frightened. I saw in him simply an educated man of the world, a man of the highest society, and I don't care at all about his rank.

The Mayor. Oh, well, you would—women! That word explains everything. Everything is just silly nonsense to you. Wait till he blurts out something all of a sudden. You'll get off with a whipping, but your husband—that will be the last you'll ever see of him. You, my love, treated him as freely as though he were some Dobchinsky.

Anna. I shouldn't worry about that if I were you, my dear. We know a thing or two. . . . [*Looks at her daughter.*]

The Mayor [*alone*]. Oh, what's the use of talking to them! What an extraordinary business, though! Haven't recovered from my fright yet. [*Opens door and speaks to someone at the other side of it.*] Mishka, call Constables Svistunov and Derzhimorda. They must be somewhere about. Near the gates perhaps. [*After a short pause.*] How strange everything is now in the world: You'd expect a man of his position to look imposing, not a thin, insignificant-looking fellow like that. How is one to know who he really is? If he'd been an army officer, he'd at least be something to look at, but in his swallowtail he looks just like a fly with its wings snipped off. And he did try to throw dust in my eyes at the inn this morning. Every second word he uttered was a lie or a quibble. I should never have been able to make any sense of it. But in the end he had given in. In fact, he said more than was necessary. You can see he's young.

Enter Osip. *All run toward him, beckoning.*

Anna. Come here, my good man.

The Mayor. Sh-sh! Well? Well? Is he asleep?

Osip. No, sir. He's still stretching himself a little.

Anna. What's your name?

Osip. Osip, ma'am.

The Mayor [*to his wife and daughter*]. That will do. [*To* Osip.] Well, friend, have they given you a good dinner?

Osip. Yes, sir. Thank you very much. A very good dinner.

Anna. Tell me, I suppose a great many counts and princes come to see your master?

Osip [*aside*]. What am I to say? If they've given me a good dinner now, they may give me a better one later. [*Aloud.*] Yes, there are counts too.

Maria. Darling Osip, how good-looking your master is.

Anna. Tell us, Osip, please, how does he—

The Mayor. Do be quiet, please. You're only hampering me with your silly questions. Well, how are you, my friend?

Anna. And what's your master's rank?

Osip. The usual sort of rank, ma'am.

The Mayor. Good Lord, how you do keep on with your silly questions! You won't let one say a word about what matters. Well, my man, what is your master like? Is he strict? Is he fond of ticking people off?

Osip. Yes, he likes good order in everything. He likes everything to be in tiptop condition.

The Mayor. I like your face, my man. I'm sure you must be a good man. Well. . . .

Anna. Tell me, Osip, does your master wear a uniform at home, or does he go about—

The Mayor. Oh, do be quiet, you chatterboxes! This is a serious matter, a matter of life and death. . . . [*To* Osip.] Well, my friend, I really do like you, you know. On a journey, you know, an extra cup of tea does not come amiss, does it? It's a bit cold now, as a matter of fact. Well, then, here's a couple of rubles for tea.

Osip [*accepting the money*]. Thank you very much, sir. May the Lord grant you health and happiness. I'm a poor man, and you've been good to me.

The Mayor. That's all right. Pleased to do it. Well, my friend. . . .

Anna. Tell me, Osip, what sort of eyes does your master like best?

Maria. Osip, you're so sweet! What a charming little nose your master has.

The Mayor. For goodness' sake, will you let me say a word to him. [*To* OSIP.] Tell me, friend, what does your master take particular notice of? I mean, what does he like best when he's traveling?

Osip. Well, sir, it all depends. What he likes best is to be well received and well entertained.

The Mayor. Well entertained?

Osip. Yes, sir. You see, sir, I'm only a serf, but he sees to it that I'm well entertained, too. He does that, sir. Sometimes, when we've been staying somewhere, he says to me, "Well, Osip," he says, "have you been well looked after?" "No, sir," I says, "very badly." "Oh," he says, "Osip, that was a bad man. Remind me," he says, "when we get home." "Oh," I thinks to myself [*with a wave of the hand*], "what does it matter? I'm a plain man."

The Mayor. Good. Good! You're right there. I gave you something for tea, so here's something more for a couple of buns.

Osip. Thank you very much, sir. I'm sure I don't deserve it. [*Puts the money in his pocket.*] I'll drink to your health, sir.

Anna. Come and talk to me, Osip. I'll give you something, too.

Maria. Osip, darling, kiss your master for me.

KHLESTAKOV *is heard coughing in the next room.*

The Mayor. Sh-sh! [*Walks on tiptoe; the rest of the scene is conducted in an undertone.*] For God's sake don't make a noise! You'd better go now. That's enough, that's enough.

Anna. Come, Maria. I'll tell you what I've noticed in our visitor, something we can only talk about by ourselves.

The Mayor. Oh, I can imagine the sort of thing they'll

be talking about. I expect if you listened to them long enough, you'd be glad to stop up your ears. [*Turning to* Osip.] Well, friend. [*Enter* Derzhimorda *and* Svistunov.] Sh-sh! Clumsy bears! Trampling with your feet! Come staggering in as if they'd just dropped a ton out of a cart. Where the devil have you been?

Derzhimorda. Acting on your instructions I—

The Mayor. Sh-sh! [*Puts his hand over his mouth.*] Listen to the croaking raven. [*Mimicking him.*] Acting on your instructions! Bellows as though from inside a barrel. [*To* Osip.] Well, friend, you'd better run along and get everything ready for your master. Ask for anything we have in the house. [Osip *goes out.*] And as for you, stand at the front door and don't budge from there. Don't let anyone come into the house, especially any of the shopkeepers. If you let a single one of them in, I'll. . . . As soon as you see anyone coming with a petition, or even without a petition, but looking like a man who might want to present a petition against me, throw him out by the scruff of his neck. Kick him out. Like this! Let him have it! [*Showing with his foot.*] Do you hear? Sh-sh! [*Tiptoes out after the constables.*]

Curtain.

ACT FOUR

The same room in The Mayor's *house. Enter cautiously, almost on tiptoe:* Lyapkin-Tyapkin, Zemlyanika, The Postmaster, Khlopov, Dobchinsky *and* Bobchinsky, *all in full-dress uniform.*

The whole scene is conducted in an undertone.

Lyapkin-Tyapkin [*arranging them all in a semicircle*]. For God's sake, gentlemen, hurry up and form a circle. Try to conduct yourselves correctly. Don't forget, he's received at the palace and bullies the State Council! Stand in military formation. Yes, in military formation. You,

Dobchinsky, run along over there and you, Bobchinsky, stand there.

BOBCHINSKY *and* DOBCHINSKY *run on tiptoe to take up their places.*

Zemlyanika. Say what you like, Judge, we ought to do something.

Lyapkin-Tyapkin. What exactly?

Zemlyanika. Well, we all know what.

Lyapkin-Tyapkin. Slip something into his hand?

Zemlyanika. Yes. Why not?

Lyapkin-Tyapkin. It's risky, damn it. He might start shouting. A great man like that! Couldn't we do it in the form of a subscription from the nobility for some memorial?

The Postmaster. Well, what about saying to him, "Here's some money, sir, sent by post some time ago, and we don't know who it belongs to."

Zemlyanika. You'd better look out he doesn't pack you off by post to a place from which you'd find it difficult to return. Now, you listen to me. These things are not done like that in a well-run state. Why's there a whole regiment of us here? We ought to introduce ourselves to him one by one, and while alone with him in the room— er—do what's necessary, so that no one gets wind of it. That's the way you do things in a well-regulated society. Now, you, Lyapkin-Tyapkin, ought to be the first to start the ball rolling.

Lyapkin-Tyapkin. No, you'd better start. Our distinguished visitor has had lunch in your establishment.

Zemlyanika. No, I think it really ought to be Khlopov as the person responsible for spreading enlightenment among our youth.

Khlopov. No, gentlemen, I can't, I can't. You see, I've been brought up in such a way that if I'm addressed by someone who is one grade above me in the service, I go all to pieces and my tongue sticks in my throat. No, gentlemen, you must let me off. Please, let me off.

Zemlyanika. I'm afraid, Lyapkin-Tyapkin, it must be you. There's no one else. As soon as you open your mouth, it might be Cicero himself making a speech.

Lyapkin-Tyapkin. Good Lord, Cicero indeed! The things

you think of! Though, it's true, I do get carried away sometimes when talking about hounds or retrievers. . . .

All [surrounding him]. No, no, not only about hounds. You can talk about the Tower of Babel as well. No, sir, no, sir! Don't fail us. Be a father to us. No, no, sir!

Lyapkin-Tyapkin. Leave me alone, gentlemen!

Sounds of footsteps and coughing in KHLESTAKOV'S *room. All rush to the other door, getting in each other's way, and trying to get out first, there is a crush at the door, and suppressed cries can be heard.*

Bobchinsky's Voice. Oh, dear, Dobchinsky, you've trodden on my foot.

Zemlyanika's Voice. Don't crush me, gentlemen, for goodness' sake! Let me go.

There are a few more cries of "Oh, dear, oh, dear!" At last they squeeze their way out of the door, and the stage is left empty.

KHLESTAKOV *enters, looking sleepy.*

Khlestakov. I seem to have had a good snooze. Where do they get such mattresses and feather beds? I'm wet with perspiration. They must have given me something strong to drink at lunch yesterday. My head's still throbbing. One might spend one's time very pleasantly here. I do like hospitable people. I don't mind confessing that I'd much rather people tried to please me out of pure kindness and not from self-interest. And the Mayor's daughter isn't at all bad-looking and her mother, too, might still—er— Well, I don't know, but I do like this kind of life.

Enter LYAPKIN-TYAPKIN.

Lyapkin-Tyapkin [stops dead, to himself]. Lord, oh Lord, do get me out of it satisfactorily. My knees are knocking together. [*Aloud, drawing himself up and putting his hand on his sword.*] I have the honor to introduce myself, sir. Lyapkin-Tyapkin, Collegiate Assessor and Judge of the District Court.

Khlestakov. Please sit down. So you're the Judge here?

Lyapkin-Tyapkin. I was elected by the nobility in 1816 for three years and I've carried on with my duties ever since.

Khlestakov. Tell me, is the post of a judge profitable?

Lyapkin-Tyapkin. After serving three terms of three years each, I was presented with the order of Vladimir of the fourth class with the approval of my superiors. [*Aside.*] The money is in my fist, and my fist feels as if it were on fire.

Khlestakov. I like the Vladimir. Now the St. Anne of the third class is not nearly as nice.

Lyapkin-Tyapkin [*pushing forward his clenched fist gradually. Aside*]. Dear Lord, I don't know if I'm coming or going. I feel as if I were sitting on hot coals.

Khlestakov. What have you got in your hand?

Lyapkin-Tyapkin [*panicking and dropping the notes on the floor*]. Nothing, sir.

Khlestakov. Nothing? Why, I can see you've dropped some money.

Lyapkin-Tyapkin [*trembling all over*]. Why, not at all, sir. [*Aside.*] Oh, Lord, I feel as if I were on trial already and the cart had come to take me to prison!

Khlestakov [*picking it up*]. Yes, it is money.

Lyapkin-Tyapkin [*aside*]. Well, it's all over. I'm done for. I'm done for.

Khlestakov. I'll tell you what. Lend it to me.

Lyapkin-Tyapkin [*hurriedly*]. Certainly, sir. Certainly. . . . With the greatest of pleasure. [*Aside.*] Come, courage, courage, man! Oh, pull me through, Holy Virgin!

Khlestakov. I'm afraid I've spent all my money on the journey. On one thing and another. But I'll send it to you as soon as I get to my estate.

Lyapkin-Tyapkin. Why, not at all, sir. Don't give it another thought. It's such an honor. . . . Of course, I shall do my best to deserve your commendation by my zeal and loyalty to my superiors, sir. As far as my poor health, sir— [*Rises from his chair and stands to attention.*] I won't trouble you any longer with my presence, sir. Have you any orders to give me?

Khlestakov. What sort of orders?

Lyapkin-Tyapkin. I mean, sir, have you no orders to give to the district court?

Khlestakov. Why, no. I don't think there is any need for it at the moment.

Lyapkin-Tyapkin [*bowing and going out, aside*]. Well, the town is ours!

Khlestakov [*alone*]. A good fellow—the Judge.

THE POSTMASTER *enters in uniform, stands to attention with his hand on his sword.*

The Postmaster. I have the honor to introduce myself, sir. Court Councilor Shpekin.

Khlestakov. Pleased to meet you. I'm very fond of good company. Do sit down, sir. You've always lived here, I suppose?

The Postmaster. Yes, sir.

Khlestakov. I like this town. Of course, it's not a very populous town, but what does that matter? It's not a capital city, is it?

The Postmaster. No, sir.

Khlestakov. Why, it's only in the capital that you get refined society and no provincial oafs. Don't you think so, sir?

The Postmaster. Yes, sir. [*Aside.*] He doesn't seem a bit proud. Asks one about everything.

Khlestakov. But you must admit, sir, that one can live very happily in a little provincial town, too, can't one?

The Postmaster. Yes, sir.

Khlestakov. Now, to my mind, what does a man want? All he wants is to be respected and to be genuinely liked, isn't that so?

The Postmaster. Perfectly true, sir.

Khlestakov. I must say I'm awfully glad you're of the same opinion as I. Of course people may think that I'm a little eccentric, but then that's the sort of man I am. [*Staring straight at him, says to himself.*] Why not ask the Postmaster for a loan? [*Aloud.*] Such an extraordinary thing happened to me. I've spent all my money on the journey. You couldn't lend me three hundred rubles, could you?

The Postmaster. Why, certainly, sir. I shall consider it a great honor. Here's the money, sir. Please, accept it. I'm very glad to be of service.

Khlestakov. Thank you very much. You see, sir, I dislike doing without all sorts of things on the journey. There is no point in it, is there?

The Postmaster. No, sir. [*Gets up, draws himself up, holding on to his sword.*] Not wishing to trouble you further with my presence, sir. . . . Have you no observation to make with regard to the post office, sir?

Khlestakov. No, none whatever.

THE POSTMASTER *bows and goes out.*

Khlestakov [*lighting a cigar*]. The Postmaster, too, I believe is a very good fellow. At least he's very obliging. I like such people.

KHLOPOV *enters. He is almost pushed into the room through the door. Behind him someone is heard saying almost aloud:* "What are you afraid of?"

Khlopov [*drawing himself up, not without trepidation, with his hands on his sword*]. I have the honor to introduce myself, sir. Khlopov, Titular Councilor, Inspector of Schools.

Khlestakov. Ah, I'm very pleased to meet you. Sit down, sit down. Won't you have a cigar? [*Offers him a cigar.*]

Khlopov [*to himself, irresolutely*]. How do you like that? That I never expected. Ought I to take it or not?

Khlestakov. Take it, take it. It's quite a good cigar. Of course, not what you'd get in Petersburg. There, my dear sir, I smoke cigars at twenty-five rubles a hundred—you feel like kissing your hands when you've smoked one. Here's a light. Light it. [*Holds a candle to him.* KHLOPOV *tries to light the cigar, but his hand is trembling violently.*] Not from that end!

Khlopov [*dropping the cigar in his panic, saying with a wave of his hand to himself in disgust*]. The devil take it! My damned timidity has ruined everything.

Khlestakov. I can see you're not very fond of cigars, sir. I'm afraid they're a weakness of mine. That's also true of the fair sex, sir. Can't resist them. What about you? Which do you like best? Blondes or brunettes? [KHLOPOV *is completely at a loss and does not know what to say.*] Come, tell me frankly, blondes or brunettes?

Khlopov. I'm afraid I don't know, sir.

Khlestakov. Come, come, don't try to wriggle out of it. I'd like very much to know which you prefer.

Khlopov. May I make so bold, sir, as to inform you . . .
[*Aside.*] I don't know what I'm saying.

Khlestakov. Ah! You won't say. I suppose some ravishing little brunette has taken your fancy. Confess, has she?
[KHLOPOV *is silent.*] Oh, I see, you're blushing. Yes, you are! Why won't you say?

Khlopov. I—I—I—I'm scared, your—hon—your rev—reverence—excel— [*Aside.*] That damned tongue of mine has betrayed me.

Khlestakov. Scared? Well, you know, there really is something about my eyes that makes people feel scared. At least, I know there isn't a woman who can hold out against them. Don't you think so?

Khlopov. Yes, sir.

Khlestakov. You know, a most extraordinary thing has happened to me: I've spent all my money on the journey. You couldn't lend me three hundred rubles, could you?

Khlopov [*clutching at his pockets, to himself*]. Oh, dear, I hope I've got it! Yes, I have, I have! [*Takes out notes and hands them over with a shaking hand.*]

Khlestakov. Thank you very much.

Khlopov [*drawing himself up, with his hand on the sword*]. I dare not trouble you any longer with my presence, sir.

Khlestakov. Good-by.

Khlopov [*rushes out almost at a run, saying aside*]. Thank God! Perhaps he won't look into the schoolrooms.

Enter ZEMLYANIKA, *drawing himself up and holding his sword.*

Zemlyanika. I have the honor to introduce myself, sir. Zemlyanika, Court Councilor, Superintendent of Charitable Institutions.

Khlestakov. How do you do? Sit down, please.

Zemlyanika. I had the honor of accompanying you and receiving you in person at the infirmary committed to my care.

Khlestakov. Oh, yes, I remember. You gave me an excellent lunch.

Zemlyanika. I'm glad to deserve well of my country, sir.

Khlestakov. I confess I like a good cuisine. It's a weak-

ness of mine. Tell me, please, weren't you a little shorter
yesterday?

Zemlyanika. Quite possibly, sir. [*After a short pause.*] If
you don't mind my saying so, sir, I don't spare myself and
perform my duties zealously. [*Draws his chair up closer
and speaks in an undertone.*] Now, the Postmaster here
does nothing at all: he neglects his duties terribly, keeps
back dispatches and so on. I think you ought to look into
it, sir. Our Judge, too, who was here a short while ago,
does nothing but course hares and keep dogs in the courtroom. And to be quite frank with you, sir, his conduct is
not entirely as it should be. You see, sir, I feel it is my duty
to tell you this for the good of my country, although he
is a relative and a friend of mine. Yes, sir, his conduct is
most reprehensible. There's a landowner here, one Dobchinsky. I believe you've seen him. Well, as soon as this Dobchinsky leaves his house, the Judge is there, sitting with his
wife. . . . I'm ready to take my oath on it, sir. Why, you
have only to look at his children: not one of them is like
Dobchinsky, but every one, even the little girl, is the
spitting image of the Judge.

Khlestakov. You don't say! I should never have thought
it of him.

Zemlyanika. Now, take the Inspector of Schools, sir. I
simply don't know how the authorities came to entrust him
with such a post. Why, he's worse than a Jacobin. The
pernicious ideas he puts into the heads of our youth are
simply beyond words. Would you like me, sir, to put it all
into writing?

Khlestakov. Yes, by all means, put it into writing. I shall
be very pleased to have it. You see, when I am bored, I
like to read something amusing. . . . What is your name?
I keep forgetting.

Zemlyanika. Zemlyanika.

Khlestakov. Oh, yes, Zemlyanika. And tell me, please,
have you any children?

Zemlyanika. Why yes, sir. Five. Two of them are
grown up.

Khlestakov. Grown up! And what are they . . . I mean,
what are they—

Zemlyanika. You mean, sir, what are their names?

Khlestakov. Yes. What are their names?

Zemlyanika. Nikolai, Ivan, Elizaveta, Maria, Perpetua.

Khlestakov. Very nice.

Zemlyanika. Not daring to trouble you with my presence, sir, and waste your time devoted to sacred duties. . . . [*Bows and is about to go out.*]

Khlestakov [*seeing him to the door*]. No, it's quite all right. What you have been telling me is very amusing, you know. Come and talk to me another time. . . . I like that kind of thing very much. [*Goes back and, opening the door, shouts after him.*] Hey, you, what's your name? I keep forgetting.

Zemlyanika. Zemlyanika.

Khlestakov. Do me a favor, Mr. Zemlyanika. A very extraordinary thing happened to me. I've spent all my money on the journey. You couldn't let me have a small loan, could you? About four hundred rubles?

Zemlyanika. Yes, sir.

Khlestakov. How very convenient! Thank you very much.

ZEMLYANIKA *goes out. Enter* BOBCHINSKY *and* DOBCHINSKY.

Bobchinsky. I have the honor to introduce myself. Peter Ivanovich Bobchinsky, a resident of this town.

Dobchinsky. Peter Ivanovich Dobchinsky, landowner.

Khlestakov. Ah, I've seen you before, haven't I? I believe it was you who slipped and fell on the floor. How's your nose?

Bobchinsky. Thank you, it's healed up. Yes, it's quite all right now.

Khlestakov. Ah, I'm glad to hear it. [*Suddenly and abruptly.*] You haven't any money on you, have you?

Bobchinsky. Money? How do you mean, sir?

Khlestakov [*aloud and quickly*]. A thousand rubles to lend me.

Bobchinsky. I'm afraid I haven't got so much money on me, sir. You don't happen to have it, do you, Dobchinsky?

Dobchinsky. I'm afraid I haven't. You see, my money, if you care to know, is all in the hands of the public trustee.

Khlestakov. Oh, well, if you haven't a thousand, let me have a hundred.

Bobchinsky [*fumbling in his pockets*]. Haven't you got a hundred rubles, Dobchinsky? All I've got is forty rubles in notes.

Dobchinsky [*looking in his wallet*]. All I've got is twenty-five rubles.

Bobchinsky. Have a good look, Dobchinsky. I know you have a hole in your right-hand pocket, and some money might have slipped through into the lining.

Dobchinsky. No, there's nothing there.

Khlestakov. Oh, well, never mind. I thought I'd just ask. Sixty-five rubles will do very well. It will be quite all right. [*Accepts money.*]

Dobchinsky. If you don't mind, sir, I'd like to ask your aid in a most delicate matter.

Khlestakov. Oh? What is it?

Dobchinsky. It's a most delicate matter, sir. My eldest son, you see, was born before I was married.

Khlestakov. Was he?

Dobchinsky. I mean, it's only in a manner of speaking. He was born exactly as though in lawful wedlock, and I made it all right by the lawful bonds of matrimony. So, you see, sir, I'd like him to become altogether my legitimate son to bear the same name as I: Dobchinsky.

Khlestakov. All right, let him bear your name. There's no law against it.

Dobchinsky. I wouldn't have troubled you, sir, but he's such a bright boy, you know. It would be a pity to sacrifice his talents. He's very promising indeed. He can recite all sorts of poems by heart and if he gets hold of a penknife he can make you a little carriage as skillfully as a conjuror. Mr. Bobchinsky here knows all about it.

Bobchinsky. Yes, he's a very gifted boy.

Khlestakov. Very well, very well, I'll see what I can do about it. I'll speak about that . . . I hope—er—everything will be arranged in the best possible way. Yes, yes. . . . [*Turning to* BOBCHINSKY.] You haven't anything to tell me, have you?

Bobchinsky. I have, sir, I have a very humble request to make, sir.

Khlestakov. What about?

Bobchinsky. I'd like to ask you, sir, when you go back to

Petersburg, to say to all the grand gentlemen there—senators and admirals, that "you know, Your Highness or Your Excellency, in such and such a town lives one Peter Ivanovich Bobchinsky." Please just say that: "lives one Peter Ivanovich Bobchinsky."

Khlestakov. Very well.

Dobchinsky. I'm sorry to have troubled you with my presence, sir.

Bobchinsky. I'm sorry to have troubled you with my presence, sir.

Khlestakov. It's perfectly all right. I'm very glad to have met you. [*Gets rid of them. Alone.*] There's a great number of civil servants here. I can't help thinking that they have taken me for someone of great importance in the government. I must have spun them a fine yarn yesterday. What fools! I must write and tell Tryapichkin about it. He contributes articles to the press—let him write them up properly. Hey, Osip, bring me some paper and ink. [OSIP *looks in at the door, says:* "At once, sir."] If Tryapichkin gets his knife into anyone, the poor fellow had better look out. He wouldn't spare his own father for the sake of a witty remark and he's fond of money, too. Still, they are good fellows, these officials. I mean, it was nice of them to have lent me all this money. Let me see, how much have I got? Three hundred from the Judge, three hundred from the Postmaster, that makes six hundred, seven hundred, eight hundred . . . What a greasy note! Eight hundred, nine hundred! Oho, over a thousand! Now, my dear captain, let me just come across you now, and we'll see who'll get the better of whom this time.

Enter OSIP *with ink and paper.*

Khlestakov. Well, you see, you fool, how they receive and entertain me here. [*Begins writing.*]

Osip. Yes, thank God. Only, do you know what, sir?

Khlestakov [*writing*]. What?

Osip. You'd better get away from here. It's high time we were gone.

Khlestakov [*writing*]. What nonsense! Why?

Osip. I think we ought to, sir. We've had enough of them all. You had a good time here for a couple of days

—well, that's enough. What's the good of having anything
to do with them? Have done with them. You never know
what may happen. Somebody else may arrive. . . . Please,
sir. And the horses here are first class—we could be racing
along.

Khlestakov [*writing*]. No. I'd rather stay here a bit
longer. Tomorrow will do.

Osip. Why tomorrow, sir? Let's go today, please, sir.
It's true it's a great honor for you, but we'd better get
away as soon as possible. You see, sir, they've mistaken you
for somebody else. . . . And your father, too, will be
angry with you for taking so long to get home. We would
roll along famously, sir. They'll give us excellent horses
here.

Khlestakov [*writing*]. Oh, very well. Only take this
letter to the post first. And you may as well get my order
for post horses. Only make sure we have good horses now.
Tell the drivers I'll tip them a ruble each to drive me like
a courier and sing songs! [*Goes on writing.*] I can imagine
how Tryapichkin will split with laughing.

Osip. I'll give your letter to the man here to post, sir.
I'd better start packing so as not to lose time.

Khlestakov [*writing*]. Very well. Only bring me a candle.

Osip [*goes out and speaks behind the scenes*]. I say, take
this letter to the post and tell the Postmaster not to
charge for it. Tell them to send around at once the very
best horses, the express ones. And say my master doesn't
pay the fare. He travels at the government's expense. And
tell them to look sharp, or my master will be angry. Wait
a minute, the letter isn't ready yet.

Khlestakov [*goes on writing*]. I wonder where he lives
now. In Post Office Street or Gorokhovy Street. He, too,
likes changing his lodgings frequently and not paying his
rent. Oh, I'll change it and address it to Post Office Street.
[*Folds up the letter and addresses it.*]

Osip *brings the candle.* Khlestakov *seals the letter. At
that moment* Derzhimorda's *voice is heard:* "Where are
you barging in, beard? I tell you, I've orders to admit no
one."

Khlestakov [*gives letter to* Osip]. Here, take it.

Voices of Shopkeepers. Let us in, Constable! You can't refuse. We're here on business.

Derzhimorda's Voice. Get out of here, get out. He's not seeing anyone. He's asleep! [*The noise grows louder.*]

Khlestakov. What's going on there, Osip? Have a look what the uproar's about.

Osip [*looking out of window*]. It's some shopkeepers trying to come in, but the constable won't let them. They're waving papers about. I expect they want to see you.

Khlestakov [*going up to the window*]. What is it, good people?

Voices of Shopkeepers. We appeal to you, Your Excellency. Please accept our petition.

Khlestakov. Let them in, let them in! Let them come in. Osip, go and tell him to let them in. [OSIP *goes out.* KHLESTAKOV *accepts petitions through the window, opens one and reads.*] "To his Most Noble Highness, the Master of Finances, from Abdulin, merchant. . . ." Dear me, what nonsense! There is no such title.

The SHOPKEEPERS *come in with a basket of wine bottles and loaves of sugar.*

Khlestakov. What can I do for you, good people?

Shopkeepers. We ask you humbly to listen to us, sir.

Khlestakov. What do you want?

Shopkeepers. Do not ruin us, sir. We're suffering constant persecution for no reason at all.

Khlestakov. Who from?

One of the Shopkeepers. Why, sir, it's all the Mayor here. There's never been a mayor like him, sir. There are no words to describe the wrong he does to people like us. He has ruined us all by billeting soldiers on us. We can't carry on any longer. He doesn't treat us fairly. He pulls a man by the beard and shouts, "Oh, you Tartar!" Yes, indeed, sir. And it isn't as if we were forgetting our duty to him. We've always done what's expected of us. We don't mind giving what is necessary for the dresses of his wife and daughter. But that's not enough for him, sir. Oh, no! He walks into the shop and takes everything he fancies. If he sees a piece of cloth, he says, "Aha, my dear man, that's a nice piece of cloth you've got there. Send it around to my house." Well, of course, you have to send it, and there may be as much as fifty yards in the piece.

Khlestakov. You don't say! Oh, what a scoundrel!

Shopkeeper. It's quite true, sir. We never had such a mayor within living memory. You have to hide everything in the shop when you see him coming. For you see, sir, it isn't only the dainty things he goes for: he'll take any rubbish. Prunes that have lain seven years in the barrel that my shop assistants wouldn't touch. He eats them by the handful. His name-day is St. Anthony's, and on that day we take all sorts of things to his house. There's nothing that he hasn't got, but no! He wants more. He says, "St. Onufry's is my name-day, too." Well, sir, what can we do about it? We have to take presents to him on that day, too.

Khlestakov. Why, he's nothing but a brigand!

Shopkeepers. Yes, indeed, sir. And if you try to cross him, he'll billet a whole regiment on you. And if you protest, he'll have the doors of your house locked. "I'm not going to flog or torture you," he says, "for that's against the law," he says, "but we're going to put you on a diet of red herrings, my dear fellow!"

Khlestakov. Oh, what a rogue! Why, he should be sent to Siberia for treating you like that.

Shopkeepers. Send him wherever you think fit, sir, so long as it is a long way off. Do not refuse our humble offerings, sir. Please accept this sugar and this basket of wine with our good wishes.

Khlestakov. No, no, don't think of it. I take no bribes. But, of course, if you were to let me have a loan of three hundred rubles, that would be a different matter: I shall be glad to take a loan.

Shopkeepers. Why, by all means, sir. [*Take out the money.*] But why only three hundred? Take five hundred. Only help us.

Khlestakov. Very well. I've nothing against a loan. I'll take a loan.

Shopkeepers [*offer him money on a silver tray*]. Please, accept the tray with it.

Khlestakov. Oh, I suppose I may as well take the tray, too.

Shopkeepers [*bowing*]. Why not take the sugar as well, sir?

Khlestakov. Oh, no! I never take bribes.

Osip. Why not take the sugar, sir? Take it. It will come in handy on the journey. Let's have the sugar loaves and the basket. Let's have the lot. It will all come in useful. What's that? A piece of string? Let's have the piece of string. String comes in handy on a journey, too. If the carriage or anything else breaks, you can tie it up with a piece of string.

Shopkeepers. So don't forget, sir, to do what we ask. If you won't help us, we don't know what's going to happen to us. We are in a desperate plight, sir.

Khlestakov. Why, certainly! certainly! I'll do my best.

The Shopkeepers *go out. A woman's voice is heard:* "No, you daren't turn me away. I'll complain of you to the gentleman himself. Don't you push me. You hurt me."

Khlestakov. Who's that? [*Goes up to the window.*] Oh, I see. What is it, my good woman?

Voices of Two Women. Help us, kind sir. Tell them to let us through. We want you to hear what we have to say.

Khlestakov [*at the window*]. Let her in.

Enter the Locksmith's Wife *and the* Sergeant's Widow.

Locksmith's Wife [*bowing low*]. I beg your help, kind sir.

Sergeant's Widow. I beg you to help me, too, sir.

Khlestakov. Who are you?

Sergeant's Widow. I'm Mrs. Ivanov, a sergeant's widow, sir.

Locksmith's Wife. Fevronya Petrova Poshlyopkina, sir, wife of a locksmith, a tradeswoman of the town.

Khlestakov. Wait, speak one at a time. What do you want?

Locksmith's Wife. I beg you to help me, sir. Protect me from the Mayor. May the Lord punish him. May neither his children nor he, the rascal, nor his uncles, nor his aunts prosper.

Khlestakov. Why, what has he done?

Locksmith's Wife. He pressed my husband into the army and it wasn't his turn. It's against the law to take a married man.

Khlestakov. How could he do that?

Locksmith's Wife. He did it, the villain, he did it. May the Lord smite him in this world and the next. May the plague take him and his aunt, too, if he has one, and his father, if he's living. May he, the blackguard, die like a dog, or may he choke, the rascal. It was the tailor's son who should have been taken, a drunken fellow, too. But, you see, his parents gave the Mayor a handsome present, so he picked on the son of Panteleyeva, the draper's woman, but she sent his wife three pieces of linen, so he came to me. "What do you want a husband for?" he says to me. "He's no more good to you," he says. Well, I know whether he's any good to me or not. That's my business, the scoundrel. "He's a thief," he says. "He may have stolen nothing yet," he says, "but all the same," he says, "he's sure to steal one day, and he'll be pressed into the army next year, anyway." "But what am I to do without a husband, you rascal? I'm a weak woman, you scoundrel! May none of your relations see the light of day! And if you have a mother-in-law, I hope she'll. . . ."

Khlestakov. All right, all right. [*Shows the old woman out.*] Well, and what about you?

Locksmith's Wife [*going out*]. Do not forget, sir. Take pity on me.

Sergeant's Widow. I've come to lodge a complaint against the Mayor, sir.

Khlestakov. Well, what has he done to you? Tell me, and be brief.

Sergeant's Widow. He flogged me, sir.

Khlestakov. What?

Sergeant's Widow. By mistake, sir. You see, sir, some of our women were fighting in the market. The police didn't get there in time, so they arrested me, and they whipped me so mercilessly that I couldn't sit down for two days.

Khlestakov. So what's to be done about it now?

Sergeant's Widow. Well, sir, you couldn't do anything about it now, of course. But make him pay me damages for the mistake. It's not every day a lucky chance like that comes one's way. The money would come in very handy just now.

Khlestakov. All right, all right. You can go now. I'll see about it. [*Hands with petitions are thrust in at the window.*] Who else is there? [*Goes up to the window.*] No more, no more. [*Moves away from the window.*] I'm sick of them all, damn it. Don't let them in, Osip.

Osip [*shouts through the window*]. Go away, go away! No time now! Come tomorrow! [*The door opens, and a figure appears in a frieze coat, with an unshaven chin, a swollen lip and a bandage around the face. Behind it can be seen several other figures.*] Be off, be off. Where are you barging into? [*Lays both hands on the stomach of the first figure and pushes him out into the passage, slamming the door behind him.*]

Enter MARIA.

Maria. Oh!

Khlestakov. What are you so frightened about?

Maria. No, sir, I wasn't frightened.

Khlestakov [*showing off*]. Why, I'm very pleased that you have taken me for a man who. . . . But may I ask where you were going?

Maria. Why, sir, I wasn't going anywhere.

Khlestakov. And why weren't you going anywhere?

Maria. I thought Mother was here.

Khlestakov. No, no, I'd like to know why you weren't going anywhere.

Maria. I'm sorry I'm disturbing you. I see you're engaged in important business.

Khlestakov [*showing off*]. But your eyes are worth more than important business. . . . You can't possibly disturb me. No, ma'am, on the contrary, your presence can only give me pleasure.

Maria. You talk like a man of the world.

Khlestakov. To such a ravishing creature as yourself. May I have the happiness of offering you a chair? But, no, you should have a throne, not a chair.

Maria. I really don't know, sir. I ought to be going now. [*Sits down.*]

Khlestakov. What a lovely fichu.

Maria. I'm afraid you're making fun of me, sir. I suppose you must enjoy making fun of us provincials.

Khlestakov. How I'd like to be that fichu, ma'am, to embrace your lily-white neck.

Maria. I don't understand what you're talking about, sir. What fichu? What strange weather we're having today.

Khlestakov. And your lips, ma'am, are better than any weather.

Maria. You do say such things. I'd like to ask you to write a few verses in my album. You must know lots of them.

Khlestakov. I'll do anything for you, ma'am. Tell me, what kind of verses do you like?

Maria. Oh, any verses, sir. Nice ones. New ones.

Khlestakov. Verses? Oh, I know lots of them.

Maria. Oh, do tell me what you will write for me!

Khlestakov. But why tell them? I know them well enough, anyhow.

Maria. Oh, I do love poetry.

Khlestakov. Oh, I've got lots of poems of every kind. What do you say to this one? "O man, who in thy hour of sorrow in vain against thy Lord dost murmur!" And there are plenty of others. Can't remember them now. Still, it doesn't matter. Instead, I'd better offer you my love which your eyes have— [*Draws up his chair.*]

Maria. Love? I don't understand love. . . . I never knew what love means. . . . [*Moves her chair away.*]

Khlestakov [*moves up his chair*]. Why do you move your chair away? We'd be happier sitting close to one another.

Maria [*moves her chair away*]. Why close? Isn't it the same if we aren't so near?

Khlestakov [*moves his chair nearer*]. Why? We might just as well be close.

Maria. But why?

Khlestakov [*moves nearer*]. You only imagine it's close. You may as well imagine that we're far apart. How happy I'd be, ma'am, if I could hold you in my arms.

Maria [*looking out of the window*]. What bird flew past the window just now? Was it a magpie or some other bird?

Khlestakov [*kisses her shoulder and looks out of the window*]. A magpie.

Maria [*gets up indignantly*]. No, that's too much! How dare you, sir!

Khlestakov [*detaining her*]. I'm sorry. I did it because I love you. Yes, indeed, I love you.

Maria. You think that because I am a provincial girl you can. . . . [*Tries to get away.*]

Khlestakov [*still detaining her*]. I love you. Indeed, I do. I meant no harm. I did it just out of fun. Please, don't be angry. I'm ready to beg your pardon on my knees. [*Falls on his knees.*] Please, forgive me. I'm sorry. You see, I'm on my knees.

Enter ANNA.

Anna [*seeing* KHLESTAKOV *on his knees*]. Good heavens!

Khlestakov [*getting up*]. Damnation!

Anna [*to her daughter*]. What does this mean, miss? What sort of behavior is this?

Maria. Why, Mother. . . .

Anna. Leave the room at once! Do you hear? Go on, go on, and don't let me set eyes on you here again. [MARIA *goes out in tears.*] I must say I'm astonished, sir!

Khlestakov [*aside*]. She, too, is an appetizing morsel. Not bad-looking at all. [*Kneels.*] Madam, you see I'm dying of love.

Anna. What? You're on your knees again? Do get up, sir! Please get up. The floor is anything but clean.

Khlestakov. No, ma'am, on my knees! It must be on my knees! I want to know my fate: is it life or death?

Anna. I'm sorry, I don't quite understand the meaning of your words. If I'm not mistaken, you're asking for my daughter's hand.

Khlestakov. No, I'm in love with you. My life is hanging by a thread. If you will not requite my undying love, I don't deserve to go on living any longer. With my heart aglow, I ask your hand.

Anna. But allow me to observe, sir, that I'm in a certain sense, er—married.

Khlestakov. That doesn't matter. Love knows of no such distinctions. As Karamzin said: "The law alone condemns it." We shall retire to some shady nook beside a running brook. . . . Your hand, I ask your hand.

MARIA *runs in suddenly.*

Maria. Mother, Father says you are to. . . . [*Seeing* KHLESTAKOV *on his knees, utters a little scream.*] Good heavens!

Anna. Well, what do you want? What is it? What have you come in for? How flighty can you be? Rushing in like a scalded cat! What do you find so surprising about it? What are you imagining? Really, you behave just like a child of three. Why, my dear, nobody, nobody would ever take you for a girl of eighteen. I don't know when you'll learn some sense, when you will learn to conduct yourself as a well-bred girl should, when you will understand what is meant by good manners and conduct befitting a young lady.

Maria [*through tears*]. Really, Mother, I didn't know.

Anna. There's always a sort of wind blowing about your head. You're always copying the Lyapkin-Tyapkin girls. Why copy them? There's no need for you to copy them. There are plenty of other people to copy—your mother, for one.

Khlestakov [*seizing the daughter's hand*]. Madam, do not oppose our happiness. Give your blessing to our eternal love.

Anna [*dumbfounded*]. So it's with her you're in—

Khlestakov. Decide: is it life or death?

Anna. There now, you see, you silly, it's for you, a worthless girl like you, that our distinguished visitor was on his knees. And you come running in like a mad thing. Well, it would serve you right if I refused. You don't deserve such happiness.

Maria. I won't do it again, Mother. Really, I won't.

THE MAYOR *runs in breathlessly.*

The Mayor. Your Excellency, don't ruin me, don't ruin me!

Khlestakov. What's the matter with you?

The Mayor. The shopkeepers have been complaining to Your Excellency. I can assure you on my honor, sir, that not half of it is true. It is they who cheat and give short measure. The sergeant's widow told you a lie when she said I flogged her. I never flogged her. She flogged herself!

Khlestakov. To blazes with the sergeant's widow. I've something better to think of now.

The Mayor. Don't believe it, sir, don't believe it. They're such liars that a child wouldn't believe them. They're known all over the town for their lying. As for swindling, let me tell you, sir, that the world has never known such swindlers!

Anna. Do you know the honor Mr. Khlestakov is doing us? He's asked for our daughter's hand in marriage.

The Mayor. What are you talking about? You must be out of your mind, my love. Don't be angry, Your Excellency. She's a bit touched in the head. Her mother, too, was the same.

Khlestakov. But, sir, I really ask your daughter's hand. I love her.

The Mayor. I can't believe it, Your Excellency.

Anna. But when he tells you so!

Khlestakov. I'm in dead earnest, sir. I might lose my reason from love.

The Mayor. I can't believe it, sir. I am unworthy of such an honor.

Khlestakov. But, sir, if you refuse me your daughter's hand, God knows what I may not do.

The Mayor. I can't believe it, sir. Your Excellency is joking.

Anna. Oh, what a blockhead you are! Isn't he telling you so himself?

The Mayor. I can't believe it.

Khlestakov. Consent, sir, consent! I'm a desperate man! I may do anything. If I shoot myself, you may be put on trial.

The Mayor. Oh, dear, I assure you I'm not to blame for anything. Please do not be angry. Do as Your Excellency thinks fit. My head. . . . I really don't know what's going on there. I feel a greater fool than I've ever felt in my life.

Anna. Well, give them your blessing.

Khlestakov *goes up to him with* Maria.

The Mayor. May God bless you. It's not my fault.

KHLESTAKOV *and* MARIA *exchange kisses.* THE MAYOR
stares at them.

The Mayor. Good Lord, then it's really true! [*Rubbing his eyes.*] They're kissing each other. Good heavens, then he is engaged to my daughter! [*He utters a cry and jumps for joy.*] Bravo, Anton! Well done, Mayor! So that's how things have turned out!

Enter OSIP.

Osip. The horses are ready.

Khlestakov. Ah, very good. I'm coming.

The Mayor. What do you mean, sir? Are you leaving us?

Khlestakov. Yes, I'm afraid so.

The Mayor. But when. . . . That is . . . er. . . . Didn't you yourself mention a wedding, sir?

Khlestakov. Oh, that! I'm only going for a short while. For a day. To see my uncle. He's a rich old man. I shall be back tomorrow.

The Mayor. Well, in that case I shouldn't dream of detaining you, sir. We shall look forward to your safe return.

Khlestakov. Of course, of course. I shan't be away long. Good-by, my love. I simply can't express what I feel. Good-by, my darling. [*Kisses her hand.*]

The Mayor. But don't you need anything for the journey, sir? I believe you're a little short of money, aren't you?

Khlestakov. Oh, no, I'm sure I'm not. [*After a moment's reflection.*] However, why not?

The Mayor. How much would you like?

Khlestakov. Oh, well, you lent me two hundred, I mean, not two but four hundred. I don't want to take advantage of your mistake. So perhaps you could let me have the same again to make it a round eight hundred.

The Mayor. Why, of course. [*Takes the money out of his wallet.*] There you are! As luck would have it, all brand-new notes!

Khlestakov. Thank you. [*Takes the notes and examines them.*] That is nice. You know, they say new notes bring good luck.

The Mayor. Yes, indeed, sir.

Khlestakov. Good-by, sir. I'm very much obliged for your hospitality. I can say it with all sincerity. I've never had such a fine reception anywhere. Good-by, ma'am! Good-by, my darling Maria!

They go out. KHLESTAKOV'S *voice behind the scenes.*

Khlestakov's Voice. Good-by, Maria, my darling angel.

The Mayor's Voice. You're not traveling by the ordinary post-chaise?

Khlestakov's Voice. Yes, I'm used to it. Springs make my head ache.

Driver's Voice. Whoa!

The Mayor's Voice. At least put a rug on your seat. Shall I have a rug fetched for you?

Khlestakov's Voice. No, why? It doesn't matter. However, perhaps you might let them fetch a rug.

The Mayor's Voice. Hey, Avdotya, go to the storeroom and fetch a rug, the best you can find, the Persian one with the blue ground. Quickly!

Driver's Voice. Whoa!

The Mayor's Voice. When are we to expect you back, sir?

Khlestakov's Voice. Tomorrow or the day after.

Osip's Voice. That's the rug? Give it here. Put it there. Now, put some straw this side.

Driver's Voice. Whoa!

Osip's Voice. Here, this side! Here, some more. That's right. That's fine. [*Pats the rug with his hand.*] Now sit down, sir.

Khlestakov's Voice. Good-by, sir.

The Mayor's Voice. Good-by, Your Excellency.

Women's Voices. Good-by, Ivan Alexandrovich.

Khlestakov's Voice. Good-by, Mother.

Driver's Voice. Gee-up, my hearties. [*Harness bells tinkle.*]

Curtain.

ACT FIVE

The same room. THE MAYOR, ANNA *and* MARIA.

THE MAYOR. Well, my love, eh? Did you expect such a thing? What a catch, damn it! Well, tell me frankly, did you ever dream of such a thing? From being just a mayor's wife and suddenly—damn it all!—to be allied with a devil like that!

Anna. Not at all. I knew it all along. You're surprised simply because you're an ordinary man and have never mixed with decent people.

The Mayor. I am a decent person myself, my love. But really, come to think of it, what fine birds we've become now—you and I! Eh, Anna, my love? At the top of the tree, eh? Damn it! You wait, I'll show 'em, I'll show all those who fell over themselves to lodge complaints and denunciations against me. Hey! Who is there? [*Enter a* CONSTABLE.] Oh, it's you, Ivan Karpovich. Fetch me those shopkeepers. I'll show them, the swine. Complain about me, will they? Oh, the damned Judases! You wait, my dear fellows! Before you had it easy, now it'll be much worse for you. Make a list of the people who came to complain about me, and especially those damned scribblers who wrote down their petitions. And don't forget to tell them all what a great honor God has bestowed on me. Let them all know that the Mayor's daughter is not marrying any clodhopper but someone occupying a great position in the world who can do anything, anything! Tell them all. Let them all know it. Shout it from the housetops! Ring the church bells, damn it! If you're going to celebrate, then let's celebrate it properly! [*The* CONSTABLE *goes out.*] So that's how things are now, Anna, my love. What do you think? Where are we going to live now? Here or in Petersburg?

Anna. Naturally, in Petersburg. We couldn't very well stay here, could we?

The Mayor. Well, if it's to be in Petersburg, then Petersburg it shall be! It could be very nice here, too, though. What do you think, my love? I suppose it's to hell with the mayor's office now, eh, my love?

Anna. Why, of course! You don't want to be a mayor now, do you?

The Mayor. What do you think, my love? I might get promoted to a higher rank now, mightn't I? For, you see, as he's on familiar terms with Cabinet ministers and is at the palace every day, he may get me promoted even to the rank of general with time. What do you think, my love? Is there a chance of my becoming a general?

Anna. I should think so! Of course there is.

The Mayor. Oh, hang it all, it would be nice to be a general with a sash over one's shoulder. Which do you like best, my love—the red or the blue?

Anna. The blue, of course, is best.

The Mayor. Aha, so that's what you've set your heart on! I shouldn't mind the red one. For why does one want to be a general? Because if you happen to go anywhere, couriers and adjutants gallop ahead of you, calling for horses, and at the posting stations they won't give them to anyone, they all have to wait—titular councilors, captains, mayors—but you don't care a damn. You dine at the Governor's and there—stand up, Mayor! Ha, ha, ha! [*Roars with laughter.*] That's what so tempting about it, damn it.

Anna. You always like something coarse. You must remember that we shall have to change completely our present mode of life, that in future your friends will not be some judge who's crazy about dogs and with whom you go coursing hares, or some Zemlyanika. On the contrary, all your friends will be men of the most refined manners: counts and people in the highest society. . . . But I can't help feeling uneasy about you. You use the most dreadful expressions, such as you never hear in good society.

The Mayor. What does it matter? Words do no harm.

Anna. Yes, that was all very well while you were the Mayor, but there life will be quite different.

The Mayor. Yes, I'm told there are two sorts of fish there, smelt and sig, which simply melt in your mouth.

Anna. All he thinks of is fish. I'm quite determined that ours shall be the smartest house in Petersburg. In my drawing room there shall be such a perfume that the moment you enter it, you close your eyes like this. [*Closes her eyes and sniffs.*] Oh, how delicious!

Enter SHOPKEEPERS.

The Mayor. Ah, how do you do, my fine fellows!

Shopkeepers [*bowing*]. We wish you good health, sir.

The Mayor. Thank you, my dear fellows, thank you. How are you today? How is business? Why, you tea-swilling samovar-sellers, you counter-jumpers, so you're complaining about me, are you? You dirty scoundrels, you arch-swindlers, you sneaking frauds, complaining, are you? Well, have you gained much by it? So you thought I'd be clapped into jail? May seven devils and one witch choke you!

Anna. Good gracious, Anton, what language!

The Mayor [*displeased*]. What does it matter? Do you know that the official you complained to about me is going to marry my daughter? What do you say to that, eh? I'll show you now. Ugh! You cheat people, you get a government contract and defraud the treasury of a hundred thousand rubles by supplying rotten cloth, then give me twenty yards and expect a reward for it! Why, if the authorities knew, they'd. . . . Shoves his big belly in front of him—he's a merchant if you please. Don't you dare touch him! "We're as good as the nobility," they say. Why, a nobleman—why, you ugly brute—a nobleman is an educated man: he may be thrashed at school, but it's to some purpose, it's to teach him something useful. And what are you? You start with petty frauds, and your master beats you if you don't know how to cheat properly. When you are small boys, before you can repeat the Lord's Prayer, you know how to give short measure. And as soon as you grow a big belly and stuff your pockets full of money, you start giving yourself airs. Dear me, what a fine fellow! Because you empty sixteen samovars a day you think you're an important fellow. Why, I don't give a fig for your dignity and your air of self-importance.

Shopkeepers [*bowing*]. We're very sorry, sir.

The Mayor. Complaining, are you? And who helped you to defraud the government when you were building a bridge and charged twenty thousand for the timber when you didn't use even a hundred rubles' worth? I helped you, you goat beard. Forgotten, have you? If I'd reported you, I could have you sent to Siberia. What do you say to that, eh?

One of the Shopkeepers. We are very sorry, sir. The devil tempted us. We swear we'll never complain again. We're ready to give you any satisfaction you like, only don't be angry.

The Mayor. Don't be angry? You're groveling at my feet now. Why? Because I've got the whip hand. But if you'd got the better of me even a little bit, you'd have trampled me in the mud, you swine. And rolled a log on top of me.

Shopkeepers [*bowing low*]. Don't ruin us, sir.

The Mayor. Now it's don't ruin us, don't ruin us! But what was it before? Why, I'll. . . . [*With a wave of the hand.*] Oh, never mind, may God forgive you! That's enough! I'm not vindictive. Only, be more careful in future. I'm marrying my daughter not to any ordinary nobleman. Mind, your congratulations are. . . . Understand? Don't try to get off with a filet of sturgeon or a loaf of sugar. Well, you can go now.

The SHOPKEEPERS *go out. Enter* LYAPKIN-TYAPKIN *and* ZEMLYANIKA, *followed by* RASTAKOVSKY.

Lyapkin-Tyapkin [*in the doorway*]. Am I to believe the rumors, Mr. Mayor? Have you really come in for this extraordinary good fortune?

Zemlyanika. Let me congratulate you on your great good fortune, sir. I was heartily glad when I heard of it. [*Goes up to* ANNA *and kisses her hand.*] Maria Antonovna!

Rastakovsky [*comes in*]. I congratulate you, sir. May God give you and the happy pair long life and happiness and lots and lots of grandchildren and great-grandchildren. Anna Andreyevna! [*Goes up to* ANNA *and kisses her hand.*] Maria Antonovna! [*Goes up and kisses her hand.*]

Enter Korobkin, *his wife and* Lyulyukov.

Korobkin. Let me congratulate you, Mr. Mayor! And you, Anna Andreyevna. [*Goes up to* Anna *and kisses her hand.*] And you, Maria Antonovna. [*Goes up to* Maria *and kisses her hand.*]

Mrs. Korobkin. My warmest congratulations, my dear Anna, on your new happiness.

Lyulyukov. Accept my congratulations, Anna Andreyevna. [*Goes up to kiss her hand, then turns to the audience and clicks his tongue with an air of bravado.*] Maria Antonovna, let me congratulate you. [*Goes up to her and kisses her hand, turns to the audience with the same air of bravado.*]

A great number of guests in frock coats and swallowtails enter, first go over to Anna, *kiss her hand and say:* "Anna Andreyevna!" *and then go up to* Maria *and say:* "Maria Antonovna!" Bobchinsky *and* Dobchinsky *push their way through the crowd.*

Bobchinsky. Congratulations.

Dobchinsky. Congratulations, Mr. Mayor.

Bobchinsky. On the most propitious occasion.

Dobchinsky. Anna Andreyevna!

Bobchinsky. Anna Andreyevna!

Both go up to kiss her hand at the same moment and knock their heads together.

Bobchinsky. Maria Antonovna! [*Goes up to kiss her hand.*] Congratulations! You'll be very happy. You will walk about in a dress of gold, have all sorts of delicate soups, and have a most amusing time.

Bobchinsky [*interrupting him*]. Maria Antonovna, congratulations! May the Lord grant you all prosperity and lots of money and a baby boy no bigger than this. [*Shows with his hand.*] Little enough to sit in your hand. Yes, ma'am, the little boy will keep on crying "Wah, wah!"

A few more visitors come in and go up to kiss the ladies' hands, followed by Khlopov *and his wife.*

Khlopov. Congratulations.

Mrs. Khlopov [*runs forward to* Anna]. Congratulations, my dear! [*They kiss.*] You can't imagine how delighted I was to hear the good news. They told me the Mayor's daughter is being married! Thank God, I thought to myself, and I was so delighted I said to my husband, "Look here, darling, that's a piece of good fortune for Anna Andreyevna!" Well, I thought to myself, thank God! And I said to him, "I'm so delighted that I can't wait to tell Anna Andreyevna herself." "Goodness," I thought to myself, "Anna Andreyevna always expected a good match for her daughter and now it's come true." Yes, it happened just as she wanted and really I was speechless with delight. I cried and cried, I positively sobbed. Luka said to me: "What are you crying for, darling?" "Luka, darling," I said, "I don't know, the tears are simply streaming down my cheeks."

The Mayor. Please sit down, ladies and gentlemen. Mishka, bring more chairs. [*The visitors sit down. The* POLICE SUPERINTENDENT *and the* CONSTABLES *come in.*]

Police Superintendent. Accept our congratulations, sir, and allow me to wish you long life and prosperity.

The Mayor. Thank you, thank you. Please sit down, gentlemen. [*The visitors sit down.*]

Lyapkin-Tyapkin. Tell us, Mr. Mayor, how it all happened. Tell us in detail, please.

The Mayor. It was most extraordinary. He himself was so good as to make the proposal in person.

Anna. In the most respectful and delicate manner. He expressed himself exceedingly well. "Anna Andreyevna," he said, "it's entirely out of respect for your great virtues that I. . . ." And what a marvelous well-bred person he is! A man of the most noble principles. "Believe me, Anna Andreyevna," he said, "life isn't worth a farthing to me. I'm doing it simply out of respect for your rare qualities."

Maria. But, Mother, he said that to me.

Anna. Hold your tongue, you know nothing about it. And, please, don't interfere in something that does not concern you. "I'm amazed," he said, and he used such flattering expressions. And when I tried to say that we dared not hope for such an honor, he suddenly fell on his knees and exclaimed in the most refined way: "Madam, don't make me the unhappiest of men. Consent to reciprocate my feelings or I will put an end to my life!"

Maria. Really, Mother, he said that to me.

Anna. Why, of course. He said something to you, too. I don't deny it.

The Mayor. He really frightened us. Kept saying he would shoot himself. "I'll shoot myself, I'll shoot myself!"

Visitors. Good Lord!

Lyapkin-Tyapkin. What a thing to say!

Khlopov. It's fate all right.

Zemlyanika. Not fate, my dear sir. Fate's a silly hussy. It's merit that was the cause of it. [*Aside.*] A swine like that is always lucky.

Lyapkin-Tyapkin. I'll sell you the puppy you were so keen on, Mr. Mayor.

The Mayor. I'm afraid I've other things on my mind now.

Lyapkin-Tyapkin. Well, if you don't want it, we might agree on some other dog.

Mrs. Korobkin. Oh, I'm so pleased about your good fortune, Anna. You can't imagine how delighted I am.

Korobkin. Where is our distinguished guest, may I ask? I've heard he's gone away for some reason.

The Mayor. Yes, he's left us for a day or two on very important business.

Anna. To see his uncle and ask his blessing.

The Mayor. To ask his blessing, but tomorrow. . . . [*He sneezes. A general hum of* "Bless you, bless you."] Thank you, thank you. But he'll be back tomorrow. [*Sneezes. A general hum of* "Bless you!"]

Voice of Police Superintendent. Good health, sir.

Bobchinsky. May you live to be a hundred and have sackfuls of gold sovereigns.

Dobchinsky. May you live to be a hundred and twenty, sir.

Zemlyanika. Damn you!

Mrs. Korobkin. The devil take you.

The Mayor. Thank you very much. The same to you.

Anna. We intend to live in Petersburg now. The atmosphere here, I must say, is a little too countrified. It's not very pleasant. My husband, too, will be made a general there.

The Mayor. Yes, I admit, ladies and gentlemen, I should very much like to be a general, damn it.

Khlopov. God grant you will be.

Rastokovsky. A man may find it impossible, but with God everything is possible.

Lyapkin-Tyapkin. A great ship asks deep waters.

Zemlyanika. A well-deserved honor.

Lyapkin-Tyapkin [aside]. I can imagine the things he'll do when he does become a general. The rank of general suits him like a saddle on a cow. No, sir, it'll take a long, long time. There are better men than you here who aren't generals yet.

Zemlyanika [aside]. Good Lord, fancy him a general, and damn it, he might well become one, too. He's conceited enough for it, the devil take him. [*Turning to the Mayor.*] I hope you won't forget us, Mr. Mayor.

Lyapkin-Tyapkin. And if anything goes wrong, if for instance, we want any help, don't leave us without your patronage, my dear sir.

Korobkin. Next year I shall be taking my son to Petersburg to enter him in the service, so please be so good as to take him under your patronage. Treat the boy as if you were his father.

The Mayor. For my part, I'm quite ready to do what I can.

Anna. You're always ready to make promises, Anton. To begin with, you won't have time to think of it. And, besides, how can you, why should you burden yourself with such promises?

The Mayor. But why not, my love? One should do someone a good turn occasionally.

Anna. One should, of course, but you can't give your patronage to all sorts of small fry.

Mrs. Korobkin. You hear what she thinks of us!

A Woman Visitor. Yes, she was always like that. I know her. Sit her at a table and she'll put her feet on it.

THE POSTMASTER *comes in, breathless, holding an open letter in his hand.*

The Postmaster. A most extraordinary thing, ladies and gentlemen! The civil servant we took to be the Government Inspector, is not the Government Inspector at all.

All. Not the Government Inspector?

The Postmaster. No, not at all. I've discovered it from a letter.

The Mayor. What are you talking about? From what letter?

The Postmaster. Why, from his own letter. A letter was brought to the post office. I looked at the address and I saw it was addressed to Post Office Street. I was thunderstruck. There, I thought, he must have discovered some irregularities in the post office and is informing the authorities. So I unsealed it.

The Mayor. How could you?

The Postmaster. I don't know how. I must have been impelled by some supernatural force. I was about to call for the courier to despatch it by express delivery. But I was overcome by a curiosity such as I've never experienced in my life before. "You can't do it, you can't do it!" I heard a voice within me saying. "You must, you must open it," another voice whispered in my ear. "Take care, don't open it! You'll be done for if you do!" But some devil seemed to be whispering in the other ear: "Open it, open it!" And when I broke the seal, I felt as though a flame ran through my veins, and when I opened it, an icy shiver passed down my spine. My hands trembled, I felt dizzy.

The Mayor. But how dared you open the letter of a personage in such a position of authority?

The Postmaster. Well, you see, that's just the point: he's not a personage and not in a position of authority.

The Mayor. What is he then in your opinion?

The Postmaster. He's neither the one nor the other. Goodness only knows what he really is.

The Mayor [*vehemently*]. What do you mean, sir? How dare you say goodness only knows what he is? I'll put you under arrest.

The Postmaster. Who, you?

The Mayor. Yes! Me!

The Postmaster. Just try and do it!

The Mayor. Do you know he's going to marry my daughter, that I shall be a great personage myself and can pack you off to Siberia, if I like?

The Postmaster. Oh, my dear sir, why talk of Siberia? Siberia's a long way off. I'd better read you the letter. Ladies and gentlemen, have I got your permission to read this letter?

All. Read it, read it!

The Postmaster [*reads*]. "My dear Tryapichkin, I hasten to tell you of the marvelous things that have been happening to me. I was cleaned out on the way by an infantry captain, and the innkeeper here was about to send me to prison. Then, all of a sudden, the whole town took me for a governor general simply because of my Petersburg countenance and clothes. And now I'm staying at the Mayor's, having the time of my life and carrying on desperate flirtations with his wife and daughter. I haven't made up my mind, though, which one to go for first. I think I'll start with the mother. I think she's ready for anything. Do you remember how hard up we used to be, how we had to use our wits to get a decent dinner and how a confectioner once took me by the scruff of the neck because I'd had some pastries at the expense of the King of England? Things have taken quite a different turn now. Everybody lends me as much money as I ask for. They're a queer lot. You'd simply die laughing. I know you write articles for the press. Put them in one of them. First of all, there's the Mayor, as stupid a donkey as you ever saw."

The Mayor. I don't believe it. It isn't there.

The Postmaster [*showing him the letter*]. Read it yourself.

The Mayor [*reads*]. "As stupid a donkey as you ever saw." I can't believe it. You must have written it yourself.

The Postmaster. How could I have written it?

Zemlyanika. Read!

Khlopov. Read it!

The Postmaster [*continuing to read*]. "The Mayor, as stupid a donkey as you ever saw. . . ."

The Mayor. Damn it all, man, must you repeat it? We know it's there.

The Postmaster [*continuing to read*]. Hmmm . . . hmmm . . . hmmm. . . . Stupid donkey. . . . The Postmaster is a good fellow. Hmmm. . . . [*Pausing.*] Oh, well, here he says something rude about me, too.

The Mayor. Go on, read it.

The Postmaster. Why should I?

The Mayor. No, damn it, if you're going to read it, then read it all.

Zemlyanika. Let me read it! [*Puts on spectacles and reads.*] "The Postmaster is the spitting image of our hall porter, Mikheyev. I expect he, too, must be an inveterate drunkard, the scoundrel."

The Postmaster [*turning to the audience*]. Well, he's just a street urchin who should be given a good thrashing, that's all!

Zemlyanika [*goes on reading*]. "The Superintendent of Infirmaries and—er—er—" [*Stutters.*]

Korobkin. Why did you stop?

Zemlyanika. Why, it's illegible here. One can see he's a scoundrel, though.

Korobkin. Give it to me. I have better eyes than you. [*Takes hold of the letter.*]

Zemlyanika [*holding on to the letter*]. No, we can leave out this bit. It's more legible further on.

Korobkin. Let me have it. I know. I can read it.

Zemlyanika. I can read it myself. Only it's more legible further on.

The Postmaster. No, read it all. You read it all so far.

All. Give it him, give him the letter. Read it! [*To* KOROB-KIN.] Read it.

Zemlyanika. One moment. [*Gives him the letter.*] Here, please. [*Puts his finger over the letter.*] Start reading from here. [*They all turn toward him.*]

The Postmaster. Read it, read it! Nonsense! Read it all!

Korobkin [*reading*]. "The Superintendent of Infirmaries, Zemlyanika, is a perfect pig in a skullcap."

Zemlyanika [*to the audience*]. That's not even funny! A pig in a skullcap! Have you ever seen a pig in a skullcap?

Korobkin [*goes on reading*]. "The Inspector of Schools reeks of onions."

Khlopov [*to the audience*]. I swear I never touch an onion.

Lyapkin-Tyapkin [*aside*]. Thank God, at least there's nothing there about me!

Korobkin [*reads*]. "The Judge—"

Lyapkin-Tyapkin. Good Lord! [*Aloud.*] *Ladies and gentlemen,* I think the letter is too long anyway. Besides, hang it all, what's the use of reading such rubbish.

Khlopov. No!

The Postmaster. No, read it!

Zemlyanika. No, you'd better read it.

Korobkin [*goes on*]. "The Judge, Lyapkin-Tyapkin, is most decidedly *mauvais ton.*" [*Pauses.*] That must be a French expression.

Lyapkin-Tyapkin. Goodness knows what it means. I wouldn't mind if it only meant a scoundrel, but I suspect it must mean something much worse.

Korobkin [*goes on reading*]. "All the same, they're a hospitable and good-natured lot. Good-by, Tryapichkin, old fellow. I'd like to follow your example and take up literary work. It's boring to go on living like this. After all, one must have food for the mind. I see I really ought to devote myself to something of a higher nature. Write to me to the province of Saratov and address it to the village of Podkatilovka." [*Turns over the letter and reads the address.*] "To Ivan Vassilyevich Tryapichkin, Post Office Street, No. 97, through the yard, 3rd Floor, turning to the right, St. Petersburg."

One of the Ladies. What an unexpected blow!

The Mayor. The fellow has murdered me, murdered me! Killed me, stabbed me to death! I can see nothing. I can only see pigs' snouts instead of faces, and nothing more. . . . Fetch him back! Fetch him back! [*Waves his hand.*]

The Postmaster. How can you fetch him back? I told the stationmaster to give him the fastest team of horses. And I sent forward orders to give him the best horses, damn it!

Mrs. Korobkin. What an embarrassing situation!

Lyapkin-Tyapkin. But, damn it all, gentlemen, he borrowed three hundred rubles from me.

Zemlyanika. Four hundred rubles from me!

The Postmaster [*sighing*]. And three hundred from me.

Bobchinsky. And sixty-five rubles in notes from Dobchinsky and me. Yes, indeed.

Lyapkin-Tyapkin [*spreading out his hands in a gesture of complete perplexity*]. How did it all happen, gentlemen? How could we have made such a stupid mistake?

The Mayor [*slapping his forehead*]. How could I? How could I, old fool that I am? How could I have taken leave of my senses, stupid dolt that I am? Thirty years I've been in the service: not a single merchant, not a contractor has ever got the better of me. I've cheated first-class rogues, outwitted the most cunning scoundrels who would have swindled the whole world. Tripped them all up. I've hoodwinked three governors! Governors? [*With a contemptuous wave of the hand.*] Governors are easy game.

Anna. But this is impossible, Anton. Why, he is engaged to our Maria. . . .

The Mayor [*angrily*]. Engaged! Rubbish! Engaged, indeed! What are you coming to me with your engagement for at such a moment! [*In a frenzy.*] Come and look, look, all the world, all the Christian world, all of you, look what a fool the Mayor has been made of! Call him a fool to his face, the old rascal. [*Shakes his fist at himself.*] Oh, you—you with your fat nose, to take a milksop, a nincompoop like that for an important personage! He's now racing along the road with his harness bells ringing. He'll spread the tale all over the world. You'll not only be made a laughingstock, but some scribbler, some cheap hack, will come along and put you in a comedy. That's what is so humiliating. He won't spare my rank or my calling. Everyone will grin and clap. [*To the audience.*] What are you laughing at? You're laughing at yourselves! Oh, you fools! [*Stamps on the floor in a fury.*] I know what I'd do to all these scribblers! Oh, you cheap hacks, you damned liberals, you devil's brood, I'd tie you all in a knot, I'd grind you all into powder and stuff you into the devil's coat, shove you into his cap. [*Shakes his fist and stamps on the floor. After a short pause.*] I still can't get over it. Truly, those whom God would punish he first deprives of reason. Why, what was there in that young whippersnapper in the least like a Government Inspector? Nothing at all! He resembled one as much as my little finger does! And all of a sudden everyone was crying: the Government Inspector, the Government Inspector! Who was it that first spread the rumor that he was the Government Inspector? Answer! Answer!

Zemlyanika [*spreading his hands in a gesture of be-*

wilderment]. Damned if I know how it happened. It's just as if we were all befogged, just as though the devil confounded us.

Lyapkin-Tyapkin. Who spread the rumor? Why, these two fine fellows here! [*Pointing to* BOBCHINSKY *and* DOB-CHINSKY.]

Bobchinsky. It wasn't me. I never thought—

Dobchinsky. I had nothing to do with it, nothing at all. . . .

Zemlyanika. Of course it was you.

Khlopov. To be sure it was. They came running here like mad from the inn: "He's come! He's come! Doesn't pay his bill!" Found an important personage!

The Mayor. Of course it was you. You're the town gossips, you damned liars.

Zemlyanika. The devil take you with your Government Inspector and your tales.

The Mayor. All you do is prowl around the town, confuse everybody, you damned chatterboxes. Spread all sorts of scandal, you bobtailed magpies!

Lyapkin-Tyapkin. You dirty mischief-makers!

Zemlyanika. You dunces! [*They all surround them.*]

Bobchinsky. I swear it wasn't me. It was Dobchinsky.

Dobchinsky. Oh, no, my dear fellow, you were the first. . . .

Bobchinsky. Oh, no, my dear fellow, you were the first. . . .

Enter a GENDARME.

Gendarme. The official who has arrived from Petersburg with instructions from the Emperor summons you to his presence. He's staying at the inn.

These words fall like a thunderbolt upon all. An exclamation of astonishment rises simultaneously to the lips of the ladies; the whole group suddenly changes its attitude and remains petrified. Dumb show.

THE MAYOR *stands in the middle like a post with arms outstretched and head flung back. On his right hand are his wife and daughter turning impetuously toward him; behind them is* THE POSTMASTER, *transformed into a note of interrogation addressed to the audience. Next to him is*

KHLOPOV *in a state of innocent bewilderment; next to him at the very edge of the stage, three lady visitors, leaning against each other with the most satirical expression aimed directly at* THE MAYOR's *family. On the left side of* THE MAYOR *stands* ZEMLYANIKA, *his head bent a little on one side, as though listening to something; next to him is the* JUDGE, *with his hands flung out, squatting almost on the ground and making a movement with his lips as though he were going to whistle and say:* "Here's a nice how-d'ye-do!" *Next to him,* KOROBKIN, *facing the spectators with a wink and a caustic sneer at* THE MAYOR; *next to him at the very edge of the stage* BOBCHINSKY *and* DOBCHINSKY, *their hands stretched out toward one another, their mouths open and their eyes staring at each other. The other visitors remain standing simply like posts; for almost a minute and a half the petrified group retains its position.*

Curtain.

THE STORM

A Tragedy in Five Acts by

ALEXANDER OSTROVSKY

CHARACTERS

SAVEL PROKOPYEVICH DIKOY, *a rich merchant, a man of great importance in town*

BORIS GRIGORYEVICH, *his nephew, a young man, well educated*

MARFA IGNATYEVNA KABANOV, *a rich widow*

TIKHON IVANYCH KABANOV, *her son*

KATHERINE, *his wife*

BARBARA, *Tikhon's sister*

KULIGIN, *an artisan, a self-taught watchmaker, trying to discover the secret of* perpetuum mobile

VANYA KUDRYASH, *young man employed in Dikoy's office*

SHAPKIN, *a young artisan*

FEKLUSHA, *a pilgrim woman*

GLASHA, *maid in Mrs. Kabanov's house*

A GENTLEWOMAN *with two footmen, about seventy and in her dotage*

TOWNSPEOPLE *of both sexes*

The action takes place in the town of KALINOV *on the banks of the* VOLGA, *in summer. Between Acts Three and Four there is an interval of ten days.*

THE STORM

ACT ONE

A public park on the high bank of the Volga. Beyond the Volga stretches the view of the countryside far away in the distance. On the stage two benches and a number of bushes.

KULIGIN *sits on a bench and admires the view.* KUDRYASH *and* SHAPKIN *are strolling about.*

KULIGIN [*hums*]. "Mid quiet valleys, on the mountain-tops. . . ." [*Stops humming.*] What a wonderful view! Lord, the beauty of it! Kudryash, just have a look at it! I've been admiring this magnificent view across the Volga for fifty years and I can never get tired of it.

Kudryash. What's so wonderful about it?

Kuligin. The view, my dear fellow. The view is so wonderful! Lord, the beauty of it! Makes my heart leap with joy.

Kudryash. Does it now?

Kuligin. It's a miracle! And you with your "does it now"! You've got used to it, that's the trouble. Or else you don't realize how beautiful nature is and how glorious are her works.

Kudryash. Oh, what's the use of talking to you? You're a queer one all right. A chemist!

Kuligin. Not a chemist, my dear fellow. A mechanic. A self-taught mechanic.

Kudryash. Same thing, isn't it?

A pause.

Kuligin [*pointing in one direction*]. I say, who's that man over there waving his arms about?

Kudryash. That one? That's Dikoy telling off that nephew of his.

Kuligin. In a public park of all places.

Kudryash. It makes no difference to him. He doesn't mind. He isn't afraid of anybody. If he finds someone to bully, he goes right ahead and bullies him.

Shapkin. You won't find a man like Dikoy anywhere for telling a man off. He'll do it for nothing at all.

Kudryash. A loud-voiced peasant.

Shapkin. Old Mrs. Kabanov isn't much better.

Kudryash. At least she does it under cover of religion, but that one just barks like a dog that's slipped his chain.

Shapkin. There's no one to put him in his place. That's why he's always on the warpath.

Kudryash. A pity there aren't many more young fellows like me in this town. We'd show him how to kick up a row.

Shapkin. A fat lot of good you could do with the likes of him.

Kudryash. Oh, couldn't we? We'd put the fear of God into him all right.

Shapkin. Would you now?

Kudryash. We would all right. Four or five of us. Corner him in some dark alley and have a heart-to-heart talk with him. He'd be as smooth as silk after that and he wouldn't dare tell anyone about the lesson we'd taught him. He'd just watch his step.

Shapkin. No wonder he wanted to enlist you in the army.

Kudryash. He may have wanted it but he hasn't done it, has he? That's the same as if he had done nothing. He won't enlist me. He can smell with that dirty nose of his that I'm not going to sell my freedom as cheap as that. It's fellows like you who're afraid of him. A fellow like me knows how to use the kind of language he understands.

Shapkin. Do you?

Kudryash. I do indeed. I'm supposed to be a roughneck, but he doesn't sack me, does he? Why not? Because he can't do without me—that's why. And if that's so, I'm not afraid of him. Let him be afraid of me.

Shapkin. Listen to him! Doesn't he swear at you at all?

Kudryash. Of course he does. He can't do without swearing till he's blue in the face. But I just don't let him get away with it. I give him a dozen words for the one he gives me. So he just spits in disgust and clears off. No, sir, I'm not going to crawl on my belly for the likes of him.

Kuligin. But you oughtn't to take him as an example, my dear fellow. I'd rather put up with him than pay him back in his own coin.

Kudryash. Well, of course, if you're so clever, you'd better teach him manners first and come and teach us some afterwards. What a pity his daughters are all just kids. Wouldn't it be fun if one of them was grown up?

Shapkin. Why? What would you have done?

Kudryash. I'd have given him something to holler about. I'm fond of the ladies, I am.

Dikoy *and* Boris *enter.* Kuligin *takes off his cap.*

Shapkin [*to* Kudryash]. Let's be off. We don't want him to start on us, do we? [*They walk off upstage.*]

Dikoy. Taking things easy, aren't you? What's the idea of coming to live with me if you don't want to do an honest day's work? You're a loafer. A good-for-nothing loafer. To hell with you!

Boris. Today's a holiday, sir. There's nothing I could do at the office.

Dikoy. You'd find something to do if you tried hard enough. I've told you a hundred times if I've told you once: don't get in my way! Why do you always pop up where you're not wanted? Is this town too small for you? I can't take a step without running into you. Get out of my sight, damn you. What are you standing like some blasted dummy for? Am I talking to you or not?

Boris. Yes, sir. And I'm listening to you, sir. What else can I do?

Dikoy [*glaring angrily at* Boris]. Go to blazes! I don't want to waste my breath on a Jesuit like you! [*Mutters while going off.*] Can't shake him off at all! [*Spits and goes off.*]

Kuligin. Why do you have anything to do with him, sir? We can't make it out at all. What do you want to live with him and put up with his foul language for?

Boris. I'm sure I don't want to. But I'm afraid I can't do anything about it.

Kuligin. Why can't you do anything about it, sir? I'd like you to tell me, if you don't mind, that is, sir.

Boris. I don't mind telling you. You knew my grandmother Anfissa, didn't you?

Kuligin. Of course I knew her.

Kudryash. I should say we did, sir.

Boris. Well, she quarreled with my father for marrying a gentlewoman. That's why my father and mother lived in Moscow. My mother used to say that she couldn't bear to live with my father's relations. Everything about them appeared so uncivilized to her.

Kuligin. Uncivilized? I should think so, sir. You have to be used to that kind of life to put up with it.

Boris. In Moscow my parents gave me and my sister a first-class education. I was sent to the commercial institute, and my sister to boarding school. Then my parents died during a cholera epidemic, and my sister and I were left all alone in the world. Then we learned that our grandmother had died in this town and left us money in her will. Our uncle was to give us the money when we came of age. On one condition, though.

Kuligin. And what was that condition, sir?

Boris. The condition was that we should never behave disrespectfully to him.

Kuligin. In that case, sir, you will never see your money.

Boris. Ah, but that's not the worst of it. He'll first vent his spite on us; do everything in his power to make our life a hell on earth. And even then he won't give us anything, or at most only a few pennies. And he'll go about telling everybody that he's given us the few pennies only out of the goodness of his heart, for by rights he oughtn't to have given us anything at all.

Kudryash. That's one of the oldest customs among our tradespeople, sir. Even if you were to show him the greatest respect in the world, nobody could prevent him from saying that you didn't treat him with proper respect.

Boris. Naturally. Even now he sometimes says to me, "I've children of my own, so why should I give my money away to strangers? That would mean robbing my own flesh and blood, wouldn't it?"

Kuligin. Well, sir, it seems your goose is as good as cooked.

Boris. I wouldn't mind if it were only myself. It's my sister I'm worried about. My uncle wanted to send for her, too, but fortunately my mother's relations wouldn't let her go. They wrote back to say that she was ill. It makes me shudder to think the kind of life she'd have had here.

Kudryash. That's about right, sir. How can you expect a man like him to behave in a human way?

Kuligin. What exactly is your position at his office, sir?

Boris. I have no position of any kind. "Live with me, do what you're told and I'll pay you any wages I think proper," he told me. Which means, I suppose, that in a year's time, if I'm lucky, he'll give me something.

Kudryash. Yes, sir, that's how it is with him. None of us fellows at the office dares even mention a raise. It only makes him fly off the handle and swear himself blue in the face. "How do you know," says he, "what I mean to do about your wages? You don't know what's in my mind, do you? Maybe I'll raise your wages to five thousand if I feel like it." What can you do with a man like that? All we know is that so far he hasn't felt like it even once in his life.

Kuligin. Well, what's to be done about it, sir? You must try your best to please him.

Boris. That's the trouble, Kuligin. You couldn't please him however hard you tried. Even his own children find it impossible to please him. So how can I hope to?

Kudryash. Who can please a man whose whole life is one quarrel after another, especially over money? He doesn't give a penny to anyone without sending him to the devil first. Some people would sooner keep out of his way than ask him for the money he owes them. And Heaven help you if he happens to fall foul of someone in the morning. Then he'll find fault with everybody all day long.

Boris. Every morning my poor aunt implores the people in the house not to make him cross. "Please, children," she keeps saying, "don't do anything to make your father cross!"

Kudryash. But you can't help making him cross. That's just it. Watch him when he goes to the market: he won't let a single peasant pass without cursing him. Sell him at a loss and he'd still curse you. And afterwards he'll go on cursing and swearing all day long.

Shapkin. Yes, a warrior, that's him.

Kudryash. And what a warrior!

Boris. He gets furious when someone he can't abuse gets the better of him. His wife and children had better look out then.

Kudryash. You should have seen the fun when a hussar told him off on the Volga ferry the other day. Didn't he let himself go that day!

Boris. Yes, and think what his wife and children must have had to put up with. They had to hide themselves in the attic and the boxrooms for two weeks.

Kuligin. What's the matter? Are they coming back from evening Mass already?

Several men and women pass across the back of the stage.

Kudryash. Come on, Shapkin. It's time to have a drink. What's the use of standing about here? [*They take their leave and go out.*]

Boris. Oh, Kuligin, it's a hard life for me here all right. And I'm not used to it, worse luck! Everyone looks strangely at me just as if I were not wanted here. As if I were in their way. I don't know your customs here. I realize that it's the sort of thing one must expect from us Russians, but I can't get used to it all the same.

Kuligin. You'll never get used to it, sir.

Boris. Why not?

Kuligin. Well, sir, the people in our town are a cruel lot. A very cruel lot. Among the working-class people and the shopkeepers you won't find anyone who knows the meaning of good manners. And how indeed can you expect good manners from people whose lives are crushed by grinding poverty? We working-class people, sir, will never be able to lift ourselves out of this dreadful bog.

For we can never hope to earn anything more than our daily bread by honest work. And those who have their money, sir, are doing their damnedest to grind the faces of the poor so as to make more and more money by cheaper and still cheaper labor. Do you know, sir, what your uncle said to our mayor the other day? Some peasants came to complain to our mayor about the way your uncle always cheated them out of their pay. Well, sir, so the mayor says to your uncle, "Look here, Dikoy, why don't you pay the peasants what you owe them in full? Every blessed day they come running to me with their complaints!" Well, your uncle just slapped the mayor on the back and said, "Why waste time discussing such trifles, Your Worship? I deal with hundreds of peasants every year. Now, just think: if I can manage to do each one of them out of only one penny, it adds up to thousands for me. So you see, Your Worship, my way of dealing with peasants pays me excellent dividends!" That's how it is, sir. And how do our big businessmen treat each other? They're always at each other's throats. Not so much from greed as from envy. Always fighting each other in the courts. They seek out some drunken lawyers and dine and wine them in their big houses. And what lawyers they choose, sir! Men who have lost all semblance of human beings. Men who don't look like human beings any more. And for a small fee scoundrels like them will not scruple to file fraudulent claims against their fellow men. They don't mind scribbling anything on their stamped papers. That's how all these lawsuits are started, sir. That's the beginning of their troubles. At first the action is heard in our courts here. Then it's transferred to our county courts. There, of course, they are welcomed with open arms by more lawyers. Well, sir, to cut a long story short, the lawyers keep hauling them from one court to another and they seem actually to enjoy it. They don't ask for anything better. "I don't grudge the expense," they say, "so long as it costs the other fellow a pretty penny, too." Do you know, sir? I was even going to write a poem about it.

Boris. Do you write poetry?

Kuligin. Rather old-fashioned poetry, sir. I've read our old poets, sir. Lomonosov, Derzhavin. . . . Lomonosov was a very wise man, sir. A great student of nature. He was one of us, sir. A man of the common people.

Boris. Why don't you write your poem? It would be fun to read.

Kuligin. I couldn't do that, sir. They'd flay me alive. As it is, I'm constantly getting into hot water for talking too much. But I can't help it, sir. I like to have a heart-to-heart talk with people. I'd like to tell you about our family life here, but perhaps I'd better leave it for another occasion. It's an instructive subject, sir. Very instructive.

Enter FEKLUSHA *and another woman.*

Feklusha. It's just grand, dearie, just grand. Real Christian charity, dearie, that's what it is. It's in the promised land you live here. And the merchants of this town, dearie, are such God-fearing folk. Virtuous and generous. Spending thousands on the poor. Up to their necks in good deeds they are, God bless them. I can't tell you, dearie, how pleased I am to be here again. Always looking after us, servants of the Lord. Never tired of ministering to our needs. May the Lord reward them a hundredfold and especially Mrs. Kabanov and her household. [*They go out.*]

Boris. Mrs. Kabanov?

Kuligin. A sanctimonious old woman, sir. Always bestowing something on the poor, but showing no mercy to her own flesh and blood. [*Pause.*] If only I could discover the secret of *perpetuum mobile*, sir.

Boris. Why? What would you do then?

Kuligin. Oh, well, sir, the English would give me a million for it, and I'd use it to found a society to assist the poor. I'd help the working people to get employment. You can't do much with your bare hands, sir.

Boris. And do you hope to discover the secret of *perpetuum mobile?*

Kuligin. I'm sure I shall, sir. If only I could scrape together a little money to build a model. So long, sir. [*Goes out.*]

Boris [*alone*]. I'd hate to disillusion him. He's such a good man! Lives in a world of his own and is happy. As for me, I shall probably waste my youth in this awful hole. I'm more dead than alive already, and to make things worse I must go and fall in love. Of all the idiotic things that had to happen to me. What good can a love affair be to me? And with whom? With a woman I shall never get a chance of saying even a few words to. [*Pause.*] I can't get her out of my head all the same. I can't. I can't. Good Lord, here she comes. Her husband and her mother-in-law with her. Well, am I not a damned fool? I'll have a look at her from behind some tree and go home. [*Goes out.*]

From the opposite direction enter MRS. KABANOV, TIKHON, KATHERINE *and* BARBARA.

Mrs. Kabanov. If you'll take your mother's advice, dear, you'll do as I tell you directly you arrive there.

Tikhon. But Mother, I wouldn't dream of disobeying you!

Mrs. Kabanov. Children aren't so anxious to honor their parents nowadays.

Barbara [*aside*]. Honor you!

Tikhon. Have I ever done anything without asking your permission first, Mother?

Mrs. Kabanov. I'd be glad to believe you, son, if I didn't see with my own eyes and hear with my own ears how much children honored their parents today. If only they'd realize how much their mothers have to put up with from their children.

Tikhon. But, Mother, I. . . .

Mrs. Kabanov. If your mother does sometimes say something which hurts your feelings, I should have thought you could put up with it without a murmur. Well, what do you say, son?

Tikhon. But when didn't I put up with it, Mother?

Mrs. Kabanov. Your mother may be a silly old woman and you young people are, of course, so clever. Why should you pay any attention to fools like us?

Tikhon [*sighs, aside*]. Oh, Lord! [*To his mother.*] But really, Mother, would we ever dream of such a thing!

Mrs. Kabanov. Why, if your parents are strict with you, it's because they love you. If they chide you, it's also because they love you. Everything they do is for your own good. But, of course, all this is considered old-fashioned nowadays. No wonder you hear children spreading wicked tales about their mothers: the mother's a scold, the mother

is an interfering busybody, the mother blights their lives.
And God forbid, if a mother-in-law should just happen to
displease her daughter-in-law by saying something or other!
Everyone will start saying that the mother-in-law is trying
to crush her spirit.

Tikhon. But, Mother, who has ever said such a horrid
thing about you?

Mrs. Kabanov. I can't say I've heard anyone say that
about me, son. No, I can't say that. I don't want to tell
a lie. If I did hear it, I'd have had quite a different kind
of talk with you, dear. [*Sighs.*] Oh, we're such dreadful
sinners, son, such dreadful sinners. Before you know it,
you've committed a dreadful sin. Talk to someone about
something that concerns you deeply, and you can't help
losing your temper and there you are—you've committed
a sin. No, no, son! Say anything you like about me. You
can't stop anyone saying what he likes, can you? If they
don't say it to your face, they'll say it behind your back.

Tikhon. May my tongue cleave to—

Mrs. Kabanov. Don't! Don't tempt Providence, son! It's
a sin. I've noticed for some time that your wife is dearer
to you than your mother. Since your marriage I can't help
feeling that you don't care for me as much as you did
before.

Tikhon. But what have I done, Mother, to make you
feel like that?

Mrs. Kabanov. Why, it's as plain as can be, son. And
don't forget, dear, that what a mother doesn't see with her
eyes she feels with her heart. Her poor heart divines every
little thing. It isn't your wife who is taking you away
from me, is it?

Tikhon. Why, no, Mother! What are you saying?

Katherine. But really, Mother, I've never made any
distinction between you and my own mother. Tikhon, too,
loves you as well as he ever did.

Mrs. Kabanov. If I were you, dear, I wouldn't speak
till spoken to. Don't try to take his part, my dear. I'm not
going to do anything that would hurt him, don't you
worry. He's my son, isn't he? Well, then, don't you forget
it, my dear. And why are you so very anxious to defend
him? Is it because you want the whole world to see how

much you love your husband? Why, my dear, they all know that. Gracious me, you're doing your best to make everyone believe it, aren't you? At least when there are people about.

Barbara [*aside*]. Found a place to lecture people.

Katherine. You've no right to speak about me like that, Mother. Whether there are people about or not I'm always the same. I'm not trying to make anyone believe anything.

Mrs. Kabanov. Why, my dear, I didn't intend to talk about you in particular. I just happened to mention it.

Katherine. Well, even if you just happened to mention it, there's no reason why you should try to hurt my feelings, is there?

Mrs. Kabanov. Hurt your feelings, have I? Well, well, what a terrible thing, to be sure.

Katherine. No one likes to hear oneself wrongly accused.

Mrs. Kabanov. I know, I know very well that my words are not to the liking of any of you, but what's to be done about it? I'm not a stranger to you exactly, am I? Can I help it if my heart aches for you? I realized long ago that you want to live your own lives. Well, why not? Have patience and wait till I'm dead and then you will live your own lives. Then you'll be able to do what you like. There won't be anyone in authority to interfere with you. But, who knows, maybe it will just be then that you will remember me.

Tikhon. But, Mother, we're praying the good Lord day and night to send you health and happiness and success in business.

Mrs. Kabanov. Come, stop pretending, son. Before your marriage you may have loved your mother but now you've no time to think of me. You've got a young wife, son.

Tikhon. One thing needn't interfere with the other, Mother. A wife is one thing and as for you, Mother, I've always respected you.

Mrs. Kabanov. So you're ready to let your wife take the place of your mother, are you? I shall never believe it, never.

Tikhon. But who ever said anything about that? I love you both.

Mrs. Kabanov. Of course, of course! Tell me another! I can see, son, that I'm in your way and in your wife's.

Tikhon. You can think what you like, Mother. No one can do anything about that. Only what I'd like to know is what did I do to deserve it? Why can't I do anything to please you?

Mrs. Kabanov. Don't pretend to be such a poor helpless creature! What are you sniveling about? What kind of a husband are you? Just look at yourself. How can you expect your wife to be afraid of you after making such a disgraceful spectacle of yourself?

Tikhon. But why should my wife be afraid of me? I'm quite happy if she loves me.

Mrs. Kabanov. Why should she be afraid of you? What do you mean? Have you gone out of your mind, son? If she isn't afraid of you, she won't be afraid of me, either. What will it be like in our house then? Aren't you her lawful wedded husband, or doesn't the law mean anything to you? And if you have such silly notions in your head, you shouldn't blurt them out in front of her and in front of your unmarried sister. She, too, will have to get married one day, and if she takes your silly talk seriously, her husband won't thank us for it afterwards. See what a clever fellow you are? And you want to be allowed to live as you like.

Tikhon. But I don't want to live as I like, mother. I shouldn't know how to carry on by myself.

Mrs. Kabanov. Well, then, so you think that a wife should be ruled by kindness? Are you afraid to raise your voice? Or tell her off?

Tikhon. But, Mother—

Mrs. Kabanov [*warmly*]. Do you want her to get herself a lover, eh? I suppose you wouldn't mind that, would you? Well, speak up!

Tikhon. But really, Mother. . . .

Mrs. Kabanov [*in a cool, matter-of-fact voice*]. You are a fool! [*Sighs.*] What's the use of talking to a fool? It only makes you lose your temper. [*Pause.*] I'm going home.

Tikhon. We, too, shall be going home in a moment, Mother. We'll just take a turn on the boulevard.

Mrs. Kabanov. All right, but mind I don't have to wait for you too long! You know I don't like it!

Tikhon. Of course not, Mother. I'd never dream of being late.

Mrs. Kabanov. That's better. [*Goes out.*]

Tikhon. You see, I'm always getting into hot water with Mother because of you. What an awful life!

Katherine. It isn't my fault, is it?

Tikhon. I don't know whose fault it is.

Barbara. You wouldn't.

Tikhon. Before my marriage she made my life miserable with her continual, "It's time you got married! It's time you got married! I'd like to see you married before I die," and now she goes on nagging and nagging me. Doesn't let me be for a moment—and all because of you!

Barbara. How can you blame her for that? Mother is always attacking her and now you, too, are turning against her. And you go on saying that you love your wife. Makes me sick to look at you. [*She turns away.*]

Tikhon. What's the use of talking? What am I to do, I'd like to know?

Barbara. Mind your own business—hold your tongue if you can't do anything better. What are you standing like a fool for, shuffling from one foot to the other? I can tell from the look on your face what you'd like to do.

Tikhon. Well, what?

Barbara. That's an easy one, my lad. You'd like to run off to Dikoy to have a drink with him. Am I right?

Tikhon. You're right first time, old girl.

Katherine. Do come back quickly, dear, or Mother will make a scene again.

Barbara. Yes, you'd better be quick about it, my lad, or you'll catch it all right.

Tikhon. Don't I know it.

Barbara. And remember, we don't like to catch it because of you.

Tikhon. I'll be back in a jiffy. Wait for me here. [*Goes out.*]

Katherine. So you feel sorry for me, Barbara?

Barbara [*looking away*]. Of course I'm sorry for you.

Katherine. Then you love me, don't you? [*She hugs and kisses her.*]

Barbara. Why shouldn't I love you?

Katherine. Well, thank you. You're a darling. I, too, love you very much. [*Pause.*] Do you know what I've just thought of?

Barbara. What?

Katherine. Why don't people fly?

Barbara. I don't know what you're talking about.

Katherine. I mean, why don't people fly like birds? You know, sometimes I imagine I am a bird. When I stand on the top of a hill I can't help wishing I could fly. I feel like taking a run, lifting my arms and flying away. Shall I try it now? [*Is about to run.*]

Barbara. What strange ideas come into your head, my dear.

Katherine [*sighing*]. I used to be so full of life. I seem to have lost all my high spirits in your house.

Barbara. Do you think I haven't noticed it?

Katherine. I wasn't at all like this! I lived without a care in the world, as free as a bird. Mother couldn't do enough for me. She used to dress me up like a doll. She wouldn't let me do any hard work. I used to do anything I liked. Do you know how I used to spend my time before I was married? Listen, I'll tell you. I used to get up early. In summer, I'd run down to the spring to wash, then bring water into the house and water all the flowers. We used to have lots and lots of flowers in our house. Then I'd go to church with Mother and everyone else, including the women pilgrims. Our house was always full of women pilgrims. And when we came home from church, we'd sit down to needlework, mostly embroidering velvet with gold thread. And the women pilgrims would tell us all sorts of wonderful stories about where they had been, what they had seen, or about the lives of the saints. Or else they'd sing hymns. That's how we'd spend our time till dinner. Afterwards the old women would lie down to have a nap, and I'd go for a stroll in our garden. Then we'd go to Vespers, and in the evening we'd have more stories and more singing. Oh, it was so wonderful.

Barbara. But it's much the same thing in our house, isn't it?

Katherine. Yes, but here everything seems to be done under compulsion. How dearly I loved to go to church! I used to feel as if I were in Paradise. I saw no one and I didn't know how the time passed or when the service was over. It was just as if it only lasted a second. Mother used to say that everyone in church had been staring at me, wondering what was the matter with me. But, you know, on a sunny day, a bright shaft of light would come down from the dome, and the smoke from the incense would go up like a cloud through it, and sometimes I would see angels flying up and down that shaft of light and chanting so gloriously. And sometimes, my dear, I used to get up in the middle of the night—we also had lights burning in front of the holy images in our house, and I used to kneel in some corner and pray and pray till dawn. Or, perhaps, early in the morning I'd go out into the garden just as the sun was rising, fall down on my knees and pray and weep without knowing what I was praying and weeping for. And there they would find me. And what I prayed for and what I asked for I really couldn't tell myself. For, you see, there was nothing I wanted. I had everything my heart could desire. And what dreams I used to dream! What wonderful dreams! Golden temples and enchanted gardens, ringing with the voices of invisible singers and fragrant with the smell of cypresses. And hills and trees such as you never saw anywhere in the world, but just like those you see painted in the sacred pictures. And sometimes I seemed to be flying through the air. I have dreams even now, but not very often, and not at all like those I used to have at home.

Barbara. Oh, what are your dreams like now?

Katherine [*after a moment's silence*]. I'm going to die soon.

Barbara. Good heavens, what are you talking about!

Katherine. I know I shall die soon. Oh, my dear, something terrible is happening to me . . . something—something miraculous. I never felt anything like it before. It's as if I'm beginning to live again or—I don't know.

Barbara. What is the matter with you?

Katherine [*takes her by the hand*]. I'll tell you what it is, my dear. Something dreadful is going to happen. I'm so frightened, my dear, I'm so terribly frightened. I feel as if I were standing at the edge of a precipice and somebody was pushing me over and there's nothing I can hold on to, nothing. [*Clutches her head.*]

Barbara. What is the matter with you? You aren't ill, are you?

Katherine. I'm all right. . . . I wish I was ill, though, for something is terribly wrong. Something keeps coming into my head. Some queer idea. And I can't get rid of it. It's a kind of obsession. I do my best to think of something else, but my thoughts seem to wander. I try to pray, but even prayers won't get it out of my head. I murmur the words of prayer with my lips, but my mind is somewhere else. It is—it is as if the devil himself were whispering in my ears, urging me to do all sorts of abhorrent things. And then I get such strange fancies that I feel ashamed of them myself. What is the matter with me? I don't know. The only thing I'm certain of is that something dreadful is going to happen. I can't sleep at night, my dear. All the time I seem to hear someone speaking in whispers to me, oh, so tenderly, so tenderly, like the cooing of a dove. I don't dream any more of the trees of Paradise and the hills in the world of the blessed spirits but of someone holding me in a passionate embrace, someone leading me somewhere, and I—I can't resist him, I follow him blindly, I go with him. . . .

Barbara. Yes?

Katherine. But why am I telling you all this? You're still a girl.

Barbara [*looking around*]. Tell me! I'm much worse than you.

Katherine. Well, what is there to tell? I'm so ashamed.

Barbara. Don't be silly, my dear. Please tell me.

Katherine. I feel so stifled at home. So stifled that I want to run, run, run! And then the thought occurs to me that if I were free to do as I liked, I'd go sailing on the Volga, singing songs, or go for a drive in the country in a carriage with a team of three swift horses, with my arms around—

Barbara. Not your husband?

Katherine. How do you know?

Barbara. How indeed!

Katherine. Oh, my dear, my head is so full of wicked thoughts! You don't know how miserable I am. How much I wept. How hard I tried to get those thoughts out of my head. But I shan't escape doing what I know to be a sin. I know I shan't, I know it. It is a great sin, darling, isn't it? I mean, for a married woman to be in love with another man.

Barbara. Well, my dear, I'm certainly not one to condemn you. I'm not such a paragon of virtue myself.

Katherine. But what am I to do? I haven't the strength to resist. Where am I to go? I shall do something dreadful to myself from sheer despair.

Barbara. Don't talk such nonsense, my dear. Wait a little longer. My brother will be going away tomorrow, then we'll try to think of something. Maybe you'll be able to meet him.

Katherine. No, no, never! How can you suggest such a thing! God forbid!

Barbara. What are you so frightened of?

Katherine. If I met him only once, I'd run away from home. I'd never come back. Never.

Barbara. You'd better wait. We'll see.

Katherine. No, no! Please don't say anything more to me. I don't want to listen to another word!

Barbara. But what's the use of wearing yourself to a shadow? Even if you died of a broken heart, they'd never be sorry for you. Of course you'd better wait till you meet him. What's the use of tormenting yourself?

Enter elderly GENTLEWOMAN, *leaning heavily on a stick and followed by two footmen in three-cornered hats.*

Gentlewoman. Well, my beauties? What are you doing here? Waiting for your lovers? You're happy? Happy? Happy because you're beautiful? [*Pointing in the direction of the Volga.*] That's where beauty leads. There, there! Right into the whirlpool! [BARBARA *smiles.*] What are you smiling at, my pretty one? There's nothing to be pleased about! [*Thumps her stick on the ground.*] You'll all burn on the everlasting fire! You'll all be writhing in pain in the burning lake of brimstone! [*Going away.*] There, there! That's where beauty leads. [*Goes out.*]

Katherine. Oh, how she frightened me! I'm trembling all over. I feel as if she's just told my future.

Barbara. It's her own future she's foretold, the old witch!

Katherine. What did she say? What was it? What did she say?

Barbara. It's all nonsense. Why do you want to listen to what she's jabbering about? She says the same thing to everyone she meets. She's been a fast one, she has. Led a gay life as a girl, she did. Ask anyone you like and they'll tell you all about her. No wonder she's afraid to die. She's trying to frighten others with the things she fears herself. Even the little boys in the streets run away from her. She waves her stick at them and shouts [*mimicking the old* GENTLEWOMAN], "You'll all burn in the everlasting fire."

Katherine [*closing her eyes*]. Stop, stop! I'm going to faint.

Barbara. Found something to be frightened of! A silly old woman. . . .

Katherine. I am frightened, I'm terribly frightened. I seem to see her before my eyes all the time.

Barbara [*looking around*]. Where's Tikhon? I wish he'd come back. Look, there's a storm coming.

Katherine [*in dismay*]. A storm? Let's run home! Quick!

Barbara. What's the matter with you? Gone off your head? How can we go home without Tikhon?

Katherine. No, no! Let's go home at once. I don't want to wait for him.

Barbara. It's a bit too soon to be frightened. The storm is a long way off.

Katherine. Oh, well, if it's a long way off I suppose we'd better wait a little longer. But really I'd rather we went now. Please let's go.

Barbara. But if anything does happen, you won't be able to hide yourself from it even at home.

Katherine. I'd feel happier there all the same. It's quieter there. At home I can kneel before the icons and pray.

Barbara. I never knew you were so afraid of a storm.
Look at me. I'm not a bit afraid.

Katherine. How can you help being afraid, my dear?
Everyone ought to be afraid. It's not being struck by
lightning and killed that's so terrible. What I'm afraid of
is to be carried off suddenly, just as I am with all my
sins and wicked thoughts. I'm not afraid to die, but when
I think that I may have to appear suddenly before God
just as I am here with you now, after what I've just told
you—that's what frightens me. For what am I thinking
of? What dreadful sin! I dread even to put it into words!
[*Thunder.*] Oh!

TIKHON *comes in.*

Barbara. Here he is at last! [*To* TIKHON.] Hurry up!

Thunder.

Katherine. Oh! Quick, quick!

Curtain.

ACT TWO

A room in the house of MRS. KABANOV.

GLASHA *is collecting clothes into bundles and* FEKLUSHA
enters.

FEKLUSHA. Always hard at work, dearie? What are you
doing now?

Glasha. I'm getting master's things ready for his journey.

Feklusha. Why, is he going on a journey, the dear boy?

Glasha. He is.

Feklusha. Will he be away a long time, dearie?

Glasha. No, I shouldn't think that's likely.

Feklusha. Well, good luck to him. What do you think,
dearie? Will your mistress be howling when her husband
leaves?

Glasha. I don't know, I'm sure.

Feklusha. Doesn't she ever howl?

Glasha. I'm sure I've never heard her.

Feklusha. I'm ever so fond of hearing a body raise a real honest-to-goodness howl, dearie. [*Pause.*] If I was you, dearie, I'd keep an eye on that beggarwoman in the house. See she doesn't pinch something.

Glasha. To tell you the truth, Feklusha, I can't be sure which of you godly folk is honest and which isn't. You're always telling tales on each other. Seems to me you're not exactly starving. In this house all you pilgrims always get the best of everything but you're always quarreling and telling awful tales about each other. You ought to be ashamed of yourselves, you ought, really. It's such a sin, too, it is.

Feklusha. But, dearie, which of us is without sin? We live in a sinful world. Now listen to me, my pretty one. You ordinary folk have only one devil each to tempt you, but us saintly folk have six devils, and some of us even twelve specially sent down to lead us down into sin. That's why we have such a big struggle to fight them all. It isn't so easy to get the better of the lot of them, dearie.

Glasha. Why do you have so many devils, Feklusha?

Feklusha. The evil one does it on purpose, dearie. Out of sheer spite, I should say. You see, it's because we are leading such a life of righteousness. But I, dearie, am not quarrelsome. I'm not guilty of that sin. Mind, there is one sin I am guilty of, that's true enough. I know I am. You see, I like good food and plenty of it. Well, what of it? It's all on account of my infirmity. And the good Lord takes pity on his handmaiden and sends me to a house where I can indulge my only weakness.

Glasha. Have your travels taken you far, Feklusha?

Feklusha. No, dearie, I haven't ventured out too far on account of my infirmity, but I hear all sorts of tales— lots of tales. They say, dearie, there are countries which aren't governed by orthodox Tsars but by Sultans. In one country the Turkish Sultan Makhnut sits on the throne and in another the Persian Sultan. And bless my soul, dearie, them Sultans judge high and low just as their fancy takes them! And whatever judgment they give it's sure to be wrong, for they can't judge righteously, dearie. They can't because such is the cruel fate imposed on them from on high. You see, all the laws in our country are righteous, but in their country every law they have is unrighteous. What our laws decide one way, theirs always decide contrariwise. And all the judges in their countries are also unrighteous so that when they write a petition to them, they always put down: "Will it please Your Lordship to judge me unrighteously." And then of course, dearie, there is a country where all the people have dogs' heads.

Glasha. Why dogs' heads, Feklusha?

Feklusha. On account of their being infidels, dearie. I shall be going along now to see if the God-fearing folk among the rich shopkeepers can spare something for the poor and the needy. Good-by for the present.

Glasha. Good-by. [FEKLUSHA *goes out.*] Fancy that! What strange places there are in the world, to be sure. What a good thing there are some people who hear about things. Otherwise we'd just sit about here and know nothing, but now you meet one of them and you hear what's going on in the wide world. Without them we'd be fools till our dying day.

Enter KATHERINE *and* BARBARA.

Barbara [*to* GLASHA]. Take the bundles outside, Glasha. The coach has arrived. [GLASHA *goes out.*] What a pity, Katherine, they married you off so soon. You had no time to enjoy yourself properly, poor darling. No wonder your heart keeps hankering after all sorts of things.

Katherine. My heart will always be hankering after something or other.

Barbara. Why should it?

Katherine. I'm afraid I was born like that, my dear. I'm so impetuous. I remember when I was only a child of six and do you know what I did? Somebody at home hurt my feelings. It was already dark outside at the time. I ran out of the house, went straight to the Volga, scrambled into a boat and pushed off. They found me next morning miles away from home.

Barbara. Well, and did the boys make eyes at you at all?

Katherine. Of course they did.

Barbara. And what about you? Weren't you ever in love with any of them?

Katherine. No, of course not. I just laughed at them.

Barbara. But, my dear, you're not in love with Tikhon, are you?

Katherine. Of course I am. I'm so sorry for him.

Barbara. Oh, no, you don't love him. If you feel sorry for him, you can't be in love with him. And why indeed should you be in love with him? And you needn't conceal your feelings from me. I noticed a long time ago that you're in love with another man.

Katherine [*in dismay*]. How could you have noticed that?

Barbara. You're so funny, my dear. What do you take me for—a baby? Here's the first infallible sign: as soon as you see him, your face becomes transformed. [KATHERINE *drops her eyes.*] And if that's not enough, darling. . . .

Katherine [*without raising her eyes*]. Well, who is it?

Barbara. But really, darling, why should I tell you? You know it yourself. Why mention names?

Katherine. No, please, tell me! Tell me his name!

Barbara. Boris.

Katherine. Yes, it's him. Oh, my dear, it's him. Only for God's sake. . . .

Barbara. Of course I shan't tell anyone. It's you who ought to be more careful. Don't for Heaven's sake give yourself away without meaning to.

Katherine. I can't conceal anything from anyone. When it comes to deceiving people, I'm quite hopeless, I'm afraid.

Barbara. But, my dear child, you can't do without it. Remember where you live. Our whole life in this house is built on deception. Do you think I liked to deceive people at first? But when it became necessary I learned how to. I was out last night and I met your sweetheart. I had a long talk with him.

Katherine [*after a short pause, without raising her eyes*]. Well, what about it?

Barbara. He asked me to remember him to you. "It's such an awful shame," he said, "I can't meet her anywhere."

Katherine [*looking more confused than ever*]. Where could we meet? And, besides, what's the use?

Barbara. He's so unhappy. . . .

Katherine. Don't talk to me about him. Please don't say another word. I don't want to know him. I shall always love my husband. Darling Tikhon, I shall never give you up for anyone! I didn't want to think of it, but you keep on upsetting me.

Barbara. Well, so far as I'm concerned, you needn't give him another thought. Who is forcing you, anyway?

Katherine. You don't have pity on me, Barbara. One moment you say don't think of him, and the next you remind me of him. You don't think I want to think of him, do you? But what can I do if I can't get him out of my head? Whatever I'm thinking of he's always at the back of my mind. I try to pull myself together but it's no use. Last night, you know, the evil one was tempting me again. I—nearly ran away from home.

Barbara. You're a strange one, Katherine. What did you want to do that for? In my opinion do what you like so long as not a soul knows about it.

Katherine. No, I don't want it that way. Besides, what's the good of it? I'd rather go on suffering as long as I possibly can.

Barbara. And if you can't stand it any longer? What are you going to do then?

Katherine. What am I going to do?

Barbara. Yes, what are you going to do?

Katherine. I shall do anything I like.

Barbara. Just you try! They'll flay you alive here.

Katherine. I don't care. I'll run away and they'll never be able to find me.

Barbara. But where will you go? Don't forget you're a married woman.

Katherine. Oh, my dear, how little you really know me. Of course, I'd just hate it to happen, but if things get too unbearable for me, no power on earth will be able to keep me here. I'll throw myself out of a window or drown myself in the Volga. If I make up my mind not to live here any more, I shan't live here any more not even if they kill me.

Pause.

Barbara. You know what, Katherine? Let's sleep in the summerhouse in the garden as soon as Tikhon leaves.

Katherine. But why?

Barbara. What difference does it make to you?

Katherine. I'm afraid to sleep in a strange place.

Barbara. What are you afraid of? Anyway, Glasha will be with us.

Katherine. All the same, I don't like it. However, I suppose it's all right.

Barbara. I shouldn't have asked you, my dear, but Mother would never let me sleep there alone and I've got to.

Katherine [*looking at her*]. Why have you got to?

Barbara [*laughing*]. Why, we'll be able to tell each other's fortunes there.

Katherine. You're joking, of course?

Barbara. Of course I'm joking. You don't really believe it, do you?

A pause.

Katherine. Where could Tikhon be all this time, I wonder?

Barbara. What do you want him for?

Katherine. Oh, well, I was just wondering. He should be leaving soon.

Barbara. He's with Mother. Locked up in her room. She's nagging the life out of him now. Eating him slowly away as rust does iron.

Katherine. But why?

Barbara. Goodness only knows, my dear. Telling him what to do, I suppose. You see, he'll be away for two whole weeks and that's a very long time for a man who is tied to her apron strings to be away. You can imagine how Mother will be eating her heart out simply because all that time her darling boy will be able to do what he pleases. That's why she's now dinning all sorts of instructions into his ears, telling him exactly what he is to do, or else. . . . Then she's going to take him to the holy icon and make him swear a solemn oath to carry out all her instructions faithfully.

Katherine. So even when he is away from her he can't call his soul his own.

Barbara. Can't he? As soon as he is out of her sight he'll start drinking, and he'll keep on drinking till it's time for him to come back. He's listening to her now but all the time he's thinking about how to cut loose as soon as possible.

Enter MRS. KABANOV *and* TIKHON.

Mrs. Kabanov. Well, do you remember everything I've told you? You'd better. Make a note of it.

Tikhon. Of course I remember, Mother.

Mrs. Kabanov. Well, everything's ready now. The coach is at the door. Say good-by and be off with you.

Tikhon. Yes, Mother, it's time I was off.

Mrs. Kabanov. Well?

Tikhon. What is it, Mother?

Mrs. Kabanov. What are you standing about like a ninny for? Don't you know what you have to do? Tell your wife how she should behave while you're away.

KATHERINE *drops her eyes to the ground.*

Tikhon. I suppose she knows that herself.

Mrs. Kabanov. Don't talk rubbish, son. Come on, tell her. Give her her orders. I want to hear you giving her her orders. Afterwards, when you come back, you can ask her to give you a full account of everything.

Tikhon [*standing in front of* KATHERINE]. Do as Mother tells you, Katherine.

Mrs. Kabanov. Tell her not to be rude to her mother-in-law.

Tikhon. Don't be rude.

Mrs. Kabanov. Tell her to honor her mother-in-law like her own mother.

Tikhon. Honor my mother like your own mother.

Mrs. Kabanov. Tell her not to sit about with her hands on her lap like a grand lady.

Tikhon. Do some work while I'm away.

Mrs. Kabanov. Tell her not to spend all her time looking out of the window.

Tikhon. But, Mother, she never—

Mrs. Kabanov. Well?

Tikhon. Don't look out of the window.

Mrs. Kabanov. Tell her not to make eyes at young men while you're away.

Tikhon. Really, Mother, how can you say a thing like that.

Mrs. Kabanov [*severely*]. Don't be a fool, son. Do what your mother tells you. [*With a smile.*] It's all for the best, son. I know what I'm talking about.

Tikhon [*overcome with confusion*]. Don't make eyes at young men, Katherine.

KATHERINE *looks sternly at him.*

Mrs. Kabanov. Well, now you'd better talk things over between yourselves. Come along, Barbara. [*They go out.*]

KATHERINE *remains standing rooted to the floor as though in a trance.*

Tikhon. Darling, you're not angry with me, are you?
Katherine [*after a short pause, shaking her head*]. No.
Tikhon. Why are you like that? I'm sorry, forgive me.
Katherine [*still the same, shaking her head slowly*]. Never mind. [*Covers her face with her hands.*] She hurt me!

Tikhon. If you're going to take everything to heart like this, you'll soon worry yourself into the grave. Why pay any attention to her? All she wants is to have her say. Well, let her talk. All you have to do is to let it go in one ear and out the other. Well, good-by, Katherine.

Katherine [*throwing herself on her husband's neck*]. Please don't go, darling. Please don't go! I beg you not to go, darling.

Tikhon. I can't stay, Katherine. If Mother sends me, I have to go.

Katherine. Well, if you have to, then take me with you. Please take me with you.

Tikhon [*freeing himself from her embrace*]. I can't do that.

Katherine. Why can't you, darling?

Tikhon. A nice time I'm going to have if I take you with me. All of you just about nag me to death here. I can hardly wait for the moment when I can get out of here. And you're trying to foist yourself on me.

Katherine. Don't you love me any more?

Tikhon. Of course I love you, Katherine. But anyone who has to put up with this kind of life would run from home however beautiful a wife he left behind him. Don't you understand? I may be a rather feeble sort of person, but I'm a man for all that. Rather than spend my whole life like this I'd run away even from my wife. You don't know what it means to me that for the next two weeks there won't be any storm breaking over me, that I shan't be chained hand and foot. How can you expect me to think of my wife now?

Katherine. But how can you expect me to love you if that's the way you talk to me?

Tikhon. Talk, talk, talk! What way do you want me to talk to you? I don't know what you're afraid of. You won't be left here alone. You'll be with my mother.

Katherine. Don't speak of her to me! Don't break my heart! Oh, dear, oh dear! [*Cries.*] What am I to do with myself? Who am I to ask for help? Oh, Lord, oh, Lord, what will become of me?

Tikhon. Come, come, it's not as bad as all that.

Katherine [*goes up to her husband and clings to him*]. Darling, if you agreed to stay or take me with you, oh, how I should love you! Oh, how I should cherish you, my darling. [*Caresses him.*]

Tikhon. I can't make you out at all, Katherine. Usually I can't get a tender word out of you, let alone a caress, and now you're simply falling all over yourself to be nice to me.

Katherine. Tikhon, think who you're leaving me with. There's going to be trouble when you are away. Serious trouble.

Tikhon. But if it can't be helped, it can't be helped.

Katherine. Well, in that case, promise me one thing. Make me swear a terrible oath. . . .

Tikhon. What sort of oath?

Katherine. This sort of oath: that while you're away I shouldn't dare to talk to any stranger on any account, that I shouldn't see anyone, that I shouldn't dare to think of anyone except you.

Tikhon. But why, Katherine, why?

Katherine. Just to ease my mind, darling. Do me this little favor, please.

Tikhon. But how can one answer for oneself? All sorts of ideas may come into one's head.

Katherine [*falling on her knees before him*]. May I never see my father and mother again, may I die without repentance, if I—

Tikhon [*raising her from the floor*]. What are you talking about, Katherine? What is it all about? Why, it's wicked to talk like that. I refuse to listen to you!

Mrs. Kabanov [*behind the scenes*]. It's time to go, Tikhon!

Enter MRS. KABANOV, BARBARA *and* GLASHA.

Mrs. Kabanov. Well, Tikhon, it's time you were off. May the Lord bless you, son. [*Sits down.*] Sit down all of you. [*All sit down. A pause.*] Well, good-by, son. [*Gets up, followed by the rest.*]

Tikhon [*goes up to his mother*]. Good-by, Mother.

Mrs. Kabanov [*points to the ground*]. Bow to me! Bow to me! [TIKHON *bows low to her, then exchanges kisses with her.*] Now say good-by to your wife.

Tikhon. Good-by, Katherine!

KATHERINE *throws herself on his neck.*

Mrs. Kabanov. What are you hanging around his neck for, your shameless hussy? You're not saying good-by to your lover. He's your husband. Your lord and master. Don't you know how to behave decently? Bow down to him!

KATHERINE *bows low to him.*

Tikhon. Good-by, sister. [*Exchanges kisses with* BARBARA.] Good-by, Glasha. [*Exchanges kisses with* GLASHA.] Good-by, Mother. [*Bows.*]

Mrs. Kabanov. Good-by, my son, good-by. Go on, we don't want to stand about shedding tears for you.

TIKHON *goes out followed by* KATHERINE, BARBARA *and* GLASHA.

Mrs. Kabanov [*alone*]. Oh, these young people! It fairly makes you laugh to look at them. If they weren't my own flesh and blood I'd split my sides laughing. They don't know anything. They don't know how to behave with decorum. They can't even take leave properly. Households where there are still older people are lucky. But for them everything would be turned upside down in the house. So long as they're alive everything at any rate is all right. And yet the silly fools are dying to be their own masters. But let them have their own way and they're quite helpless unless someone tells them what to do. They only make the whole world laugh at them. Of course, some people may be sorry for them, but mostly they just laugh at them. And indeed you can't help laughing at them. They invite guests and they don't know how to seat them. What's more, they leave out some of their relations as likely as not. It's a joke, that's what it is. A real joke. That's how the good old customs die out. Already there are houses one doesn't care to visit. And if you do visit them, it fairly makes you sick and you're glad to get away as quickly as possible. What will happen when the old people are dead, how the world will be able to carry on, I really don't know. Well, anyway, I'm thankful I shan't be here to see it.

Enter KATHERINE *and* BARBARA.

Mrs. Kabanov. A short while ago you were boasting that you loved your husband. I can see now how much you really love him. Another woman in your place, a woman who did love her husband, would have collapsed in tears on the front steps after seeing him off and lain there for an hour and a half, crying her eyes out. But you don't seem to care, do you?

Katherine. Why should I give such a performance? Besides, I can't do it. I should only make a spectacle of myself.

Mrs. Kabanov. It isn't much, is it? If you really cared for him, you'd soon learn. If you don't know how a wife should behave on such occasions, you should at least have pretended for the sake of appearances. It's more decent like that. As it is, you only say you love him. Oh, well, I'd better go and say my prayers now. Don't interrupt me, please.

Barbara. I'm going out, Mother.

Mrs. Kabanov. I don't care what you do. Go, if you

like. Have a good time while you still may. You'll be a long time married! [*Goes out.*]

Katherine [*alone, dreamily*]. Well, now everything will be as quiet as the grave in the house. Oh dear, how dull. If only there were children in the house. What a pity I have no children of my own. I'd have spent all my time with them, playing with them. I like talking to children— the little angels. [*Pause.*] It would have been far better if I'd died when I was a little child. I'd have been looking down from Heaven now and been happy, or I'd have been flying off somewhere, anywhere I took a fancy to, without being seen by anyone. I would fly into a meadow and flutter about like a butterfly from one flower to another. [*Sinks into thought.*] Yes, that's what I'm going to do. I'm going to do some work, as I promised. Go to the stores, buy some material and start making clothes and then give it to the poor. They will pray to God for me. I'll tell Barbara about it and we'll do it together. We shan't even notice how quickly the time passes and before we know it Tikhon will be back.

Barbara [*putting on kerchief before looking glass*]. I'm going out now. Glasha is going to make up our beds in the summerhouse. Mother has given her permission. There's a gate behind the raspberry bushes in the garden. Mother usually keeps it locked and hides away the key. I've got it, and I've put another in its place so that she won't notice it. Here, take it. You may need it. [*Gives her the key.*] If I see him, I'll tell him to wait for you at the gate.

Katherine [*pushes key away in dismay*]. No, no, I don't want it.

Barbara. Well, if you don't want it, I most probably will. Take it, it won't bite you.

Katherine. What are you planning to do, you wicked girl? Have you thought what it might lead to? Take it back, take it back.

Barbara. Well, I'm not going to waste my time talking to you. Besides, I'm in a hurry. It's time I had some fun. [*Goes out.*]

Katherine [*alone, holding key in her hand*]. What is she trying to do? What is she up to now? Oh, she must be mad, she must be mad. This key will be my ruin. I'm sure of it. I'd better get rid of it, throw it into the river, so that no one could find it, ever. It burns my hand like a piece of live coal. [*After a moment's thought.*] Yes, that's what leads a woman to her ruin. Who can be happy shut in like a prisoner? No wonder one gets all sorts of ideas. Any other woman in my position would, I suppose, jump at such a chance: she'd take it without a moment's hesitation. But how can one do such a thing without first considering it carefully? It doesn't take long to get into trouble. And then what? Cry one's eyes out for the rest of one's days? Live in torment for years and years to come? Life between four walls would seem even more insupportable then. And life between four walls can be bitter—oh, how bitter! Who can bear to put up with it without tears? Least of all a woman. What sort of life do I lead now? A life without hope, without happiness. Torturing myself, without any chance of escape. And I shall never, never know what real life is like. The longer it goes on, the worse it will be. And now this awful thing must happen to me. [*Sinks into thought.*] Oh, if only it were not for my mother-in-law! She has wrecked my life. She has made me loathe my own home. Even these walls have become hateful to me. [*Looks thoughtfully at the key.*] Throw it away? Of course, I must throw it away. How did I get hold of it? It was given me to tempt me, to destroy me. [*Listening.*] Someone's coming. Lord, what shall I do. [*Hides key in pocket.*] No . . . no one. . . . Why did I get so frightened? I even hid the key away. . . . Oh, well, let it stay there now. It's fate, it seems. And anyway, what sort of sin is it if I do look at him from a distance just once? And even if I say a few words to him, what does it matter? But what about my husband? Haven't I. . . . But he himself didn't want me to. Such a chance may not occur again. Never again in a lifetime. I should be sorry then. I should never forgive myself: you had your chance but you let it slip by. But what am I talking about? Why am I deceiving myself? Even if I were to die for it, I must see him. Why pretend to myself? Throw away the key? Not for anything in the world! It's mine now, mine. I'm going to see Boris whatever happens. Oh, if it were night already!

Curtain.

ACT THREE

SCENE I—*A street. Gates in front of* MRS. KABANOV'S *house. A bench in front of the gates.*

MRS. KABANOV *and* FEKLUSHA *are sitting on the bench.*

FEKLUSHA. The day of judgment is at hand, dearie, according to every sign. Of course, here in your town everything's quiet and peaceful, but everywhere else, in every town I've been to, it's like a second Sodom, dearie: such a terrible din, such a frenzied rushing about, such a mad scurrying of horses and carriages! The people darting about, hither and thither, poor wretches.

Mrs. Kabanov. Why should we be rushing about, my dear? We're in no particular hurry to get anywhere, are we? That's why everything is so quiet and peaceful here.

Feklusha. No, dearie, that isn't the real reason. Shall I tell you why everything is so quiet and peaceful in your town? It's because many people here, and you, dearie, in particular, are adorned with virtues as with flowers. That's why everything here is done so sober and respectable like. For, bless my soul, dearie, what does all this rushing to and fro signify? Why, what else but vanity! You've only to look at Moscow, dearie. There the people always rush about as if they've taken leave of their senses. That's what vanity means. Puffed up with pride, they all are. That's why they're always in such a rush. Ask any one of them what's his hurry, and he'll tell you he's running about on business. He's so flurried and flustered, the poor wretch, he doesn't recognize his own friends. He fancies somebody's beckoning to him, but when he gets there he finds no one there, not a living soul. He's just been imagining it all, so he walks away with sorrow in his heart. And someone else fancies he's overtaking somebody he knows. But any stranger, seeing him dashing along like mad, could have told him that there's no one there. But the poor man, afflicted with the curse of vanity, really believes that he's about to catch up with someone he knows. You see, dearie, vanity's the same as a fog in which people grope about blindly. Here, in your town, on this lovely evening, you rarely see anyone sitting outside the gates of a house. But in Moscow, dearie, the people at this hour are fairly mad with excitement and up to their necks in dissipation. In the streets the noise is like a never-ending roll of thunder. Why, the very earth seems to groan. And would you believe it, dearie, they've even started harnessing a fiery serpent to carriages on iron wheels. All, you see, for the sake of making everything move faster.

Mrs. Kabanov. Yes, yes, my dear. I've heard of it, I have.

Feklusha. But I saw it with my own eyes, dearie. Of course, they can't see anything because of vanity, so that it looks like an engine to them, and they call it an engine. But I saw with my own eyes how that fiery serpent crawled about on his paws like that. [*She spreads out her fingers.*] And the terrible groans he lets out, dearie, which only people who are worthy in the sight of the Lord can hear.

Mrs. Kabanov. They can call it by any name they like. People are such fools they'd believe anything. If they like, they can call it an engine. But even if I were to be offered a fortune, I'd never travel in that engine of theirs.

Feklusha. Heaven forbid, dearie! May the Lord preserve and protect you from such a calamity. And there's something else I must tell you, dearie. Last time I was in Moscow I had a vision. I was taking a walk early in the morning. The sun was just rising, and there on the roof of a very high building I saw some weird figure of a man with a face as black as soot. I needn't tell you, dearie, who that was. I could see him doing something with his hands, as though scattering seeds, but the funny thing was that I could see no seeds at all coming down. It was then that I realized that he was scattering all kinds of weeds in daytime for the people to pick up unbeknown to themselves, blinded as they are by vanity. That's why they are rushing about like mad and that's why their women are nothing but skin and bone and a hank of hair. For the seeds the devil has been scattering don't let them put on fat, poor souls. So they walk about as if they've lost something or as if they're looking for something, their faces so mournful it fairly makes you feel sorry for them.

Mrs. Kabanov. I can well believe it, my dear. Nothing can surprise me any more, not in these days.

Feklusha. Aye, dearie, our times are times of tribulation and sorrow, times of grievous tribulation and great sorrow. Time itself, dearie, is beginning to show signs of shortening.

Mrs. Kabanov. Shortening, my dear?

Feklusha. Yes, shortening. Of course, we can't be expected to have noticed it ourselves because we're blinded by vanity. But wise men have noticed that time's getting shorter and shorter. In the old days, dearie, summer and winter went on and on, seemingly never coming to an end and, indeed, you were thankful when they did come to an end. But today they're gone before you've time to look around. The days and the hours seem to have remained the same as ever, but time is getting shorter and shorter. That's what the wise men are saying.

Mrs. Kabanov. Mark my words, my dear, much worse than that is to come.

Feklusha. All I can say is I hope we shan't live long enough to see it.

Mrs. Kabanov. Maybe.

Enter DIKOY.

Mrs. Kabanov. Good heavens, Mr. Dikoy, why are you out so late?

Dikoy. Who's going to stop me, I should like to know?

Mrs. Kabanov. Stop you? Who wants to stop you?

Dikoy. Very well, why make such a damned song and dance about it? I'm not taking orders from anybody. What the devil are you trying to insinuate, anyway? What's all this blasted nonsense?

Mrs. Kabanov. Don't you bawl at me, Saul Dikoy. Find somebody who is of less account in this town to shout at. I'm too big for you. Go on, carry on with your stroll. Come along, Feklusha, let's go in. [*Gets up.*]

Dikoy. Wait, woman, wait! No need to get huffy, is there? What are you in such a devil of a hurry for, you're not miles away from your home, are you? There it is, behind you.

Mrs. Kabanov. If you want to talk business, then don't shout and talk sense.

Dikoy. I've no business to discuss with you. I'm a bit tipsy, see?

Mrs. Kabanov. You don't want me to give you a pat on the back for that, do you?

Dikoy. Good Lord, no. Don't pat me on the back, but mind, don't scold me, either. I just want you to know that I'm tipsy, that's all. Until I get up tomorrow morning there's nothing anyone can do about it.

Mrs. Kabanov. Then why don't you go to bed?

Dikoy. Where can I go?

Mrs. Kabanov. Where? How do you like that? Home, of course.

Dikoy. But what if I don't want to go home?

Mrs. Kabanov. Why shouldn't you want to go home, tell me that?

Dikoy. Because there's a war going on in my home.

Mrs. Kabanov. Who's waging this war? Aren't you the only warrior in the house?

Dikoy. What if I am a warrior, what does that matter?

Mrs. Kabanov. It doesn't matter a bit. For there's precious little glory you can get fighting with women all your life. That's how it is, my dear sir.

Dikoy. Well, that means that they must all do as I like. You don't expect me to do as they like, do you?

Mrs. Kabanov. I'm surprised at you, Saul Dikoy. There are so many people in your house, and yet they don't seem to be able to do anything to please you.

Dikoy. And what about you?

Mrs. Kabanov. What can I do for you?

Dikoy. Talk to me until this raging temper of mine simmers down. You're the only person in this town who can talk to me like that.

Mrs. Kabanov. Run along, Feklusha, ask Glasha to get something ready for Mr. Dikoy. [FEKLUSHA *goes out.*] Won't you come in?

Dikoy. No, ma'am, I won't. I'm sure I'll feel much worse inside.

Mrs. Kabanov. What have they done to put you in such a temper?

Dikoy. Oh, it's been going on since morning.

Mrs. Kabanov. I suppose they must have been asking you for money.

Dikoy. Blast them, they all seem to have conspired to provoke me today. They kept pestering me all day long.

Mrs. Kabanov. They must have wanted something very badly if they kept pestering you.

Dikoy. I realize that, but what the blazes can I do if I have such a devil of a temper? I know damned well that I have to part with some of my money but I can't part with it without kicking up a hell of a row. You may be one of my best friends, and I know very well that I must pay it back to you, but if I saw you coming to me for your money, I'd call you all the names under the sun before giving it back to you. If you just mention money to me, my heart blazes up in me and I can't do anything about it. It's then I'm ready to revile anyone for no reason at all.

Mrs. Kabanov. The trouble is you've no one older than yourself to keep you in check. That's why you go on bullying everyone.

Dikoy. Don't talk, woman! Hold your tongue and listen to me. This is the sort of thing that happens to me during Lent. While I was observing the fast, the devil would send some peasant to see me: came for his money, had sold me some logs and now he wanted to be paid. He would come just at such a time! Well, of course, I could not help committing a sin. I cursed him as I never cursed anyone in my life before, and he was damned lucky I didn't beat him up as well. That's the sort of devilish temper I have. Afterwards, of course, I asked him to forgive me. Went down on my bended knees before him, I did. It's the truth I'm telling you, woman, gospel truth. I, Saul Dikoy, went down on my bended knees before a miserable clodhopper of a peasant. And all because of my uncontrollable temper. Crawled about in the mud in my own yard, in front of everybody, imploring him to forgive me.

Mrs. Kabanov. And why do you work yourself up into such a rage? You do it on purpose, too, don't you? That's not nice at all.

Dikoy. What do you mean, I do it on purpose?

Mrs. Kabanov. I know, I've seen you in one of your fits. Every time you see anyone who wants to ask you for something you purposely pick a quarrel with your wife or one of your children just to work yourself up into one of your rages. For you know perfectly well that no one would dare ask you for something when you're in a temper. That's what it is, my dear man.

Dikoy. So that's what it is, is it? Well, what of it? Can't a fellow even be sorry to part with his money?

GLASHA enters.

Glasha. The table is laid, ma'am.

Mrs. Kabanov. Well, won't you come in and have a bite of whatever the good Lord has sent us?

Dikoy. Thank you, I think I will.

Mrs. Kabanov. Come along, then.

MRS. KABANOV *ushers* DIKOY *through the gates and follows him into the house.* GLASHA *remains standing at the gates with her arms folded.*

Glasha. There's Mr. Dikoy's nephew. Has he come to fetch his uncle or is he just out for a stroll? Must be out for a stroll.

Enter BORIS.

Boris. Is my uncle at your house?

Glasha. Yes, sir. Do you want him, sir?

Boris. No, no. They asked me at home to find out where he was, but if he is at your place, then let him stay there. Who wants him, anyway? At home they're beside themselves with joy because he's gone out.

Glasha. I bet you if my mistress married him, she'd soon make a different man of him. But I mustn't stand talking to you, sir. Good-by, sir. [*Goes out.*]

Boris. Oh, if only I could have one look at her. I can't very well walk into the house. No one calls on them without an invitation. Lord, what a life! We live in the same town, almost next door to each other, and I can see her only once a week perhaps, and that, too, in church or in the street. In this town when a woman gets herself married she might as well get herself buried—it comes to the same thing. I'm sure I'd be much happier if I never set eyes on her again. As it is, I can see her only in snatches

and in the presence of people who're staring at you with
prying eyes. It nearly breaks your heart. And, besides, I can
no longer manage to keep myself under control. If I go
out for a walk, I invariably find myself outside these gates.
And what's the use of my coming here? I can't see her
anyway, and if I'm not careful people will start talking
and I may make things worse for her. What a confounded
town I've got to! [*Is about to go off,* KULIGIN *meets him
halfway.*]

Kuligin. Hello, sir! Out for a walk?

Boris. Yes, I'm out for a walk, the weather is lovely,
isn't it?

Kuligin. Very nice weather indeed, for a walk, sir. It's
so quiet, the air is so balmy, you can smell the flowers in
the meadows across the Volga, the sky, too, is so clear.

While barred clouds bloom the soft dying day
And touch the stubble plains with rosy hue. . . .

Let's have a walk along the promenade, sir. There's not a
soul there now.

Boris. All right, let's go.

Kuligin. What a terrible place this town of ours is, sir.
We lay out a boulevard, but no one ever thinks of taking
a walk along it. They only go out for walks on holidays
and that, too, merely to show off their smart clothes. The
only man you're likely to meet there now is a drunken
lawyer's clerk, staggering along on his way from the pub.
The poor, sir, have no time for taking walks. They have
to work hard, day and night. They can only afford three
hours of sleep, if that. As for the rich, sir, you'd think
there was nothing to prevent them from taking a walk for
a breath of fresh air, but no, sir, not them. They've locked
and bolted their gates hours ago and let their dogs off
their chains. You'd think they had some important business
to transact, or they're saying their prayers, but you'd be
wrong again, sir. They don't shut themselves in for fear
of burglars, but so that people shouldn't see how they
tyrannize over their own flesh and blood and ill-treat their
servants. The oceans of tears that are shed, unheard and
unseen, behind those locked gates, sir. But why am I telling you this? You know it yourself. And, sir, the horrible

debauchery and the drunken orgies that go on behind some of those locked gates! But everything is carefully covered up. Nobody sees anything and nobody knows anything, only God alone sees it. "You're welcome to look at me in public," they tell you, "I don't mind how hard you stare at me in the street. But what happens in my own home is none of your business. That's why I've got my bolts and bars and fierce dogs. The family," they say, "is not only a sacred but also a secret institution." Well, sir, we know what sort of secrets they have in mind. He alone derives any pleasure from those secrets, sir. As for the rest, let them scream their heads off if they like. And what exactly is this secret? Everyone knows it. Robbing orphans, relations, nephews, or thrashing their children within an inch of their lives so that they shouldn't let out a squeak about what's going on in their homes. That's the whole secret, but enough of that. Do you know, sir, who does take a stroll at this time of day? Our lads and lasses. They don't mind stealing an hour or more from sleep so that they can walk out in couples. Here's one couple, sir.

KUDRYASH *and* BARBARA *appear. They kiss.*

Boris. They're kissing.
Kuligin. That's as it should be, sir.

KUDRYASH *goes out while* BARBARA *walks up to the gates and beckons to* BORIS *who goes up to her.*

Kuligin. I'm off to the boulevard, sir. I don't want to be in your way. Shall I wait for you there, sir?
Boris. Yes, wait for me; I'll join you there in a minute.

KULIGIN *goes out*

Barbara [*hiding her face in her kerchief*]. Do you know the ravine behind the garden of Mrs. Kabanov's house?
Boris. I do.
Barbara. Don't fail to be there a little later tonight.
Boris. Why?
Barbara. Don't ask foolish questions. Do as I tell you. You'll find out why when you come. All right. You'd better go, your friend is waiting for you. [BORIS *goes out.*] I don't think he recognized me. Well, let him rack his brains for a while. It'll do him good. I bet anything

Katherine won't hold out: if she knows he's waiting for her, she's sure to slip out. [*Goes out through gates.*]

SCENE II—*Night. A ravine covered with bushes. On top is the fence of* MRS. KABANOV'S *garden and the gate. A path leads down from the top.*

KUDRYASH [*comes in with guitar*]. Nobody here, yet. What's keeping her, I wonder? Well, let's sit down and wait a little. [*Sits down on a stone.*] And let's have a song to while away the time. [*Sings.*]

> "Don Cossack, do not lead thy horse
>   To water down the river,
> Instead thou homeward bend thy course,
>   Sharp arrow in thy quiver!"
>
> The lusty carle comes riding fast
>   His lady wife to summon.
> "My dear, this night must be your last
>   Prepare yourself for Heaven!"
>
> "Oh, this last mercy grant me, friend,
>   Our babes to sleep to lay,
> Before my soul to Heaven thou send,
>   And thy dear wife do slay.
>
> "Past midnight must thou do thy will,
>   When all my neighbors kind,
> Are sound asleep and think no ill,
>   Till they my body find."

Enter BORIS.

Kudryash [*stops singing*]. Well, of all the— Look who's here! You'd think butter wouldn't melt in his mouth, but he's started sowing his wild oats, too.

Boris. Is that you, Kudryash?

Kudryash. It's me, sir.

Boris. What are you doing here?

Kudryash. Me, sir? I expect I must have some sort of business here, if I'm here, sir. If I had no business to be here, why, then I shouldn't be here. Where are you making for, sir?

Boris [*looking around*]. Look here, Kudryash, I'd like to stay here a little by myself. Would you mind, if it's all the same to you, going somewhere else?

Kudryash. Oh, but it isn't all the same to me, sir. I can see you're here for the first time. But I, sir, I've established a kind of right of ownership over this place. Do you see that path, sir? Well, sir, as a matter of fact, I've made it. I like you very much, sir, and I'd be glad to do anything for you, but don't you ever cross me on this path at night or, God forbid, something untoward might happen. Now that's a fair warning, sir.

Boris. What's the matter with you, Vanya?

Kudryash. Don't you Vanya me. I know my name's Vanya. Just keep to your side of the road, that's all. Get yourself a girl of your own and have a good time with her and it's nobody's business. But lay off somebody else's girl. That's a strict rule among us fellows, sir. I should strongly advise you to observe it, if you don't want to be crippled for life. If anyone tried to get my girl away from me I'd . . . Well, I hardly know myself what I'd do to him. Cut his throat, I would, and that's a fact.

Boris. You're wasting your breath, old man, I haven't the slightest desire to get your girl away from you. I shouldn't have come here at all if I hadn't been told to.

Kudryash. Who told you to come here?

Boris. I couldn't make out who it was. It was too dark. A girl stopped me in the street and told me to come here, at the back of Mrs. Kabanov's garden, near the path.

Kudryash. Who could it have been, sir?

Boris. Now, look here, Kudryash, can I speak frankly to you? You won't give me away, will you?

Kudryash. Never fear, sir. You can talk to me as frankly as you wish. I'm as silent as the grave.

Boris. I'm afraid I don't know all your customs here, or how you order your affairs, and the business, you see, is rather . . .

Kudryash. Have you fallen in love with someone, sir?

Boris. Yes, Kudryash.

Kudryash. Well, there's nothing terrible about that, sir. We're quite broadminded about those things in our town. Girls can run about with boys as much as they like, and mothers and fathers close an eye to their daughters' goings on. It's different with married women, though. They're kept under lock and key.

Boris. Well, that's the trouble, you see.

Kudryash. You mean, sir, you've fallen in love with a married woman?

Boris. I'm afraid so, Kudryash.

Kudryash. Well, sir, if you take my advice you'll forget all about it.

Boris. It's easy to say—forget all about it! It wouldn't matter much to you, perhaps; you'll throw one over and run off with another. But I can't do that. Once I've fallen in love . . .

Kudryash. But don't you realize, sir, that if you carry on with it, it'll mean her undoing?

Boris. Good heavens, no! God preserve me from doing a thing like that. No, Kudryash, I'd never dream of doing that. Would I do anything that would lead to her undoing? All I want is to be able to see her somewhere. I don't want anything else.

Kudryash. But how can you be sure of yourself, sir? And if anything does happen, well, you know the kind of people they are here. They'll make short shrift of her. They won't be satisfied until they've driven the last nail into her coffin.

Boris. Please don't talk like that, Kudryash. Don't try to scare me.

Kudryash. But is she in love with you, sir?

Boris. I don't know.

Kudryash. But you have seen her, haven't you?

Boris. I've only paid one visit to her house with my uncle. Otherwise I only see her in church or I may meet her on the boulevard occasionally. Oh, Kudryash, if you could only see her saying her prayers! What an angelic smile she has! Her whole face seems to be radiant with an inner light.

Kudryash. So it's the young Mrs. Kabanov, isn't it, sir?

Boris. Yes, Kudryash.

Kudryash. I see! So that's how things are. Well, sir, accept my congratulations.

Boris. What on?

Kudryash. Why, don't you realize, sir? Things must be

going along very nicely if you've been told to come here.

Boris. You don't think it was she who told me to come?

Kudryash. Who else?

Boris. Oh, you're joking. I can't believe it. [*Clutches at his head.*]

Kudryash. What's the matter with you, sir?

Boris. I shall go raving mad with happiness.

Kudryash. So that's how it is. You've found something to go raving mad about, sir. You'd better watch your step. You might land yourself into an awful mess and you might get her into proper trouble, too. It's true, her husband is a damned fool, but her mother-in-law is a mighty fierce dragon, sir.

BARBARA *comes out of the gate.*

Barbara [*sings*].

> Beyond the swift rapids my Vanya's hieing,
> There my Vanya's hieing. . . .

Kudryash [*continuing*]. And fair wares he's buying! [*Whistles.*]

Barbara [*comes down the path and, covering her face with her kerchief, comes up to* BORIS]. You'd better wait here, my lad. A little bird tells me you won't be disappointed. [*To* KUDRYASH.] Come on, let's go to the Volga.

Kudryash. Why are you so late? I've been waiting for you! You know I hate being kept waiting! [BARBARA *embraces him with one arm and they go off together.*]

Boris. Am I dreaming? This lovely night, these songs, these lovers' meetings! Boys and girls walking about locked in each other's arms. All this is so new to me, it's so fine, so jolly! I, too, am waiting for something to happen. But I don't know, I can scarcely imagine what exactly is going to happen. All I know is that my heart is pounding away and that every nerve in my body is tense with expectation. I can't even think what to say to her. I'm so excited I can hardly breathe. I can hardly stand on my feet. Once my stupid heart is ablaze nothing will hold me back, nothing. Here she comes. [KATHERINE *is coming down the path unhurriedly, covered with a large white shawl, her eyes fixed on the ground.*] Is it you, Katherine? [*A pause.*] I'm so glad you've come! [*A pause.*] If only you knew how much I loved you, Katherine. [*Wants to take her by the hand.*]

Katherine [*frightened, but without raising her eyes*]. Don't touch me! Please, don't touch me!

Boris. Don't be angry with me.

Katherine. Go away! Go away! You're my evil genius! You know perfectly well that not all the prayers in the world can take away this terrible sin. It will lie like a heavy stone on my heart, like a heavy stone.

Boris. Don't send me away!

Katherine. Why did you come, why did you come, my destroyer? Don't you know I'm married? Don't you know I've vowed to be faithful to my husband till death do us part?

Boris. But didn't you tell me to come yourself?

Katherine. Till death do us part. . . . Please understand it! You're my enemy, my worst enemy!

Boris. Then I'd better not see you again.

Katherine [*excitedly*]. But do you realize what I'm preparing for myself? You know where my place should be, don't you?

Boris. Please calm yourself. [*Takes her by the hand.*] Sit down.

Katherine. Why do you want my ruin?

Boris. But how can I want you ruined, Katherine, when I love you more than anything in the world, more than myself?

Katherine. No, no, you've already ruined me!

Boris. Why, I'm not a scoundrel, am I?

Katherine [*nodding*]. Yes yes, you've ruined me, ruined me, ruined me.

Boris. God forbid, Katherine. I'd rather die a thousand deaths than let you come to any harm.

Katherine. But how can you say you haven't ruined me when I've left my home at night to come to you?

Boris. But you did it of your own free will, didn't you?

Katherine. I have no will of my own. If I had, I shouldn't have come to you. [*Raises her eyes and looks at* BORIS. *After a short pause.*] You can do anything you like with me now. You know that, don't you? [*Throws herself on his neck.*]

Boris. My darling! [*Embraces her.*]

Katherine. Do you know what? I wish I could die now.

Boris. But why should you want to die when we're so happy?

Katherine. No, I shan't live long. I know that. I shan't live long.

Boris. Please don't talk like that, darling. You're making me feel awful. . . .

Katherine. Yes, you're happy, you're a free man, but I. . . .

Boris. No one will ever find out about our love. No one in the whole world. Do you really think that I of all people won't take pity on you?

Katherine. Oh, it doesn't matter. Why take pity on me? No one's to blame. I made up my mind to come myself. Don't pity me. Ruin me! Let the whole world know about us. Let them all see what I'm doing. [*She embraces* BORIS.] If I'm not afraid of sin for your sake, do you think I'll be afraid of what people may say about me? I've heard it said that it's much better if you expiate your sin here on earth by suffering.

Boris. But why think of it at all, Katherine? Why destroy our present happiness?

Katherine. You're quite right. I'll have plenty of time to think about it and to cry over it later on.

Boris. And you know, I was really afraid a moment ago that you were going to send me away.

Katherine [*smiling*]. Send you away? How could I do that, darling? Not when I love you as much as I do with all my heart and soul. If you hadn't come, I believe I should have come to you myself.

Boris. I didn't know you were in love with me, Katherine.

Katherine. I've loved you for a long time. You seem to have come here specially to lead me astray. As soon as I saw you I became a different woman. If you'd beckoned to me the first time we met, I'd have followed you. If you'd gone to the ends of the earth, I should have gone after you without looking back.

Boris. Will your husband be away a long time?

Katherine. For two weeks.

Boris. Oh, in that case let's enjoy every moment of it! We've lots of time.

Katherine. Very well, darling. Let's enjoy every minute of it and then. . . . [*Sinks into thought*.] If they put me under lock and key again, it'll mean death to me. But if they don't, I'll find some way of seeing you, darling!

Enter KUDRYASH *and* BARBARA.

Barbara. Well, have you two made it up?

KATHERINE *hides her face on* BORIS' *chest*.

Boris. Yes, we have.

Barbara. Well, then, why not go for a walk? We'll wait for you here. Vanya will give you a shout if necessary.

BORIS *and* KATHERINE *go out*. KUDRYASH *and* BARBARA *sit down on a stone*.

Kudryash. That's a very clever trick of yours to climb over the garden gate. Extremely convenient for fellows like me.

Barbara. It was my idea.

Kudryash. I thought as much. But won't you catch it from your mother when she finds out?

Barbara. Oh, she'll never find out. It will never occur to her.

Kudryash. But if she should, worse luck—

Barbara. She sleeps like a log. She never wakes till the morning.

Kudryash. But how can you be sure? What if the devil should rouse her?

Barbara. Let him! You see, the gate leading from the house to the garden is locked. She'll knock and knock till she gets tired of it and goes back. And in the morning we'll tell her that we didn't hear a thing. Besides, Glasha is keeping watch for us. If anything happens, she'll give us a signal. I've taken every precaution. You can trust me to do that. If you don't have your wits about you in our house, you'll soon get into trouble.

KUDRYASH *strums on the guitar*. BARBARA *leans on his shoulder*. KUDRYASH *goes on playing softly without paying any attention to her*.

Barbara [*yawning*]. I wonder what the time is?

Kudryash. It's gone twelve.

Barbara. How do you know?

Kudryash. I heard the night watchman calling the hour.

Barbara [*yawning*]. It's time they came back. Give them a shout. We'll come out earlier tomorrow so that we'll have more time together.

Kudryash [*whistles and shouts in a singsong*]. All go home! All go home! But damned if I want to go home!

Boris [*behind the scenes*]. I can hear you!

Barbara [*getting up*]. Well, good night, darling! [*Yawns and kisses him coldly like a very old friend.*] See that you come earlier tomorrow. [*Looks in the direction where* BORIS *and* KATHERINE *have gone.*] Hi there, come on, will you? You're not parting forever. You'll see each other again tomorrow. [*Yawns and stretches herself.*]

KATHERINE *runs in, followed by* BORIS.

Katherine [*to* BARBARA]. Let's go, let's go! [*They walk up the path.* KATHERINE *turns around.*] Good-by.

Boris. Till tomorrow!

Katherine. Yes, yes, till tomorrow! Don't forget to tell me your dream! [*Goes up to the gate.*]

Boris. I won't.

Kudryash [*sings to the accompaniment of the guitar*].

> Go on, lassie, frolic and play,
> But be back home at close of day,
> Tra-la-la at close of day,
> You must be home at close of day!

Barbara [*at the gate*].

> No, no, mother, I'll frolic and play,
> Till the break of a new day,
> Tra-la-la, till break of day,
> I shan't be home till break of day!

BARBARA *and* KATHERINE *go out.*

Kudryash [*sings*].

> But when the next day broke all red,
> And I, poor lassie, homeward sped. . . .

Curtain.

ACT FOUR

In the foreground a narrow arcade with a vaulted roof of an ancient building slowly falling into decay. Here and there tufts of grass and bushes. In the background through the arches the bank of the Volga and the view across the river can be seen.

A few strollers of either sex pass across the stage to the other side of the arches.

FIRST STROLLER. It's beginning to drizzle. Hope there won't be a thunderstorm.

Second Stroller. There will be, you know.

First Stroller. It's a good thing we can find some shelter.

All go under the arches.

A *Woman.* Have you ever seen such big crowds on the boulevard? On a holiday everyone seems to come out for a walk. And how do you like our shopkeepers' wives? Dressed up, aren't they?

First Stroller. They, too, will run for shelter.

Second Stroller. There'll be hundreds of them here in another minute.

First Stroller [*examining walls*]. Somebody's been doing a nice bit of brushwork here. Why, some of it can still be made out.

Second Stroller. I should think so. The place was painted all over once upon a time. It's been falling to bits for some time, though. Look at the cracks in the walls, with bushes sprouting out of them. They never bothered to repair it after the fire. I don't suppose you remember the fire? It's forty years or more since it happened.

First Stroller. I wonder what was painted here? It's difficult to make head or tail of it in its present shocking state.

Second Stroller. That's the burning pit.

First Stroller. Fancy that!

Second Stroller. There are all sorts of people here on their way to hell.

First Stroller. Oh, I see. Yes, yes.

Second Stroller. People of all ranks.

First Stroller. Black men, too?

Second Stroller. Yes, black men, too.

First Stroller. And what's that?

Second Stroller. That's the Lithuanian invasion. A battle, you see. A battle between the Russians and the Lithuanians.

First Stroller. Lithuania? What's that?

Second Stroller. That's Lithuania, that is.

First Stroller. I've heard it said that the Lithuanians fell upon us from the sky.

Second Stroller. Can't say. Maybe they did and again maybe they didn't.

A Woman. Don't talk nonsense! Everybody knows they fell from the sky, and where the battle was there have been mounds put up for a memorial.

First Stroller. That's right, the lady's right. That's exactly what happened.

Enter Dikoy, *followed by* Kuligin *without a cap. All bow and assume a respectful attitude.*

Dikoy. Whew, whew. . . . Got drenched to the skin. [*To* Kuligin.] Do leave me alone, man! Leave me alone, I say! [*Angrily.*] You're a blasted fool, sir!

Kuligin. But please consider, sir. Such a thing will be very useful. All the inhabitants of our town will benefit from it.

Dikoy. Go away, man, go away. What damned use will it be to anybody? Who cares, anyway, whether it's of any use or not?

Kuligin. But wouldn't you like it, sir? Suppose it's placed on the boulevard, on a spot specially cleared for it. And it can be done almost for nothing. What indeed can such a thing cost, sir? Just a small stone pillar [*indicates with his hands the size of each thing he enumerates*], a brass plate, a round one, sir, and a style, a straight style [*shows how straight*], a very ordinary one, sir. I'd do everything, sir. I'd even cut out the figures myself. Now, just imagine for a minute, sir, that you're taking a walk, or indeed any

of our townspeople, sir, who are minded to take a
walk once in a while, and then they walk up to it,
and they can tell the right time at once. It's such a lovely
spot for a sundial, sir, and such a beautiful view, and
everything, and it looks so empty, sir. And don't forget, sir,
that we sometimes have visitors in our town who like to
go sight-seeing, and that sundial, sir, would be one of our
showpieces, an ornament for the eye, something of which
our townspeople might well be proud.

Dikoy. What the devil are you worrying the life out of
me with all sorts of nonsense for? How do you know I
even want to listen to you, let alone discuss it with you?
You ought to find out first whether I'm at all disposed to
waste my time talking to a blasted fool like you. Who do
you take me for? One of your equals? Good Lord, have
you ever heard such nonsense! A matter of public importance! How dare you shove your blasted snout into my
face?

Kuligin. If I'd come to you with my own business, sir,
you'd have been absolutely right in abusing me. But I'm
doing it for the general good, sir. What do a few rubles
matter to a whole town, sir? And it won't cost more than
that, sir.

Dikoy. You'll probably run off with the money. How
can one trust a damned rogue like you?

Kuligin. But if I'm willing to give my work for nothing,
sir, how can you suspect me of wishing to steal the money?
Why, everybody knows me here. Nobody has ever said
a word against me—nobody, sir.

Dikoy. What do I care whether they know you or not?
I don't want to know you.

Kuligin. But why insult an honest man, sir?

Dikoy. Listen to him! He wants me to give him an
account of my actions now. I shouldn't dream of giving
an account of my actions to a much bigger man than you.
If I want to form a certain opinion of you, I'll damned
well do it. You may be an honest enough man for other
people, but so far as I'm concerned, you're just a damned
blackguard. That's all. Did you want me to tell you that?
Very well, now you've heard it. I tell you again, you're a
blackguard, sir, and a blackguard so far as I'm concerned

you'll remain. Or will you perhaps sue me for slander? Very well, sue me. I tell you that to me you're a worm. If I'm so minded, I'll leave you in peace; if not—I'll crush you.

Kuligin. You can do as you like, sir. I'm a small man, sir, and it's easy to do me an injury. But I hope you won't mind my reminding you that "virtue shines even through the meanest rags."

Dikoy. Damn your impertinence! I shan't put up with any blasted sermons from the likes of you.

Kuligin. I'm not being impertinent, sir. I'm telling you that simply because one day maybe you'll want to do something for our town. You have the power to do it, all you want is the will to do a good deed. For instance, sir, we usually get quite a number of thunderstorms at this time of the year but we've got hardly any lightning conductors.

Dikoy [*haughtily*]. All that is newfangled nonsense.

Kuligin. How can you say it's newfangled nonsense when experiments have shown—

Dikoy. What lightning conductors are you talking about?

Kuligin. Steel ones, sir.

Dikoy [*angrily*]. And what else?

Kuligin. The rods, sir, are made of steel.

Dikoy [*getting angrier and angrier*]. Don't be a blasted fool, man, I heard you say that the rods were made of steel. What else, I'm asking you? Rods, indeed! What else?

Kuligin. Nothing else, sir.

Dikoy. But what's a thunderstorm in your opinion, eh? Come on, tell me.

Kuligin. It's electricity, sir.

Dikoy [*stamping his foot*]. Electricity be damned! Now, aren't you a blackguard? Don't you know that a thunderstorm is sent us as a punishment to make us repent of our sins? And you've the impudence to propose to fight it with some blasted steel rods and sticks and I don't know what else. What are you, a Tartar? Are you a Tartar, I ask you? Answer me, are you a Tartar?

Kuligin. Sir, our great poet Derzhavin said—

My body's dust and to dust it will return,
But with my mind I thunder spurn!

Dikoy. I have a good mind to haul you before the mayor for such words. He'll teach you a lesson, he will. Ladies and gentlemen, will you listen to this man for a moment.

Kuligin. Well, I suppose I have to give in. But wait till I get my million, I'll show you then! [*Goes out with a scornful wave of the hand.*]

Dikoy. Where are you going to get your million? Steal it from someone? Stop him! Stop him! He's planning to steal money from someone. You've got to be a saint not to lose your temper with such people. [*Addressing the crowd.*] That's all your fault, blast you. I made a vow this morning not to lose my temper, and then this damned fool comes along and gets my back up on purpose. To hell with him! [*Angrily.*] Is it still raining?

First Stroller. It seems to have stopped, sir.

Dikoy. How do you mean, it seems? You blasted fool, can't you poke your head out and see? It seems!

First Stroller [*emerging from under the arches*]. It has stopped, sir.

DIKOY *goes out followed by the rest. For a short time the stage is empty. Then* BARBARA *comes in hurriedly and hides in a corner under the arches, on the lookout for somebody.*

Barbara. I think it's him.

BORIS *passes in the background.*

Barbara. Psst! [BORIS *looks around.*] Come here. [*Beckons to him.* BORIS *walks up to her.*] What are we to do with Katherine? Tell me, for Heaven's sake.

Boris. What's wrong?

Barbara. Everything. Her husband has come back. Didn't you know that? We didn't expect him back so soon, but he's back all right.

Boris. No, I didn't know that.

Barbara. She's simply gone out of her mind.

Boris. It seems all I could count on was ten days of happiness while he was away. Now I don't suppose I shall see her again.

Barbara. So that's what you're worried about, is it? Listen to me, Katherine is in a terrible state. She's trembling all over just as though she were in a fever. She walks about the house like a ghost, looking for something. Her eyes are just like the eyes of a crazy woman. This morning she had a terrible fit of crying. She was sobbing her heart out. Oh, dear, oh dear, what am I to do with her?

Boris. Perhaps she'll get over it after a time.

Barbara. I shouldn't think so. She daren't look at her husband. Mother has begun to notice it. She has been casting sidelong glances at her. I think she's beginning to suspect something. She looks daggers at poor Katherine, and Katherine is not enjoying it, I can tell you. It frightens me to see her in such a state. I tell you I'm frightened.

Boris. What are you frightened of?

Barbara. You don't know her. She is a queer one. She's capable of anything. She may do something that—

Boris. Good God, what are we to do then? You ought to have a good talk to her. Can't you persuade her to be reasonable?

Barbara. I tried to, but she refuses to listen to me. I'm afraid to go near her any more.

Boris. But what do you think she's capable of doing?

Barbara. I'll tell you what. She may go down on her knees before her husband and tell him everything. That's what's worrying me.

Boris [*frightened*]. Good God, she won't do that, will she?

Barbara. Won't she? She's capable of anything.

Boris. Where is she now?

Barbara. She's gone out for a walk on the boulevard with her husband. Mother is with them. You'd better go there, too, if you like. But no, perhaps you'd better not. If she sees you, she may completely collapse. [*Distant claps of thunder.*] There's a storm coming. [*Looks out.*] Yes, it's beginning to rain. Everybody's running for shelter here. Hide yourself somewhere. I'll stand here so that nobody suspects anything.

Enter several persons of either sex of every social class, followed by MRS. KABANOV, TIKHON, KATHERINE *and* KULIGIN.

First Stroller. I suppose the young lady must be very frightened of the storm if she's in such a hurry to run for shelter.

A Woman. You can't run away from your fate, how-ever much you may hurry.

Katherine [rushes in]. Oh, Barbara! [*Grasps* BARBARA's *hand and holds on to it tightly.*]

Barbara. What's the matter with you? What's wrong?

Katherine. I'm going to die!

Barbara. Do talk some sense for a change. Pull yourself together.

Katherine. I can't, I can't! I can't do anything. My heart's bursting with pain.

Mrs. Kabanov [coming in]. Yes, my girl, if you lived so as to be prepared for everything, you wouldn't be so terrified.

Tikhon [coming in]. But, Mother, what sort of sin could she have committed? The same as the rest of us are committing every day, I'm sure of it. She's timid by nature.

Mrs. Kabanov. How do you know that? Still waters run deep.

Tikhon [jokingly]. Well, Mother, maybe something did happen while I was away, but I'm quite sure nothing's happened while I was at home.

Mrs. Kabanov. Maybe it happened while you were away, son.

Tikhon [jokingly]. You'd better confess, Katherine, dar-ling. Come, confess your terrible sin. You won't be able to hide it from me for long, you know. I should say not, my dear. I know everything.

Katherine [looking straight into TIKHON's *eyes].* Oh, my darling!

Barbara. Leave her alone, will you? Can't you see she's worried enough without your silly jokes?

BORIS *emerges from the crowd and exchanges bows with the* KABANOVS.

Katherine [utters a little scream]. Oh!

Tikhon. What are you so frightened of? Did you think it was a stranger? Why, it's an old friend of mine. How's your uncle?

Boris. He's quite well, thank you.

Katherine [to BARBARA].* What more does he want of

me? Can't he see how I suffer? [*Leans against* BARBARA *and bursts out crying.*]

Barbara [*in a loud voice so that her mother should hear*]. We are at our wit's end to know what to do with her, and complete strangers would come and bother us at such a time! [*Signals to* BORIS *who effaces himself in the crowd at the entrance.*]

Kuligin [*comes forward to the center of the stage and harangues the crowd*]. What is there to be afraid of, I ask you? Every little blade of grass, every flower, is now rejoicing, and we hide ourselves, terrified out of our wits, as though expecting some terrible calamity to befall us. The thunderstorm will kill me! Why, it's not a storm at all. It's grace abounding. Yes, grace abounding. You're afraid of everything. If the northern lights appear in the sky, do you run out into the streets and admire that miracle of nature? With gratitude in your hearts for God's great wisdom, for "from the north a dawn ariseth"—no! You're thrown into a panic. You try to invent all sorts of fearful omens. You start whispering to each other: "What does it signify? A war or a pestilence?" A comet appears— you'd think there was nothing more wonderful in the night sky! We've got used to the miracle of the starry heavens, there's no surprise left in the stars, but a comet is something new, something wonderful, so one would have thought that you would have been only too glad to look at it and marvel at its beauty. But no, to look at the sky across which a comet is trailing clouds of glory drives you into a cold sweat. You tremble all over with terror! You've transformed every grand spectacle of the heavens into a nightmare. What a people! Lord, what a people! Look at me! I'm not afraid. [*To* BORIS.] Won't you come with me, sir?

Boris. Come on, I'm more afraid to be here. [KULIGIN *and* BORIS *go out.*]

Mrs. Kabanov. Did you ever hear anything like it? What a sermon. No wonder nobody wants to listen to him. The times we live in! Are these our new preachers? If an old man talks like that, what can you expect from the young?

A Woman. The whole sky's overcast, covered by a black cloud as though by a cap.

First Stroller. Lord, look at that cloud, rolling along like smoke, for all the world like some creature was whirling round and round in it. Look, look, it's crawling toward us now. Just like a living creature about to pounce on us.

Second Stroller. Mark my words, this storm won't pass without doing some damage. I tell you I know it. It'll either kill someone or set a house on fire. You'll see. Why do I think so? Because the sky looks so unusual.

Katherine [*listening to the conversation*]. What are they saying? Did you hear? They said it was going to kill someone.

Tikhon. Don't pay any attention to them. They say the first thing that comes into their silly heads.

Mrs. Kabanov. Don't you talk like that about those who are older than you, son. They know better than you. Old men know all the signs. An old man won't utter a word in vain.

Katherine [*to her husband*]. Tikhon, I know who's going to be killed.

Barbara [*softly, to* KATHERINE]. Shut up, for goodness' sake.

Tikhon. How do you know?

Katherine. I know. It's I who will be killed. You will pray for me when it happens, won't you?

Enter the elderly GENTLEWOMAN *with two footmen.* KATHERINE *utters a piercing cry and hides herself.*

Gentlewoman. Why are you hiding from me, my pretty one? It's no use hiding yourself. You're afraid, I see. You don't want to die, do you? You want to live. Well, of course you want to live. Everyone can see what a beauty you are. Ha, ha, ha! A beauty. If I were you, my pretty one, I'd pray to God to take my beauty away from me. It will ruin you. And it will lead others astray. Then you'll be able to rejoice in your beauty. Ah, yes, my pretty one, you're going to lead many, many men astray. The young fools will be fighting duels over you, they'll be slashing each other with swords. Jolly, isn't it, my pretty one? And the old fools? Why, the old fools, the respectable old men, will forget the grave that is waiting for them, and they, too, will fall under the spell of your beauty. And who'll have to answer for all that? You, my pretty one, you'll have to answer for everything. Take my advice, child. Into the river with your beauty. It's much better so, and quickly, quickly. [KATHERINE *hides herself.*] Where are you hiding, you silly creature? You can't run away from God. All of you will burn in the everlasting fire. [*Goes out*].

Katherine. Oh, I'm dying!

Barbara. Stop torturing yourself for nothing. Here, go into a corner and say a prayer. You'll feel better.

Katherine [*walks up to the wall and falls on her knees, then quickly jumps to her feet*]. Oh, oh, the burning pit, hell-fire, hell-fire! [TIKHON, MRS. KABANOV *and* BARBARA *crowd around her.*] I can't bear it any longer. My heart is going to burst. Mother, Tikhon! I've sinned before God and before you. Didn't I swear to you, Tikhon, that I wouldn't even look at a man during your absence? You remember, Tikhon, don't you? You remember, don't you? But do you know what I did while you were away? Do you know what your worthless wife did, Tikhon? The very first night I went out of the house. . . .

Tikhon [*looks very embarrassed, almost in tears, pulls* KATHERINE *by her sleeve*]. Don't say anything, Katherine, don't say another word, there's a good girl. Can't you see Mother's here?

Mrs. Kabanov [*severely*]. Oh, no, you'd better go on, my girl, now that you've begun.

Katherine. Every night I walked out . . . [*Bursts into tears.*]

TIKHON *wants to embrace her.*

Mrs. Kabanov. Don't touch her, son. Let her go on. Who with?

Barbara. She's lying, Mother. She doesn't know what she's saying.

Mrs. Kabanov. Shut up. So that's what it was. Who is the man? Tell me.

Katherine. Boris. [*Thunder.*] Oh! [*Faints into her husband's arms.*]

Mrs. Kabanov. Well, son, now you know. That's what comes of freedom. I told you, but you wouldn't listen to me. Now I hope you are satisfied!

Curtain.

ACT FIVE

Same as Act One. Dusk.

KULIGIN *sits on a bench.* TIKHON *is walking on the boulevard.*

KULIGIN [*sings*].

> The vault of heaven with darkness
>   is veiled o'er,
> The eyes of men in sleep are closed,
>   their bodies to restore.

[*Seeing him.*] Good evening, sir. Are you going far?

Tikhon. I'm going home. You've heard of my trouble, haven't you? The whole family is at sixes and sevens.

Kuligin. I know sir, I know.

Tikhon. I went to Moscow on business, you know that, don't you? Well, my dear mother read me a long lecture before I left, but as soon as I got out of the place, I forgot all about it. I cut loose like hell. I was so glad to feel a free man for a change. I drank all the way to Moscow and when I arrived in Moscow I went on drinking. Left a trail of empty bottles behind me. You see, I had to get enough drink into ten days to last me a whole year. I never stopped to think what was happening at home. Even if I had, I should never have guessed what was going on there. You've heard, haven't you?

Kuligin. Yes, sir, I've heard.

Tikhon. I'm the most unhappy man alive now, Kuligin. It's the end. And I don't know what I did to deserve it.

Kuligin. Your mother is a bit too strict, I'm afraid.

Tikhon. Yes, of course. She's the cause of it all. But what have I done to deserve it? Tell me that. I've just been to see Dikoy. Had a drink with him. Thought I might feel better, but not a bit of it, Kuligin, not a bit of it. I feel much worse. Think what my wife has done to me! She couldn't have done anything worse, could she?

Kuligin. It's difficult to say, sir. It's difficult to blame either of you.

Tikhon. No, oh, no, wait a minute. There can't be anything worse than that. She really should be made to pay with her life. Mother said she deserves to be buried alive, to give her a chance to expiate her sin, but I love her, Kuligin. I wouldn't like to hurt a hair of her head. It's true, I did chastise her a little, but only because Mother told me to. I feel sorry for her. Do you understand that, Kuligin? Mother is nagging the life out of her. She is walking about like a shadow, looking miserable and brokenhearted. All she does is cry, and waste away. That's what's making me so miserable. I can't look at her without feeling wretched.

Kuligin. Couldn't you arrange things so that everything would come right in the end? You ought to forgive her and never mention the matter again. I don't suppose you are entirely blameless yourself, are you?

Tikhon. Of course I'm not.

Kuligin. That's it. So you see, you have to forget the whole thing and never throw it back at her even when you are drunk. She'd be a good wife to you, sir. A better wife than any other girl in the town.

Tikhon. But don't you realize, Kuligin? I'm only too willing to let bygones be bygones. But my mother . . . You can't do anything with my mother, you know.

Kuligin. It's high time you lived your own life in your own way, sir.

Tikhon. But what can I do, Kuligin? I can't become a different person, can I? They tell me I haven't got enough sense to live as I live. So what can I do but live as others tell me to? I tell you what I can do, though. I'm going to spend my last copper on drink. Drink myself silly. Then let Mother nurse her idiot boy for the rest of her life.

Kuligin. Oh, sir, what a business it is! And what about Boris? What's going to happen to him?

Tikhon. The scoundrel is being bundled off by his uncle to some hole on the Chinese border. His uncle is sending him to a business friend of his, to work at his office. He is going to spend the next three years there.

Kuligin. But how is he, sir?

Tikhon. He is also in a hell of a state, I can tell you.

Crying and wringing his hands. His uncle and I gave him
a good talking to the other day, but he didn't utter a
word. He's got a kind of wild look about him. Do anything you like with me, he says, but leave her alone. Don't
torment her. He, too, seems to be heartbroken about her.

Kuligin. He's a good fellow, sir.

Tikhon. Well, he's ready to leave the town any time
now. His things are packed and his coach is ready. He is
very cut up, the poor devil. I can see that he wants to
see her before he leaves, but he's made his bed and now
he can lie on it. Why should I be sorry for him? He's my
enemy, isn't he? I'd hang, draw and quarter him if I could.

Kuligin. We must forgive our enemies, sir.

Tikhon. You'd better tell that to my mother. She'd give
you the right answer, she would. Our family life has
been knocked into a cocked hat. We're no longer members of the same family. We're mortal enemies to one
another. Mother nagged Barbara day and night till she
couldn't stand it any longer and ran away. Just left the
house and disappeared.

Kiligin. Where has she gone to?

Tikhon. Dunno. I understand she's run off with Kudryash. He can't be found anywhere, either. That, Kuligin,
is entirely my mother's doing. She started bullying her,
locking her up in her room. "Don't lock me up," Barbara
said, "or it'll be the worse for you." And so it was. But
what am I to do now? Please tell me. Teach me how to
live now. I'm sick to death of my home. I'm ashamed to
show myself among people. If I try doing something in
our business, I make an unholy mess of it. Now I'm going
home, but do you think I'm looking forward to it?

Enter GLASHA.

Glasha. Mr. Kabanov, sir, oh, Lord, sir!

Tikhon. What now?

Glasha. There's more trouble in the house, sir.

Tikhon. Good Lord, one damned thing after another.
Tell me, what's happened?

Glasha. Your wife, sir. . . .

Tikhon. Well, what's the matter with her? She isn't
dead, is she?

Glasha. No, sir. She's gone away, sir. We can't find her

anywhere. We've looked all over the place for her, sir.

Tikhon. Come on, Kuligin, let's go and look for her. Do you know what I'm afraid of? I'm afraid she might lay hands on herself. She's so heartbroken, so heartbroken, that it's impossible to describe it. My heart breaks every time I look at her. Are you sure you've looked everywhere, Glasha? Has she been gone long?

Glasha. Not very long. I'm sorry, sir. It's my fault. But I couldn't keep an eye on her every minute of the day, could I?

Tikhon. Well, don't stand about. Go on, look for her. [GLASHA *goes out.*] Let us go, too, Kuligin. [*They go out.*]

The stage is empty for a little while. KATHERINE *enters from the opposite side and walks slowly across the stage. During this soliloquy, and throughout the following scenes,* KATHERINE *speaks as though in a trance, only half-realizing what she is saying.*

Katherine [*alone*]. No, I can't see him anywhere. My poor darling, what is he doing now? All I want is to say good-by to him. After that—after that, I don't mind what happens to me, I don't mind if I die even. Why did I get him into trouble? It doesn't make things easier for me, does it? Why should both our lives be ruined? Oh, if only mine had been ruined! But I've ruined my life and I've ruined his. I've brought dishonor on myself and I've condemned him to a life of slavery. Yes, dishonor for me and slavery for him. [*A pause.*] Let me see. What did he say to me? How did he pity me? What were the words he used? [*Clutching at her head.*] Can't remember. I've forgotten everything. It's at night, at night, that I suffer most. Everybody goes off to bed, and I, too, go off to bed, but they go to sleep and I— It's as if I were going to my grave. I get so frightened of the dark! There are such strange noises. I seem to hear people chanting as if they were burying someone, but so softly that I can barely hear it, it seems miles and miles away. . . . I'm so glad when it gets light again. But I hate to get up. I hate to face the same people, to hear the same kind of talk, to go through the same torment over and over again. Why do they look at me like that? Why don't they kill unfaithful wives any more? Why is it different now? Before they used to put them to death, why don't they take them and throw them into the Volga? I'd be glad if they did. Ah, they say, if you were put to death, your sin would be forgiven you. You must go on living, for you must expiate your sin by suffering. But haven't I expiated my sin already? How much more shall I have to suffer? What have I got to live for now? I don't desire anything more. I don't care for anything in the world. Life has become hateful to me, but death does not come. You pray for it, but it doesn't come. Whatever I hear and whatever I see merely increases my pain here. [*Pressing her heart.*] If only I could go away with him, I might still have found some kind of happiness. . . . And, anyway, what difference would it make now? Isn't my soul damned already? Oh, how I long to see him. Darling, if I never see you again, then please hear me from afar. Oh, wild winds, bear my great sorrow and my anguish to him! Oh, Lord, I am so miserable, so miserable! [*Goes up to the bank of the river and shouts in a loud voice.*] Darling, life of my heart, I love you! Answer me! [*Bursts out crying.*]

Enter BORIS.

Boris [*not noticing* KATHERINE]. Good God, I'm sure I heard her voice. Where is she?

Katherine [*runs up to him and falls on his neck*]. Found you at last! [*Buries her head on his breast and sobs.*]

A pause.

Boris. Well, Katherine, so now we've had our cry together, anyway.

Katherine. You haven't forgotten me, have you?

Boris. How could I have forgotten you?

Katherine. No, no, that's not what I meant. You're not angry with me, are you?

Boris. Why should I be angry with you?

Katherine. Well, forgive me anyway. I didn't want to cause you any trouble. I couldn't help it. I didn't know myself what I was saying or what I was doing.

Boris. Of course, of course! Don't think about it any more.

Katherine. Well, how are you? What are your plans?

Boris. I'm going away.

Katherine. Where?

Boris. Far away, Katherine. To Siberia.

Katherine. Please take me with you, take me with you!

Boris. I can't do that, Katherine. I'm not going of my own free will. My uncle is sending me away. Everything's ready. The coach, everything. I only got my uncle's permission to go out for a minute. I wanted to say good-by at least to the place where we used to meet.

Katherine. All right. I hope you will be happy, Boris. Don't worry about me. I expect you will feel lonely at first, my poor darling, but you'll soon forget me.

Boris. Why talk about me? I am a free man. What about you, Katherine? How's your mother-in-law treating you?

Katherine. She keeps tormenting me. She keeps me under lock and key. Tells everybody, even my husband, "Don't trust her, she's a cunning devil." So they all keep watching me all day and laugh in my face. Every word they utter is to reproach me with you.

Boris. And your husband?

Katherine. He is kind one minute and angry the next. He drinks all the time. Oh, I'm sick of him, so sick of him. I'd much rather he beat me than be kind to me.

Boris. You're having a bad time, aren't you, Katherine?

Katherine. Yes, I'm having a very bad time. So bad that I'd rather be dead.

Boris. Who could have known that we'd have to go through such a terrible time because we loved each other? I wish I'd run away before I'd met you.

Katherine. I met you to my sorrow, darling. I knew so little happiness, but I've paid for it with so much unhappiness, so much grief. And to think how much of it there is still in store for me. But why think of the future? I've seen you now, that they cannot take away from me. And I don't want anything more. All I wanted was to see you once again. Now I'm feeling much better. Just as if a load had been lifted from my shoulders. You see, darling, I thought you were angry with me, that you were cursing me. . . .

Boris. How could you think that of me, Katherine?

Katherine. No, no, that's not what I meant, I meant

something else. I missed you so, that's what I wanted to say. Well, I've seen you now, haven't I?

Boris. I do hope no one finds us here!

Katherine. Wait, please! There's something else I wanted to say to you. Now what is it? I can't remember it. I had to tell you something. I feel so dazed I can't remember anything.

Boris. It's time I went, Katherine.

Katherine. Wait, wait!

Boris. Well, what is it you want to tell me?

Katherine. Wait, I'll tell you in a minute. [*After a moment's thought.*] Oh, yes, oh, yes. As you go on your journey don't pass any beggar on the way without giving him something and don't forget to ask him to say a prayer for me.

Boris. Oh, if only they realized how painful this parting is to me. I only hope that one day they'll have to go through the pleasant time I'm going through now. Good-by, Katherine. [*He embraces her and is about to go.*] Oh, the monsters! If only I had the strength!

Katherine. Wait, wait, let me have a good look at you for the last time. [*Looks into his eyes.*] Well, I mustn't keep you any longer. You can go now, darling. Have a nice journey. Go, please, go!

Boris [*walks away a few steps and stops*]. Katherine, I feel there's something wrong. You're not thinking of doing something dreadful? I'll worry myself to death on the journey thinking of you.

Katherine. No, nothing's wrong. Go, darling. A happy journey. [BORIS *wants to approach her.*] No, no! Stay where you are. Enough!

Boris [*sobs*]. Well, good-by, Katherine. There's nothing left to do but to pray for a speedy deliverance. Oh, Lord, let her die rather than go on tormenting herself any longer. [*To* KATHERINE.] Good-by. [*Bows.*]

Katherine. Good-by.

BORIS *goes out.* KATHERINE *watches him go and then remains standing for a few moments lost in thought.*

Katherine [*alone*]. Where now? Go home? No, I'd rather be dead. Home and the grave are the same things

to me. It would be better in the grave. A little grave under
a little tree. . . . How wonderful! The sun warms it, the
rain washes it. . . . In the spring, grass grows over it.
Such soft grass. Birds come nesting in the tree and they
sing and they hatch their young, the flowers open up, red,
yellow and blue. . . . All sorts of flowers. [*Falls into
thought.*] All sorts of flowers. . . . It's so peaceful, so
lovely! I seem to feel much better. But I don't want even
to think of life. To go on living, no, no! I don't want it.
It isn't any good. I hate the people, I hate the house.
Even the walls are hateful to me. No, I'm not going
back there! I'm not! Never, never, never. If I went back
to them they'd be talking, talking, and I don't want any
more of that. How dark it has grown. I can hear the
chanting coming again from somewhere. What are they
chanting? I can't make out. . . . I'd like to die now. . . .
What are they chanting? What difference does it make
whether death comes for me or I myself— For I can't go
on living! A sin? They won't pray for me. Those who love
me will pray for me. They cross one's hands like that. . . .
In the coffin! Yes, like that. . . . I remember it now.
But if they find me here, they'll drag me home by
force. . . . Oh, quick, quick! [*Goes up to the bank of the
river. In a loud voice.*] My darling, life of my heart,
good-by! [*Goes out.*]

Enter MRS. KABANOV, TIKHON, KULIGIN *and a workman
with a lantern.*

Kuligin. She's been seen here, I'm told.
Tikhon. Are you sure?
Kuligin. Yes, they saw her here.
Tikhon. Well, thank God. At least they saw her alive.
Mrs. Kabanov. And you've already worked yourself up
into a panic, burst out crying! Found something to cry
about! Don't worry, she'll be a burden to us for a long
time to come.
Tikhon. Who would have thought she'd have come
here? There are always so many people about. Who'd
dream of hiding in such a place?
Mrs. Kabanov. Can't you see what she's up to, the

shameless hussy? She's merely showing again the sort of woman she is.

People appear from all directions with lanterns.

One Man in the Crowd. Have you found her?

Mrs. Kabanov. I'm afraid not. She seems to have sunk through the ground.

Several Voices. That's funny. What a strange business. Where could she have gone to?

One Man in the Crowd. She'll be found, never fear.

Another. Of course she will.

A Third. Shouldn't be surprised if she came back by herself.

A Voice [*behind the scenes*]. Hi, there, let's have a boat!

Kuligin [*from the bank*]. Who is shouting? What's the matter?

A Voice. A woman has thrown herself into the river!

KULIGIN *and a few other men run off.*

Tikhon. Good God, Mother, it's her! [*He wants to run, but* MRS. KABANOV *holds him back.*] Let me go, Mother, let me go! I'll drag her out or if not I myself— I can't live without her.

Mrs. Kabanov. I won't let you, don't you even think of it. To ruin yourself for her! Why, she isn't worth your little finger. Hasn't she already caused us enough disgrace? What more trouble is she bringing us now?

Tikhon. Let me go!

Mrs. Kabanov. There are lots of people without you. Your mother's curse on you if you go!

Tikhon [*falls on his knees before her*]. Let me just look at her, Mother.

Mrs. Kabanov. Let them fish her out first, then you can look at her.

Tikhon [*gets up and addresses the people*]. Can you see anything?

First Man. It's dark down below, sir, can't see a thing.

A confused noise behind the scenes.

Second Man. Somebody's shouting, but I can't make out a word.

First Man. They're coming here! They're bringing her!

A few people come back.

One of Those Who Came Back. A smart fellow, Kuligin. She was quite close to the bank. In a whirlpool. You can see a long way with a light. He noticed her dress and fished her out.

Tikhon. Is she alive?

Another. No, sir. She threw herself from the high bank and must have hit her head against an anchor. She's got a gash, poor thing. But otherwise she's just as if she was alive. Just a small gash on her temple, that's all. Hardly any blood at all. A few drops at most.

TIKHON *starts running but he is stopped by* KULIGIN *and others who bring in* KATHERINE'S *body.*

Kuligin. Here's your Katherine. You can do what you like with her now. Her body is here. Take it. Her soul is no longer yours. She is now before a judge who is more merciful than you. [*He puts the body down on the ground and runs off.*]

Tikhon [*rushes to* KATHERINE]. Katherine, Katherine!

Mrs. Kabanov. That will do, son. Even to weep for her is a sin.

Tikhon. Mother, it's you who have killed her! You, you, you!

Mrs. Kabanov. What are you talking about? Have you gone off your head? Have you forgotten who you're talking to?

Tikhon. You killed her! You, you, you!

Mrs. Kabanov [*to her son*]. Very well, I'll talk to you when we get home. [*Bowing low to the people.*] Thank you, good people, for your services. [*All return her bow.*]

Tikhon. You're all right now, Katherine! But I must go on living and suffering. . . . Why? Why? [*Collapses on his wife's body.*]

Curtain.

THE POWER OF DARKNESS

A Tragedy in Five Acts by

LEO TOLSTOY

CHARACTERS

PETER, *forty-two, a rich peasant, twice married, an invalid*
ANISYA, *his wife, thirty-two, fond of fine clothes*
AKULINA, *sixteen, Peter's daughter of first marriage, a little deaf, not very bright*
ANYUTA, *his second daughter, ten*
MARTHA, *his sister*
NIKITA, *twenty-five, laborer, handsome young fellow*
AKIM, *fifty, Nikita's father*
MATRYONA, *fifty, his wife*
MARINA, *twenty-two, an orphan girl*
MARINA'S HUSBAND
MITRICH, *an old laborer*
A NEIGHBOR
AKULINA'S FIANCÉ
HIS FATHER *and* MOTHER
BEST MAN
COACHMAN
POLICE OFFICER
VILLAGE HEADMAN
VILLAGE GIRLS
GUESTS, PEASANT WOMEN, ETC.

1886

THE POWER OF DARKNESS

ACT ONE

The action takes place in the autumn in a large village. The scene represents a room in PETER's *spacious cottage.*

PETER *sits on a wooden bench, mending a horse collar.* ANISYA *and* AKULINA *are spinning and singing a part song.*

PETER [*looking out of the window*]. The horses have got out again. They might kill the colt. Nikita! Hey, Nikita. Gone deaf. [*Listens. To the women.*] Shut up, I can't hear anything.

Nikita [*from the yard*]. What do you want?

Peter. Drive in the horses.

Nikita [*from the yard*]. All right. Give me time.

Peter [*shaking his head*]. Lord, these laborers! If I was well, I'd never keep any. There's nothing but trouble with them. [*Gets up and sits down again.*] Nikita! No use calling. One of you'd better go. You go, Akulina, and drive 'em in.

Akulina. The horses?

Peter. What else?

Akulina. All right. [*Goes out.*]

Peter. The lad's a loafer. A wastrel. Won't do anything if he can help it.

Anisya. You're not very quick yourself, are you? Lying about on the stove or squatting on the bench. All you do is keep asking other people to do things for you.

Peter. If one didn't keep on at you, one wouldn't have a roof over one's head in less than a year. Oh, what people!

Anisya. You ask him to do a dozen things at a time and

157

keep on swearing at him. It's easy to lie on the stove and give orders.

Peter [*with a sigh*]. Oh, if I wasn't so sick, I wouldn't keep him on another day.

Akulina [*behind the scenes*]. Gee-up, gee-up, whoa!

A *colt can be heard neighing and the horses running through the gates. The gates creak as they are closed.*

Peter. Talking—that's all he's good for. I really wouldn't keep him on.

Anisya [*mimicking him*]. Wouldn't keep him on! You'd better do something yourself for a change and then talk.

Akulina [*comes in*]. Oh, dear, just managed to drive them in. It's all that roan horse. . . .

Peter. And where's Nikita?

Akulina. Nikita? Standing about in the street.

Peter. What is he standing there for?

Akulina. What's he standing there for? Jabbering.

Peter. Can't get any sense out of her. Who's he jabbering with?

Akulina [*not hearing*]. What did you say?

PETER *gives it up with a wave of the hand.* AKULINA *sits down to her spinning.*

Anyuta [*running in, to her mother*]. Nikita's father and mother have come. They're going to take him home with them. Cross my heart.

Anisya. Don't tell lies!

Anyuta. It's true! May I die! [*Laughing.*] I was just passing, and Nikita, he says to me, "Good-by, Anne. Come to my wedding," he says. "You'll have a good time, I promise you. I'm leaving you," he says. [*Laughs.*]

Anisya [*to her husband*]. See? They don't want you very much, do they? He's going away himself. Sack him, indeed!

Peter. Let him go. I'll find someone else.

Anisya. And what about the wages you've paid him in advance?

ANYUTA *goes up to the door, stands listening for a while and goes out.*

Peter [*frowning*]. If he owes me money, he'll work it off in summer.

Anisya. I can see you're glad to let him go. Won't have to feed him, will you? You don't care if I have to work like a horse all winter, do you? That daughter of yours is not very fond of work, is she? And you, of course, will be lying on the stove. I know you.

Peter. What's the use of jabbering when we don't know yet what's going to happen?

Anisya. The yard's full of cattle. You haven't sold the cow and you've kept all the sheep for the winter. Feeding and watering them is more than a day's work, and you want to get rid of your laborer. I tell you one thing: I'm not going to do a farm laborer's work! I'll lie down on the stove same as you and let everything go to wrack and ruin! Do as you like.

Peter [*to* AKULINA]. Go and fetch the fodder, will you? It's time.

Akulina. The fodder? Oh, all right. [*Puts on a coat and takes a rope.*]

Anisya. I'm not going to work for you. I've had enough. I'm not going to. Go and work yourself.

Peter. All right. What are you in such a rage for? Like a mad sheep.

Anisya. And you're a mad dog. One gets neither work nor pleasure out of you. All you know is to nag, nag, nag. You palsied dog, you!

Peter [*spits and puts on coat*]. To hell with you! The Lord forgive me. I'd better go and find out what's going on there. [*Goes out.*]

Anisya [*after him*]. Decrepit devil with a big nose!

Akulina. What are you swearing at Dad for?

Anisya. Never mind, you fool. Hold your tongue.

Akulina [*goes up to the door*]. I know why you're swearing at him. You're a fool yourself, you bitch. I'm not afraid of you.

Anisya. What's the matter with you? [*Jumps up and looks around for something to hit her with.*] You'd better look out or I'll give you one with the poker.

Akulina [*opening the door*]. You're a bitch, a she-devil, that's what you are! She-devil, bitch, bitch, she-devil! [*Runs off.*]

Anisya [*alone*]. "Come to my wedding," he says. What

are they planning now? Marry him off? You'd better look out, Nikita. If that's your intention, I'll do myself in—I can't live without him. I won't let him go.

Nikita [*comes in and looks around. Seeing* ANISYA *alone, goes up to her quickly. In a whisper*]. Well, my dear, I'm in trouble all right. Dad's come and wants me to give up my job here. Wants me to go home. "We're going to marry you off," he says, "once and for all. We want you to live at home."

Anisya. Well, get married. What do I care?

Nikita. So that's it, is it? I'm trying to think what's best to be done, and all she says is—get married! Why this sudden change? [*Winking.*] Have you forgotten?

Anisya. Yes, get married! I don't want you, I'm sure.

Nikita. What are you so peevish about? Look at her! Won't let me stroke her even. . . . What's the matter with you?

Anisya. You want to get rid of me, don't you? Well, I don't care if you do. I can do without you. That's all there is to it.

Nikita. Good Lord, Anisya, you don't think I want to forget you, do you? Never while I live. I mean, I'll never leave you. You see, what I mean is that even if they do marry me off, I'll come back to you. I only hope he won't take me back home.

Anisya. Do you think I want you married to someone else?

Nikita. But what am I to do, my dear? I can't very well go against my father's will, can I?

Anisya. Putting the blame on your father, but you're all for it yourself, aren't you? You've been planning it with that slut of yours, Marina, for some time now. She suggested it to you, didn't she? Didn't come here for nothing the other day, did she?

Nikita. Marina? Good Lord, I don't want her! Lots of girls are making a beeline for me!

Anisya. Why then has your father come? You told him to, didn't you? You've deceived me! [*Cries.*]

Nikita. Anisya, do you believe in God or not? I never so much as dreamed of it. I tell you, I know nothing about it, nothing. It's the old man's idea.

Anisya. If you don't want to go yourself, he won't be able to force you, will he? He can't drag you there by a rope.

Nikita. Well, you see, I'm afraid it'll be impossible to go against my father. I don't want to, either.

Anisya. Refuse to budge, that's all.

Nikita. I know of a fellow who refused to budge, and he was taken to the district police station and given a good drubbing. It's very simple. I don't want it to happen to me. I'm told it's a bit prickly.

Anisya. I don't feel like listening to your jokes. Listen to me, Nikita: if you marry that Marina, I don't know what I shall do to myself. I'll kill myself! I've sinned, I've gone against the law, but it's too late to go back. As soon as you're gone, I'll do it, I tell you.

Nikita. Why should I go? If I wanted to go, I'd have gone long ago. As a matter of fact, Ivan Semyonovich offered me a job as his coachman the other day. . . . Think what a fine life I'd have had there! But I didn't go. For, you see, what I reckon is that I'm good enough for anyone. If you didn't love me, then, of course, it would be a different matter.

Anisya. That's just it. You'd better remember it. My old man, I think, will die soon. Not now, perhaps before long. We could cover up all our sins. Everything could be made legal then, and you'd be master here.

Nikita. Oh, what's the use of looking ahead? I don't mind. I work just as if I was doing it for myself. Master likes me and Mistress loves me. And if other women love me too—it's not my fault, is it? It's very simple, really.

Anisya. And you will love me?

Nikita [*embracing her*]. Like that! As you've always been in my heart. . . .

Matryona [*comes in and crosses herself a long time before the icons;* NIKITA *and* ANISYA *draw away from each other*]. What I saw, I didn't see, and what I heard, I didn't hear. Had some fun with a pretty lass—well, what of it? A calf, too, you know, likes to have a little fun. Why shouldn't one have fun when one's young? Your master has been calling for you in the yard, son.

Nikita. I only came in for the ax.

Matryona. I know, my dear, I know the sort of ax you've come in for. That ax is usually found where the women are.

Nikita [*stoops and picks up the ax*]. Well, Mother, do you really want me to marry? I mean, it's quite unnecessary. You see, I don't want to get married.

Matryona. Why, my dear, who wants to marry you? You can carry on just as you are. It's all the old man. You'd better go now, dear. We'll settle it all without you.

Nikita. Funny, though. One moment I'm to be married, and the next I'm not to be married. Can't make it out at all. [*Goes out.*]

Anisya. Well, Matryona, do you really want to marry him off?

Matryona. How can we marry him off, dearie? You know how poor we are, don't you? My old man's just talking a lot of nonsense: marry, marry! He don't understand nothing about it, dearie. Horses don't run away from oats, and folks know where their bread is buttered. That's how it is. Don't you think I can see the way the wind blows? [*Winks.*]

Anisya. Well, my dear, I don't want to hide things from you. You know all about it. I've sinned. I've fallen in love with your son.

Matryona. Well, that's no news to me. Did you really think I didn't know? Why, dearie, Matryona has seen all sorts of things in her lifetime. There's nothing I haven't been through. Matryona, let me tell you, dearie, can see what's buried three feet deep under the ground. I know everything. I know what young wives need sleeping draughts for. I've brought some along with me. [*Unties a knot in her handkerchief and takes out some powders in bits of paper.*] What's wanted I see, and what's not wanted I neither see nor hear. That's how it is. You see, I was young once, too. I, too, had to know a thing or two if I was to go on living with my old fool. I know seventy and seven dodges, I do. I can see, dearie, your old man's ailing. Aye, ailing. How is one to live with a man like him? Why, if you jabbed him with a hayfork, you wouldn't draw blood. You'll bury him before the spring. I'm sure of that. You'll have to get someone in the house then, won't you? And isn't my son a good farm hand? He's certainly not worse than anyone else. So what will I gain by taking him away from a good place? Am I my child's enemy?

Anisya. He won't go away from us, will he?

Matryona. Of course he won't, dearie. It's all nonsense. You know my old man. He changes his mind from one day to another. But sometimes he gets an idea into his head and it's just as if he wedged it with a stake. You can't knock it out of him however much you try.

Anisya. But how did it all start?

Matryona. Well, you see, dearie, the lad, as you know, is popular with the girls, and he's handsome, too—there's no denying it. Well, as you know, he worked on the railway and there they had a girl, an orphan, who worked as a cook. So that girl began running after him.

Anisya. Marina?

Matryona. Yes, the plague take her. I can't rightly say if there was anything or not, only my old man, he found out about it. Folks may have told him, or she herself may have complained to him about Nikita.

Anisya. She's a bold one, the hussy!

Matryona. Well, anyway, so my old man, the silly idiot, started shouting: "Marry her, marry her, cover up her sin! Let's take the lad home," he says, "and marry him." I tried to reason with him, but it was no good. Well, I thinks to myself, all right. I'll try something else. You see, dearie, that's the only way to get them to change their minds. You have to cheat them. Pretend you're of the same mind as them, the fools. And when it comes to the point, you turns it all your own way. A woman, dearie, has time to think seventy-seven thoughts while falling off the stove, so how can a man like him suspect anything? "Well," I says to him, "it's a good thing, only first we must think it over carefully. Let's go," says I, "and see our son and talk it over with Peter Ignatich. Let's hear what he has to say." So here we are.

Anisya. Oh, dear, but what happens if his father tells him to marry her?

Matryona. Tells him? He can tell him till he's blue in the face. Don't you worry, my dear. That will never be. I'll go and talk it over with your old man myself. Get it all thrashed out thoroughly, and there'll be nothing left of it. I came with him only to humor him. You see, dearie, my son's happily settled here and he has expectations to be more happily settled. Is it likely, I ask you, that I'd let him marry that slut? What do you think I am—a fool?

Anisya. She came running after him here, too—Marina, I mean. I tell you, Matryona, when I heard that he was going to be married, it was as if someone had stuck a knife into my heart. I can't help thinking that he's in love with her.

Matryona. Good heavens, no, dearie! He isn't a fool, is he? He won't love a homeless slut like her. I'm sure of it. Nikita has his wits about him, you see. He knows who to love. Don't you harbor any doubts about him, dearie. We'll never take him away. And we won't marry him off, either. We'd be ever so grateful to you if you could let us have a little money, though. We'll let him stay here.

Anisya. I don't mind telling you, Matryona, that if Nikita went away, I couldn't go on living.

Matryona. Aye, dearie, it's always like that when one's young. It isn't easy for you, I can see that. A woman like you, full of life, and living with a decrepit old man like your husband!

Anisya. Believe me, Matryona, I'm that sick of him, that sick of that big-nosed cur of mine that I can hardly bear to look at him.

Matryona. Yes, I'm afraid you can't help that, dearie. Now, just look here. [*In a whisper, looking around.*] You see, I've been to see that old man to get the powders from him and he gave me two kinds—look! This, he says, is a sleeping draught. Give him one of 'em and he'll sleep so sound you might walk all over him. And this here, he says, is the kind of a drug which if you give him to drink, he says, he won't be able to smell it, but its strength is very great. There are seven doses here, he says. A pinch each time. Seven times and you'll soon be a free woman.

Anisya. Oh! What is it?

Matryona. Leaves no mark, he says. Took a ruble from me, he did. Can't take less, he says. For, you see, he says, it's no easy matter to get them. I paid him out of my own pocket, dearie. I says to myself, if she don't take it, I'll let Mikhailovna have it.

Anisya. Oh, dear, but won't something bad come of it?

Matryona. What bad thing could come of it, dearie? It isn't as if your husband was hale and hearty. It's just a miracle he's still alive. He's not long for this world, you know. There are lots of such cases.

Anisya. Oh, dear, oh, dear, what am I to do? I'm afraid, Matryona. I'm afraid something terrible might come of it. It's—I can't bring myself to say what it is!

Matryona. Well, I can take it back.

Anisya. Are they to be dissolved in water like the others?

Matryona. It's best in tea, he says. You can't notice a thing, he says. No smell—nothing. He's a clever one, he is.

Anisya [taking the powders]. Oh, dear, oh, dear. I'd never do such a thing, if my life wasn't so unbearable.

Matryona. You won't forget the ruble, will you, dearie? I promised to take it to the old man. He, too, finds it hard to make a living.

Anisya. I suppose so. *[Goes to the chest and hides powders.]*

Matryona. You hide it well, dearie, so that no one knows about it. And if, God forbid, someone does find out, say it's for the black beetles. *[Takes the ruble.]* It's good for the black beetles, too, you see. *[Stops short.]*

PETER *and* AKIM *come in.* AKIM *crosses himself in front of the icon.*

Peter [sits down]. Well, then, what about it, Akim?

Akim. For the best, aye, for the best . . . I mean, as it's best. . . . For, you see, I'm afraid of—er—what-d'you-call-it. . . . I mean, mischief—aye. I'd like, I mean, to—er—what-d'you-call-it—start the lad on—er—in a good job. And if, I mean, if you'd rather—er—well, of course, then that's all right with me. All for the best, I mean. . . .

Peter. All right, all right. Sit down and let's talk it over. *[*AKIM *sits down.]* Well, then. Do you want him to marry?

Matryona. There's no hurry about marrying him, Peter Ignatich. You know how poor we are, don't you?

We can't afford to marry him. We've hardly enough to fill our bellies as it is. We just can't afford it.

Peter. You must do what you think best.

Matryona. No hurry to marry him. It'll wait. It just can't be done like that. It's not like ripe raspberries—it won't drop off by itself.

Peter. Well, if he got married, it wouldn't be such a bad thing, either.

Akim. We'd have liked it, you see. . . . For, I mean, I've got a job, a job in the town—suits me down to the ground, I mean. . . .

Matryona. Some job! Cleaning out cesspools. When he came home from work the other day, I was sick, brought up everything—oh, it was awful!

Akim. That's right—I mean, at first it does—what-d'you-call-it—knock you over a bit. I mean, the smell. But when you gets used to it, it's nothing. Just like the refuse at a distillery. I mean it's—er—what-d'you-call-it—same thing. . . . The smell, of course, it's—er—nothing for the likes of us to complain of. I mean, you can change your clothes, can't you? So we'd have liked, you see, to have Nikita with us. I mean, he must put things right. Let him put things right at home. And I'll—I mean—I'll get something in town.

Peter. You want to keep your son at home. That's all very well, but what about the advance in wages he's had?

Akim. Well, of course, I mean, that's right. It's just as you say. He's hired himself out, I mean, sold himself. So he must stay and serve his time. Only—I mean—what about him getting married? You'll have to let him off for a while to—er—I mean. . . .

Peter. Well, yes. That could be arranged.

Matryona. But, you see, we haven't agreed about it between us yet. I'll be as frank to you as before God, Peter Ignatich. Settle the dispute between me and my old man. He keeps muttering: "Let him get married, let him get married!" But who to, I ask you? If it was the right kind of wife for my son, would I be my own son's enemy? But the girl's a whore.

Akim. You—you oughtn't to say that. It's not right, I mean to say, to—to—er—give the girl a bad name. It's not right. For, you see, it's my son who's to blame. He, I mean, has done her wrong.

Peter. How d'you mean—done her wrong?

Akim. Well, you see, I mean, her and my son Nikita. With Nikita, I mean, you see. . . .

Matryona. Wait a minute. Let me tell it. I've got a readier tongue in my head. You see, the lad, as you know, worked as a porter on the railway before he came to you. Well, so that girl got stuck on him. She don't care, you see, who she goes to bed with. Marina's her name. Used to cook for the railway workers. So now she, Marina, that is, accuses my son Nikita of having seduced her.

Peter. Well, there's nothing good about that.

Matryona. But she's a trollop herself. Runs about with men. A whore. Aye, that's what she is.

Akim. Again you're—I mean—you're not—er—you're not. . . .

Matryona. That's all I hear from that fine, upstanding husband of mine—I mean—I mean. . . . He don't know what he means. You'd better ask other people, not me about that girl. Everybody will say the same. She's a homeless good-for-nothing trollop.

Peter [to AKIM]. Well, Akim, if that's how things are, there's no point in him marrying her. A daughter-in-law is not a bast shoe—you can't kick her off.

Akim [excitedly]. You're being unfair to the girl, old woman. Aye, unfair. I mean—er—the girl's a good girl. A very good girl. Aye. I mean, I feel sorry for her. Sorry for the girl.

Matryona. As the saying is: old Miriam for the whole world she grieves, but her children without bread she leaves. He's sorry for the girl, but he isn't sorry for his own son. Put her around your neck and carry her about all your life. Stop talking nonsense.

Akim. It ain't nonsense.

Matryona. You're just imagining things. Let me have my say.

Akim [interrupts]. No, it's not nonsense. You just twist everything to suit your purpose—about the girl or about yourself. You twist things to suit your purpose, but God, I mean—turns them to suit His. That's how it is.

Matryona. Oh, what's the use of talking to you!

Akim. She's a hard-working, sensible girl, and—I mean —keeps everything around her—I mean—er— And us being so poor, you see, it's a pair of hands, I mean . . . And the wedding needn't cost much. But it's the wrong done to the girl, you see, that's the chief thing. Aye—I mean—she's an orphan, the girl is. That's what she is. And he done her wrong.

Matryona. All of them tell you the same tale. . . .

Anisya. You'd better listen to us women, Uncle Akim. They can tell you a thing or two.

Akim. And God? What about God—eh? Isn't she a human being same as us? The girl, I mean. In God's sight she's, I mean, a human being, too. What do you think?

Matryona. He's off again. . . .

Peter. Look here, Uncle Akim, one can't believe all these girls say, either. And the lad's just in the yard. Let's send for him and ask him whether it's true or not. He won't wish to destroy his soul. Go and call the lad. [ANISYA *gets up.*] Tell him his father wants him. [ANISYA *goes out.*]

Matryona. That's right, dear. That's the way to deal with it: let the lad speak for himself. After all, you know, nowadays you aren't allowed to marry anyone against his will. The lad must be asked first. He'll never agree to marry her. Mark my words, he won't disgrace himself by such a marriage. If you ask me, he'd better go on living with you and serving you as his master. And there's no need for us to take him home for the summer: we can hire a help. Give us ten rubles now and let him stay.

Peter. All in good time. Let's first settle one thing before starting another.

Akim. You see, sir, I'm saying this because—er—I mean, that's how it happens. You try to fix things up as seems best for yourself and, I mean, you forget all about God. You think it's best so. You turn everything to your own advantage, but before you know where you are—I mean—you're carrying a millstone around your neck. You thought it would turn out for the best, but it's turned out for the worst—without God, I mean.

Peter. Well, of course, we must not forget God.

Akim. Aye, it turns out for the worst. But, I mean, if you act according to the law, according to God's will—I mean—it makes you feel happy. Does your heart good, I mean. So I says to myself, I'll get him to marry her, the lad, I mean. Keep him from sin, I mean. And let him live at home, according to the law, I mean, as he ought to. And as for myself, I'd get some work in town. It's not bad work. I mean, it agrees with me. According to God's laws, I mean. It's best that way. After all, she's an orphan child. Now, last summer some fellows went and stole logs from the steward. They thought they swindled the steward. And so they did, but they didn't swindle God, did they? I mean. . . .

NIKITA *and* ANYUTA *come in.*

Nikita. You sent for me? [*Sits down and takes out his tobacco pouch.*]

Peter [*in a low voice, reproachfully*]. What are you doing? Have you no manners? Your father's going to ask you a few questions and you sit down and start making yourself a cigarette. Come here. Get up!

NIKITA *gets up, leans carelessly with his elbow on the table and smiles.*

Akim. Well, Nikita, there seems to be some complaint about you. Aye, a complaint. A complaint, I mean.

Nikita. Who from?

Akim. Who from? Why, from that girl, that orphan girl. She's been complaining about the way you treated her. Marina, I mean.

Nikita [*chuckling*]. That's funny. What sort of complaint? And who's told you? Not she?

Akim. It's me who's asking, and you must know—I mean—give me an answer. You've got yourself mixed up with the girl, haven't you? I mean, you have, haven't you?

Nikita. I don't know what you're talking about. Honest, I don't.

Akim. You've been fooling around with her, haven't you? Fooling around with her, I mean.

Nikita. What about it? Why not have a little fun with the cook to while away the time? You play the concertina

and she dances. What sort of fooling around do you have
in mind, Dad?

Peter. Don't be too clever, Nikita. Answer your father's
questions properly.

Akim [*solemnly*]. Nikita, you can hide it from men, but
you can't hide it from God. You'd better think, Nikita,
and—I mean—don't tell lies. She's an orphan. So it's easy
to hurt her. An orphan, I mean. You'd better tell us what
happened.

Nikita. There's nothing to tell. Absolutely nothing. I've
told everything. [*Excitedly.*] She'll say anything. Say anything that comes into her head, just as if I didn't exist.
Why didn't she tell you about Fedka Mikishkin? How
d'you like that? Can't even have some innocent fun with
a girl nowadays! Why, of course, she's free to say what
she likes.

Akim. Mind, Nikita, a lie will out. Was there anything
or not?

Nikita [*aside*]. Why don't he leave me alone? [*To
Akim.*] I tell you I know nothing. There's been nothing
between us. [*Angrily.*] I swear by God, and may I never
move from this spot. [*Crosses himself.*] I don't know
nothing. [*A pause, after which Nikita goes on still more
excitedly.*] What do you want me to marry her for? Why,
it's—it's scandalous. Besides, you can't force a fellow to
marry nowadays. It's quite simple. I've sworn I know
nothing about it, haven't I?

Matryona [*to her husband*]. So you see, you silly fool!
He believes everything people tell him. Humiliated the
lad and all for nothing. He'd better stay here with his
master. I'm sure his master will let us have ten rubles
seeing as how badly off we are just now. And when the
time comes, we'll wed him.

Peter. Well, what do you say, Akim?

Akim [*clicking his tongue disapprovingly, to his son*].
Remember, Nikita, the tears of a wronged woman never
fall in vain—I mean—they always fall on the head of the
man who wronged her. Mind it don't—I mean. . . .

Nikita. What's there to mind? You mind yourself.
[*Sits down.*]

Anyuta. I'd better run and tell Mother. [*Runs away.*]

Matryona [*to* PETER]. It's always like that with that addlepated husband of mine. If he gets something into his head, you can't knock it out of it. I'm sorry we've troubled you all for nothing. Let the lad go on living with you as he has been. Keep him—he's your servant.

Peter. So what is it to be, Akim?

Akim. Well, sir, I mean, I—er—the lad's old enough to be his own master. I mean, I can't do nothing about it, can I? I wish I could have—I mean—

Matryona. You don't know yourself what you are blabbering about. Let him go on living here as he has done. The lad himself has no wish to leave, has he? And what do we want him with us for? We can manage ourselves.

Peter. One thing, though, Akim. If you take him away for the summer, I shan't want him for the winter. If he is to live here, it must be for the whole year.

Matryona. He'll bind himself for a year. If we want some help in the summer, we'll hire a man, but let the lad stay here. Only you must give us ten rubles now.

Peter. So what is it to be? For another year?

Akim [*sighs*]. Well, I suppose, if that's how it is—I mean, it seems, it's—er—

Matryona. So it's for another year from St. Dimitry's Day. I know you'll pay fair wages, but let's have the ten rubles now. Help us out of our difficulties. [*Gets up and bows.*]

ANISYA *and* ANYUTA *come in.* ANISYA *sits down in a far corner of the room.*

Peter. Well, if that's what you want, then it's settled. We might as well go over to the inn and have a drink. Come along, Akim, let's have a glass of vodka.

Akim. I don't drink—vodka, I mean.

Peter. Well, then, have some tea.

Akim. Aye, I like a cup of tea. That I do.

Peter. And the women will have some tea, too. And you, Nikita, drive the sheep in and clear away the straw.

Nikita. All right.

All go out except NIKITA. *It is getting dark.*

Nikita [*alone, lights a cigarette*]. Couldn't shake 'em off. Tell them how I lark about with the girls. It's a long

story. Marry her, he says. If I was to marry them all, I'd
have hundreds of wives. What do I want to get married
for? I'm as good as married now. There's many a fellow
as envies me. And it was a good idea to cross myself
before the icon. It put an end to the whole silly nonsense.
They say it's terrible to swear what's not true. It's just
foolishness. Nothing but talk. Very simple.

*Akulina [comes in in a man's coat, puts down a rope,
takes off the coat and goes into the storeroom].* You might
at least have lighted the lamp.

Nikita. To have a look at you? I can see as it is.

Akulina. Oh, to hell with you!

ANYUTA *runs in.*

Anyuta [to NIKITA *in a whisper].* Nikita, come quickly!
Someone's asking for you, cross my heart!

Nikita. Who is it?

Anyuta. Marina from the railway. She's around the
corner.

Nikita. Don't tell lies.

Anyuta. Cross my heart.

Nikita. What does she want?

Anyuta. She wants you to come out. She says she only
wants a word with you. I asked her, but she wouldn't
tell me. She only asked if it was true you was leaving us.
Well, so I told her it wasn't true. Your father wanted to
take you away, and get you married, but you refused and
you was going to stay another year with us. So she says
to me: "Send him out to me, for God's sake. I have something to tell him." She's been waiting there a long time.
You'd better go out to her.

Nikita. Oh, to blazes with her! What do I want to see
her for?

Anyuta. She says if you won't go, she'll come into the
house herself. Cross my heart! "I'll come myself," she
says.

Nikita. I don't think so. She'll wait a bit and then go
away.

Anyuta. "Do they want to marry him to Akulina?" she
says.

Akulina [comes in and goes up to NIKITA *to take her
distaff].* Marry whom to Akulina?

Anyuta. Nikita.

Akulina. Some hope. Who says it?

Nikita. Well, it seems people have been saying it. [*Looks at her and laughs.*] Well, Akulina, will you marry me?

Akulina. Who, you? Perhaps, I might have before, but not now.

Nikita. Why won't you marry me now?

Akulina. Because you won't love me.

Nikita. Why won't I?

Akulina. Because you wouldn't be allowed to. [*Laughs.*]

Nikita. Who won't allow me to?

Akulina. Who? My stepmother. She's always swearing and she keeps looking at you.

Nikita [*laughs*]. Does she? You're an observant one, aren't you?

Akulina. Me? What is there to observe? I'm not blind, am I? She's been nagging and nagging Dad all day. The fat witch! [*Goes out into the storeroom.*]

Anyuta. Look, Nikita! [*Looks out of the window.*] She's coming. Cross my heart, she is. I'm going out. [*Goes out.*]

Marina [*comes in*]. What are you doing about me?

Nikita. What am I doing? I'm doing nothing.

Marina. Want to throw me over?

Nikita [*getting up angrily*]. Well, what did you come for?

Marina. Oh, Nikita!

Nikita. You're a funny one and no mistake! What did you come for?

Marina. Nikita!

Nikita. Well, what of it? I know my name's Nikita. What do you want? Go away, I tell you.

Marina. So you want to throw me over. You want to forget me, do you?

Nikita. What's there to remember? You don't know yourself. When you stood there around the corner and sent Anyuta for me, I didn't come, did I? Well, wasn't that plain enough that I didn't want you? It's very simple. Well, go then.

Marina. You don't want me! You don't want me any more now. I believed you when you said you'd love me.

And now that you've ruined me, you don't want me any more.

Nikita. You're just wasting your breath. It's all so stupid. You've been telling all sorts of things to my father, too. Go away. Do me a favor.

Marina. You know very well I never loved anyone but you. Whether you married me or not, I wouldn't have blamed you. I've done you no wrong. Why have you fallen out of love with me? Why?

Nikita. What's the use of talking about it? You'd better go. Women are such fools!

Marina. What hurts is not so much that you deceived me, promised to marry me and went back on your promise, but that you've fallen out of love with me. And not that even, but that you've thrown me over for another. I know for whom, too!

Nikita [*walks up to her, viciously*]. Oh, what's the use of talking to the likes of you? You won't listen to reason. Go away, I tell you, or you'll make me do something you'll be sorry for.

Marina. Shall I? What? Are you going to strike me? Well, come on, strike me! Why do you turn away? Oh, Nikita!

Nikita. It wouldn't look nice if someone was to come in, would it? And, anyway, what's the use of talking?

Marina. So it's the end, is it? What's been, has been. You want me to forget. Well, Nikita, you'd better remember this: I've never known a man before you. You've ruined me for nothing. You've deceived me. You've shown no pity for an orphan girl like me. [*Cries.*] You've thrown me over. You've killed me. But I bear you no malice. God forgive you. If you find a better one, you'll forget me; if a worse one, you'll remember me. You'll remember me, Nikita. Well, good-by, if that's what you want. Oh, how I loved you! Good-by for the last time. [*She takes his head in her hands and wants to kiss him.*]

Nikita [*freeing himself from her embrace*]. Oh, what's the use of talking to you? If you won't go away, I will. You can stay here if you like.

Marina [*screams*]. You're a beast! [*In the doorway.*] God won't grant you happiness! [*Goes out weeping.*]

Akulina [*comes out of the storeroom*]. You're a real cur, Nikita.

Nikita. Why?

Akulina. How she cried, the poor thing! [*Cries.*]

Nikita. What's that got to do with you?

Akulina. What? You've hurt her. And you're going to hurt me like that, too—you cur. [*Goes out into the storeroom.*]

Nikita [*alone, a pause*]. What a damned stupid situation. I can't help loving women, but as soon as you sin with them, there's no end to your troubles.

Curtain.

ACT TWO

A village street. To the left of the spectator PETER's *cottage showing the entrance hall and the front steps in the middle; to the right the gates and part of the yard.*

In the corner of the yard ANISYA *is beating hemp. Six months have passed since the first act.*

ANISYA [*alone. Stops and listens*]. Something's mumbling again. He must have climbed down from the stove. [AKULINA *comes in with two pails on a yoke.*] He's calling. Go and see what he wants. He's screaming his head off.

Akulina. Why don't you go?

Anisya. Go, I tell you.

AKULINA *goes into the cottage.*

Anisya [*alone*]. He has tired me out. Won't tell me where the money is, won't tell me anything. He was in the passage the other day. Must have been hiding it there. Now I don't know where it is. Thank goodness he's afraid of parting with it. It's in the house then. If only I could find it. He hadn't it on him yesterday. Now I

don't know where it can be. He's driven me till I'm fit
to drop.

AKULINA *comes out, tying her kerchief over her head.*

Anisya. Where are you off to?

Akulina. Where? He's told me to go and fetch Aunt
Martha. "Fetch my sister," he says. "I'm going to die,"
he says. "I've got something to say to her."

Anisya [*aside*]. Asking for his sister! Oh dear! I suppose
he wants to give her an account of everything. What am I
to do? Oh! [*To* AKULINA.] Don't go. Where are you
off to?

Akulina. To fetch Auntie.

Anisya. Don't go, I'm telling you. I'll go and fetch her
myself. You'd better go to the stream to do the washing.
Otherwise you won't have finished it by the evening.

Akulina. But he told me to go.

Anisya. You do as I tell you. I'll go and fetch Martha
myself. Take the shirts off the fence.

Akulina. The shirts? Are you sure you'll go? He told me
to.

Anisya. Of course I'll go. Where's Anyuta?

Akulina. Anyuta? Minding the calves.

Anisya. Tell her I want her. The calves won't run away.

AKULINA *collects the washing and goes out.*

Anisya [*alone*]. If I don't go, he'll scold me; if I do,
he'll give the money to his sister. All my trouble will have
been wasted. I'm sure I don't know what to do. My head's
splitting. [*Continues to work.*]

MATRYONA *comes in with a stick and a bundle, as though
on a journey.*

Matryona. May the Lord help you, dearie.

Anisya [*looks around, stops work and throws up her
hands with joy*]. I never expected you, Matryona. The
Lord has sent me the right visitor at the right time.

Matryona. Well, how are things?

Anisya. I'm out of my mind with worry. Trouble!

Matryona. He's still alive I hear.

Anisya. Oh, don't talk to me about it! He doesn't live
and he doesn't die.

Matryona. And what about the money? He hasn't given it to anyone, has he?

Anisya. He's just sent for his sister Martha. Probably about the money.

Matryona. Why, of course! But he hasn't given it to anyone, has he?

Anisya. To no one. I've watched him like a hawk.

Matryona. But where is it?

Anisya. He won't tell me. And I can't find out in any way. He keeps hiding it in different places, and I can't do anything because of Akulina. She may be a fool, but she's also keeping watch. Keeps an eye on me, she does. Oh, my poor head. I'm exhausted.

Matryona. Well, dearie, if he gives the money away to anyone except you, you'll be sorry for it as long as you live. They'll turn you out of house and home without a penny. Poor thing, all your life you've had to put up with a man you don't love and now when you're a widow you'll have to go begging.

Anisya. No need to tell me that, Matryona. I'm sick and tired and I don't know what to do and I've no one to advise me. I told Nikita, but he's afraid. He doesn't want to have anything to do with it. All he told me yesterday was that it's hidden under the floorboards.

Matryona. Well, have you looked for it there?

Anisya. I couldn't. The old man is there himself. All I noticed is that sometimes he carries it about on himself and sometimes he hides it.

Matryona. Remember, dearie, once you let the chance slip, you'll never have it again. [*In a whisper.*] Well? Did you give him the strong tea?

Anisya. Oh! [*Is about to say something, but sees a neighbor and stops.*]

The NEIGHBOR, *a woman, passes the cottage and listens to a call from within.*

Neighbor [*to* ANISYA.] I say, Anisya, I believe your husband is calling.

Anisya. He always coughs like that, just as if he was calling someone. He's very bad.

Neighbor [*goes up to* MATRYONA]. Good afternoon, Grannie. Where have you come from?

Matryona. Straight from home, dearie. Came to see how my son was getting on. Brought him some shirts. Can't help thinking of one's own child, you know.

Neighbor. Yes, that's how it is. [*To* ANISYA.] I was thinking of bleaching the linen, but perhaps it's a bit too soon. No one has begun yet.

Anisya. What's the hurry?

Matryona. Has he been given Extreme Unction?

Anisya. Yes, of course. The priest was here yesterday.

Neighbor. I, too, had a look at him yesterday, my dear. It's a wonder how he keeps body and soul together. He's wasted away so. And the other day, my dear, he seemed to be drawing his last breath. They laid him under the icons. They had already started wailing. Got ready to lay him out.

Anisya. He recovered and got up. Now he's wandering all over the place again.

Matryona. When are you going to anoint him?

Anisya. People have been saying we ought to be doing it now. If he lives, we shall be sending for the priest tomorrow.

Neighbor. I expect you must be terribly upset, Anisya, dear. It's true what they say, that he's not sick who lies ill in bed, but he who sits over the patient in bed.

Anisya. Oh, you can't imagine what it's like. If it were only one thing or the other.

Neighbor. I can imagine how you must feel, dear. He's been dying for a whole year. You must feel bound hand and foot.

Matryona. Well, a widow's life isn't a happy one, either. It's all right so long as you're young, but who'll be sorry for you when you're old? Old age is no joy, I can tell you. Take me, for instance. I've not walked very far and yet I'm so exhausted I don't know whether I'm on my head or my heels. Where's my son?

Anisya. Ploughing. But come in and we'll get the samovar ready. You'll feel better after a cup of tea.

Matryona [*sitting down*]. Aye, I'm tired out, that's true. As to anointing him, that must be done. Folks say it's good for the soul.

Anisya. We'll send for the priest tomorrow.

Matryona. I would, dearie. We've had a wedding in our village, my dear.

Neighbor. What, in spring?

Matryona. Well, it seems it's not for nothing they say that when a poor man marries, even the night's too short. It's different with a rich man. You see, Semyon Matveyevich has wed Marina.

Anisya. So it's turned out well for her after all.

Neighbor. He's a widower. I expect there are children.

Matryona. Four. No decent girl would have wed him, so he's taken her. And she's glad. Aye, she had good reason to be.

Neighbor. I see! Does anyone know? And is he a well-to-do peasant?

Matryona. They're living well enough so far.

Neighbor. Well, who'd like to marry a widower with children? There's Mikhailo in our village, for instance. He's a sound peasant all right, my dear, but. . . .

Peasant's Voice. Hi, there, Mavra, where the hell are you? Go and drive in the cow.

The NEIGHBOR goes out.

Matryona [*while the* NEIGHBOR *is within earshot, speaks in her ordinary voice*]. Thank goodness, dearie, she's got married. At least, my fool of a husband won't go on thinking of Nikita. [*Suddenly changes into a whisper.*] She's gone! [*In a whisper.*] Well? Did you give him the tea?

Anisya. Don't speak to me about it! I wish he'd die of his own accord. He isn't dying, anyway, and I've only taken a sin upon my soul. Oh, dear, my poor head. And why did you give me those powders?

Matryona. What about the powders? They're only sleeping powders, dearie. Why not give them to him? No harm can come of them.

Anisya. I'm not talking about the sleeping powders, but of the others. The white ones.

Matryona. Well, dearie, those powders are just a medicine.

Anisya [*with a sigh*]. I know, but I'm afraid all the same. He's worried me to death.

Matryona. Did you use many?

Anisya. I gave them to him twice.

Matryona. Did you notice anything?

Anisya. I had a taste of the tea myself. Just a little bitter it was. But he drank it and said: "I can't even enjoy my tea any more." I said to him: "Everything tastes bitter to a sick man." But I felt scared, I can tell you.

Matryona. Don't think of it. Thinking makes it worse.

Anisya. I wish you'd never given it to me and not led me into sin. Every time I think of it my heart turns over. Why did you have to give it to me?

Matryona. What's the matter, dearie? How can you say a thing like that? Why are you trying to put the blame on me? Don't you try putting the blame on someone else, dearie. If anything was to happen, I had nothing to do with it. I know nothing about it. I'll take my oath I never gave you no powders and never saw none or heard or knew that such powders existed. Think it over carefully, dearie. I mean, we were talking about you the other day, about what you, poor thing, have to put up with. Your step-daughter is an idiot, your husband is on his last legs, a constant worry. What wouldn't one do in a case like that?

Anisya. I'm not thinking of denying my responsibility. A life such as mine could make you do worse things than that. Make you hang yourself or strangle him. Is this a life?

Matryona. That's just it. No time to open one's mouth. All the same you must find the money. And he must have his tea.

Anisya. Oh, my poor head! I don't know what to do. I'm so frightened. I wish he'd die of his own accord. I don't want to have it on my soul.

Matryona [*viciously*]. And why doesn't he show you where the money is? He's not going to take it with him, is he? Is no one to get it? Is that right? Good Lord! Such a lot of money to be lost for nothing. Isn't that a sin? What's he doing it for? Are you keeping an eye on him?

Anisya. I don't know myself what I'm doing. He's worried me to death.

Matryona. What is there to know? It's clear enough. If you make a slip now, you'll be sorry for it all your life.

If he gives the money to his sister, you'll never get a penny of it.

Anisya. Oh, dear, and he sent for her just now—I must go.

Matryona. Don't be in such a hurry to go. Put on the samovar first of all. We'll let him have a few cups of tea and then we'll look for the money together. I'm sure we'll find it.

Anisya. Oh, I hope nothing goes wrong.

Matryona. Why, can you think of anything else? What's the good of waiting? You don't want the money to slip through your fingers, when it's just within your grasp, do you? Do as I say.

Anisya. Well, I'll go and put the samovar on.

Matryona. Go, dearie, see that everything is done as it should be, so as to have no regrets afterwards. That's right.

ANISYA *is about to go out but* MATRYONA *calls her back.*

Matryona. One thing, though, don't tell Nikita about this business. He's stupid. God forbid he should find out about the powders. You never know what he'd do. You see, he is so softhearted. He was never able to kill a chicken. Don't tell him. He won't see it the way we do and it will only mean trouble. [*Stops horror-stricken, as* PETER *appears in the doorway.*]

Peter [*holding on to the wall, creeps out on to the front steps and calls in a faint voice*]. Can't make you hear! Oh, dear, oh, dear! Anisya, who is there? [*Drops down on the bench.*]

Anisya [*comes out from around the corner*]. What have you crawled out for? Why don't you stay in bed?

Peter. Has she gone for Martha? Oh, I feel so bad. I wish I could die soon.

Anisya. She is busy. I sent her to the stream. Wait a bit, I'll go myself when I'm ready.

Peter. Send Anyuta. Where is she? Oh, I feel dreadful. I wish I was dead!

Anisya. I've sent for her already.

Peter. Oh, dear, where is she?

Anisya. I don't know where she's got to, the plague take her.

Peter. Oh, I can't bear it any longer. My inside's on

fire. Just as if a gimlet was boring away inside me. Why have you left me alone like a dog? There's no one even to give me a drink. Oh! Send Anyuta to me.

Anisya. Here she is. Anyuta, go to your father.

ANYUTA *runs in.* ANISYA *goes around the corner of the house.*

Peter. You go—oh—to Aunt Martha, and tell her that Father wants her. Say she must come. I want her.

Anyuta. All right.

Peter. Wait. Tell her she's to come quick. Tell her I'm dying. Oh. . . .

Anyuta. I'll just get my kerchief and go. [*Runs off.*]

Matryona [*winking*]. Well, dearie, remember what you have to do. Go into the cottage, rummage about. Hunt about like a dog looking for fleas. Go through everything, and I'll search him.

Anisya [*to* MATRYONA]. I'll go right away. I feel much bolder now with you here. [*Walks up to the front steps, to* PETER.] Hadn't I better put the samovar on for you? Here's Matryona come to see her son. You can have a cup of tea with her.

Peter. Well, I suppose you'd better put it on.

ANISYA *goes into the house.* MATRYONA *walks up to the front steps.*

Peter. How are you?

Matryona. How are you, my benefactor? How are you, my dear? I can see you're still ill. My old man, too, is that sorry for you. Go, he says to me, see how he's getting on. He sends his regards to you. [*Bows again.*]

Peter. I'm dying.

Matryona. Oh, my dear, now that I look at you I can see that, as the saying has it, it isn't in the forest but among people that sickness warps. You've wasted away, wasted away, my dear, now that I come to look at you. Seems illness doesn't add to beauty.

Peter. My last hour has come.

Matryona. Oh, well, my dear, it's God's will, you know. You've been given Extreme Unction, and you're going to be anointed, God willing. Your wife, thank God, is a wise woman. They'll give you a nice burial, have

prayers said for you. Everything as nice as nice can be. My
son, too, will look after things in the meantime.

Peter. There'll be no one to give orders. She's an un-
reliable woman. Has her head full of all sorts of nonsense.
You see, I know all about it. . . . I know. . . . And my
girl is silly and young. I've got the homestead together
and now there's no one to look after things. The pity of it.
[*Whimpers*.]

Matryona. Well, if it's money or something, you can
leave orders.

Peter [*to* ANISYA *in the passage*]. Has Anyuta gone?

Matryona [*aside*]. Fancy him remembering!

Anisya [*from the passage*]. She went immediately. Come
inside, won't you? I'll help you in.

Peter. I think I'll sit here for the last time. It's so close
in there. I feel awful. My heart's burning all the time. . . .
Oh, if only I was to die today.

Matryona. If God don't take a soul, the soul won't go
by itself. In life and death, my dear, it's God's will that
matters. You can't be sure of death, either. Perhaps you'll
recover. There was a man in our village just like you on
the very point of death. . . .

Peter. No, I know I shall die soon. I feel it. [*Leans back
and shuts his eyes*.]

ANISYA *comes in*.

Anisya. Well, are you coming in or not? You do keep
people waiting, don't you? Peter! Peter, I say!

Matryona [*moves away and beckons to* ANISYA]. Well?

Anisya [*comes down the steps, to* MATRYONA]. It isn't
there.

Matryona. Have you looked everywhere? Under the
floor?

Anisya. It's not there, either. Maybe it's in the barn.
He was rummaging there yesterday.

Matryona. Go and look for it for all you're worth. Go
over everything with a fine-tooth comb. I can see he's going
to die today. His fingernails have turned blue and his face
looks earthy. Is the samovar ready?

Anisya. It's on the boil.

Nikita [*comes in from the other side and, if possible,
on horseback, up to the gate; he does not see* PETER].

How are you, Mother? Is everything all right at home?

Matryona. Thank God, son, we're all alive while there's bread in the house.

Nikita. Well, and how's the master?

Matryona. Hush! There he sits. [*Points to the front steps.*]

Nikita. Well, let him sit. What do I care?

Peter [*opens his eyes*]. Nikita! Come here, Nikita! [NIKITA *approaches.* ANISYA *and* MATRYONA *whisper together.*] Why've you come back so early?

Nikita. I've done my ploughing for today.

Peter. Have you ploughed the strip on the other side of the bridge?

Nikita. It was too far to go there.

Peter. Too far? From here it's still farther. Now you'll have to go there specially. You might have made one job of it.

ANISYA *is listening without showing herself.*

Matryona [*comes up*]. Why don't you do as your master tells you, son? Your master's sick and he relies on you. You ought to obey him as your own father. You must wear yourself to the bone for him. That's what I always told you.

Peter. Well. . . . Oh, dear! I suppose you'd better get out the seed potatoes. The women—oh, dear—will sort them out.

Anisya [*aside*]. Not likely. He wants to send everyone away from him again. He must have the money on him. Wants to hide it somewhere.

Peter. Oh, dear, oh, dear! It's time to plant them or they'll all go rotten. . . . Oh, I've not strength left. [*Rises.*]

Matryona [*runs up onto the front steps and supports Peter*]. Shall I help you into the cottage?

Peter. Yes, help me in. [*Stops.*] Nikita!

Nikita [*crossly*]. What now?

Peter. I shan't see you again. . . . I shall die today. Forgive me, in Christ's name. Forgive me if I've ever sinned against you—in word or deed. . . . There have been all sorts of things. Forgive me.

Nikita. What's there to forgive? I'm a sinner myself.

Matryona. Oh, son, don't be so hard.

Peter. Forgive me, in Christ's name. [*Weeps.*]

Nikita [*breathing heavily*]. The Lord will forgive you, Uncle Peter. I've no cause to complain against you. You never did me any wrong. You forgave me. Maybe I've sinned more against you. [*Weeps.*]

PETER *goes out whimpering.* MATRYONA *is supporting him.*

Anisya. Oh, my poor head! He didn't say it for nothing. He must have got some idea. [*Goes up to* NIKITA.] Why did you tell me the money was under the floor? It isn't there.

Nikita [*does not answer, weeps*]. I've never had anything bad from him. Nothing but good. And look what I've gone and done.

Anisya. That's enough now. Where's the money?

Nikita [*crossly*]. How should I know? Go and look for it yourself.

Anisya. What's made you so softhearted all of a sudden?

Nikita. I'm sorry for him. I'm very sorry for him. How he cried! Oh, dear!

Anisya. Look at him, overcome with pity! Found someone to pity. He's treated you like a dog and even now he was giving orders to have you turned out of the house. You'd better show me some pity.

Nikita. Why should I pity you?

Anisya. If he dies and the money's hidden away. . . .

Nikita. Don't worry, he won't hide it.

Anisya. Oh, Nikita, darling, he's sent for his sister. He wants to give it to her. We shall be in real trouble if he gives her the money. How are we going to live? They'll turn me out of the house. Why don't you try to find it? You said he went to the barn last night, didn't you?

Nikita. I saw him coming from there, but who knows where he's put it?

Anisya. Oh, my poor head! I'll go and have a look there.

Matryona [*comes out of the passage and down the steps, to* ANISYA *and* NIKITA. *In a whisper*]. Don't go anywhere. I felt him. He's got the money on him. On a string around his neck.

Anisya. Oh, my poor head!

Matryona. If you miss it now you'll never see it again. If your sister comes—you can say good-by to it.

Anisya. That's true. If she comes, he'll give it to her. What's to be done? Oh, my head!

Matryona. What's to be done? Why, look there, the samovar is boiling, go and make the tea and [*in a whisper*] pour him out a cup and then put in what's left in the paper and see he drinks it. When he's drunk the cup, take it. Don't worry, he won't tell.

Anisya. Oh, I'm afraid!

Matryona. Don't talk too much. Do it quickly. And I'll keep his sister talking here if need be. See you don't fail now. Get the money and bring it here. Nikita will hide it.

Anisya. Oh, my poor head! How am I to do it and—and—

Matryona. Don't waste your time talking that way. Do as I bid you. Nikita!

Nikita. What?

Matryona. You wait here. Sit down on the mound of earth. You may be needed.

Nikita [*waving his hand*]. Oh, the things these women think of. They'll get me into trouble properly. Oh, to hell with you all! I'll go and get the potatoes out.

Matryona [*seizes him by the hand*]. Wait, I tell you.

ANYUTA *comes in.*

Anisya. Well?

Ayuta. She's gone to her daughter's kitchen garden. She'll be coming presently.

Anisya. What are we to do if she comes?

Matryona [*to* ANISYA]. We've lots of time. Do as I tell you.

Anisya. I don't know—I know nothing. Everything's mixed up in my head. Anyuta, go and see to the calves, there's a darling. They've all run away. Oh, dear, I don't think I can bear to do it.

Matryona. Go on, the samovar must be boiling over, I expect.

Anisya. Oh, my poor head! [*Goes out.*]

Matryona [*goes up to her son*]. That's how it is, son. [*Sits down beside him on the mound of earth.*] Your business, too, must be thought over carefully. We can't leave it like that.

Nikita. What business?

Matryona. Why, what sort of life you're going to have.

Nikita. What sort of life? Others live and I shall live like them.

Matryona. I expect the old man will die today.

Nikita. Well, if he dies, let him rest in peace. What has it got to do with me?

Matryona [*keeps looking toward the front steps while she is talking*]. Oh, my son, my son, the living must think about the living. Here, too, my dear, one needs plenty of good sense. What do you think? Didn't I trudge all over the place looking after your affairs? Got footsore and bedraggled worrying about you. And you mustn't forget me when the time comes.

Nikita. And what have you been worrying about?

Matryona. About your affairs, son, about your future. If you don't see to it in good time, you'll get nothing. Do you know Ivan Moseyvich? Well, I've been to see him, too. I went there the other day. You see, I did some business for him, too. Well, so I sat there and we started talking. I asked him for his advice about a certain matter. Suppose, I said, a peasant, a widower, marries a second wife and supposing that he has a daughter by the first wife and he has another daughter by the second. When that peasant dies, I says, could another peasant marry the widow and get hold of the homestead? Could that peasant, I says, marry off the two daughters and become master of the house himself? He could, says he, only it would mean a great deal of trouble. You could manage it if he had enough money, for, he says, without money you'd better not meddle with it.

Nikita [*laughs*]. Yes, all they want is your money. Who doesn't want money?

Matryona. Well, my dear, so I told him all about you. "First of all," he said, "your son must register as a peasant of that village. That will cost some money. He'd have to treat the elders. For they will have to sign the papers." "Everything," he said, "must be done cleverly." Look! [*Unwraps her kerchief and takes out a paper.*] He's written it. Read it. You know how to read, don't you? [NIKITA *reads.* MATRYONA *watches him.*]

Nikita. Well, it's the usual sort of paper. A document. Nothing in particular.

Matryona. You listen what Ivan Moseyvich says we must do. "Above all," he says, "mind you don't let the money out of your hands. If she don't get hold of the money, they won't let her marry the lad. Money," he says, "is the key to everything." So take care, son. Things are coming to a head now.

Nikita. What has it got to do with me? It's her money, so let her worry about it.

Matryona. That's not the way to look at it, son. How can a woman manage it all? Even if she gets hold of the money, how does she know what to do with it? She's just a woman. You're a man, so you'd better hide it. After all, you've got more sense if anything should go wrong.

Nikita. Oh, you women don't know what you're doing.

Matryona. What do you mean? You grab the money. Then the woman will be in your power. If by chance she should turn nasty, you'll be able to put her in her place.

Nikita. Oh, to hell with you all! I'm going.

Anisya [*runs out of the cottage, looking pale, and around the corner to* MATRYONA]. He had it on him. Here it is. [*Points to something under her apron.*]

Matryona. Give it to Nikita. He'll hide it. Nikita, take it and hide it.

Nikita. Oh, all right, give it here.

Anisya. Oh, my poor head! I think I'd better do it myself. [*Goes toward the gates.*]

Matryona [*seizes her by the arm*]. Wait, where are you going? You'll be missed. There's his sister coming. Give it to him. He knows. Oh, you silly woman!

Anisya [*stops irresolutely*]. Oh, my poor head!

Nikita. Well, you'd better give it to me. I'll put it away somewhere.

Anisya. Where?

Nikita [*laughs*]. You're not afraid, are you?

AKULINA *comes in with the washing.*

Anisya. Oh, my poor head! [*Gives him the money.*] Mind, Nikita!

Nikita. What are you afraid of? I'll hide it away in a place where I won't be able to find it myself. [*Goes out.*]

Anisya [*in dismay*]. Oh, and what if he—

Matryona. Well, is he dead?

Anisya. Yes, I think so. I got it off him and he didn't stir.

Matryona. Go in. There's Akulina.

Anisya. Well, I've done it, and he's gone off with the money.

Matryona. Never mind that, go in. There's Martha coming.

Anisya. There now, I've trusted him. I wonder what's going to happen now. [*Goes out.*]

Martha [*comes in from one side and* AKULINA *from the other side*]. I'd have come earlier, but I had to go and see my daughter. Well, how is the old man? Is he dying?

Akulina [*puts down the clothes*]. I don't know. I've been at the river.

Martha [*pointing to* MATRYONA]. Who's that?

Matryona. I'm Nikita's mother from Zuyevo, dearie. Good afternoon to you. The poor man is wasting away, wasting away, your brother, I mean. He came out here himself. "Send for my sister," he says, "because," he says. . . . Oh, dear, is he dead?

ANISYA *runs out screaming from the cottage, holds on to a post and begins to wail.*

Anisya. Oh, who have you left me to? Who have you forsaken me for? Oh, poor miserable widow that I am—to live the rest of my life by myself. . . . He closed his bright eyes—

NEIGHBOR *comes in. The* NEIGHBOR *and* MATRYONA *catch hold of her arms.* AKULINA *and* MARTHA *go into the cottage. People begin to gather around.*

A Voice from the Crowd. Send for the women to lay out the body.

Matryona [*rolls up her sleeves*]. There's some water in the copper, isn't there? And there must still be some left in the samovar. They haven't emptied it. I'll do my bit.

Curtain.

ACT THREE

PETER'S *cottage. Winter. Nine months have passed since Act Two.*

ANISYA, *shabbily dressed, sits before a loom weaving.* ANYUTA *is on the stove.* MITRICH, *an old laborer, comes in slowly and begins to take off his overcoat.* MITRICH. Oh Lord, oh Lord! Well, hasn't the master come home yet?

Anisya. What?

Mitrich. Isn't Nikita back from town yet?

Anisya. No.

Mitrich. Having a gay time, I suppose. Oh, dear, oh, dear!

Anisya. Have you finished on the threshing floor?

Mitrich. What else? Got it all in and covered everything with straw. I don't like leaving things undone. Oh Lord! Merciful St. Nicholas! [*Rubbing his corns.*] It's time he was back.

Anisya. Why should he be in a hurry? He's got the money and, I suppose, he's having a good time with the girl. . . .

Mitrich. He's got the money so why shouldn't he have a good time? Why did Akulina go to town?

Anisya. You'd better ask her why the devil she's gone there.

Mitrich. To town? There are lots of things in town, if one's got the money. Oh Lord!

Anyuta. I heard it myself, Mum. "I'll get you a shawl," he said. Cross my heart he did. "I'll buy it for you," he said. "I'll let you choose it yourself." And she dressed herself up. Put on her best clothes, her velveteen sleeveless jacket and the French shawl.

Anisya. A girl's modesty reaches only to the threshold. As soon as she steps over it, it's gone. The shameless hussy!

Mitrich. Why, what's there to be ashamed of? If you

have money, go and have a good time! Oh Lord! I suppose it's too early for supper. [ANISYA *is silent.*] Well, I might as well get warm meanwhile. [*Climbs on the stove.*] Oh Lord, blessed Virgin Mother, holy St. Nicholas!

NEIGHBOR *comes in.*

Neighbor. Your husband hasn't come back yet, has he?
Anisya. No.
Neighbor. It's time he was back. I wonder if he's stopped at our inn? My sister says there are lots of sledges from the town standing there.
Anisya. Anyuta! I say, Anyuta!
Anyuta. What?
Anisya. Run down to the inn, there's a dear. Perhaps he's drunk and stopped there.
Anyuta [*jumps down from the stove and dresses*]. All right.
Neighbor. And he's taken Akulina with him?
Anisya. There would have been no need to go otherwise. It's because of her that he discovered he had some business in town. Must go to the bank, he says. Got to draw out some money. But it's all her doing.
Neighbor [*shakes her head*]. It's a bad business.

A *pause.*

Anyuta [*in the doorway*]. And what am I to tell him if he's there?
Anisya. You just see if he's there.
Anyuta. Oh, all right. Be back in a jiffy. [*Goes out.*]

A *long pause.*

Mitrich [*growls*]. Oh Lord, merciful St. Nicholas!
Neighbor [*with a start*]. Oh, you frightened me! Who is that?
Anisya. Why, Mitrich, our laborer.
Neighbor. How he frightened me! I'd forgotten all about him. Tell me, dear, I've heard you've been trying to get a husband for Akulina.
Anisya [*comes out from behind the loom and sits down at the table*]. Yes, someone from Dedlovo had a go at it, but it seems they've got wind of the affair even there. They had a go at it and we heard nothing more from them. So

the thing fell through. Of course, who'd want to marry a girl like that?

Neighbor. And the Lizunovs from Zuyevo?

Anisya. They sent someone to have a look, but nothing came of it, either. He won't let anyone come near her.

Neighbor. But she ought to be married.

Anisya. That she ought. I'd give anything to get her out of the house, but it's not as easy as that. You see, he doesn't want it. And she doesn't want it either. Hasn't had enough fun with his beauty, it seems.

Neighbor. Dear, dear, what goings on! Who could have thought of it? Why, he's her stepfather!

Anisya. Oh, my dear, they've got around me so cleverly, got the better of me so well, that I can do nothing about it. Fool that I am, I never noticed anything. I never suspected anything when I married him. It never occurred to me that there might already have been an understanding between them.

Neighbor. Oh, dear, what a disgraceful business!

Anisya. And as time went on, it got worse and worse, and they began to hide from me. Oh, my dear, I had a terrible time of it, I can tell you. Sick and tired of my life, I was. It's not as if I didn't love him.

Neighbor. Why, that's clear enough.

Anisya. And you can't imagine, my dear, how much it hurts me to bear such awful treatment from him! Oh, how it hurts!

Neighbor. I've heard he's getting a little too free with his fists, too.

Anisya. Yes, that's true enough. He used to be quiet when he had a drop too much. You see, he was fond of drink even before our marriage. But he was always fond of me even then, even when drunk. But now, as soon as he has a drop too much, he goes for me, threatens to trample me under his feet. The other day he got me by the hair, and I could hardly tear myself out of his hands. And the girl's worse than a serpent. I don't know how the earth bears such vixens.

Neighbor. Oh, dear! I can see you're sick. And how indeed could you put up with it? You've taken in a pauper and now he's treating you like dirt. Why do you let him carry on like this?

Anisya. Oh, my dear, what can I do? I'm still fond of him, you see. My late husband was very strict, but I could twist him around my little finger. But I can do nothing with this one. The moment I see him, my anger goes. I can't summon up enough courage to stand up to him. I go about in fear and trembling when he's at home.

Neighbor. Oh, my dear, they must have cast a spell on you. I've heard Matryona goes in for that sort of thing. It must have been her.

Anisya. Well, my dear, I can't help thinking so myself. You can't imagine how it hurts at times. I could tear him to pieces. But as soon as I set eyes on him, I can't bring myself to say a cross word.

Neighbor. It's plain enough you're bewitched. It doesn't take long to destroy a body. Now that I look at you, it's terrible the way you've been wasting away.

Anisya. My legs are beginning to look like two sticks. But look at that fool of a girl, that Akulina. She used to be a regular slattern, dirty and untidy, and now look at her! Where's it all come from I wonder? The way he's got her up! Dressed to kill, puffed up like a bubble in the water! And fool though she is, she's got it into her head that she's mistress here. "I'm the mistress," she says, "the house is mine. It was Father's intention that I should marry him!" And Lord, how vicious she is! When she gets into a rage, she's ready to tear the thatch off the roof.

Neighbor. Oh, what a terrible life yours is, my dear. And there are people who envy you. "They're rich," they say. But it seems, my dear, tears flow even over gold.

Anisya. What's there to envy? And the riches, too, will have all gone soon. He's throwing money about like water.

Neighbor. But how is it, my dear, that you've given up your money without a fight? The money's yours.

Anisya. Oh, if you knew all! You see, I made a little mistake.

Neighbor. If I were you, my dear, I'd go straight to the police. The money's yours. What right has he to squander it? There are no such rights.

Anisya. People don't pay heed to that nowadays.

Neighbor. Oh, my dear, I feel sorry when I look at you. You've grown so weak.

Anisya. Yes, my dear, I've grown weak, very weak. He's sapped my strength. I do know anything myself. Oh, my poor head!

Neighbor. I believe someone's coming. Listen!

The door opens and AKIM *enters.*

Akim [*crosses himself, knocks the snow off his bast shoes and takes off his coat*]. Peace to this household. How are you all? Are you all right, Anisya?

Anisya. How are you, Father? Have you come straight from home? Sit down. Take off your things.

Akim. Well, I thought I'd—I mean, I'd go and see my son. I—er—didn't start early, I mean, I had my dinner first. But, you see, the snow is so deep that, I mean, it was hard walking. That's why I'm so late. I'm late, I mean. And is my son at home? My son, I mean, is he at home?

Anisya. No, he's gone to the town.

Akim [*sits down on the bench*]. I've some business with him. I mean, some business, you see. I—er—told him a few days ago about—er—I mean, about the bother I've had with my horses. I mean, my horse is done for. Aye, my horse, I mean. So you see, I must get hold of a horse. Any kind of horse. Must get hold of it by hook or by crook. So that's why I've come, you see.

Anisya. Yes, Nikita told me. When he comes back you can have a talk with him. [*Gets up and goes to the stove.*] Have some supper now. He'll be here soon. Mitrich, come and have your supper. Mitrich!

Mitrich [*growls and wakes up*]. What?

Anisya. Supper!

Mitrich. Oh Lord, merciful St. Nicholas.

Anisya. Come and have some supper.

Neighbor. I'll go now. Good night. [*Goes out.*]

Mitrich [*gets down from the stove*]. Never noticed how I fell asleep. Oh Lord, holy St. Nicholas! Ah, good evening, Uncle Akim.

Akim. Hello, Mitrich, what are you—er—I mean?

Mitrich. I'm working here. Working for your son, Nikita. I live here.

Akim. Do you? So—er—I mean, you're working for my son, are you?

Mitrich. I used to live with a shopkeeper in town, but I spent all my money on drink. So now I've come back to the village. I've no place of my own, so I've hired myself out as a laborer.

Akim. Well, er—I mean, yes. . . . But what's Nikita doing? I mean, is he doing something else? I mean, that he has to hire a laborer?

Anisya. What else has he got to do? He used to manage it all by himself, but now he's other things to think of. That's why he's hired a laborer.

Mitrich. He's got money, so why shouldn't he?

Akim. That, well, I mean, that has nothing to do with it. That's—er—I mean, nothing to do with it. That's idleness.

Anisya. Yes, he's bone idle. So idle that it's just awful.

Akim. Aye, I see. I mean, I thought things would be better, but it seems they're much worse. Riches spoil a man, I mean, they spoil him.

Mitrich. Too good a life drives even a dog mad. You can't help being spoiled if you're living on the fat of the land. When I had everything I wanted, I made a mess of my life, too. Drank for three weeks nonstop. Sold my last shirt for drink. When I had no more money left, I gave it up. Now I've taken the pledge. To hell with drink.

Akim. And your wife? I mean, where is she? Your wife, I mean.

Mitrich. My wife has found her proper place. Hanging about the pothouses in town. A smart woman: one eye knocked out, another blackened and her chin twisted on one side. She's never sober. Never has a decent meal, either.

Akim. Oh, dear, how's that?

Mitrich. Where's a soldier's wife to go? She's found her proper place.

A pause.

Akim [*to* ANISYA]. What's Nikita doing in town? I mean, has he taken anything there? To sell, I mean?

Anisya [*laying the table and serving supper*]. No. He's

taken nothing there. Gone there for money. To get money from the bank.

Akim [*eating*]. Why, do you wish to put it, the money I mean, to some other use?

Anisya. No, we don't touch it. Only about twenty or thirty rubles. When the interest falls due, we take it.

Akim. Take it? Why must you take it? The money, I mean. If you take it today, then you'll take it tomorrow and so, I mean, you'll take it all.

Anisya. We get this in addition. The money's safe.

Akim. Safe? How do you mean safe? You take it, I mean, and it's safe? How can that be? You put some flour in a bin or a barn and—er—you take it from there, the flour, I mean, and it's still safe? Oh, no, it isn't. They're cheating you. You'd better look into it or they'll cheat you. Safe? I mean, you take it out and it's still safe?

Anisya. I'm afraid I don't know. Ivan Moseyvich advised us at the time. "Put your money in the bank," he said. "The money will be safe and you'll get the interest."

Mitrich [*having finished his supper*]. That's right. I've lived with a shopkeeper. They all do it. Put your money in the bank and you can lie on the stove and get it when you want it.

Akim. That's strange talk. I mean, how could you get it? And what about them? Where do they get it from, the money, I mean?

Anisya. They take the money from the bank.

Mitrich. It's like this, you see. A woman can't explain it properly. Let me explain it to you. Now, listen. Suppose you have some money, and spring is coming and I have none, and my land's idle. I've no money to buy seeds or to pay taxes. Now then, I come to you and I says to you, "Akim," I says, "let me have a ten-ruble note and when I've harvested in the autumn I'll return it to you and plough up an acre of your land for having helped me out." Now you see that I've something of my own. A horse or a cow. So you say to me, "All I want from you is two or three rubles for having obliged you and that's all." Well, I'm in a fix, but I can't help myself, so I say, "All right," and take the ten rubles. In the autumn, having sold my crop, I bring the money back to you, and you squeeze another three rubles out of me.

Akim. Yes, but this, I mean, this is the sort of thing peasants do when they forget God. That's not honest, I mean.

Mitrich. You wait. You'll see it all comes to the same thing. So now you've got that money out of me, and Anisya here has got some money lying idle. She doesn't know what to do with it and, besides, being a woman she doesn't know how to use it. So she comes to you and says, "Can't you do something with my money?" "Why, yes," you say. So you take her money and wait. Now, before the summer I come again. "Give me a ten-ruble note again," I says, "and I'll pay you for your loan." So you make sure I've still got some hide left on me, and seeing as how you can still get some money out of me, you give me Anisya's money. But suppose, for instance, that I haven't got anything. Not a penny, nothing to eat. Then seeing as how you can't get anything out of me, you say to me, "I'm sorry, my dear fellow, I can't do anything for you." So you look out for another man and lend him your own and Anisya's money and fleece him. That's what a bank is. That's how it goes round and round. You see, it's a clever piece of roguery.

Akim [*excitedly*]. Good Lord, so that's what it is like! That, I mean, that is a filthy trick. It's peasants, I mean, peasants who do it. They, too, think it's a sin. It's, it's not right. It's not right, I mean. It's a dirty trick. How can educated folk, I mean. . . .

Mitrich. Why, it's something they all like doing. Yes, sir. Just remember, if a man's not too clever or if it's a woman who can't make any use of her money, they take it to the bank and they—the devil take them—grab that money and fleece the people. It's a clever trick.

Akim [*with a sigh*]. Oh, dear, I see that if you have no money, it's—I mean—it's bad, and if you have, it's twice as bad. But why is it like that? God bid us work. And you, I mean, you put your money in the bank and you can go to sleep and your money, I mean, your money will feed you while you're idle. That's a dirty trick. It's not right, I mean.

Mitrich. Not right? Why, they don't care about what's right or wrong nowadays. If you don't look out, they'll pluck you clean. That's how it is.

Akim [*sighing*]. Aye, it seems the time, I mean, the time is drawing nigh. I've also had a look at those lavatories in town. I mean, the things they do to them. It's all so polished, so smart, I mean, just like inside an inn, and what is it all for? For nothing. Oh, dear, we've forgotten God. Aye, we've forgotten God. Forgotten, forgotten. Thank you, my dear, I've had enough.

They rise from the table. MITRICH *climbs onto the stove.*

Anisya [*clears the table and eats*]. If only his father would talk to him. But I'm ashamed to tell him.

Akim. What did you say?

Anisya. Oh, nothing. I was just talking to myself.

ANYUTA *comes in.*

Akim. There's a clever girl. Always busy. Cold, are you?

Anyuta. I'm freezing cold. Good evening, Granddad.

Anisya. Well, is he there?

Anyuta. No, but Adrian is there. He's just come back from town and he said he saw them at the inn in town. He says Dad's as drunk as a lord.

Anisya. Want anything to eat? Here you are.

Anyuta [*goes to the stove*]. Oh, it's cold. My hands are stiff with cold.

AKIM *takes off his leg bindings and bast shoes.*

Anisya [*washing up*]. Father!

Akim. Well? What is it?

Anisya. Tell me, is Marina living well?

Akim. Quite well. Yes, she's all right. She's, I mean, she's clever and quiet and, I mean, she's doing her best. She's living all right. I mean, she's a right decent woman. Aye, she's hard-working and meek. I mean, she's all right, the girl is.

Anisya. And is there talk in the village that a relative of Marina's husband is thinking of marrying our Akulina? Haven't you heard anything about it?

Akim. You mean the Mironovs? Yes, the women did talk about it. But, I mean, I can't remember what they said. I'm sorry, I can't remember. I mean, the old women were saying something, but my memory's bad. The Mironovs are all right. They're good peasants, I mean.

Anisya. Oh, I wish I could marry her off quickly.

Akim. Why?

Anyuta [*listens*]. They've come.

NIKITA *comes in, drunk, with a sack and a bundle under his arms and his purchases wrapped in a piece of paper. Opens the door and stops dead.*

Anisya. Well, leave them alone. [*Goes on washing up without turning her head when the door opens.*]

Nikita. Anisya! Wife! Who's come?

ANISYA *looks up and turns away in silence.*

Nikita [*sternly*]. Who's come? Have you forgotten?

Anisya. Stop showing off. Come in.

Nikita [*still more sternly*]. Who has come?

Anisya [*goes up and takes him by the arm*]. Well, then, my husband has come. Come inside, Nikita.

Nikita [*stubbornly*]. Ah, your husband! And what's your husband's name? Speak up!

Anisya. Oh, really—Nikita.

Nikita. Oh, I see, you ignorant woman, what's his patronymic?

Anisya. Akimych. Are you satisfied now?

Nikita [*still in the doorway*]. Ah, I see. No, you tell me what's his surname?

Anisya [*laughs and pulls him by the arm*]. Chilikin. Good Lord, what a fine gentleman you are.

Nikita. Ah, I see. [*Holds on to the doorpost.*] Now, say with which foot does Chilikin step into his cottage?

Anisya. That'll do. You're letting the cold in.

Nikita. Say with which foot does he step into the house. You've got to say it.

Anisya [*aside*]. He'll plague me to death now. Well, the left. Come in.

Nikita. Ah, I see!

Anisya. Look who is here.

Nikita. Father? Well, I'm not ashamed of my father. I can pay my respects to my father. How are you, Father? [*Bows to him and puts out his hand.*] My respects to you.

Akim [without answering]. So that's what drink does to a man. I mean, look at him. The nastiness of it!

Nikita. Drink? You mean, I've been drinking? Well, I'm sorry, Father. It's my fault. My fault entirely. I had a drink with a friend. I had to congratulate him.

Anisya. You'd better go and lie down.

Nikita. Wife, tell me where am I standing now?

Anisya. Oh, all right, go and lie down now.

Nikita. No, I'll first have some tea with my father. Put on the samovar. Akulina, come in!

Akulina [comes in all dressed up, carrying their purchases. To NIKITA]. Why have you thrown everything about? Where's the yarn?

Nikita. The yarn? The yarn's there. Hey, there, Mitrich! Where are you? Asleep? Go and put the horse away.

Akim [does not see AKULINA, *but looks at his son].* What is he doing? The old man's tired out. I mean, he's been threshing and he—he's putting on airs. Take away the horse, indeed! Dear me, what nastiness.

Mitrich [climbs down from the stove and puts on felt boots]. Oh, dear Lord! Where's the horse? Outside? Oh, I'm so tired. He's been swilling it up to his neck. Oh Lord, holy St. Nicholas. [*Puts on sheepskin and goes out.*]

Nikita [sits down]. I'm sorry, Father. I've been drinking, that's true, but what of it? Even a hen drinks, isn't that so? You must forgive me. Look at Mitrich. He doesn't mind. He'll put away the horse.

Anisya. Shall I really put on the samovar?

Nikita. Yes, Father's come and I want to talk to him. [*To* AKULINA.] Have you brought in all the parcels?

Akulina. The parcels? I've brought in mine, the others are in the sledge. You take this, that's not mine. [*Throws a parcel on the table and puts the others in her trunk.* ANYUTA *watches* AKULINA *while she is putting her things away.* AKIM *does not look at his son, but puts his leg bindings and bast shoes on the stove.*]

Anisya [goes out with the samovar]. Her trunk is full as it is, and he's bought her more things.

Nikita [pretending to be sober]. Don't be angry with me, Father. You think I'm drunk. Well, I can do everything. Everything. For, you see, you can drink as much as you like so long as you keep your wits about you. I can talk to you about anything you like, Father. I remember everything. You want some money, don't you? Your horse is no good any more. I remember that. Well, I can help you. It can be managed. Now if you'd wanted a big sum of money, you might have had to wait, but that I can manage. Here's the money.

Akim [goes on busying himself with his leg bindings]. Eh, lad, I mean, it's thawing. It's not, I mean, good for traveling.

Nikita. What do you mean by that? You mean it's no good talking to a man who's drunk? But you needn't worry. We'll have some tea and you'll see I can settle everything. Absolutely. Put everything right.

Akim [shakes his head]. Oh, dear, oh, dear!

Nikita. Your money, here it is. [*Puts his hand into his pocket, pulls out wallet, fingers the notes and gets out a ten-ruble note.*] Take this to buy a horse. Go on, take it. I can't let down my father, can I? I shall never leave him in the lurch, because, you see, he's my father. Here, take it. It's very simple. I don't grudge it. [*Goes up to* Akim *and offers him the money.* Akim *refuses to take it.* Nikita *catches hold of his hand.*] Take it, I tell you. When I give it to you, it means that I don't grudge it.

Akim. I can't take it. I mean, I can't. And I can't talk to you, because, I mean, you're not yourself.

Nikita. I won't let you go. Take it. [*Puts money into* Akim's *hand.*]

Anisya [comes in and stops]. You'd better take it. You see, he won't let you be unless you take it.

Akim [takes the money, shaking his head]. Oh, what drink does to man! I mean, he isn't a human being any more.

Nikita. Ah, that's better. Repay me or not, I don't care. That's the sort of fellow I am. [*Sees* Akulina.] Akulina, show us your presents.

Akulina. What?

Nikita. Show us your presents.

Akulina. The presents? What's the use of showing them? I've put them away.

Nikita. Get them out, I tell you. Anyuta may like to see

them. Show them to Anyuta. Undo the shawl. Give it here.

Akim. Oh, makes you sick to look at it! [*Climbs on the stove.*]

Akulina [*gets out her presents and puts them on the table*]. Well, there you are. What's the good of looking at them?

Anyuta. Oh, it's lovely! It's as good as Stepanida's.

Akulina. Stepanida's? Why, Stepanida's is not half as good as this. [*Brightening up and undoing the parcels.*] Look at it. What excellent material. It's French.

Anyuta. And the print's beautiful. Mary has a dress like that, only it's lighter and on a blue ground. Oh, it's ever so lovely.

Nikita. Aye, so it is!

ANISYA *walks angrily into the storeroom and returns with a tablecloth and the chimney of the samovar and goes up to the table.*

Anisya. That'll do, cluttering up the table.

Nikita. But look at it.

Anisya. What do I want to look at it for? Haven't I seen anything like it before? Put it away. [*Sweeps the shawl on to the floor with her hands.*]

Akulina. What are you throwing things about for? Throw your own things about. [*Picks it up.*]

Nikita. Anisya, look here.

Anisya. What am I to look at?

Nikita. You think I've forgotten you? Look here. [*Shows her a parcel and sits down on it.*] It's a present for you. Only you must deserve it first. Wife, where am I sitting?

Anisya. Stop fooling. I'm not afraid of you. Whose money do you think you're having a good time with and buying that fat slut presents on? It's mine!

Akulina. Yours, indeed! You were going to steal it, but you didn't succeed. Get out of my way! [*Pushes her aside while trying to pass.*]

Anisya. Who are you pushing? I'll teach you to push. [*Pushes against her.*]

Nikita. Now, then, women, that'll do. [*Steps between them.*]

Akulina [*also pushing herself forward*]. She's pushing, too! You ought to keep quiet. Remember what you've done. You think no one knows?

Anisya. What do they know? Tell me, tell me! What do they know?

Akulina. I know something you've done.

Anisya. You're a slut who lives with another's husband.

Auklina. And you've murdered yours.

Anisya [*throwing herself on* AKULINA]. You're lying!

Nikita [*holding her back*]. Anisya, have you forgotten?

Anisya. What are you trying to scare me for? I'm not afraid of you.

Nikita. Get out! [*Turns* ANISYA *around and pushes her out.*]

Anisya. Where am I to go? I won't go out of my own house.

Nikita. Get out, I say. And don't you dare to come in here again.

Anisya. I won't go. [NIKITA *pushes her out.* ANISYA *cries and screams, clinging to the door.*] Am I going to be thrown out of my own house? What are you doing, you villain? I'll have the law on you! You wait!

Nikita. Now, then!

Anisya. I'll go to the village headman! To the police!

Nikita. Get out, I tell you. [*Pushes her out.*]

Anisya [*from behind the door*]. I'll hang myself!

Nikita. You won't.

Anyuta. Oh, oh, Mother, dear, darling. [*Cries.*]

Nikita. I'm not frightened of her. What are you crying for? She'll come back, don't worry. Go and see to the samovar.

ANYUTA *goes out.*

Akulina [*collects her present and folds it*]. Just look how she creased it all, the pig. You wait, I'll cut up her jacket for her! You see if I don't.

Nikita. I kicked her out, what more do you want?

Akulina. She messed up my new shawl, the bitch. If she hadn't gone out, I'd have torn her eyes out.

Nikita. Pipe down, will you? What do you want to be angry for? I'm not in love with her, am I?

Akulina. In love with her! Who'd be in love with that

ugly fat face of hers? If you had thrown her over at that
time, nothing would have happened. I'd have sent her to
the devil. The house is mine, anyway, and the money is
mine. She's the mistress, she says. Some mistress! What
sort of mistress was she to her husband? She's a murderess,
that's what she is. She'll murder you, too.

Nikita. Oh, you can't stop a woman's mouth, can you?
You don't know yourself what you are talking about.

Akulina. Yes, I do. I'm not going to live with her.
I'll turn her out of the house. She can't live here with me.
The mistress indeed! She is not the mistress, she's a jail-
bird.

Nikita. That's enough. You've got nothing to share with
her, have you? Don't take any notice of her. You look to
me, I'm master here. I do as I like. I've stopped loving her,
and now I love you. I love who I like. I have the power
here. She has to do what I damned well like. That's where
I keep her. [*Points to his feet.*] Oh, what a pity I've no
concertina. [*Sings.*]

> There's loaves on the stove,
> There's porridge on the step,
> So we'll live,
> So we'll be merry and gay,
> And when death comes, we'll die.
> There's loaves on the stove,
> There's porridge on the step. . . .

MITRICH *comes in, takes off his outdoor clothes and climbs
on the stove.*

Mitrich. Seems the women have had a fight again.
Scratching their eyes out. Oh Lord, holy St. Nicholas!

Akim [*sitting on the edge of the stove, takes his leg
bindings, his bast shoes and begins putting them on*]. Come
on, get into the corner.

Mitrich. Seems they can't share things out between
them. Oh Lord!

Nikita. I'll get out the brandy. We'll have some with
our tea.

Anyuta [*comes in, to* AKULINA]. The samovar is just boiling over.

Nikita. And where's your mother?

Anyuta. She's standing in the passage and crying.

Nikita. Is she? Go and tell her to bring in the samovar. And you, Akulina, get the tea things.

Akulina. The tea things? Oh, all right. [*She puts out the cups and saucers.*]

Nikita [*fetches the brandy, ring-shaped rolls and salt herrings*]. That's for myself. This is yarn for the wife. The paraffin is out there in the passage. And here's the money. One moment, though. [*Takes an abacus.*] I'll add it up. [*Clicks the abacus counters.*] Wheat flour, eighty kopeks; lenten oil . . . ten rubles to Father. Father, come and let's have some tea.

Silence. AKIM *sits on the stove and winds the leg bindings around his legs.*

Anisya [*comes in with the samovar*]. Where shall I put it?

Nikita. Put it on the table. Well, have you been to see the headman? I see! Biting off more than you can chew. Oh, well, don't be angry. Sit down and drink this. [*Fills a wineglass for her.*] And here's your present. [*Hands her the parcel he has been sitting on.* ANISYA *takes it silently and shakes her head.*]

Akim [*climbs down from the stove and puts on his sheepskin, then walks up to the table and puts down the money*]. Here, take your money. Put it away.

Nikita [*does not see the money*]. Where're you going? Why have you put on your things?

Akim. I'm going, I'm going. I mean, forgive me, in Christ's name. [*Takes up his cap and belt.*]

Nikita. How do you like that? Where are you going to at this time of night?

Akim. I can't stay here. I mean, I can't stay in your house. I can't, I mean. I can't. Sorry.

Nikita. So where are you going? And without having your tea?

Akim [*fastening his belt*]. I'm going because it's not right here, in your house, I mean. It's not right, I mean, Nikita, in your house. It's not right. I mean, the sort of life you lead, Nikita, is bad. I'll go.

Nikita. Oh, don't talk so much! Sit down and have your tea.

Anisya. Really, Father, what will the neighbors say? Why are you offended?

Akim. I'm not offended. I mean, no offense meant, only I can see my son, I mean, I can see that you're on the road to ruin, my son. On the road to ruin, I mean.

Nikita. What ruin? Prove it.

Akim. Ruin. Aye, ruin. You're on the road to ruin, you are. What did I tell you that time, Nikita?

Nikita. You told me all sorts of things.

Akim. I told you, I mean, I told you about that orphan girl. The orphan girl Marina, whom you'd wronged, I mean.

Nikita. Oh, so you've remembered that, have you? It's an old story. It's finished.

Akim [*excitedly*]. Finished? No, sir, it's not finished. Sin, I mean, sin is fastening on to sin and dragging you down after it. You're stuck fast in sin, Nikita. Aye, stuck fast. Up to your neck, I mean.

Nikita. Sit down and drink your tea. And for God's sake, shut up.

Akim. I can't. I mean I can't have tea with you. Because, you see, because of that filth of yours. I mean, it makes me sick. Aye, sick. I can't, I mean. I can't have tea with you.

Nikita. Good Lord, how he carries on! Come on, sit down at the table.

Akim. You're in your riches same as in a net. Aye, caught in a net, I mean. It's the soul, Nikita, the soul, I mean, that matters.

Nikita. What right have you to reproach me in my own house? What are you badgering me for? What do you think I am, a child you can pull by the hair? People don't do these things nowadays.

Akim. Aye, that's true. I've heard that nowadays, I mean, nowadays children pull their fathers' beards! But that's the road to ruin. Aye, the road to ruin.

Nikita [*angrily*]. We don't want anything from you. It's you who've come begging to us.

Akim. Money? There's your money. I'd rather go begging, I mean, before I take it.

Nikita. That's enough from you. I don't know why

you're angry. Upsetting everybody! [*Tries to detain him by the arm.*]

Akim [*yells*]. Let go, I'm not staying here! I'd rather sleep under some fence than in your filth. Ugh! God forgive me! [*Goes out.*]

Nikita. How do you like that? [AKIM *opens the door.*]

Akim. Come to your senses, Nikita. Remember, it's the soul that matters. [*Goes out.*]

Akulina [*taking the cups*]. Well, shall I pour out the tea?

They are all silent.

Mitrich [*growls*]. Oh Lord, have mercy on me, miserable sinner that I am!

They all start.

Nikita [*lies down on a bench*]. Oh, I'm bored. Akulina, where's the concertina?

Akulina. The concertina? Have you forgotten? You took it to be mended. I've poured out your tea. Drink it.

Nikita. I don't want it. Put out the light. . . . Oh, I'm so bored, so bored! [*Cries.*]

Curtain.

ACT FOUR

Autumn. Evening. The moon is shining. In the foreground the yard of NIKITA'S *cottage. In the middle, the passage. To the right, the winter half of the cottage and the gate. To the left, the summerhouse and the cellar. Loud talk and drunken cries come from inside the cottage.*

PEASANT WOMAN *comes out of the passage and beckons to* ANISYA'S NEIGHBOR.

PEASANT WOMAN. Why hasn't Akulina come out?

Neighbor. Why? She'd have been glad to but she's too ill, you see. Her suitor's relatives have come to have a look at her, but she, poor thing, is lying in the cold cottage and can't come out.

Peasant Woman. But why not?

Neighbor. I'm told she's under the spell of an evil eye. She has a pain in her stomach.

Peasant Woman. Has she now?

Neighbor. Why, what else do you think it could be? [*Whispers in her ear.*]

Peasant Woman. Good gracious! What a business! His relatives are sure to find out.

Neighbor. They won't find out. They're all drunk. All they're after is her dowry. Do you know what they are giving with the girl? Two fur coats, six dresses, a French shawl as well as pieces of linen and, I'm told, two hundred rubles.

Peasant Woman. Even money can't cover up this sort of trouble. Such disgrace!

Neighbor. Sh-sh! That's the suitor's father coming!

They stop talking and go into the passage. The SUITOR'S
FATHER *comes out of the passage, hiccuping.*

The Father. I'm sweating all over. Terribly hot. I think I'd better cool off a little. [*Stands fanning himself.*] I don't know. There's something wrong here. I don't feel happy. Well, it's my old woman's affair.

Matryona [*comes out from the passage*]. So that's where you are, dearie. I was wondering where the father was. Well, thank God, everything has gone off well. One mustn't boast when arranging a match, and I've never known how to boast, but as you've come to do the right thing, so with the Lord's help you'll be grateful to me all your life. Akulina, you know, is a fine girl. You won't find anyone like her in all the district.

The Father. That may be so, but what about the money?

Matryona. Don't worry about the money. All she's had from her father goes with her. And it isn't little as things are nowadays. Three times fifty rubles.

The Father. We don't complain, but we have to think of our child. We want to get the best we can.

Matryona. I tell you, if it hadn't been for me, you'd never have found anyone like her. It's the truth I'm telling you. You see, they've had an offer from the Koromilins, but I stood out for you. As for the money, I tell you, and it's the truth I'm telling you, that when her father, the Lord rest his soul, was dying, he gave orders that his widow should take Nikita into the house and that the money should go to Akulina. You see, I know everything through my son. Someone else might have refused to part with the money, but Nikita is giving her everything to the last penny. And it isn't just a few coppers. It's big money.

The Father. I've heard people say that she was left much more money. The lad's a sharp one, too.

Matryona. Why, a morsel always looks big in other people's hands. All she had they are giving her. I tell you, stop worrying. Clinch the deal. Think what a girl you're getting. She's as pretty as a picture.

The Father. That may be so, but my old woman and I were wondering about the girl. Why hasn't she come out? She isn't sickly, is she?

Matryona. Good heavens, no! She sickly! Why, there's no healthier girl in the whole district. Sound as a bell. You won't find any fault with her. But, why, you saw her the other day. And she's a wonderful worker. She's a little deaf, it's true, but one blemish on a red apple doesn't mean it's bad. As for her not coming out, it's, you see, it's because of an evil eye. A spell has been cast on her, and I know the bitch who's responsible for it. You see, they knew of the betrothal, so they bewitched her. But I know a counter spell. The girl will get up tomorrow. Don't you worry about the girl.

The Father. Well, of course, the thing is settled.

Matryona. And so it is. Don't you try even to think of getting out of it. And don't forget me, either. This thing has given me a lot of trouble. So don't forget me.

A Woman's Voice from the Passage. If you're going then let's go. Come on, Ivan.

The Father. Coming. [*Goes out.*]

Guests crowd together in the passage and drive away.

Anyuta [*runs out of the passage and calls to* ANISYA]. Mother!

Anisya [*from inside*]. What?

Anyuta. Mother, come here, or they'll hear.

ANISYA *comes out and they go together to the shed.*

Anisya. Well, what is it? Where's Akulina?

Anyuta. She's gone into the barn. Oh, it's awful! The things she's doing there! Cross my heart. "Can't bear it," she says. "I'll scream," she says. "I'll scream out loud," cross my heart.

Anisya. She'd better wait. First we must see off our guests.

Anyuta. Oh, Mother, she feels so bad. And she's angry, too. "They won't sell me," she says, "however much they drink. I'm not going to marry," she says. "I'll die." What if she does die, Mother? Oh, I'm so afraid.

Anisya. Don't worry, she won't die. But you'd better not go near her. Come along.

ANISYA *and* ANYUTA *go out.*

Mitrich [*comes in at the gate and starts collecting the scattered hay*]. Oh Lord, holy St. Nicholas, the spirits they drank and the horrible smell they made! Stinks even out here. But I don't want it. To hell with it. Look at them! The hay they've scattered about. They don't eat it, they only trample it underfoot. Before you know where you are, a whole truss has gone. Oh, the stink. Just under my nose! Oh, to hell with it! [*Yawns.*] Time to turn in, but I don't like to go into the hut. The stink seems to float under my nose. [*The guests can be heard driving off.*] Well, they're gone at last. Oh Lord, holy St. Nicholas. Worrying themselves to death, cheating each other and all for nothing.

Nikita [*comes in*]. Mitrich, you can go off to your stove and I'll clean up here.

Mitrich. All right, give it to the sheep. Well, seen them off?

Nikita. Yes, I've seen them off, but there's something wrong. I don't know what to do.

Mitrich. What a mess! But I shouldn't worry if I was you. There's the foundlings' home for that. Anyone can drop it there, and they're sure to pick it up. You can give them as many as you like. No questions asked. They even pay you if the mother goes in as a wet nurse. It's very easy now.

Nikita. Mind, Mitrich, don't you go talking about it.

Mitrich. It's none of my business. Cover up the tracks as best you can. Lord, how you stink of liquor. I'd better go in. [*Goes out yawning.*] Oh Lord!

A long pause. NIKITA *sits down on a sledge.*

Nikita. What a mess! [ANISYA *comes out.*]

Anisya. Where have you been?

Nikita. Here.

Anisya. What are you sitting here for? We've no time to lose. We must take it out at once.

Nikita. What are we to do?

Anisya. I've told you what to do. Do it.

Nikita. You'd better take it to the foundlings' home—if anything.

Anisya. Take it there yourself, if you like. You don't mind getting a girl into trouble, but you're not so keen when it comes to cleaning up the mess afterwards.

Nikita. What's to be done?

Anisya. I'm telling you. Go down into the cellar and dig a hole.

Nikita. But can't you manage it somehow?

Anisya [*mimicking him*]. Somehow! We can't and that's all there is to it. You should have thought of that before. Go and do it.

Nikita. What a business!

Anyuta [*comes in*]. Mother, the midwife's calling. I expect Akulina's got a baby. Cross my heart, it cried.

Anisya. What are you talking about? Plague take you. It's the kitten crying there. Go to bed or I'll give it to you.

Anyuta. It's true, Mother, I swear.

Anisya [*making as though to hit her*]. I'll give it to you! Go to bed and don't let me catch sight of you again. [ANYUTA *runs off. To* NIKITA.] Go and do as you're told, or else there's going to be trouble. [*Goes out.*]

Nikita [*alone*]. Oh, what a mess! These women. "You should have thought of it before," she says. When was I to think of it? A year ago Anisya began pestering me. What was I to do? I'm not a monk, am I? The master died, and I covered up my sin as was proper. I was not to be blamed there. There are lots of such cases. And then

those powders. Did I put her up to it? Why, had I known
what the bitch was up to, I should have killed her! Yes,
killed her. She's made me her partner in this crime, the
dirty bitch! And she became hateful to me after that.
Hateful! As soon as Mother told me about it, I couldn't
bear to look at her. So how could I live with her? And
then this business started. That girl threw herself on my
neck. What was I to do? If it hadn't been me, it would
have been someone else. And now it's this. Again, am I
to blame for it? Oh, what a mess! [*Sits thinking.*] Those
women! They're afraid of nothing! What a thing to think
of! No, I'm not going to do it.

MATRYONA *comes in with a lantern and spade, in a hurry.*

Matryona. What are you sitting there like a broody hen
for? What did your wife tell you to do? Get it all ready.

Nikita. And what are you going to do?

Matryona. We know what to do. You do your job.

Nikita. You're getting me into a proper mess.

Matryona. Why, you're not trying to back out, are you?
Now that it's come to this, you want to back out, do you?

Nikita. But think what you're trying to make me do!
It's a living soul.

Matryona. A living soul, indeed! Why, it's more dead
than alive. What are we going to do with it? Take it to a
foundlings' home? It'll die all the same, and people will
talk, and everything will come out, and the girl will be
left on our hands.

Nikita. And what if they found out?

Matryona. It's in your house, isn't it? We can do it here.
We'll manage it so that there won't be a chance of anyone finding out. Just do as I tell you. We can't do it
without a man. There, take the spade, go down into the
cellar and get it done. I'll hold the light.

Nikita. What have I got to do?

Matryona [*in a whisper*]. Dig a hole, then we'll bring
it out and you get rid of it quickly. There, she's calling
again. Now, go for Heaven's sake. I'll follow you.

Nikita. Is it dead then?

Matryona. Of course it's dead. Only it must be done
quickly or people will notice. They're still up. All they

want is to hear or see something, the swine. The police officer has passed by this evening. I tell you what to do. [*Gives him the spade.*] Go down to the cellar and dig a hole in the corner. The earth is soft there and you can smooth it over afterwards. Mother earth will not tell anyone. She'll lick it over with her tongue like a cow. Go! Go, my dear.

Nikita. You'll get me into proper trouble. I wish you'd leave me alone. I'll go away. Do it yourselves as best you can.

Anisya [*through the door*]. Well, has he dug it?

Matryona. Why did you go away? Where have you put it?

Anisya. I've covered it with rags, so that no one can hear it. Well, has he dug it?

Matryona. He won't do it.

Anisya [*runs out in a rage*]. He won't do it! And how would he like feeding lice in jail? I'll go straight and tell everything to the police. Let's all be ruined. I'll tell them everything.

Nikita. What will you tell?

Anisya. What? Everything. Who took the money? You did. [NIKITA *is silent.*] And who gave the poison? I did! But you knew. You knew. I did it with your consent.

Matryona. That'll do. Why are you so obstinate, Nikita? What's to be done now? We'll have to go through with it. Go, my dear.

Anisya. Look at him! He doesn't want to dirty his hands. You've treated me like scum long enough! Trampled me underfoot! Now it's my turn. Go, I say, or else I'll do what I said. . . . Take the spade. Take it. Go.

Nikita. Keep away from me. What are you pestering me for? [*Takes the spade but is still undecided.*] I won't go if I don't choose to.

Anisya. You won't go? [*Begins to shout.*] Come here, good people, hey!

Matryona [*puts her hands over her mouth*]. What are you doing? Have you gone stark raving mad? He'll go. Go, my son, go.

Anisya. I'll call for help.

Nikita. Oh, stop it. What a woman! You'd better be

quick. I suppose if you're all in it . . . I may as well. [*Goes toward the cellar.*]

Matryona. Well, son, that's how it is: you've had a good time, now you must pay for it.

Anisya [*still excitedly*]. He kept jeering at me, he and that slut of his. All right, I've had enough. I'm not going to be the only one. Let him, too, be a murderer. He'll know what it feels like.

Matryona. All right, all right. What's the use of being in a rage now? Instead of flying into a rage, you'd better do things quietly and see that they're done well. Go to the girl. He'll see to everything. [*Follows* NIKITA *to the cellar with a lantern.* NIKITA *goes down into the cellar.*]

Anisya. I'll make him strangle that damned brat of his. [*Still excitedly.*] Worried myself to death, I have, with Peter on my conscience. Let him, too, know what it's like. I won't spare myself. I've said I won't spare myself.

Nikita [*from the cellar*]. Let me have a light.

Matryona [*holds up the lantern. To* ANISYA]. He's digging. Go and bring it.

Anisya. You stay with him, or he'll go away, the wretch. I'll go and bring it.

Matryona. Mind, don't forget to baptize it first, or else I'll do it. Have you got a cross?

Anisya. I'll find one. I know how to do it. [*Goes out.*]

Matryona [*alone*]. Also taken the bit between her teeth, like a silly woman. She's had a lot to put up with, though. But, thank God, we'll cover up this business and there'll be an end to it. We'll get rid of the girl without anyone knowing of her sin. My son will be able to live in comfort then. They've got plenty of everything, thank God, and he won't forget me, either. Where would they have been without Matryona? They wouldn't have been able to think of anything. [*Into the cellar.*] Is it ready, son?

Nikita [*puts his head out of the cellar*]. What are you doing there? Why don't you bring it? What are you wasting your time for? If it's to be done, let it be done quickly.

Matryona [*goes toward the passage and meets* ANISYA *who comes out with a baby wrapped in rags*]. Well, have you christened it?

Anisya. Of course I have. I couldn't get it away from

her. She wouldn't give it to me. [*Walks up to the cellar and gives it to* Nikita.]

Nikita [*refuses to take it*]. Take it down yourself.

Anisya. Take it, I tell you. [*Throws the baby down to him.* Nikita *catches it.*]

Nikita. It's alive! Good Lord, it's moving! What am I going to do with it?

Anisya [*snatches the baby from him and throws it into the cellar*]. Strangle it quickly, and it won't be alive. [*Pushes* Nikita *down.*] It's your doing and you must finish it.

Matryona [*sitting down on the doorstep*]. He's so soft-hearted. He finds it hard, poor dear. But then, after all, it's also his sin, isn't it? [Anisya *stands over the cellar.* Matryona *sits on the steps, looks at her and speaks.*] Good Lord, how frightened he was. But what's to be done? It may be a hard thing to do, but it has to be done all the same. Where else could we have put it? And then again, just think how often people pray to God to have children. But God doesn't give them to them. They're all stillborn. Take the priest's wife. And here where it's not wanted, it's born alive. [*Looks in the direction of the cellar.*] I expect he must have finished it off now.

Anisya. Well? [*Looking into the cellar.*] He's put a board on it and is sitting on it. It must be finished.

Matryona. Oh, dear Lord. One would be glad not to sin, but what is one to do?

Nikita [*comes out of the cellar, trembling all over*]. It's still alive. I can't do it. It's alive!

Anisya. Alive, is it? Where are you off to? [*Wants to stop him.*]

Nikita [*rushes at her*]. Go away. I'll kill you. [*Seizes her by the arm. She tears herself free. He runs after her with the spade.* Matryona *runs toward him and stops him.* Anisya *runs to the front steps.* Matryona *tries to take the spade from him.* Nikita *brandishes it at his mother.*] I'll kill you, too! Go away! [Matryona *runs away to* Anisya *on the front steps.* Nikita *stops.*] I'll kill you! I'll kill you all!

Matryona. He acts like this because he's frightened. Never mind. It'll pass.

Nikita. What have they done? What have they done to me? It cried so. . . . How it crunched under me. What have they done to me? And it's alive! It's still alive! [*Listens in silence.*] It's crying. It's still crying. [*Runs to the cellar.*]

Matryona [*to* ANISYA]. He's going. I think he means to bury it. Nikita, take the lantern.

Nikita [*without answering, listens at the cellar*]. Can't hear it. I must have fancied it. [*Moves away and stops.*] Oh, how the little bones scrunched under me! Crr. . . . Crr. . . . What have they done to me? [*Listens again.*] It's crying again. Yes, it's crying. What's this? Mother, mother! [*Goes up to* MATRYONA.]

Matryona. What is it, son?

Nikita. Mother, dear, I can't bear it any longer. I can't do anything. Mother, have pity on me.

Matryona. Lord, how frightened you are, dearie. Come, come, have a drop to give you courage.

Nikita. Mother, it seems my time has come. What have you done to me? How the little bones crunched and how it cried. Mother, what have you done to me? [*Moves away and sits down on the sledge.*]

Matryona. Go, my dear, have a drink. It does seem fearful at night, but when day comes you won't feel so bad. And after a couple of days you won't even think of it. Just wait a little. We'll marry off the girl and we'll forget all about it. You'd better go now and have a drink. I'll go and put things straight in the cellar.

Nikita [*shakes himself*]. Is there any drink left? Perhaps I can drink it off.

ANISYA, *who was standing at the passage all the time, makes way for him silently.*

Matryona. Go, go, my dear. I'll see to it myself. I'll go down and bury it. Where has he thrown the spade? [*Finds the spade and goes down into the cellar.*] Anisya, you'd better come here and hold the light.

Anisya. And what about him?

Matryona. He's too frightened. You've been too hard on him. Leave him alone and he'll come to his senses. Never mind him. I'll do it myself. Just put the lantern here. I can see. [*Matryona disappears into the cellar.*]

Anisya [*looking toward the door through which* NIKITA *has gone into the cottage.*] Well, have you had enough of a good time? What a fine fellow! Now you'll know what it feels like. You won't be so full of yourself any more.

Nikita [*rushes out of the cottage and runs toward the cellar.*] Mother, Mother!

Matryona [*puts her head out of the cellar*]. What is it, son?

Nikita [*listening*]. Don't bury it! It's alive! Can't you hear it? It's crying. There! Quite clearly.

Matryona. How can it cry? Why, you've flattened it to a pancake. Smashed in his little head.

Nikita. What is it then? [*Stops up his ears.*] It's still crying. I'm lost, I'm lost. What have they done to me? Where am I to go? [*Sits down on the step.*]

Curtain.

ACT FIVE

SCENE I—*A thrashing floor. A corn stack; to the left, the threshing ground, to the right, a barn. The barn doors are open. Straw is strewn about in the doorway. In the background a yard, and the sound of songs and a tambourine can be heard. Two girls are walking past the barn to the cottage.*

FIRST GIRL. You see, we've managed to pass by without dirtying our shoes. But it's terribly muddy by the road.

They stop and wipe their shoes on the straw.

First Girl [*looks at the straw and sees something*]. What's that?

Second Girl [*looking*]. It's Mitrich, their laborer. Look how drunk he is.

First Girl. Why, I thought he didn't drink.

Second Girl. It seems he doesn't till someone stands him a drink.

First Girl. Look, he seems to have come here for the straw. See, he's got a rope in his hands. He's fallen asleep.

Second Girl. They're still singing in honor of the bride and bridegroom. I don't suppose they've been given the blessing yet. I'm told Akulina didn't even wail.

First Girl. Mother says she's marrying against her will. Her stepfather threatened her, or else she wouldn't have agreed to for anything. Why, the things they've been saying about her!

Marina [catching up with the girls]. How are you, girls?

Girls. How are you, Marina?

Marina. Going to the wedding, my dears?

First Girl. Why, it's nearly over. We're just going to have a look.

Marina. Please tell my husband I want him. Semyon, from Zuyevo. I think you know him.

First Girl. Of course, we know him. He's a relative of the bridegroom's, isn't he?

Marina. Yes, of course. The bridegroom is my husband's nephew.

Second Girl. Why don't you go there yourself? Fancy not going to a wedding.

Marina. I don't want to, my dear, and I haven't got the time, either. It's time we went home. We didn't mean to go to the wedding. We were taking oats to the town. We only stopped to feed the horse, and my husband was invited in.

First Girl. Where did you put up? At Fyodorovich's?

Marina. Yes. I'm going to wait here and so would you please tell him I'm waiting. Call him out, my dear, and tell him his wife, Marina, says he has to come now. His mates are harnessing the horse.

First Girl. Well, all right. If you don't want to go yourself.

The girls walk off along the path to the yard. The sound of songs and tambourines can be heard.

Marina [alone, pensively]. I could have gone, but I don't want to, for I haven't seen him since the day he threw me over more than a year ago. I'd have liked to

have a look and see how he lives with his Anisya. People
say they're always fighting. She's a coarse woman, a stubborn one. I expect he must have remembered me more
than once. Hankering after a good life he was. Gave me
up for her. Ah, well, never mind. I don't harbor any ill-
feeling against him. I did feel hurt at the time. Very hurt.
But now it's all worn off and I've forgotten it. Still, I'd
have liked to have a look at him. [*Looks toward the house
and sees* NIKITA.] Good Lord, why is he coming here?
Have the girls told him? Why has he left his guests? I'd
better go.

NIKITA *comes in, hanging his head, waving his arms and
muttering something.*

Marina. He looks so gloomy.

Nikita [*sees* MARINA *and recognizes her*]. Marina! Darling Marina, what are you doing here?

Marina. I've come for my husband.

Nikita. Why didn't you come to the wedding? You
might have had a look and a laugh at me.

Marina. Why should I have a laugh at you? I've come
for my husband.

Nikita. Oh, my darling! [*Tries to embrace her.* MARINA
pushes him away angrily.]

Marina. Stop that, Nikita. What's been has been. I've
come for my husband. Is he at your place?

Nikita. I mustn't remember the past, must I? You
don't want me to.

Marina. It's no use recalling the past. What's been has
been.

Nikita. And it can never return?

Marina. Never. But why have you gone away? You, the
master of the house, and gone away from the wedding?

Nikita [*sits down in the straw*]. Why have I gone away?
Oh, if only you knew. Oh, Marina, I'm bored. I'm so
bored, I can't tell you. I got up from the table and went
away. Got away from the people. Didn't want to see
anyone.

Marina [*coming nearer to him*]. Why? What's the
matter?

Nikita. Why? Because I can't eat, I can't drink, I can't
sleep. Oh, I feel sick, I feel so sick! And the reason why

I feel so sick, Marina, dear, is that I have no one to share my grief.

Marina. You can't live your life without grief, Nikita. I've wept over mine and it's gone.

Nikita. But that's a long time ago. That's an old story. Oh, my friend, you've wept over it and it's gone, but I've got mine up to here.

Marina. But what's the matter?

Nikita. I'm sick to death of my life. That's what it is. I'm sick to death of myself. Oh, Marina, you didn't know how to keep me and now you've ruined me and yourself. Is this life?

Marina [*stands by the barn, cries, but restrains herself*]. I'm not complaining about my life, Nikita. God grant everyone a life like mine. I do not complain. I told everything to my husband at the time. He forgave me. And he doesn't reproach me. I've nothing against my life. My old man is quiet and is fond of me. I keep his children clothed and clean. He, too, is sorry for me, so why should I complain? It seems it was God's will. But what's the matter with your life? You're rich. . . .

Nikita. My life? It's only that I don't want to disturb the wedding or I'd take this rope here [*picks up the rope from the straw*], throw it across that rafter, make a noose, climb up on the rafter, put it around my neck and jump down. That's what my life is like.

Marina. Don't talk like that!

Nikita. You think I'm joking? You think I'm drunk? I'm not drunk. Today I can't even get drunk. I'm sick at heart. Aye, my heart is heavy. I'm that sick of my life I care for nothing any more. Oh, Marina, it's only with you that I've ever really lived. You remember how we used to while away the nights on the railway?

Marina. Don't open old sores, Nikita. I'm a married woman now, and you're married, too. My sin has been forgiven. Don't stir up the past.

Nikita. But what can I do with my heart? Where am I to turn to?

Marina. Well, what's to be done? You have a wife, don't go running after others, but take care of your own. You loved Anisya. Well, go on loving her.

Nikita. Oh, Anisya is gall and wormwood to me now. She's wound herself around my feet like rank weeds.

Marina. Whatever she is, she's still your wife. But what's the use of talking about it? You'd better go back to your guests and send my husband back to me.

Nikita. Oh, if only you knew the whole business! But why talk about it?

Marina's Husband [*comes in, red and tipsy*]. Marina, wife, where are you?

Nikita. There's your husband calling you. You'd better go.

Marina. And what about you?

Nikita. Me? I'll lie down here for a while. [*Lies down on the straw.*]

Marina's Husband. Where is she?

Anyuta [*comes in*]. There she is, Uncle. Near the barn.

Marina's Husband. What are you standing there for? Go to the wedding feast. They want you to come and do them honor. The wedding party is just going to start and then we can go, too.

Marina [*going toward her husband*]. I didn't want to go.

Marina's Husband. Go, I tell you. You'll drink a glass to the health of our nephew Peter, the rascal. Our hosts are offended. There's plenty of time for business. [MARINA'S HUSBAND *puts his arms around her and, staggering, goes out with her.*]

Nikita [*rises and sits down in the straw*]. Oh, now that I've seen her I feel more sick than ever. The only time I ever really enjoyed life was with her. I've ruined my life for nothing. I'm done for! [*Lies down.*] Where am I to go now? Oh, if only the ground would open up and swallow me!

Anyuta [*sees* NIKITA *and runs toward him*]. Daddy, they're looking for you. Her godfather and all of them have already blessed her. Cross my heart, they've already blessed her. They're getting angry.

Nikita [*aside*]. Where am I to go?

Anyuta. What? What did you say?

Nikita. I didn't say anything. What are you pestering me for?

Anyuta. Daddy, are you coming? [NIKITA *is silent and*

she pulls him by the hand.] Daddy, you must go and give them your blessing. I tell you they are angry, they are swearing.

Nikita [*pulls his hand away*]. Leave me alone.

Anyuta. Come on.

Nikita [*threatens her with the rope*]. Go, I say, or I'll give it to you.

Anyuta. Then I'll send Mother. [*Runs off.*]

Nikita [*alone, rises*]. How can I go? How can I take the icon in my hand? How can I look her in the face? [*Lies down again.*] Oh, if there was a hole in the ground, I'd jump in. No one would see me and I would see no one. [*Rises again.*] No, I won't go. . . . To hell with them all. I won't go. [*Takes off his boots and picks up the rope. Makes a noose and puts it around his neck.*] That's the way.

MATRYONA *comes in.* NIKITA *sees his mother, takes the rope off his neck and lies down on the straw again.*

Matryona [*comes in hurriedly*]. Nikita, Nikita! He won't even answer. What's the matter with you? Are you drunk? Come, my son. Come, Nikita, dear. The people are tired of waiting.

Nikita. Oh, what have you done with me? I'm no longer a human being.

Matryona. What's the matter with you? Come, my dear. Come, give them your blessing, as is right and proper, and then you can do what you like. You see, the people are waiting.

Nikita. How can I give the blessing?

Matryona. You know how. In the usual way.

Nikita. I know, I know. But who is it I'm to bless? What have I done to her?

Matryona. What have you done? What's the use of remembering that? No one knows about it, not a living soul. And the girl is going of her own free will.

Nikita. But why is she going?

Matryona. Because she's afraid, of course. But she's going all the same. But what's to be done? She should have thought of it sooner. Now she can't afford to be stubborn. Besides, his parents can't back out, either. They

came to see the girl twice and they got the money for her.
No one knows about anything. Everything is safe.

Nikita. But what's in the cellar?

Matryona [laughs]. In the cellar? Why, cabbages, mushrooms, potatoes, I suppose. Why keep harping on the
past?

Nikita. I wish I could forget it, but I can't. Every time
I think of it I can hear. Oh, what have you done with me?

Matryona. What are you making such a fuss about?

Nikita [turns over on his face]. Mother, don't torture
me. I've got it up to here.

Matryona. But it has to be done. As it is, people are
talking. And then the father suddenly goes away and
refuses to give his blessing. They'll be putting two and
two together at once. As soon as they see you're getting
frightened, they'll start guessing. In a crowded street a
man's no thief, but when you run away from a wolf, you're
sure to bump into a bear. Above all, son, don't show it.
Don't lose heart or they'll find out all the more.

Nikita. Oh, you've got me into a proper mess.

Matryona. Enough of that. Let's go. Come! Come and
give your blessing. Do everything just as is right and
proper, and that will be the end of the matter.

Nikita [lies with his face downward]. I can't.

Matryona [aside]. What has come over him? Everything
seemed to be all right and suddenly this comes over him.
He seems to be bewitched. Nikita, get up! Look, there's
Anisya coming. She's left the guests.

*Anisya [comes in, dressed up, red in the face and a little
tipsy].* Everything's so nice, Mother. So nice and proper.
And how pleased everyone is! But where is he?

Matryona. He's here. Lain down on the straw, and there
he lies. He refuses to come.

Nikita [looking at his wife]. Look at her! She, too, is
drunk. I look at her and my heart turns over within me.
How can I live with her? [*Again turns over on his face.*]
I'll kill her someday. It will be worse then.

Anisya. Fancy him lying down on the straw! Drunk, is
he? [*Laughs.*] I'd lie down there with you, but I've no
time. Come on, I'll take you back. Oh, it's so nice in the
house. It's a treat to look at. And the concertina! The

women are singing so beautifully. They're all drunk. All
so respectable, so nice.

Nikita. What's so nice about it?

Anisya. The wedding. Such a gay wedding. Everyone
says it's quite out of the ordinary. So respectable, so nice.
Come along, come along, we'll go together. I've had a
drop, but I can help you along. [*Takes his hand.* Nikita
pulls his hand back with disgust.]

Nikita. Go alone. I'll come.

Anisya. What are you glaring at me like that for? We've
got rid of all our troubles. Married off the girl who has
come between us. We've nothing to do now but to live
and be merry. Everything is so respectable and legal. I'm
so glad. I can't tell you how glad I am. Just as if I was
going to marry you a second time. And, dear me, how
pleased the people are. They're all thanking us. And the
guests are all of the best. Ivan Moseyvich and the police
officer. They, too, made speeches praising us.

Nikita. Well, go and stay with them then. What have
you come here for?

Anisya. I suppose I'd better go back. Else what would
it look like? The hosts have gone and left the guests to
fend for themselves, and the guests are all of the best.

Nikita [*gets up and brushes the straw off himself*]. Go.
I'll come at once.

Matryona. The night cuckoo has outcuckooed the day
cuckoo. He wouldn't listen to me, but he followed his
wife at once. [Matryona *and* Anisya *turn to go.*] Well,
are you coming?

Nikita. I'll be coming along directly. You go, I'll follow
you. I'll come and give my blessing. [*The women stop.*]
Go. Go on. I'll follow you. Go! [*The women go out.*
Nikita *follows them with his eyes and sinks into thought.
Sits down and takes off his boots.*] Yes, wait till I come!
Some hope! You'd better look at the rafter for me. Put
the noose around my neck, jump off the rafter and—then
you can look for me. Thank goodness the rope was here.
[*Ponders.*] I would have shaken it off, however great my
grief, I would have shaken it off, but this thing is here—
in my heart—and I can't take it out, however much I try.
[*Gazes intently at the yard.*] Good Lord, she isn't coming

again, is she? [*Mimicking* ANISYA.] It's so nice, so nice, I could lie down with you! Oh, you dirty baggage! Well then, come, cuddle me when they've taken me down from the rafter. There's only one way out. [*Takes the rope and pulls it.*]

Mitrich [*tipsy, sits up and won't let go of the rope*]. I won't give it to you. I won't give it to anyone. I'll bring it myself. I said I'll bring the straw and I'll bring it. Is that you, Nikita? [*Laughs.*] Damn! Have you come for the straw?

Nikita. Give me the rope.

Mitrich. No, you wait. The peasants sent me. I'll bring it. [*Rises to his feet and begins getting the straw together, but staggers, straightens himself and then falls down.*] It's got the better of me. It's stronger than me.

Nikita. Give me the rope.

Mitrich. I told you I wouldn't. Oh, Nikita, you stupid pig. [*Laughs.*] I love you, but you're stupid. You think I'm drunk? Well, I don't care a damn about you. You think I need you. Just look at me. I'm a sergeant. Fool! You can't say it, can you? I'm a sergeant of Her Majesty's first regiment of grenadier guards. I've served my king and country faithfully and loyally. And who am I? You think I'm a warrior? No, I'm no warrior. I'm the humblest of men. I'm an orphan. I'm a lost man. I've taken the pledge and now I've broken it. Well, what do you think? I'm afraid of you? No, I'm not afraid of you. I'm not afraid of no one. I've taken to drinking again, so I'm going to drink! I'm going to drink for a whole fortnight. I'm going to sell my last shirt for drink. And my cap. And my cross. I'll pawn my passport, too. I'm not afraid of no one. They flogged me in the army to stop me drinking. They whipped and whipped me. "Well," they said, "won't you stop?" "No," says I. Why should I be afraid of dirt like them? That's the sort of man I am. Such as I am, so God's made me. I took the pledge and I didn't drink. Now I took to drink and I'm going to drink. And I'm not afraid of no one. For you see, I don't lie, but I'm telling the truth. Why should I be afraid of the dirty scum? That's the sort of fellow I am. A priest told me the devil was the biggest boaster. As soon as you begin to boast, he said, you get frightened, and as soon as you get frightened of people, he, the hoofed one, will grab you and push you where he likes. But as I don't fear man I feel easy in my mind. I'll spit in his beard, the horned beast. And at his mother, too, the dirty sow. He can't do nothing to me. There, put that in your pipe and smoke it.

Nikita [*crossing himself*]. Good Lord, what was I going to do? [*Throws down the rope.*]

Mitrich. What?

Nikita [*rising*]. You tell me not to fear man?

Mitrich. Why should you fear them, the dirty rotters? You have a look at them in the bathhouse. They're all made of the same dough. One has a bigger belly and another a smaller one, but that's all the difference. Yes, sir, why be afraid of them? To hell with them.

Matryona [*comes in from the yard*]. Well, aren't you coming?

Nikita. Yes, it's much better so. Yes, I'm coming.

Curtain.

SCENE II—*Same as Act One. The cottage is full of people, some sitting around tables and others standing. In the front corner* AKULINA *with her* FIANCÉ. *At one of the tables— icons and a loaf of bread. Among the visitors are* MARINA, *her* HUSBAND, *and a* POLICE OFFICER. *The women are singing.*

ANISYA *carries around the drinks. The singing stops.*

COACHMAN. If we are to go, let's go. The church isn't so near.

The Best Man. Don't be in such a hurry. Let her step-father give his blessing first. But where is he?

Anisya. He's coming, he's coming at once. Have another glass, all of you. Please.

The Matchmaker. Why is he so long? We've been waiting for hours.

Anisya. He's coming. Coming directly. He'll be here in a minute. Have a drink, please. [*Takes the drinks around.*] He's coming. Another song, my beauties.

Coachman. But they've sung all their songs waiting for him.

The women sing. NIKITA *and* AKIM *come in in the middle of their song.*

Nikita [*holds his father's arm and pushes him in before him*]. Go, Father, I can't do it without you.

Akim. I don't like it. I mean. . . .

Nikita [*to the women*]. Enough. Be quiet. [*Looks around at all the people in the cottage.*] Marina, are you here?

The Matchmaker. Come, take the icon, and give them your blessing.

Nikita. Wait, give me time. Akulina, are you there?

The Matchmaker. What are you calling them for? Where do you think she is? Lord, he looks queer.

Anisya. Good gracious, he's barefoot.

Nikita. Father, are you here? Look at me. Christian people, you're all here and I'm here. Here I am. [*Falls on his knees.*]

Anisya. Nikita, darling, what's the matter with you? Oh, my poor head!

The Matchmaker. Well, I declare!

Matryona. I said he was drinking too much of that French wine. Come to your senses, son! What's the matter with you? [*They try to lift him, but he pays no attention to them, staring in front of him.*]

Nikita. Christian people, I have sinned, and I wish to confess.

Matryona [*drags him by his shoulder*]. Have you gone off your head? Dear people, he's gone crazy. He must be taken away.

Nikita [*shakes her off*]. Leave me alone. And you, Father, listen. To begin with, Marina, look here. [*Bows to the ground to her and rises.*] I've wronged you. I had promised to marry you. I seduced you. I deceived you. I threw you over. Forgive me, in Christ's name.

Anisya. What are you making such a song and dance about? It ill becomes you. No one is asking you about it. Get up. What are you trying to do? What are you up to?

Matryona. Oh, someone's cast a spell on him. How did it happen? He's bewitched. Get up! What nonsense are you talking? [*Pulls him.*]

Nikita [*shakes his head*]. Don't touch me. Forgive my sin toward you, Marina, forgive me in Christ's name. [MARINA *covers her face with her hands and is silent.*]

Anisya. Get up, I tell you. What are you up to? Found a time to remember the past! Found a time for showing off! Aren't you ashamed of yourself? Oh, my poor head! He's gone crazy.

Nikita [*pushes his wife away and turns to* AKULINA]. Akulina, I'm speaking to you now. Listen, Christian people. I'm a damned soul. Akulina, I'm guilty toward you. Your father didn't die a natural death. He was poisoned!

Anisya [*screams*]. Oh, my head, what is he talking about!

Matryona. The man's beside himself. Take him away. [*People come up and try to seize him.*]

Akim [*waves them away*]. Wait, wait, boys. I mean, wait.

Nikita. Akulina, I poisoned him. Forgive me in Christ's name.

Akulina [*jumps up*]. He's telling lies. I know who poisoned him.

The Matchmaker. Don't interfere! Sit down.

Akim. Oh, Lord, what a sin, what a sin!

Police Officer. Seize him and send for the elder and for the witnesses. We must draw up a statement. Get up, you, and come here.

Akim [*to the* POLICE OFFICER]. You, I mean, you, bright buttons, I mean, go away. Let him have his say, I mean.

Police Officer [*to* AKIM]. Don't you interfere, old man. I warn you. I have to draw up an official statement.

Akim. Ah, what a fellow you are, to be sure! I mean, wait, I say. Don't talk of your statement now. I mean, here's God's work being done. A man's confessing, I mean. And you with your statement!

Police Officer. Get the headman.

Akim. Let God's work be done first, I mean. Then you do your business, I mean.

Nikita. And another thing, Akulina, I've committed a great sin toward you. I've seduced you. Forgive me in Christ's name. [*Bows low to her.*]

Akulina [*leaves the table*]. Let me go. I'm not going to get married. He told me to, but I'm not going to now.

Police Officer. Repeat what you said.

Nikita. Wait, sir, let me finish.

Akim [*with rapture*]. Speak, my son, tell everything. You'll feel better. Confess to God. Don't be afraid of men. God—God. It's He—

Nikita. I poisoned the father and ruined his daughter, cur that I am. She was in my power, and I ruined her and her baby.

Akulina. That's true, too.

Nikita. I smothered her baby in the cellar with a board. I sat on it—smothered it—and its little bones crunched. [*Weeps.*] And I buried it. I alone.

Akulina. He's lying. I told him to.

Nikita. Don't shield me. I fear no one now. Forgive me, Christian people. [*Bows to the ground.*]

Police Officer. Bind him. Your marriage, it seems, is off.

Men come up with belts.

Nikita. Wait. Plenty of time. [*Bows to the ground before his father.*] Father, you, too, forgive me, damned that I am. You told me from the first moment I took to this path of evil and wickedness, you told me if one claw is caught, the bird is lost, but I didn't listen to you, and it has turned out as you said. Forgive me in the name of Christ.

Akim. God will forgive you, my son. [*Embraces him.*] You have had no pity on yourself, but he will have pity on you. God—God. It is He—

ELDER *comes in.*

Elder. There are enough witnesses here, too.

Police Officer. Take down his statement at once.

NIKITA *is bound.*

Akulina [*goes up to stand by his side*]. I shall tell the truth. Take a statement from me, too.

Nikita [*bound*]. No need to take a statement from her. I did it all myself. I planned it all and I carried it out. Take me where you like. I won't say another word.

Curtain.

UNCLE VANYA

Country Scenes in Four Acts by

ANTON CHEKHOV

CHARACTERS

ALEXANDER VLADIMIROVICH SEREBRYAKOV, *a retired university professor*

YELENA ANDREYEVNA SEREBRYAKOV, *his wife, aged twenty-seven*

SOPHIA (SONIA) ALEXANDROVNA, *his daughter by his first marriage*

MARIA VASSILYEVNA VOYNITSKY, *the mother of the professor's first wife*

IVAN PETROVICH VOYNITSKY, *her son*

MIKHAIL LVOVICH ASTROV, *a country doctor*

ILYA ILYICH TELEGIN, *an impoverished landowner*

MARINA, *an old nurse*

A LABORER

The action takes place on SEREBRYAKOV's *estate.*

UNCLE VANYA

ACT ONE

*A garden. Part of the house can be seen with the veranda.
Under an old poplar, by the avenue of trees, a table set for
tea. Benches, chairs; a guitar on one of the benches. Not
far from the table—a swing. About three o'clock in the
afternoon. An overcast sky.*

MARINA, *a heavily built old woman, who moves with
difficulty, sits by the samovar, knitting a sock, and* ASTROV
is walking up and down near her.

MARINA [*pours out a glass of tea*]. Have some tea, dear.

    Astrov [*accepts the glass reluctantly*]. Thank you, I don't
feel like it, somehow.

    Marina. You wouldn't like a drop of vodka, would you?

    Astrov. No, thank you. I don't drink vodka every day,
you know. Besides, it's so close. [*Pause.*] How long have we
known each other, Nanny?

    Marina [*thinking it over*]. How long? Dear me, let me
think. . . . You first came here—into these parts—when?
—Sonia's mother was still living then. You visited us
regularly for two winters before she died. Well, that makes
eleven years to my way of reckoning. [*After a moment's
thought.*] Perhaps even longer.

    Astrov. Have I changed much since then?

    Marina. Yes, I'm afraid you have, dear. You were young
and handsome then, but now you look much older. And
you aren't as handsome as you used to be. If you don't
mind me mentioning it, you drink a lot, too.

Astrov. Yes. . . . In ten years I've grown a different man. And the reason? Overwork, Nanny. Overwork. On my feet from morning till night. Don't know the meaning of rest. And at night I lie awake under the bedclothes in constant fear of being dragged out to a patient. Haven't had a single free day ever since I've known you. I couldn't help growing old, could I? And, besides, life here is dull, stupid, sordid. . . . This sort of life wears you down. You're surrounded by cranks—cranks, all of them. Spend two or three years with them and gradually, without noticing it, you become a crank yourself. It's inevitable—sure as fate. [*Twisting his long mustache.*] Just look at this enormous mustache I've grown. An idiotic mustache. I've become a crank, Nanny. . . . Haven't grown stupid yet, thank God, there's nothing wrong with my brains, but my feelings have, I'm afraid, grown numb. I want nothing, I need nothing, there's no one I'm fond of—except, perhaps, you, Nanny. [*Kisses her on the head.*] I had a nurse like you when I was a little boy.

Marina. You wouldn't like something to eat, would you?

Astrov. No, thank you. In the third week in Lent I went to Malitskoye. There was an epidemic there. Spotted fever. In the cottages people were lying side by side on the floor. . . . Filth, stench, smoke. . . . Calves, too, lying about on the floor, among the sick. And pigs. Spent a whole day there looking after the patients without sitting down and without a bite of food, and when I got back home, they wouldn't let me rest. Brought a signalman from the railway. I got him on the table and was about to operate on him when damned if he didn't go and die on me under the chloroform. It was then, when I didn't want them, that my feelings awakened and my conscience pricked me, as though I had killed him on purpose. . . . I sat down, closed my eyes like this and thought to myself: will those who will be living a hundred or two hundred years after us spare a thought for us who are now blazing a trail for them? Will they have a good word to say for us? No, Nanny, they won't, they won't!

Marina. Men won't, but God will.

Astrov. Thank you, Nanny. You spoke well.

VOYNITSKY *enters.*

Voynitsky [comes out of the house; he has had a nap after lunch and looks rumpled; sits down on a bench and straightens his fashionable tie]. Yes. . . . *[A pause.]* Yes. . . .

Astrov. Had a good sleep?

Voynitsky. Yes—very. *[Yawns.]* Ever since the professor and his wife have come to live with us, our life has been turned upside down. . . . I go to sleep at the wrong time, at lunch and dinner I eat all sorts of fancy concoctions, drink wine—all this can't be good for me! Before I hadn't a free minute to myself. Sonia and I worked like Trojans, but now only Sonia works, while I sleep, eat and drink—it's too bad!

Marina [shaking her head]. Shameful's what I call it! The professor gets up at twelve o'clock, and the samovar's kept on the boil all morning waiting for him. Before they came, we used to have dinner at one o'clock, like everybody else, but now we're having it at about seven. The professor spends the night reading and writing and all of a sudden at two in the morning he rings his bell. Why, what is it? Tea, if you please! Wake the servants for him. Put on the samovar. Shameful—that's what it is!

Astrov. And are they going to stay here long?

Voynitsky [whistles]. A hundred years. The professor has decided to stay here for good.

Marina. Same thing now. The samovar has been on the table for the last two hours, and they've gone for a walk.

Voynitsky. They're coming, they're coming. Keep calm, Nanny.

Voices are heard; from the far end of the garden, returning from their walk, enter SEREBRYAKOV, YELENA, SONIA *and* TELEGIN.

Serebryakov. Excellent, excellent. . . . Wonderful scenery.

Telegin. Remarkable, sir.

Sonia. We'll go to the plantation tomorrow, Father. Would you like to?

Voynitsky. Let's have tea, ladies and gentlemen.

Serebryakov. My friends, be so kind as to send my tea up to my study. I've still some work to do today.

Sonia. I'm sure you'll like the plantation, Father.

YELENA, SEREBRYAKOV *and* SONIA *go into the house;* TELE-
GIN *goes up to the table and sits down beside* MARINA.

Voynitsky. It's hot, close, and our eminent scholar
walks about in an overcoat and galoshes, wearing gloves
and carrying an umbrella.

Astrov. Which shows that he takes good care of himself.

Voynitsky. But how lovely she is, how lovely! I've never
seen a more beautiful woman in my life.

Telegin [*to* MARINA]. Whether I drive through the
fields or take a walk in the shade of the trees in the garden
or look on this table, I experience a feeling of indescrib-
able bliss! The weather is enchanting, the birds are singing,
we all live in peace and harmony—what more do we want?
[*Accepting a glass from* MARINA.] I'm infinitely obliged to
you!

Voynitsky [*dreamily*]. Her eyes. . . . A wonderful
woman!

Astrov. Tell us something.

Voynitsky [*phlegmatically*]. What do you want me to
tell you?

Astrov. Is there nothing new at all?

Voynitsky. Nothing. Everything's old. I'm the same
as I was. Grown worse, I daresay, for I've grown lazy, do
nothing, just grumble like an old fogey. My mother, the
old crow, still goes about croaking about women's emanci-
pation. She's got one foot in the grave, but she's still looking in her clever books for the dawn of a new life.

Astrov. And the professor?

Voynitsky. The professor, as always, spends all his time
from morning till late at night in his study—writing.
"Racking his wits, with furrowed brow, odes, odes, odes we
write, without one word of praise for them or us, our
labor to requite." Pity the poor paper! He'd much better
write his autobiography. What a wonderful subject! A retired professor, you understand, an old dry-as-dust, a
learned minnow. . . . Gout, rheumatism, migraine. Got
himself an enlarged liver from jealousy and envy. . . .
This minnow lives on the estate of his first wife. Lives
there against his will, for he can't afford to live in the town.
Always complaining of his hard luck, though as a matter
of fact he's damned lucky. [*Nervously.*] Just think how

lucky he is! The son of an ordinary sacristan, a divinity student, he obtained all sorts of degrees and was given a chair at a university. Now he is the son-in-law of a senator, and so on, and so on. All that is not important, though. What is important is this: the man has been lecturing and writing about art for exactly twenty-five years and yet he doesn't know a thing about art. For twenty-five years he's been chewing over other men's ideas about realism, naturalism and all sorts of other nonsense. For twenty-five years he has been lecturing and writing on things intelligent people have known about for ages and stupid people aren't interested in, anyway. Which means that for twenty-five years he's been wasting his time. And yet the self-conceit of the man! What pretensions! He has retired, and not a living soul knows or cares about him. He's totally unknown, which means that for twenty-five years he's been doing somebody else out of a job. But look at him: struts about like a demigod!

Astrov. You're jealous!

Voynitsky. Yes, I'm jealous! And the success he has with women. No Don Juan has ever known such amazing success! His first wife, my sister, a sweet, gentle creature, pure as this blue sky, noble, generous, a woman who had had more admirers than he has had students, loved him as only pure angels can love beings as pure and beautiful as themselves. My mother, his mother-in-law, dotes on him to this day, and he still inspires a feeling of reverential awe in her. His second wife, a beautiful, clever woman— you've just seen her—married him when he was already an old man. She sacrificed her youth, her beauty, her freedom, her brilliance to him. Whatever for? Why?

Astrov. Is she faithful to the professor?

Voynitsky. Unfortunately, yes.

Astrov. Why unfortunately?

Voynitsky. Because that loyalty of hers is false from the beginning to end. There's a lot of fine sentiments in it, but no logic. To be unfaithful to an old husband whose company is insufferable—that is immoral. But to try to stifle your unhappy youth and your natural feelings—that's not immoral. . . .

Telegin [*in a tearful voice*]. Vanya, I don't like to

hear you talk like that. Really, you know, anyone who be-
trays a wife or husband is a person you cannot trust, a
person who might betray his country, too!

Voynitsky [*with vexation*]. Dry up, Waffles!

Telegin. No, listen, Vanya. My wife ran away from me
with her lover the day after our wedding because of my
unprepossessing appearance. I never swerved from my
duty after that. I still love her and I'm still faithful to her.
I do all I can to help her. I gave her all I had for the
education of her children by the man she loved. My happiness may have been ruined, but I've still got my pride.
And what about her? She's no longer young, under the
influence of the laws of nature her beauty has faded, the
man she loved is dead. . . . What has she got left?

Enter SONIA *and* YELENA: *a little later enter* MARIA VOY-
NITSKY *with a book; she sits down and reads; she is given
tea and she drinks it without raising her head.*

Sonia [*hurriedly to nurse*]. Some peasants have come,
Nanny. Please, go and talk to them. I'll see to the tea
myself. [*Pours out the tea.*]

The nurse goes out. YELENA *takes her cup of tea and
drinks, sitting on the swing.*

Astrov [to YELENA]. I've really come to see your husband.
You wrote to me that he was very ill—rheumatism and
something else, but it seems there's nothing the matter
with him at all.

Yelena. He felt very depressed last night. Complained
of pains in his legs. But today he's quite all right.

Astrov. And I've galloped like mad for twenty miles!
Oh, well, never mind. It's not the first time. I can stay
with you now till tomorrow and at least have a good night's
sleep.

Sonia. Yes, do. It's not often you stay the night with us.
I don't expect you've had dinner, have you?

Astrov. No, as a matter of fact I haven't.

Sonia. Well, in that case you will have some dinner,
too. We dine at about seven now. [*Drinks.*] The tea's cold!

Telegin. I'm afraid the temperature has dropped con-
siderably in the samovar.

Yelena. Never mind, Ivan Ivanych, we'll drink it cold.

Telegin. Beg your pardon, ma'am, but I'm not Ivan Ivanych. I'm Ilya Ilyich—er—Ilya Ilyich Telegin, ma'am, or just Waffles, as some people call me because of my pock-marked face. I stood godfather to Sonia, and your husband knows me very well. I live here now, ma'am, on your estate. I expect—er—the fact that I dine with you every day has not escaped your notice.

Sonia. Mr. Telegin is our assistant, our right-hand man. [*Tenderly.*] Won't you have another cup, dear godfather?

Maria. Good heavens!

Sonia. What's the matter, Granny?

Maria. I forgot to tell Alexander. . . . I'm afraid it must have slipped my memory. . . . I had a letter from Kharkov today—from Pavel Alexandrovich. He's sent me his new pamphlet.

Astrov. Interesting?

Maria. Yes, but rather peculiar. He flatly contradicts everything he defended seven years ago. This is terrible!

Voynitsky. There's nothing terrible about it. Drink your tea, Mother.

Maria. But I want to talk!

Voynitsky. You've been talking for fifty years, talking and reading pamphlets. Time you put a stop to it.

Maria. I don't know why you always seem to find my conversation disagreeable. I'm sorry, Jean, but you've changed so much during the last year that I simply cannot recognize you. You used to be a man of definite convictions, a man of enlightened views. . . .

Voynitsky. Oh yes, to be sure! I was a man of enlightened views which did not enlighten anyone. . . . [*Pause.*] A man of enlightened views! What a cruel joke! I'm forty-seven now. Till a year ago I did my best to hoodwink myself with that pedantic stuff of yours so as not to see what real life was like. And I thought I was doing the right thing! And now, if you only knew! I can't sleep at night, so vexed, so furious am I with myself for having so stupidly frittered away my time when I could have had everything that my age now denies me!

Sonia. Uncle Vanya, this is boring!

Maria [*to her son*]. You seem to be putting all the blame for something on your former convictions. But it is not they that are at fault but yourself. You seem to forget that convictions are nothing by themselves, a dead letter. You should have been doing some real work.

Voynitsky. Some real work? Not everyone has the ability to be some sort of scribbling *perpetuum mobile* like that Herr Professor of yours.

Maria. What are you suggesting by that, pray?

Sonia [*imploringly*]. Granny, Uncle Vanya, please!

Voynitsky. All right, all right. I'll shut up and apologize.

Pause.

Yelena. It's such a lovely day today. . . . Not too hot. . . .

Voynitsky. A lovely day to hang oneself. . . .

TELEGIN *tunes his guitar.* MARINA *walks near the house, calling a hen.*

Marina. Chuck-chuck-chuck. . . .

Sonia. What did the peasants come for, Nanny?

Marina. Oh, always the same thing. About the wasteland again. Chuck-chuck-chuck. . . .

Sonia. Which one are you calling?

Marina. Old Speckly has gone off with her chicks. . . . The crows might get them. . . . [*Goes out.*]

TELEGIN *plays a polka; they all listen in silence; enter a* LABORER.

Laborer. Is the doctor here? [*To* ASTROV.] If you please, sir, they've sent for you.

Astrov. Where from?

Laborer. From the factory.

Astrov [*with vexation*]. Thank you very much. Well, I suppose I'd better go. [*Looks around for his cap.*] A pity, though, damn it.

Sonia. What a shame you have to go. Do come back to dinner from the factory.

Astrov. Afraid it'll be too late. Yes, afraid so. . . . Afraid so. . . . [*To the* LABORER.] Look here, be a good chap and fetch me a glass of vodka. [*The* LABORER *goes out.*] Afraid so. . . . Afraid so. . . . [*Finds his cap.*] There's a character in one of Ostrovsky's plays who has a big mustache but little wit. . . . Well, that's me. Oh,

well, good-by, ladies and gentlemen. [*To* YELENA.] If you
care to look me up sometimes with Sonia, I'd be delighted
to see you. I have a little estate of about eighty acres, but,
if you're interested, there's a model orchard and nursery
such as you wouldn't find within a thousand miles. Next to
my estate is the government plantation. The forester there
is old and always ill, so it's I who have really to look
after things there.

Yelena. I've been told already that you make a hobby
of forestry. I suppose it could be of the greatest use, but
don't you think it interferes with your real work? After all,
you're a doctor.

Astrov. God alone knows what our real work is.

Yelena. Do you find it interesting?

Astrov. Yes, it's interesting work.

Voynitsky [*ironically*]. Very!

Yelena [*to* ASTROV]. You're still a young man. You
don't look more than—well, thirty-six or thirty-seven and
—I don't suppose it's really as interesting as you say.
Nothing but trees and trees. Must be awfully monotonous,
I should think.

Sonia. Oh no, it's extremely interesting. Dr. Astrov is
planting new forests every year and already he's been
awarded a bronze medal and a diploma. He does his best to
prevent the destruction of the old forests. If you listen to
him, you'll agree with him entirely. He says forests adorn
the earth, teach man to understand the beautiful and instill
in him a lofty attitude of mind. Forests temper the sever-
ity of the climate. In countries with a mild climate less
energy is spent in the struggle with nature and that is why
men there are beautiful, supple, more sensitive, their
speech refined and their movements graceful. Art and learning flourish there. Their outlook on life is not so gloomy
and their attitude to women is full of exquisite refine-
ment. . . .

Voynitsky [*laughing*]. Bravo, bravo! All this is charming
but hardly convincing, so that [*to* ASTROV] allow me, my
friend, to go on stoking my stoves with logs and building
my barns of wood.

Astrov. You can stoke your stoves with peat and build
your barns of brick. Well, all right, cut down the woods, if

you have to, but why destroy them? The Russian forests echo with the sound of the ax, millions of trees are perishing, the homes of wild animals and birds are being laid waste, the rivers are growing shallow and running dry, exquisite scenery is disappearing forever, and all because men are too lazy and too stupid to bend down and pick up their fuel from the ground. [*To* YELENA.] Isn't that so, Madam? One has to be a reckless barbarian to burn this beauty in one's stove, to destroy what we cannot create. Man has been endowed with reason and creative powers to increase what has been given him, but so far he has not created but destroyed. There are fewer and fewer forests, the rivers are drying up, the game birds are becoming extinct, the climate is ruined, and every day the earth is becoming poorer and more hideous. [*To* VOYNITSKY.] Here you're looking at me ironically and you don't think that what I am telling you is serious—and perhaps I really am a crank, but when I walk past the peasants' woods I saved from the ax, or when I hear a young wood planted with my own hands rustling over my head, I realize that the climate is to some extent in my power and that if in a thousand years men are happy and contented I shall have done my bit toward it. When I plant a birch tree and then see its green branches swaying in the wind, I cannot help feeling proud and thrilled with the thought that I— [*Seeing the* LABORER, *who has brought a glass of vodka on a tray.*] However—[*drinks*] it's time I was going. All that is, I suppose, just the talk of a crank when all is said and done. Good-by! [*Goes toward the house.*]

Sonia [*takes his arm and goes with him*]. When are you coming again?

Astrov. Don't know.

Sonia. Not for another month again?

ASTROV *and* SONIA *go into the house;* MARIA *and* TELEGIN *remain sitting at the table;* YELENA *and* VOYNITSKY *go toward the veranda.*

Yelena. And you, Vanya, have again been behaving disgracefully. What did you want to irritate your mother for with your talk about the *perpetuum mobile?* And at lunch today you quarreled with Alexander again. All this is so petty!

Voynitsky. But if I hate him!

Yelena. There's no reason why you should hate Alexander. He's just like everybody else. No worse than you.

Voynitsky. Oh, if you could only see your face, your movements! You're too lazy to be alive! Too lazy!

Yelena. Oh, dear, lazy and bored! Everyone's abusing my husband, everyone looks at me with compassion: poor woman, she has an old husband! This tender concern for me—oh, how well I understand it! As Astrov said just now: you're all recklessly destroying the forests and soon there will be nothing left on the earth. And in the same way you're recklessly destroying human beings and, thanks to you, there will be no more loyalty, no more purity, nor any capacity for self-sacrifice. Why can't you ever look with indifference at a woman if she doesn't happen to belong to you? Why? Because—again the doctor is right—there's a devil of destruction in all of you. You don't care what happens to the forests, nor to the birds, nor to women, nor to one another. . . .

Voynitsky. I don't like this sort of talk! [*Pause.*]

Yelena. That doctor has a tired, sensitive face. An interesting face. Sonia quite obviously finds him attractive. She's in love with him, and I quite understand her. This is the third time he's been here since we arrived, but I feel shy with him and I have never really been nice to him or spoken to him as I should have liked. He must think I'm a detestable creature. I expect the reason why we are such good friends is that we are both such tiresome, such dull people! Tiresome! Don't look at me like that! I don't like it!

Voynitsky. How else can I look at you if I love you? You're my happiness, my life, my youth! I know the chances that you should return my feeling are nil, but I'm not asking for anything. All I want is to be allowed to look at you, to listen to your voice. . . .

Yelena. Shh. . . . They might hear you! [*Goes toward the house.*]

Voynitsky [*following her*]. Let me talk to you of my love. Don't drive me away. That alone will make me the happiest man on earth. . . .

Yelena. This has gone far enough! [*Both go into the house.*]

TELEGIN *strikes a chord on the guitar and plays a polka;* MARIA *writes something on the margin of the pamphlet.*

Curtain.

ACT TWO

A *dining room in* SEREBRYAKOV's *house. Night. The* WATCHMAN *can be heard knocking in the garden.*

SEREBRYAKOV *is sitting in an armchair before an open window, dozing.* YELENA *is sitting beside him, also dozing.*

Serebryakov [*waking*]. Who's there? You, Sonia?

Yelena. It's me.

Serebryakov. You, darling. . . . Oh, what excruciating pain!

Yelena. Your rug has fallen on the floor. [*Wraps the rug around his legs.*] I think I'd better close the window, Alexander.

Serebryakov. No, don't. I can't breathe. I dropped off just now and I dreamed that my left leg did not belong to me. I was awakened by the frightful pain. No, it's not gout. More likely rheumatism. What's the time?

Yelena. Twenty past twelve. [*Pause.*]

Serebryakov. Please find Batyushkov for me in the library in the morning. I believe we've got his works.

Yelena. I'm sorry, what did you say?

Serebryakov. See if you can find Batyushkov for me in the morning. I seem to remember we had his works. But why can't I breathe?

Yelena. You're tired. You haven't slept for two nights.

Serebryakov. I've been told Turgenev got angina pectoris from gout. I'm afraid I may get it, too. This damnable, disgusting old age! The devil take it. Ever since I've become ill, I've become disgusting to myself. And I shouldn't be in the least surprised if you all find me repugnant.

Yelena. You talk of your old age as though it were our fault that you are old.

Serebryakov. You most of all, I expect, must find me odious.

YELENA *gets up and sits down farther away.*

Serebryakov. And you're quite right, of course. I'm not a fool and I understand. You're a young, healthy, beautiful woman. You want to live. And I'm an old man, practically a corpse. Isn't that so? Don't I realize it? And, of course, it's stupid of me to go on living. But wait, I shall soon set you all free. I shan't last much longer.

Yelena. I can't stand it any more. For God's sake, be quiet.

Serebryakov. What it comes to is that, thanks to me, everyone is worn out, bored, wasting their youth, and only I am satisfied and enjoying life. Why, of course!

Yelena. Do be quiet! You've exhausted me!

Serebryakov. I've exhausted everyone. Of course.

Yelena [*through tears*]. It's unbearable! Tell me, what do you want of me?

Serebryakov. Nothing.

Yelena. Well, in that case be quiet. I beg you.

Serebryakov. It's a funny thing but every time Ivan or that old idiot Maria starts talking, no one objects, everyone listens. But I've only to open my mouth and everyone begins to feel miserable. Even my voice disgusts them. Well, suppose I am disgusting, suppose I am an egoist, a despot, but haven't I got some right to be an egoist even in my old age? Haven't I earned it? Haven't I the right, I ask, to enjoy a quiet old age, to be treated with consideration by the people around me?

Yelena. No one's disputing your rights. [*The window bangs in the wind.*] The wind is rising. I'd better close the window. [*Closes window.*] It's going to rain soon. No one disputes your rights.

A pause; the watchman in the garden knocks and sings.

Serebryakov. All my life I've worked in the interests of learning, I got used to my study, my lecture room, my colleagues, and now I find myself buried alive in this tomb and every day I'm obliged to see stupid people and listen

to their absurd talk. I want to live! I like success, I like
fame, I like people to talk about me, and here—why, it's
like living in exile! Every minute to be grieving for the
past, watching others making a name for themselves, being
afraid of death. . . . I can't put up with it! I haven't the
strength. And here they won't even forgive me for being
old!

Enter SONIA.

Sonia. You told me to send for Dr. Astrov yourself,
Father, and now that he's here you won't see him. It's
not nice. We seem to have troubled him for nothing.

Serebryakov. What good is your Astrov to me? He
knows as much about medicine as I do about astronomy.

Sonia. You don't want us to send for the whole medical
faculty for your gout, do you?

Serebryakov. I refuse even to talk to that crazy fellow.

Sonia. Just as you like. [*Sits down.*] I don't care.

Serebryakov. What's the time?

Yelena. Nearly one o'clock.

Serebryakov. I can't breathe. . . . Sonia, fetch me the
drops from the table!

Sonia. Here you are. [*Gives him the drops.*]

Serebryakov [*irritably*]. Good Lord, not those! You can't
ask anyone for anything!

Sonia. Kindly keep your temper. Some people may put
up with it, but I won't. So spare me, for goodness sake. I
haven't the time, either. I have to get up early in the
morning. We are haymaking.

Enter VOYNITSKY *in dressing gown with a candle.*

Voynitsky. There's going to be a storm. [*Lightning.*]
Dear me, what a flash! Helen, Sonia, go to bed. I've come
to take your place.

Serebryakov [*frightened*]. No, no! Don't leave him with
me. He'll talk me to death!

Voynitsky. But you must let them have some rest! It's
the second night they've had no sleep.

Serebryakov. Let them go to bed, but you go, too.
Thank you. I implore you. In the name of our past friendship don't raise any objections. We'll talk another time.

Voynitsky [*with a grin*]. Our past friendship. . . . Past—

Sonia. Do be quiet, Uncle Vanya.

Serebryakov [*to his wife*]. Darling, don't leave me alone with him! He'll talk me to death.

Voynitsky. This is really becoming absurd.

Enter MARINA *with a candle.*

Sonia. Why don't you go to bed, Nanny? It's late.

Marina. I can't very well go to bed while the samovar's still on the table, can I?

Serebryakov. No one's asleep, everyone's exhausted, I'm the only one to have a hell of a good time.

Marina [*goes up to* SEREBRYAKOV, *tenderly*]. What's the matter, sir? Does it hurt very badly? I've a gnawing pain in my legs, too, it keeps on gnawing something terrible. [*Puts his rug right.*] You've had this trouble for a long time, sir. I remember Sonia's mother sitting up night after night with you. She took it so much to heart, poor dear. Aye, she was very fond of you, she was. [*Pause.*] The old are just like children. They want someone to be sorry for them. But no one ever cares for the old. [*Kisses* SEREBRYAKOV *on the shoulder.*] Come along, sir, come along to bed. . . . Come along, love. I'll give you some lime tea and warm your poor legs. . . . Say a prayer for you, I will. . . .

Serebryakov [*deeply touched*]. Let's go, Marina.

Marina. I've a gnawing pain in my legs, too, sir. Keeps on gnawing something terrible. [*Leads him away together with* SONIA.] Sonia's mother used to worry over you so much, poor dear. Cried her heart out, she did. You were only a silly little girl then, Sonia. . . . Come along, sir, come along. . . .

SEREBRYAKOV, SONIA *and* MARINA *go out.*

Yelena. I'm absolutely worn out with him. I can hardly stand on my feet.

Voynitsky. You with him and I with myself. This is the third night I've had no sleep.

Yelena. There's something the matter with this house. Your mother hates everything except her pamphlets and the professor. The professor is in a state of exasperation: he doesn't trust me and he's afraid of you. Sonia is angry with her father, angry with me, and hasn't spoken to me for a fortnight. You hate my husband and don't conceal your contempt for your mother. I am exasperated and was about to burst into tears a dozen times today. . . . There's something the matter with this house.

Voynitsky. Let's drop this silly talk!

Yelena. You, Vanya, are an educated and intelligent person, and I should have thought you ought to understand that the world is not being destroyed by bandits and by fires, but by hatred, enmity and all these petty squabblings. You ought to stop grumbling and try to reconcile everyone.

Voynitsky. Reconcile me to myself first! Oh, my dear— [*Presses his lips to her hand.*]

Yelena. Don't do that! [*Takes her hand away.*] Go away!

Voynitsky. The rain will be over in a moment, and everything in nature will be refreshed and breathe freely. I alone will not be refreshed by the storm. Day and night the thought that my life has been hopelessly wasted weighs upon me like a nightmare. I have no past. It has been stupidly wasted on trifles. And the present frightens me by its senselessness. That's what my life and my love are like: what on earth am I to do with them? My whole inner life is being wasted to no purpose, like a ray of sunshine in a pit, and I'm running to waste, too.

Yelena. When you talk to me about your love it somehow makes me go all dead inside and I don't know what to say. I'm sorry, but I've nothing to say to you. [*Is about to go out.*] Good night.

Voynitsky [*barring her way*]. Oh, if you knew how miserable I am at the thought that by my side in this very house another life is being wasted—yours! What is it you're waiting for? What damned reason prevents you from doing something? Understand, do understand—

Yelena [*looks at him intently*]. Vanya, you're drunk!

Voynitsky. Possibly, possibly. . . .

Yelena. Where's the doctor?

Voynitsky. He's in there. He's staying the night with me. Possibly, possibly—everything is possible!

Yelena. Have you been drinking today again? Why do you do it?

Voynitsky. At least it's something like life. Don't stop me, Helen.

Yelena. You never used to drink before and you never used to talk so much before. Go to bed! You bore me.

Voynitsky [*presses his lips to her hand*]. My darling—my wonderful one!

Yelena [*with vexation*]. Leave me alone, please. This really is the end! [*Goes out.*]

Voynitsky [*alone*]. She's gone. . . . [*Pause.*] Ten years ago I used to meet her at my sister's. She was seventeen then and I—thirty-seven. Why didn't I fall in love with her then and propose to her? I could have married her easily! And now she would have been my wife. . . . Yes. . . . Now we should have both been awakened by the storm. She'd have been frightened by the thunder, and I'd have held her in my arms and whispered: "Don't be afraid, darling, I'm here." Oh, what wonderful thoughts! I can't help laughing, so happy do they make me feel. Oh, dear, I'm getting all confused. . . . Why am I old? Why doesn't she understand me? Her fine phrases, her lazy morals, her absurd, her lazy ideas about the ruin of the world—oh, I hate it all so much! [*Pause.*] Oh, how I've been cheated! I adored that professor, that miserable, gouty nonentity; I worked for him like a horse. Sonia and I squeezed the last penny out of the estate. Like greedy peasants we haggled over linseed oil, pease, curds, half starving ourselves to save up every farthing and send him thousands of rubles. I was proud of him and his learning. He was everything in the world to me! Everything he wrote, every word he uttered, seemed the highest achievement of genius to me. . . . Good God, and now? Now he has retired and now one can see what his life's work amounts to. He won't leave behind a single worth-while page; he is a mere cipher—a soap bubble! And I have been cheated. I can see it now. Stupidly cheated. . . .

Enter ASTROV, *without waistcoat and tie; he is tipsy; he is followed by* TELEGIN *with the guitar.*

Astrov. Play!

Telegin. But everyone's asleep.

Astrov. Play, damn you!

TELEGIN *begins playing softly.*

Astrov [*to* VOYNITSKY]. All alone? No ladies? [*Arms akimbo, sings softly.*] "Dance cottage, dance stove, dance bed, I've nowhere where to lay my head. . . ." You see, the storm woke me. Lovely drop of rain. What's the time?

Voynitsky. Hanged if I know.

Astrov. I thought I heard Helen's voice.

Voynitsky. She was here a minute ago.

Astrov. A gorgeous woman. [*Examines bottles on table.*] Medicines. Good Lord, look at these prescriptions! From Kharkov, from Moscow, from Tula. . . . Every town must be sick and tired of his gout. Is he ill or is he shamming?

Voynitsky. He's ill. [*Pause.*]

Astrov. Why are you so down in the mouth today? Not sorry for the professor, are you?

Voynitsky. Leave me alone.

Astrov. Or can it be that you're in love with the professor's wife?

Voynitsky. She's my friend.

Astrov. Already?

Voynitsky. What do you mean—already?

Astrov. A woman can be a man's friend in the following sequence: first a good companion, then a mistress, and only then a friend.

Voynitsky. What a vulgar idea!

Astrov. Oh? Well, yes, I admit I'm growing vulgar. Besides, as you see, I'm drunk, too. As a rule, I get drunk like this once a month. When in this condition, I become as brazen and insolent as you please. I don't care a damn for anything then. I don't hesitate to do the most difficult operations and I do them beautifully. I make the most ambitious plans for the future. At such a time I do not think of myself as a crank and I believe that I'm being of enormous service to humanity—enormous! At such a time, too, I have my own special philosophic system, and all of you, my friends, seem to me such teeny-weeny insects— such microbes. [*To* TELEGIN.] Play, Waffles!

Telegin. My dear chap, I'd be only too glad to play for you, but please understand—everyone's asleep!

Astrov. Play, damn you!

TELEGIN *plays softly.*

Astrov. We really must have a drink. Come along, we've still got some brandy left. And as soon as it's daylight we'll go to my place. All right? [*Seeing* SONIA *entering.*] Excuse me, I have no tie on. [*Goes out quickly;* TELEGIN *follows after him.*]

Sonia. And you have again got drunk with the doctor, Uncle Vanya. Birds of a feather. Thick as thieves. Oh, well, he's always like that, but what made you do it? At your age it certainly doesn't suit you.

Voynitsky. Age has nothing to do with it. When there's no real life, one has to live on illusions. It's better than nothing, anyway.

Sonia. The hay is all cut, it rains every day, it's all rotting, and you're amusing yourself with illusions. You don't care about the estate at all any more. I'm the only one who does any work here, and I'm all done up. [*Alarmed.*] Uncle, you have tears in your eyes.

Voynitsky. Tears? Not at all—nonsense. You looked at me just now as your mother used to do. My dear! [*Kisses her hands and face.*] My sister, my dear, dear sister. . . . Where is she now? Oh, if she knew! If only she knew!

Sonia. What? Knew what, Uncle?

Voynitsky. Oh, I feel so miserable—so unhappy. . . . Never mind. . . . Later. . . . I'm going. . . . [*Goes out.*]

Sonia [*knocks on the door*]. Doctor, you're not asleep, are you? Please, come out for a minute!

Astrov [*behind the door*]. One moment! [*A minute later comes out with waistcoat and tie on.*] What can I do for you?

Sonia. You can drink yourself, if you don't think it's disgusting, but please don't let my uncle drink. It's bad for him.

Astrov. All right. We won't drink any more. [*Pause.*] Not a drop. I'm going home now. By the time the horses are harnessed it will be daylight.

Sonia. It's raining. Wait till morning.

Astrov. The storm is passing over, we shall get only the tail end of it. I'm going. And please don't send for me to see your father again. I tell him it's gout, and he tells me it's rheumatism. I ask him to stay in bed, and he will sit in a chair. And today he refused to talk to me at all.

Sonia. He's spoiled. [*Looks in the sideboard.*] Won't you have something to eat?

Astrov. Thank you, I think I will.

Sonia. I like to have a bite of something at night. I think we shall find something here. They say Father has been a great favorite with the ladies and they've spoiled him. Here, have some cheese. [*Both of them stand at the sideboard and eat.*]

Astrov. I've had nothing to eat today. I've only been drinking. Your father is a very difficult man. [*Takes a bottle from the sideboard.*] May I? There's no one here, so I can speak frankly. You know, I don't think I'd survive a month in your house. The atmosphere would stifle me. Your father can think of nothing but his gout and his books, Uncle Vanya with his depressions, your grandmother and, last but not least, your stepmother. . . .

Sonia. What's wrong with my stepmother?

Astrov. In a human being everything ought to be beautiful: face, dress, soul, thoughts. She is very beautiful, there's no denying it, but—all she does is eat, sleep, go for walks, fascinate us all by her beauty and—nothing more. She has no duties. Other people work for her. Isn't that so? And an idle life cannot be pure. [*Pause.*] However, I may be too hard on her. Like your Uncle Vanya, I'm dissatisfied with life, and both of us have become a pair of old grumblers.

Sonia. Are *you* dissatisfied with life?

Astrov. I love life in general, but I simply can't stand our Russian provincial, philistine life. I have the utmost contempt for it. And as for my own personal life, I wish to goodness I could say there was something good in it. But there's absolutely nothing. You know, if there's only one glimmer of light in the distance as you walk through the woods on a dark night, you don't notice your weariness, nor the darkness, nor the thorns and twigs that strike

your face as you pass. . . . I work harder than anyone
in our district, fate is forever hitting out at me and sometimes I suffer unbearably, but there's no light gleaming in
the distance for me. I don't expect anything for myself
any more. I dislike people and it's years since I cared for
anyone.

Sonia. Not for anyone?

Astrov. No, not for anyone. I feel a certain affection only
for your old nurse—for old times' sake. There doesn't
seem to be much to distinguish one peasant from another.
They're all undeveloped, and they all live in squalor; and
I find it difficult to get on with our educated people. They
make me tired. Our dear old friends all have petty minds
and petty feelings, and they don't see further than their
noses. In fact, they are simply stupid. And those who are
bigger and more intelligent are hysterical, given to self-
analysis and morbid introspection. They whine, hate and
slander each other, sidle up to a man, look at him askance
and decide: "He has a bee in his bonnet!" or "He's a
windbag!" And when they don't know what label to
stick on me, they say: "He's a queer fellow, a queer one!"
I like forests—that's queer; I don't eat meat, that's queer,
too. They no longer have a spontaneous, pure and objective
attitude to nature or to men. . . . None whatever! [*Is
about to drink.*]

Sonia [*prevents him*]. Don't, please. I beg you. Don't
drink any more.

Astrov. Why not?

Sonia. Because you're not that kind of man. You have
such natural good manners, such a nice, gentle voice, and
—and more than that. You're unlike anyone I know: you
are—the salt of the earth! Why do you want to be like
ordinary people who drink and play cards? Oh, please,
don't do it, I beseech you! You keep on saying that people
do not create but only destroy what Heaven has given
them. Then why do you destroy yourself? You mustn't,
you mustn't—I beseech you, I beg you!

Astrov [*holds out his hand to her*]. I won't drink any
more.

Sonia. Give me your word.

Astrov. My word of honor.

Sonia. [presses his hand warmly]. Thank you!

Astrov. No more! I've come to my senses. You see I'm quite sober now and I shall remain sober to the end of my days. [*Looks at his watch.*] And so, let's continue. I say: my time is over, it's too late for me. . . . I've grown old, I've worked too hard, I've become vulgar, all my feelings have become blunted, and I don't think I could form an attachment to anyone any more. I don't love anyone and I don't think I shall ever love anyone. The only thing that still continues to exercise the strongest possible appeal on me is beauty. I just can't remain indifferent to it. I can't help feeling that if, for example, Helen wanted to, she could turn my head in one day. . . . But then that's not love. That's not affection. [*Covers his eyes with his hands and shudders.*]

Sonia. What's the matter?

Astrov. Oh, nothing. . . . In Lent one of my patients died under chloroform.

Sonia. It's time you forgot about it. [*Pause.*] Tell me, if—if I had a friend or a younger sister and if you were to discover that—well, that she had fallen in love with you, what would your reaction be to that?

Astrov [shrugging]. Don't know. I'd give her to understand that I couldn't care for her and—er—that I had other things on my mind. Well, if I am to go, I must go now. Good-by, my dear child, or we shall not finish till morning. [*Presses her hand.*] I'll go through the drawing room, if I may, or I'm afraid your uncle will detain me. [*Goes out.*]

Sonia [alone]. He has said nothing to me. . . . His heart and his mind are still hidden from me, but why do I feel so happy? [*Laughs happily.*] I told him: you're fine, you're noble, you have such a gentle voice. . . . Shouldn't I have said that? His voice trembles, it is so caressing. . . . I—I can still almost feel it in the air. But when I spoke to him about a younger sister, he didn't understand. . . . [*Wringing her hands.*] Oh, how awful it is not to be beautiful! How awful! And I know that I'm not beautiful. I know. I know. Last Sunday, when people were coming out of church, I heard them talking about me, and one woman said: "She's such a good and generous girl, but what a pity she is so plain." So plain. . . .

Enter YELENA.

Yelena [*opens the window*]. The storm is over. What sweet air! [*Pause.*] Where's the doctor?

Sonia. Gone. [*Pause.*]

Yelena. Sophia!

Sonia. Yes?

Yelena. How long are you going to be cross with me? We've done one another no harm. Why should we be enemies? Don't you think it's time we made it up?

Sonia. Oh, I've been wishing it myself. . . . [*Embraces her.*] Don't let's be cross ever again.

Yelena. That's different. [*Both are agitated.*]

Sonia. Has Father gone to bed?

Yelena. No, he's sitting in the drawing room. . . . You and I haven't been speaking to one another for weeks and goodness only knows why. . . . [*Seeing that the sideboard is open.*] What's this?

Sonia. The doctor has had something to eat.

Yelena. And there's wine, too. Come, let's drink to our friendship.

Sonia. Yes, let's.

Yelena. Out of one glass. . . . [*Fills it.*] That's better. Well, so now we're friends?

Sonia. Yes. [*They drink and kiss each other.*] I've been wanting to make it up with you for so long, but I felt ashamed, somehow. [*Cries.*]

Yelena. So what are you crying for?

Sonia. Oh, nothing. I—I can't help it.

Yelena. There, there. . . . [*Cries.*] Oh, dear, I'm so silly, I'm crying too. [*Pause.*] You're angry with me because you think I married your father for selfish reasons. But please believe me, I swear I married him for love. I fell in love with him because he was such a famous man. It was not real love. It was all so insincere, so artificial, but, you see, it seemed real to me at the time. It's not my fault. And since our marriage you have never stopped accusing me with those clever, suspicious eyes of yours.

Sonia. Well, we've made it up now, so let's forget it.

Yelena. You mustn't look at people like that—it's not at all like you. One must trust people, or life becomes impossible. [*Pause.*]

Sonia. Tell me honestly, as a friend—are you happy?

Yelena. No, I'm not.

Sonia. I knew that. One more question. Tell me frankly. Don't you wish your husband were young?

Yelena. What a child you are! Of course, I do! [*Laughs.*] Well, ask me another one—come on.

Sonia. Do you like the doctor?

Yelena. Yes, I like him very much.

Sonia [*laughs*]. I have such a silly look on my face, haven't I? You see, he's gone, but I can still hear his voice and his footsteps, and I have only to look at the dark window and I see his face. Do let me tell you more about it. . . . But I can't speak so loud—I feel ashamed. Let's go to my room and talk there. Do you think I'm being silly? Tell me truly. . . . Tell me something about him.

Yelena. What do you want me to tell you?

Sonia. Well, he's clever—he knows everything—he can do everything. . . . He's not only a doctor, he plants forests, too.

Yelena. It's not only a question of forests or medicine. My dear, don't you understand? It's his genius that matters! And do you know what that means? Courage, an independent mind, bold initiative. . . . He plants a tree and already he's thinking what will be the result of it in a thousand years. Already he's dreaming of the happiness of humanity. . . . Such people are rare, one must love them. . . . He drinks and occasionally he is a little coarse, but what does that matter? A gifted man cannot keep himself entirely spotless in Russia. Just think what sort of life that doctor has! Muddy, impassable roads, frosts, blizzards, enormous distances, coarse, savage peasants, widespread poverty, diseases—how can you expect a man of forty to have kept himself sober and spotless working and struggling like that, day in, day out, and in such surroundings? [*Kisses her.*] I wish you all the happiness in the world, my dear—you deserve it. [*Gets up.*] As for me, I'm just a tiresome character—an episodic character. . . . In my music, in my husband's house, in all my love affairs —everywhere, in fact, I was only an episodic character. Come to think of it, Sonia, and I mean it seriously, I'm very, very unhappy. [*Paces up and down the stage in agitation.*] There's no happiness for me in this world—none whatever! What are you laughing at?

Sonia [*laughs, hiding her face*]. I'm so happy—so happy!

Yelena. I'd like to have some music. I'd like to play something.

Sonia. Yes, do! [*Embraces her.*] I don't feel like going to bed. Please, play!

Yelena. I will in a moment. Your father isn't asleep. Music irritates him when he is not well. Go and ask him if I may. If he agrees, I'll play. Go on.

Sonia. All right. [*Goes out.*]

The WATCHMAN *is knocking in the garden.*

Yelena. I haven't played for ages. I'll play and cry, cry like a fool. [*In the window.*] Is that you, Yefim?

Voice of Watchman. Yes, ma'am, it's me.

Yelena. Don't knock, the master's ill.

Voice of Watchman. All right, ma'am. I'll be on my way now. [*Whistles.*] Here, good dog. Here, lad! Good dog! [*Pause.*]

Sonia [*returning*]. No!

Curtain.

ACT THREE

Drawing room in SEREBRYAKOV'*s house. Three doors: one on the right, one on the left and one in the middle. Daytime.*

VOYNITSKY *and* SONIA *seated and* YELENA *pacing up and down the stage, deep in thought about something.*

VOYNITSKY. The Herr Professor has been so good as to express the wish that we should meet him in this room at one o'clock today. [*Looks at his watch.*] It's a quarter to one. He wishes to make some communication to the world.

Yelena. I suppose it's some business matter.

Voynitsky. He has no business matters. All he does is write rubbish, grumble and be jealous. Nothing else.

Sonia [in a reproachful voice]. Uncle!

Voynitsky. All right, all right, I'm sorry. [*Motioning toward* YELENA.] Look at her: a sight for the gods! Walks about, swaying lazily. Very charming! Very!

Yelena. You sit there buzzing and buzzing all day long —aren't you sick of it? [*Miserably.*] I'm bored to death. I don't know what to do.

Sonia [shrugging]. There's plenty to do, if you really wanted to.

Yelena. For instance?

Sonia. You could do some of the work on the estate. You could teach. You could take up nursing. Plenty of things you could do. When Father and you weren't here, Uncle Vanya and I used to go to the market and sell flour.

Yelena. I'm afraid I'm not much good at that sort of thing. And, besides, it's not interesting. It's only in serious novels that people teach and nurse sick peasants. How on earth do you expect me to become a nurse or a teacher just like that?

Sonia. Well, and I just can't understand how one can refuse to go and teach the peasants. You wait. You'll soon be doing it yourself. [*Puts her arm around her.*] Don't be bored, my dear. [*Laughing.*] You're bored, you don't know what to do with yourself, and boredom and idleness are catching. Look: Uncle Vanya does nothing but follow you about like a shadow. I've left my work and come to talk to you. Oh, dear, I've grown lazy and the worst of it is I can't help it! Dr. Astrov used to come and see us very rarely before—once a month. It was difficult to coax him into coming. But now he's here every day. Neglects his forests and his patients. You must be a witch.

Voynitsky. Why are you in such a state? [*Eagerly.*] Come, my dear, my precious one, be sensible! You have mermaid blood in your veins—well, then, be a mermaid! Let yourself go for once in your life, fall head over ears in love with some water goblin, plunge headlong into the whirlpool with him and leave the Herr Professor and all of us gasping with surprise!

Yelena [*angrily*]. Leave me alone! How can you be so cruel? [*Is about to go out.*]

Voynitsky [*barring her way*]. Come, come, my sweet, forgive me. I'm sorry. [*Kisses her hand.*] Peace.

Yelena. You must admit you'd try the patience of a saint.

Voynitsky. As a sign of peace and harmony I'll fetch you a bunch of roses. I gathered them for you this morning. Autumn roses: so sad and so lovely. . . . [*Goes out.*]

Sonia. Autumn roses: so sad and so lovely. . . . [*Both look out of the window.*]

Yelena. September already. How are we going to live through the winter here? [*Pause.*] Where's the doctor?

Sonia. In Uncle Vanya's room. He's writing something. I'm glad Uncle Vanya has gone out. I want to talk to you.

Yelena. What about?

Sonia. What about? [*Lays her head on* YELENA's *bosom.*]

Yelena. There—there. . . . [*Stroking her head.*] There. . . .

Sonia. I'm not beautiful.

Yelena. You have beautiful hair.

Sonia. No! [*Turning her head to have a look at herself in the looking glass.*] No! When a woman is not good-looking she's told: You've beautiful eyes, you've beautiful hair. I've loved him for six years. I love him more than my own mother. Every minute I can hear his voice, feel the touch of his hand. I keep looking at the door and waiting—expecting him to come in. And—well—you see, I always come running to you to talk about him. Now he's here every day, but he doesn't look at me—doesn't see me. Oh, I can't bear it! I have no hope—no hope at all! [*In despair.*] Oh, God, give me strength. . . . I've been praying all night. . . . I often go up to him, begin talking to him, look into his eyes. . . . I've lost all my pride, I've lost control over my feelings. . . . I told Uncle Vanya yesterday that I love him. Couldn't help myself. And all the servants know that I love him. Everybody knows.

Yelena. Does he?

Sonia. No. He doesn't notice me.

Yelena [*pondering*]. He's a strange man. . . . Look, why not let me talk to him? I'll be very careful—just a hint. [*Pause.*] Honestly, how much longer are you to remain in uncertainty? Please, let me.

SONIA *nods.*

Yelena. That's settled then. It won't be difficult to find out whether he loves you or not. Don't worry, darling. Don't be so uneasy. I'll sound him out so discreetly that he won't even notice it. All we have to find out is—yes or no. [*Pause.*] If it's no, then he'd better stop coming here. Don't you think so?

SONIA *nods.*

Yelena. It would be much better not to see him. It's no use putting it off: I shall question him right away. He promised to show me some maps. Go and tell him that I want to see him.

Sonia [*in violent agitation*]. You will tell me the whole truth, won't you?

Yelena. Yes, of course. I can't help thinking that truth, however unpalatable, is not so dreadful as uncertainty. You can rely on me, my dear.

Sonia. Yes, yes. . . . I'll tell him that you want to see his maps. . . . [*Is going but stops at the door.*] No, uncertainty is much better. . . . At least, there's hope. . . .

Yelena. What did you say?

Sonia. Nothing. [*Goes out.*]

Yelena [*alone*]. There's nothing worse than knowing somebody else's secret and being unable to help. [*Musing.*] He's not in love with her—that's clear, but why shouldn't he marry her? She's not good-looking, but for a country doctor at his age she'll make a splendid wife. She's so intelligent, so kind and so pure-minded. . . . No, no, that's not the point. . . . [*Pause.*] I understand the poor child. In the midst of so much desperate boredom, living among walking gray shadows instead of men and women, listening to vulgar talk of people whose only aim in life is to eat, drink and sleep—and here's a man who is so unlike the others, handsome, interesting, fascinating—like a bright moon rising in the darkness. To fall under the spell of such a man, to forget oneself. . . . I believe I'm a little in love with him myself. Yes, I certainly feel bored when he's not here. I find myself smiling when I think of him. That Uncle Vanya says I've mermaid blood in my veins. "Let yourself go for once in your life. . . ." Well, why not? Perhaps that's what I really ought to do. Oh, if I could fly away like a bird from you all, from your somnolent faces, from your talk—forget your very existence! But I'm timid, cowardly. . . . My conscience will not let me rest. . . . He comes here every day, and I can guess why he's here, and already I've got a guilty feeling. I'm ready to throw myself on my knees before Sonia and beg her to forgive me. . . .

Astrov [*comes in with a map of the district*]. How do you do? [*Shakes hands with her.*] You wanted to see my drawings?

Yelena. You promised yesterday to show me your work. Can you spare the time?

Astrov. Yes, of course. [*Spreads the map on a card table and fastens it with drawing pins.*] Where were you born?

Yelena [*helping him*]. In Petersburg.

Astrov. And where did you study?

Yelena. At the conservatoire.

Astrov. I'm afraid you won't find this interesting.

Yelena. Why not? It's true I don't know anything about country life, but I've read a lot about it.

Astrov. I have my own table in this house. In Vanya's room. When I'm thoroughly exhausted, to the point of stupor, I leave everything and run over here and amuse myself for an hour or two with this. . . . Vanya and Sonia click away at their counting frame, and I sit beside them at my table daubing—and I feel warm and cozy, and the cricket keeps singing. . . . But I don't allow myself to indulge in this pleasant pastime too often—only once a month. [*Pointing to the map.*] Now, look here. This is a picture of our district as it was fifty years ago. The dark and light-green show the forests: half of the whole area was covered with forest. Where those red lines crisscross each other over the green—elks and wild goats used to roam. . . . I show both the flora and the fauna here. On this lake there were swans, geese and ducks and, according to the old people, "a power" of all sorts of birds, thousands of them, clouds of them flying about. Besides the villages and hamlets, as you can see, little settlements were dotted about here and there, small farms, hermitages of Old Believers, water mills. . . . There were lots of cattle and horses. It's all shown in blue. Now, for instance, in this small administrative area, comprising only a few farmsteads, there's a thick smudge of blue: there were whole droves of horses here, and every homestead had on the average three horses. [*Pause.*] Now look lower down. That's what the district was like twenty-five years ago. There was only a third of the area under timber. There are no wild goats, but there are still some elks left. The blue and green colors are paler. And so on. Now let's have a look at the third section. This is the map of the district as it is now. There are still bits of green here and there, but only in small patches. The elks, the swans and the capercaillies have disappeared. There's no trace left of the old settlements and farms and hermitages and water mills. It is, as a matter of fact, a picture of gradual and unmistakable degeneration, which, I suppose, will be complete in another ten or fifteen years. You may say this shows the influence of civilization, that the old life must naturally give way to the new. Well, I admit that if there were highroads and railways on the site of these ruined forests, if factories, workshops and schools were built there, the common people would be healthier, better off and more intelligent. But there's nothing of the kind here! There are still the same swamps and mosquitoes, the same impassable roads, the same poverty, typhus, diphtheria, and the same outbreaks of fire. . . . It's, I'm afraid, a case of degeneration as a result of too severe a struggle for existence. A degeneration caused by apathy, ignorance and the complete absence of a sense of responsibility. The sort of thing a cold, hungry and sick man does to save what is left of his life and to keep his children alive when he clutches instinctively and unconsciously at anything that will warm him and relieve his hunger and destroys everything without thinking of the future. Nearly everything has been destroyed already, but nothing has as yet been created to take its place. [*Coldly.*] I can see from your face that this doesn't interest you.

Yelena. I'm afraid I understand so little about it.

Astrov. There's nothing to understand. You're simply not interested.

Yelena. To tell the truth I was thinking of something else. I'm sorry. I ought to put you through a little interrogation and I'm not quite sure how to begin.

Astrov. An interrogation?

Yelena. Yes, an interrogation, but—a rather harmless one. Let's sit down. [*They sit down.*] It concerns a certain young lady. We will talk like honest people, like good friends, without beating about the bush. We'll have our talk and then forget all about it. Agreed?

Astrov. Agreed.

Yelena. What I want to talk to you about is my stepdaughter Sonia. Do you like her?

Astrov. Yes, I think highly of her.

Yelena. But do you like her as a woman?

Astrov [*after a short pause*]. No.

Yelena. A few words more and I've done. You've noticed nothing?

Astrov. No.

Yelena [*taking him by the hand*]. You don't love her. I can see it from your eyes. She's terribly unhappy. Please, understand that and—stop coming here.

Astrov [*gets up*]. I'm afraid I'm too old for this sort of thing. I have no time for it, anyway. [*Shrugging.*] When could I . . . ? [*He looks embarrassed.*]

Yelena. Oh, dear, what an unpleasant conversation! I'm shaking all over just as though I'd been dragging a ton weight. Well, thank goodness, that's over. Let's forget it just as though we'd never spoken about it and—please go away. You're an intelligent man—you'll understand. . . . [*Pauses.*] Goodness, I'm hot all over.

Astrov. If you'd told me that two or three months ago, I might perhaps have considered it, but now. . . . [*Shrugs.*] But if she's unhappy, then of course. . . . There's one thing I can't understand, though. What made you undertake this interrogation? [*Looks into her eyes and shakes a finger at her.*]

Yelena. What do you mean?

Astrov [*laughing*]. A sly one! Suppose Sonia is unhappy, I'm quite ready to admit it, but what did you want this interrogation for? [*Not letting her speak, eagerly.*] Please, don't look so surprised. You know perfectly well why I'm here every day. Why I am here and who brings me here. You know that perfectly well. You sweet little beast of prey, don't look at me like that! I'm an old hand at this sort of game. . . .

Yelena [*bewildered*]. Beast of prey? I don't know what you're talking about.

Astrov. A beautiful, furry little beast of prey. . . . You must have your victims. Here I've dropped everything and done nothing for a whole month. I'm mad with desire for you, and you're awfully pleased about it—awfully! Well, I'm conquered. You knew that even before your interrogation. [*Folding his arms and bowing his head.*] I surrender. Come and eat me up!

Yelena. You're crazy!

Astrov [*laughs through his teeth*]. And you are—afraid. . . .

Yelena. Oh, I'm much better and more honorable than you think, I assure you! [*Tries to go out.*]

Astrov [*barring her way*]. I'm going away today. I won't come here again, but—[*takes her hand and looks around*] tell me: where can we meet? Where? Tell me quickly. Someone may come in. Tell me quickly. . . . [*Passionately.*] Oh, you're so beautiful, so lovely. . . . One kiss. . . . Let me just kiss your fragrant hair. . . .

Yelena. I assure you—

Astrov [*not letting her speak*]. Why assure me? There's no need. No need of unnecessary words. . . . Oh, how beautiful you are! What lovely hands! [*Kisses her hands.*]

Yelena. That's enough—go away, please. . . . [*Takes her hands away.*] You're forgetting yourself.

Astrov. But tell me, tell me where shall we meet to-morrow? [*Puts his hand around her waist.*] Darling, you see it's inevitable. We must meet. [*Kisses her; at that moment* VOYNITSKY *enters with a bunch of roses and stops dead at the door.*]

Yelena [*not seeing* VOYNITSKY]. For pity's sake let me go. . . . No! [*Tries to go out.*]

Astrov [*holding her back by the waist*]. Come to the plantation tomorrow—at two o'clock. . . . Yes? Yes? Darling, you will come, won't you?

Yelena [*seeing* VOYNITSKY]. Let me go! [*In great confusion goes to the window.*] This is awful!

Voynitsky [*puts down the bunch of flowers on a chair; agitatedly wipes his face and his neck with his handkerchief*]. It's all right—yes—it's quite all right. . . .

Astrov [*trying to brazen it out*]. Not a bad day today, my dear sir. A bit cloudy in the morning, looked like rain, but it's nice and sunny now. . . . To be quite fair, we haven't had such a bad autumn this year—the winter corn isn't too bad at all. [*Rolls up the map.*] There's one thing, though: the days are drawing in. . . . [*Goes out.*]

Yelena [*goes quickly up to* VOYNITSKY]. You must see to it, you must do your utmost to arrange that my husband and I leave here today. Do you hear? Today!

Voynitsky [*wiping his face*]. What? Why, yes, of course. . . . I saw it all, Helen, all. . . .

Yelena [*tensely*]. You understand? I must get away from here today—today!

Enter SEREBRYAKOV, SONIA, TELEGIN *and* MARINA.

Telegin. I'm afraid, sir, I am not feeling very well myself. Been out of sorts for the last two days. My head's not quite—

Serebryakov. Where are the others? I hate this house. It's a sort of labyrinth. Twenty-six huge rooms, people are all over the place, and you can never find anyone you want. [*Rings.*] Ask my mother-in-law and my wife to come here.

Yelena. I am here.

Serebryakov. Please sit down, everybody.

Sonia [*going up to* YELENA, *impatiently*]. Well, what did he say?

Yelena. I'll tell you later.

Sonia. You're trembling? You're agitated? [*Looks searchingly at her.*] I see. . . . He said he won't come here again. . . . Yes? [*Pause.*] Tell me—yes?

YELENA *nods.*

Serebryakov [*to* TELEGIN]. I don't mind ill-health so much—after all, one can't help that, can one?—what I can't stand is the way people live in the country. I have a feeling as though I've dropped off the earth and landed on a strange planet. Sit down, please, all of you. Sonia! [SONIA *does not hear him; she stands with her head bowed sor-*

rowfully.] Sonia! [*Pause.*] She doesn't hear. [*To* Marina.] You, too, nurse, sit down. [*The nurse sits down, knitting a sock.*] Now, if you please, suspend, as it were, your ears on the nail of attention. [*Laughs.*]

Voynitsky [*agitated*]. You' don't want me here, do you? Do you mind if I go?

Serebryakov. Yes, it's you I want here most of all.

Voynitsky. What do you want with me, sir?

Serebryakov. Sir? Why are you so cross? [*Pause.*] If I'm to blame for anything I did to you, then I'm deeply sorry.

Voynitsky. Drop that tone. Let's get down to business. . . . What do you want?

Enter Maria Voynitsky.

Serebryakov. Ah, here's mother-in-law at last. . . . Now I can begin. [*Pause.*] I have invited you here, ladies and gentlemen, to announce that the Government Inspector is about to pay us a visit. However, this is no time for joking. This is a serious matter. I've invited you here to ask for your help and advice and, knowing your unfailing kindness, I feel sure that I shall receive both. I am a scholar, I have spent all my life among books and have always been a stranger to practical affairs. I cannot dispense with the assistance of people who've had practical experience of business, and I beg you, Ivan, you, Mr. Telegin, and you, mother-in-law—er— You see, what I'm driving at is that *manet omnes una nox*, I mean, that we are all in God's hands. . . . I'm old and ill, and so I think that the time has come when I ought to settle my worldly affairs in so far as they concern my family. My life's over. I'm not thinking of myself. But I have a young wife and an unmarried daughter. [*Pause.*] I'm afraid I cannot possibly go on living in the country. We are not made for country life. On the other hand, to live in town on the income we derive from this estate is impossible. If, for instance, we were to sell the woods, it's just an emergency measure that cannot be repeated every year. We have, therefore, to look for some means which would ensure to us a permanent and more or less stable income. I have thought of one such scheme and I shall be glad to submit it to your consideration. Leaving aside the details, I shall give you a general idea of it. Our estate returns on average not more than two per cent of its capital value. I propose to sell it. By investing the money in gilt-edged securities we should get from four to five per cent. I think there might be even a surplus of a few thousand which will enable us to buy a small country house in Finland.

Voynitsky. One moment. . . . I think my ears must be deceiving me. Repeat what you've said.

Serebryakov. Invest the money in gilt-edged securities and use the surplus to buy a small country house in Finland.

Voynitsky. Never mind Finland. There was something else you said.

Serebryakov. I propose to sell the estate.

Voynitsky. Yes, that's it. You're going to sell the estate. That's rich! An excellent idea! And how do you propose to dispose of me and my old mother and Sonia here?

Serebryakov. We shall discuss it all in good time. You don't expect me to settle everything at once, do you?

Voynitsky. One moment. It seems to me that up to now I haven't shown a grain of common sense. Up to now I've been fool enough to believe that the estate belonged to Sonia. My father bought this estate as a dowry for my sister. Up to now I've been so naïve as to believe that our laws were not made in Turkey and that the estate passed from my sister to Sonia.

Serebryakov. Yes, the estate belongs to Sonia. I'm not disputing it. Without Sonia's consent I shouldn't dream of selling it. Besides, I'm proposing to do it for Sonia's benefit.

Voynitsky. It's beyond everything—beyond everything! Either I've gone stark, staring mad, or—

Maria. Don't contradict Alexander, Jean. Believe me, he knows much better than you or me what's good and what isn't.

Voynitsky. No, he doesn't! Give me some water, please. [*Drinks water.*] Say what you like, what you like!

Serebryakov. I don't understand why you're so upset. I I don't say that my plan is ideal. If all of you think it's no good, I will not insist on it. [*Pause.*]

Telegin [*looking embarrassed*]. I've always had a great reverence for learning, sir, and, if I may say so, my feelings for it have a certain family connection. You see, sir, my brother's wife's brother, Konstantin Lacedaemonov, as you perhaps know, is an M.A.

Voynitsky. Just a moment, Waffles, we're discussing business. Wait a little—later. . . . [*To* SEREBRYAKOV.] Just ask him. The estate was bought from his uncle.

Serebryakov. Why should I ask him? Whatever for?

Voynitsky. The estate was bought at the prices current at the time for ninety-five thousand. My father paid only seventy thousand and twenty-five thousand remained on mortgage. Now, listen. . . . This estate would not have been bought if I hadn't given up my share in the inheritance in favor of my sister, whom I loved dearly. What's more, for ten years I've worked like a horse and paid off all the mortgage.

Serebryakov. I'm sorry I ever started this discussion.

Voynitsky. The estate is clear of debt and is in good order thanks only to my own personal exertions. And now, when I'm beginning to get old, I'm to be kicked out of it!

Serebryakov. I don't see what you're getting at.

Voynitsky. I've been managing this estate for twenty-five years. I've worked and sent you the money like a most conscientious agent and not once during all that time has it occurred to you to thank me. All that time—both when I was young and now—I've received from you five hundred rubles a year in salary—a mere pittance! And not once did it occur to you to add a ruble to it!

Serebryakov. My dear fellow, how was I to know? I'm not a practical man and I don't understand anything about these things. . . . You could have increased your salary by as much as you pleased.

Voynitsky. You mean, why didn't I steal? Why don't you all despise me because I didn't steal? That would be only fair and I shouldn't have been a pauper now!

Maria [*sternly*]. Jean!

Telegin. Vanya, my dear chap, don't—don't—I'm trembling all over. . . . Why spoil good relations? [*Kisses him.*] Please, don't.

Voynitsky. For twenty-five years I sat like a mole within

these four walls with this mother of mine. . . . All our thoughts and feelings belonged to you alone. By day we talked about you and your work. We were proud of you. We uttered your name with reverence. We wasted our nights reading books and periodicals for which I have now the utmost contempt!

Telegin. Don't, Vanya, don't. . . . I can't stand it.

Serebryakov [*angrily*]. What is it you want?

Voynitsky. We looked upon you as a being of a higher order and we knew your articles by heart. . . . But now my eyes are opened. I see it all! You write about art, but you don't understand a thing about art! All those works of yours which I used to love aren't worth a brass farthing! You've humbugged us!

Serebryakov. Won't any one of you stop him? I—I'm going!

Yelena. Be silent, Vanya! I insist. Do you hear?

Voynitsky. I won't be silent! [*Stopping in front of* SEREBRYAKOV *and barring his way.*] Wait, I haven't finished! You've ruined my life! I haven't lived! I haven't lived at all! Thanks to you I've wasted, destroyed the best years of my life! You're my worst enemy!

Telegin. I can't stand it—I can't . . . I'm going. . . . [*Goes out in great agitation.*]

Serebryakov. What do you want from me? And what right have you to talk to me like this? Nonentity! If the estate is yours, take it! I don't want it!

Yelena. I shall run away from this hell this very minute! [*Screams.*] I can't stand it any longer!

Voynitsky. My life's ruined! I'm gifted, I'm intelligent, I have courage. . . . If I had lived a normal life, I might have been a Schopenhauer, a Dostoyevsky—but I'm talking nonsense! I'm going mad. Mother, I'm in despair! Mother!

Maria [*sternly*]. Do as Alexander tells you!

Sonia [*kneels before* MARINA *and clings to her*]. Darling Nanny! Darling Nanny!

Voynitsky. Mother, what am I to do? Oh, never mind, don't tell me! I know myself what I must do. [*To* SEREBRYAKOV.] You will not forget me in a hurry! [*Goes out through middle door.*]

MARIA *follows him.*

Serebryakov. This is really going a bit too far! Take that lunatic away! I can't live under the same roof as he. He's always there [*points to the middle door*], almost beside me. . . . Let him move into the village or to the cottage in the grounds, or I will move myself, but stay in the same house as he, I cannot!

Yelena [*to her husband*]. We're leaving this place today! We must make all the arrangements at once.

Serebryakov. An utter nonentity!

Sonia [*on her knees, turns to her father, talking excitedly*]. You must be charitable, Father! Uncle Vanya and I are so unhappy! [*Restraining her despair.*] One must be charitable! Remember how, when you were younger, Uncle Vanya and Granny sat up all night translating books for you, copying your papers—they used to do it every night, every night! Uncle Vanya and I worked without a moment's rest, afraid to spend a penny on ourselves, and sent it all to you. . . . We earned our keep! I'm sorry, I seem to be saying it all wrong, but you must understand us, Father. One must be charitable!

Yelena [*agitatedly, to her husband*]. For Heaven's sake, Alexander, go and talk it over with him. . . . I beg you.

Serebryakov. Very well, I'll have a talk with him. I'm not accusing him of anything and I'm not angry. But you must admit that, to say the least of it, his behavior is extraordinary. Very well, I'll go to him. [*Goes out through middle door.*]

Yelena. Be gentle with him. Try to calm him. . . . [*Follows him.*]

Sonia [*clinging to nurse*]. Darling Nanny! Darling Nanny!

Marina. Don't worry, child. The ganders will gaggle and get tired of it. Gaggle and—get tired of it.

Sonia. Darling Nanny!

Marina [*stroking her head*]. You're trembling as though you were out in the frost. There, there, my orphan child, the Lord's merciful. A cup of lime tea or raspberry tea and it will pass. . . . Don't grieve, child. . . . [*Looking at the middle door, angrily.*] What a row these ganders make, drat 'em!

A shot behind the scenes; a shriek is heard from YELENA; SONIA *shudders.*

Marina. Oh, drat 'em!

Serebryakov [*runs staggering in, looking terrified*]. Stop him! Stop him! He's gone mad!

YELENA *and* VOYNITSKY *struggle in the doorway.*

Yelena [*trying to snatch the revolver away from him*]. Give it me! Give it me, I tell you!

Voynitsky. Let go of me, Helen! Let go of me! [*Freeing himself, runs in and looks for* SEREBRYAKOV.] Where is he? Ah, there he is! [*Fires at him.*] Bang! [*Pause.*] Missed him! Missed him again! [*Furiously.*] Oh, damn, damn, damn! [*Bangs revolver on the floor and sinks exhausted in a chair.* SEREBRYAKOV *is stunned;* YELENA *leans against the wall, almost fainting.*]

Yelena. Take me away from here! Take me away—kill me. . . . I can't stay here. . . . I can't!

Voynitsky [*in despair*]. Oh, what am I doing! What am I doing!

Sonia [*softly*]. Darling Nanny! Darling Nanny!

Curtain.

ACT FOUR

VOYNITSKY's *room; it is his bedroom as well as the estate office. At the window—a large table with account books and all sorts of papers, a bureau, cupboards, scales. A smaller table for* ASTROV *with paints and drawing materials; beside it—a portfolio. A cage with a starling in it. On the wall a map of Africa, apparently of no use to anyone. An enormous sofa covered with American cloth. On the left a door leading to the inner rooms; on the right a door leading into the hall; near the door on the right a doormat for the peasants to wipe their feet on.*

An autumn evening. All is quiet. TELEGIN *and* MARINA
sit facing each other, winding wool.

TELEGIN. You'd better hurry up, Marina, or they'll soon be
calling us to say good-by. The carriage has already been
ordered.

Marina [*trying to wind more rapidly*]. There's not much
more of it left.

Telegin. They're going to Kharkov. They're going there
to live.

Marina. So much the better.

Telegin. Got scared. Helen keeps saying, "I won't stay
here another hour—let's go—let's go at once. In Kharkov,"
she says, "we'll have a good look around and then send for
our things." They're not taking many things with them.
So it seems, Marina, they're not going to stay here. No,
they're not. A divine dispensation of Providence.

Marina. So much the better. All that row this morning,
shooting and God knows what—the disgrace of it!

Telegin. Yes, a subject worthy of the brush of Ayva-
zovsky.

Marina. Never seen the like of it before. [*Pause.*] We'll
live again as we used to do in the old days. Tea at eight
o'clock in the morning, dinner at one, and sit down to
supper in the evening. Everything as it should be, like
other folk, like good Christians. [*With a sigh.*] Haven't
tasted noodles for a long time, sinner that I am.

Telegin. Aye, it's a very long time since we've had
noodles for dinner. [*Pause.*] A long time. As I was walking
through the village this morning, Marina, the shopkeeper
shouted after me: "Hey, you, sponger!" It made me feel
bad I can tell you.

Marina. You shouldn't take any notice of that, dear.
We're all spongers in the sight of God. You, Sonia, the
master—none of us sits about doing nothing. We all work
hard, we do. All of us. Where is Sonia?

Telegin. In the garden. Still going around with the
doctor looking for Vanya. They're afraid he may lay hands
on himself.

Marina. And where's his pistol?

Telegin [*in a whisper*]. I've hidden it in the cellar!

Marina [*with a smile*]. Such goings-on!

VOYNITSKY *and* ASTROV *come in from outside.*

Voynitsky. Leave me alone. [*To* MARINA *and* TELEGIN.] And you, too, please go. Can't I be left alone for a single hour? I hate being kept under observation.

Telegin. I'll go at once, Vanya. [*Goes out on tiptoe.*]

Marina. Look at the gander: ga-ga-ga! [*Gathers her wool and goes out.*]

Voynitsky. Won't you go?

Astrov. With the greatest of pleasure. I ought to have gone long ago, but I tell you again I won't go till you give me back what you took from me.

Voynitsky. I took nothing from you.

Astrov. Seriously, don't detain me. I ought to have gone hours ago.

Voynitsky. I tell you, I took nothing from you. [*Both sit down.*]

Astrov. No? Well, I'll give you a little longer and I hope you won't mind too much if I have to use force then. We'll tie you up and search you. I'm quite serious about it, I tell you.

Voynitsky. As you please! [*Pause.*] To have made such a fool of myself: fired twice and missed him! That I shall never forgive myself!

Astrov. If you're so keen on shooting people, why don't you go and shoot yourself?

Voynitsky [*shrugs*]. Here I make an attempt to commit murder and no one thinks of arresting me and putting me on trial. Which, of course, can only mean that I'm regarded as a madman. [*With a bitter laugh.*] It is I who am mad but not those who hide their stupidity, their mediocrity and their flagrant heartlessness under the mask of a professor, a learned pundit. Those who marry old men and then deceive them under the eyes of everyone are not mad—oh no! I saw you kissing her! I saw!

Astrov. Yes, I did kiss her and be damned to you!

Voynitsky [*glancing at the door*]. No, it's the earth that's mad to let such people as you go on living on it!

Astrov. That's a damned silly thing to say!

Voynitsky. Well, I'm mad, I'm not responsible for my actions, so I have a right to say damned silly things.

Astrov. That's an old trick. You're not mad. You're just a crank. A damned fool. Before, I used to regard every crank as a mental case, as abnormal, but now I've come to the conclusion that it is the normal condition of a man to be a crank. You're quite normal.

Voynitsky [*buries his face in his hands*]. Oh, the shame of it! Oh, if only you knew how ashamed I am! No pain can be compared with this acute feeling of shame. [*Miserably.*] It's unbearable! [*Bends over the table.*] What am I to do? What am I to do?

Astrov. Nothing.

Voynitsky. Give me something! Oh, God! I'm forty-seven; if I live to be sixty, I have another thirteen years. It's devilishly long! How can I live through those thirteen years? What shall I do? What shall I fill them with? You see [*squeezing* ASTROV's *hand convulsively*], you see, if only you could live what is left of your life in some new way. Wake up on a still, sunny morning and feel that you've begun your life all over again, that all your past was forgotten, vanished like a puff of smoke. [*Weeps.*] To begin a new life. . . . Tell me how to begin it—what to begin it with. . . .

Astrov [*with vexation*]. Oh, you and your new life! A new life indeed! My dear fellow, our position—yours and mine—is hopeless.

Voynitsky. Are you sure?

Astrov. I'm quite sure of it.

Voynitsky. Give me something. . . . [*Pointing to his heart.*] I've a burning pain here.

Astrov [*shouts angrily*]. Stop it! [*Softening.*] Those who will live a hundred or two hundred years after us and who will despise us for living such damned stupid, such insipid lives, will perhaps discover a way of being happy. But as for us . . . There's only one hope left for you and me, one hope only. The hope that when we are at rest in our graves, we may, perhaps, be visited by visions that will not be unpleasant. [*With a sigh.*] Yes, old man, in the whole of this district there were only two decent, intelligent men, you and I. But in the course of some ten years this humdrum, this rotten life has worn us down. It's foul vapors have poisoned our blood, and we've become just as vulgar as the rest. [*Eagerly.*] But don't you try to put me off! Give me what you took from me.

Voynitsky. I took nothing from you.

Astrov. Yes, you did. You took a bottle of morphia out of my traveling medicine case. [*Pause.*] Look here, if you've really made up your mind to make an end of yourself, why don't you go into the woods and blow your brains out? But you must give me back my morphia or else people will start talking, putting two and two together and end up by saying that I gave it to you. . . . It will be quite enough for me to have to do your post-mortem. You don't suppose I shall enjoy that, do you?

Enter SONIA.

Voynitsky. Leave me alone.

Astrov [*to* SONIA]. Your uncle has filched a bottle of morphia from my medicine case and he refuses to give it back. Tell him that it's—well, not very clever. Besides, I'm in a hurry. I ought to be going.

Sonia. Uncle Vanya, did you take the morphia? [*Pause.*]

Astrov. He did. I'm certain of it.

Sonia. Give it back. Why do you frighten us? [*Tenderly.*] Give it back, Uncle Vanya! I may be just as unhappy as you, perhaps, but I don't give way to despair. I can bear it and I shall go on bearing it until my life comes to its natural end. You must bear it, too. [*Pause.*] Give it back! [*Kisses his hands.*] Darling Uncle, give it back! [*Cries.*] You are kind, you will have pity on us and give it back, won't you? Bear up, Uncle! Bear up!

Voynitsky [*takes the bottle out of the table drawer and gives it to* ASTROV]. Here, take it! [*To* SONIA.] I must set to work at once, I must do something immediately, or I can't bear it—I can't. . . .

Sonia. Yes, yes, work. As soon as we've seen them off, we shall sit down to work. [*Nervously sorting out the papers on the table.*] We've let everything go. . . .

Astrov [*puts the bottle into his medicine case and tightens the straps*]. Now I can set off.

Yelena [*enters*]. Vanya, are you here? We're leaving now. Go to Alexander. He wants to say something to you.

Sonia. Go, Uncle Vanya. [*Takes* VOYNITSKY *by the arm.*] Let's go. Father and you must make it up. It must be done.

SONIA *and* VOYNITSKY *go out.*

Yelena. I'm going away. [*Gives* ASTROV *her hand.*] Good-by!

Astrov. So soon?

Yelena. The carriage is at the door.

Astrov. Good-by.

Yelena. You promised me today that you'd go away.

Astrov. I haven't forgotten. I'm just going. [*Pause.*] Frightened? [*Takes her hand.*] Is it so terrible?

Yelena. Yes.

Astrov. Why not stay? What do you say? And tomorrow in the plantation. . . .

Yelena. No. . . . It's all settled. . . . And I look at you so bravely because it is settled. . . . There's only one thing I'd like to ask you: think well of me. Yes, I'd like you to respect me.

Astrov. Oh, blast! [*Makes a gesture of impatience.*] Do stay. Please! You must realize that there's nothing in the world you can do, that you've no aim in life, that you've nothing to occupy your mind and that sooner or later your feelings will get the better of you—that's inevitable. So don't you think it had better be here in the country and not in Kharkov or somewhere in Kursk? It's more poetical, at all events. And the autumn here is beautiful. There's the plantation and the half-ruined country houses Turgenev was so fond of describing. . . .

Yelena. How absurd you are! I'm angry with you, but— I shall remember you with pleasure all the same. You're an interesting, an original man. We shall never meet again, so—why conceal it? I was a little in love with you—that's quite true. So let's shake hands and part friends. Don't think too badly of me.

Astrov [*pressing her hand*]. Yes, I suppose you'd better go. [*Musingly.*] I believe you're a good, warmhearted person and yet there seems to be something peculiar about you, something that is part of your very nature. The moment you came here with your husband all of us, instead of going on with our work, instead of doing something, creating something, leave everything and do nothing all the summer except to attend to you and your husband's gout. You and your husband have infected us all with your idleness. I became infatuated with you and have done nothing for a whole month, and all the time people have been ill and the peasants have been grazing their herds in my newly planted woods. And so, wherever you and your husband go, you bring ruin and destruction in your wake. . . . I'm joking, of course, but all the same it's—it's strange, and I'm quite sure that if you had stayed here much longer, the devastation would have been enormous. I should have been done for, but—you, too, would not have got off scot free. Well, go. *Finita la comedia!*

Yelena [*takes a pencil from his table and hides it quickly*]. I shall keep this pencil to remember you by.

Astrov. It's all so strange. . . . We've met and, suddenly, for some unknown reason, we shall never see each other again. Everything in the world is like that. . . . But while there's no one here, before Uncle Vanya comes in with his bunch of flowers, let me—kiss you. . . . A farewell kiss. . . . Yes? [*Kisses her on the cheek.*] Well—that's the end of that.

Yelena. I wish you all the happiness in the world. [*Looking around.*] Oh, I don't care! For once in my life! [*Embraces him impulsively and both at once draw quickly away from each other.*] I must go.

Astrov. Hurry up and go. If the carriage is ready, you'd better set off.

Yelena. I think they're coming. [*Both listen.*]

Astrov. Finita!

Enter SEREBRYAKOV, VOYNITSKY, MARIA VOYNITSKY *with a book,* TELEGIN *and* SONIA.

Serebryakov [*to* VOYNITSKY]. Let bygones be bygones. After all that has happened, during these few hours, I've been through so much and I've thought over so much that I believe I could write a whole treatise on the art of living for the benefit of posterity. I gladly accept your apologies and I apologize myself. Good-by. [*He and* VOYNITSKY *kiss each other three times.*]

Voynitsky. You will receive the same amount you received before regularly in the future. Everything will be as it used to be.

YELENA *embraces* SONIA.

Serebryakov [*kisses* MARIA VOYNITSKY's *hand*]. Mother-in-law. . . .

Maria. Do have your photograph taken again, Alexander, and send it to me. You know how dear you are to me.

Telegin. Good-by, sir. Don't forget us!

Serebryakov [*kissing his daughter*]. Good-by. . . . Good-by, everyone! [*Shaking hands with* ASTROV.] Thank you for the pleasure of your company. I respect your way of looking at things, your enthusiasms, your impulses, but please permit an old man like me to add just one single observation to my farewell: we must work, ladies and gentlemen, we must work! Good-by! [*Goes out, followed by* MARIA VOYNITSKY *and* SONIA.]

Voynitsky [*kisses* YELENA's *hand warmly*]. Good-by. . . . Forgive me. . . . We shall never meet again. . . .

Yelena [*deeply moved*]. Good-by, my dear. [*Kisses him on the head and goes out.*]

Astrov [*to* TELEGIN]. Tell them, Waffles, to bring my carriage around, too.

Telegin. Certainly, my dear fellow. [*Goes out. Only* ASTROV *and* VOYNITSKY *remain.*]

Astrov [*collects his paints from the table and puts them away in his suitcase*]. Why don't you go and see them off?

Voynitsky. Let them go. I—I can't. . . . I'm sick at heart. . . . I must get to work quickly. Do something— anything. . . . To work, to work! [*Rummages among the papers on the table.*]

Pause; the sound of harness bells can be heard.

Astrov. They've gone. The professor must be jolly glad, I shouldn't wonder. You won't get him to come here again for all the tea in China.

Marina [*comes in*]. They've gone. [*Sits down in an easy chair and knits her sock.*]

Sonia [*comes in*]. They've gone. [*Wipes her eyes.*] I hope they'll be all right. [*To her uncle.*] Well, Uncle Vanya, let's do something. . . .

Voynitsky. Work, work. . . .

Sonia. It seems ages since we sat at this table together. [*Lights the lamp on the table.*] I don't think there's any ink. . . . [*Takes the inkstand, goes to the cupboard and fills it with ink.*] I can't help feeling sad now that they've gone.

Maria [comes in slowly]. They've gone! [*Sits down and becomes absorbed in her pamphlet.*]

Sonia [sits down at the table and turns the pages of the account book]. First of all, Uncle Vanya, let's make up the accounts. We've neglected them terribly. Today someone sent for his account again. Let's start. You do one account and I another.

Voynitsky [writes]. To the account of—Mr.— [*Both write in silence.*]

Marina [yawns]. I'm ready for bye-byes. . . .

Astrov. Silence. The pens scratch and the cricket sings. Warm, cozy. . . . No, I don't want to go. . . . [*The sound of harness bells is heard.*] There's my carriage. . . . Well, my friends, all that's left for me to do is to say good-by to you, say good-by to my table, and—be off! [*Puts away maps in portfolio.*]

Marina. What's the hurry? Sit down.

Astrov. Sorry, Nanny, I can't.

Voynitsky [writes]. Balance from previous account two rubles, seventy-five kopecks. . . .

Enter LABORER.

Laborer. Your carriage is waiting, Doctor.

Astrov. I know. [*Hands him the medicine case, the suitcase and portfolio.*] Take these and, mind, don't crush the portfolio.

Laborer. Very good, sir. [*Goes out.*]

Astrov. Well, that's that. . . . [*Goes to say good-by.*]

Sonia. When shall we see you again?

Astrov. Not before next summer, I'm afraid. Hardly in the winter. Naturally, if anything should happen, you'll let me know and I'll come. [*Shakes hands.*] Thank you for your hospitality and for your kindness, for everything, in fact. [*Goes up to the nurse and kisses her on the head.*] Good-by, old woman.

Marina. You're not going without tea?

Astrov. I don't want any, Nanny.

Marina. You'll have a glass of vodka, though, won't you?

Astrov [hesitantly]. Thank you. Perhaps I will. . . .

MARINA *goes out.*

Astrov [*after a pause*]. My trace horse is limping a bit.
I noticed it yesterday when Petrushka was taking it to
water.

Voynitsky. You must change its shoes.

Astrov. I suppose I'd better call at the blacksmith's in
Rozhdestvenskoye. Yes, I'll have to, it seems. [*Goes up to
the map of Africa and looks at it.*] I expect down there
in Africa the heat must be simply terrific now. Terrific!

Voynitsky. I expect so.

Marina [*comes back with a tray on which there is a
glass of vodka and a piece of bread*]. Here you are!

ASTROV *drinks the vodka.*

Marina. To your health, dear. [*Makes a low bow.*] Have
some bread with it.

Astrov. No, thank you, I like it as it is. Well, good-by
all! [*To* MARINA.] Don't bother to see me off, Nanny.
There's no need.

He goes out; SONIA *follows him with a candle to see him
off;* MARINA *sits down in her easy chair.*

Voynitsky [*writes*]. "February the second: linseed oil;
twenty pounds. . . . February the sixteenth—linseed oil
again—twenty pounds. . . . Buckwheat meal. . . ."
[*Pause*].

The sound of harness bells is heard.

Marina. He's gone.

Pause.

Sonia [*comes back, puts candle on table*]. He's
gone. . . .

Voynitsky [*counts on the abacus and writes*]. Total—
fifteen—twenty-five. . . .

SONIA *sits down and writes.*

Marina [*yawns*]. Mercy on us. . . .

TELEGIN *comes in on tiptoe, sits down near the door and
softly tunes the guitar.*

Voynitsky [*to* SONIA, *passing his hand over her hair*].

My child, I'm so unhappy! Oh, if only you knew how unhappy I am!

Sonia. It can't be helped, we must go on living however unhappy we are! [*Pause.*] We shall go on living, Uncle Vanya. We shall live through a long, long round of days and dreary evenings; we shall bear with patience the trials which fate has in store for us; we shall work without resting for others now and in our old age, and when our time comes, we shall die without complaining; and there, beyond the grave, we shall say that we have wept and suffered, that we had a hard, bitter struggle, and God will have pity on us, and you and I, Uncle dear, will see a new life, a bright, lovely and happy life; and we shall rejoice and shall look back with a deep feeling of tenderness and a smile upon our present sufferings and tribulations, and —and we shall rest. . . . I believe that, Uncle, fervently, passionately believe it!

TELEGIN *plays softly on the guitar.*

Sonia. We shall rest! We shall hear the angels, we shall see all heaven bright with many stars, shining like diamonds, we shall see all our sufferings and all earthly evil dissolve in mercy that will fill the whole world, and our life will be peaceful, tender and sweet as a caress. I believe that, I do, I believe it. [*Wipes away his tears with her handkerchief.*] Poor, poor Uncle Vanya, you are crying. . . . [*Through tears.*] You knew no happiness in your life, but wait, Uncle Vanya, wait. . . . We shall rest. . . . [*Embraces him.*] We shall rest!

TELEGIN *plays softly;* MARIA VOYNITSKY *writes on the margin of her pamphlet;* MARINA *knits her sock.*

Sonia. We shall rest!

The curtain descends slowly.

THE LOWER DEPTHS

by

MAXIM GORKY

CHARACTERS

MIKHAIL IVANOVICH KOSTYLYOV, *fifty-four, keeper of a doss house*

VASSILISA KARPOVNA, *his wife, twenty-six*

NATASHA, *her sister, twenty*

ABRAM MEDVEDEV, *their uncle, a policeman, fifty*

VASSILY PEPEL, *twenty-eight*

ANDREY MITRICH KLESHCH, *locksmith, forty*

ANNA, *his wife, thirty*

NASTYA, *a girl, twenty-four*

KVASHNYA, *meat dumpling seller, not yet forty*

BUBNOV, *hatter, forty-five*

THE BARON, *thirty-three*

SATIN
THE ACTOR } *approximately of the same age; not yet forty*

LUKA, *a pilgrim, sixty*

ALYOSHKA, *a shoemaker, twenty*

KRIVOY ZOB
THE TARTAR } *porters*

A few nameless tramps without dialogue

THE LOWER DEPTHS

ACT ONE

A basement resembling a cave. A heavy vaulted stone ceiling, grimy, with peeling plaster. The light comes from a square window to the right of the spectators. The right corner is occupied by PEPEL's *room, partitioned off from the rest of the basement by thin boards.* BUBNOV's *bunk is near the door of that room. In the left corner is a large Russian stove; in the left brick wall is the door into the kitchen where* KVASHNYA, THE BARON *and* NASTYA *live. Between the stove and the door at the wall—a large bed concealed by dirty cotton curtains. Everywhere along the walls are bunks. In the foreground by the left wall stands a wooden block with a vice and a small anvil attached to it and another wooden block a little farther toward the back.* KLESHCH *is sitting on the latter in front of the anvil, fitting keys into old locks. At his foot are two large bundles of keys of different sizes strung on wire rings, a battered tin samovar, a hammer, files. In the middle of the doss house is a large table, two benches and a stool, all of dirty unpainted wood.* KVASHNYA *is busying herself with the samovar at the table.* THE BARON *is munching a piece of black bread, and* NASTYA, *on the stool, reads a battered book, leaning with her elbows on the table.* ANNA *lies coughing on the bed behind the curtains.* BUBNOV *is seated on his bunk and is trying to cut up a pair of old trousers on a hat block, which he holds between his knees. All around him are torn bits of cardboard, from which he makes the peaks for his caps, as well as bits of American*

*cloth and all sorts of rags. SATIN, who has just awakened,
lies on his bunk, grunting. THE ACTOR, invisible to the
audience, tosses about and coughs on the stove.*

An early spring morning.

THE BARON. Go on!

Kvashnya. No, sir, I says, don't come to me with such
proposals. I've been through it before, I says, and I
wouldn't marry again if you gave me a hundred baked
lobsters. . . .

Bubnov [to SATIN]. What are you grunting like a pig
for?

SATIN *grunts.*

Kvashnya. That I, a free woman and my own mistress,
I says, should register my name in somebody else's passport and sell myself, I says, into slavery to a man—no,
sir! Why, if he was an American prince, I wouldn't dream
of marrying him, I wouldn't.

Kleshch. Wouldn't you?

Kvashnya. What did you say?

Kleshch. You'll marry Abram all right, that's what I
said.

*The Baron [snatching the book from NASTYA and read-
ing the title].* "Ill-fated Love." [*Laughs uproariously.*]

Nastya [holding out her hand]. Come on, give it back!
Come on—don't be silly!

THE BARON *looks at her, waving the book in the air.*

Kvashnya [to KLESHCH]. You ginger goat! So I'll marry
him, will I? You've got some cheek, I must say!

The Baron [striking NASTYA on the head with the book].
You're a damned fool, Nastya!

Nastya [snatching the book away]. Give it me!

Kleshch. A grand lady, ain't you? You'll marry Abram
all right—that's what you're out for.

Kvashnya. Why, of course! To be sure! Look at you—
nearly driven your wife to death, haven't you?

Kleshch. Shut your mouth, you old bitch! It's none of
your business!

Kvashnya. Oho! Can't stand the truth, can you?

The Baron. It's started! Nastya, my sweet, where are you?

Nastya [*without raising her head*]. What do you want? Oh, go away!

Anna [*putting her head through the curtains*]. The day's started! For God's sake—don't shout—do stop squabbling!

Kleshch. Whining again!

Anna. Every blessed day—let me die in peace, can't you?

Bubnov. Noise never stopped nobody from dying.

Kvashnya [*walking up to* ANNA]. How ever have you managed to live with a good-for-nothing bully like that, dear?

Anna. Go away—leave me alone, please.

Kvashnya. Well, well. . . . Oh, you poor thing—a real saint, that's what you are—a real saint! How's the pain in your chest, love? Any better?

The Baron. Kvashnya, time to go to market!

Kvashnya. Coming—half a minute! [*To* ANNA.] Like some hot dumplings, love?

Anna. No, thank you. What do I want to eat for?

Kvashnya. You must eat, my dear. Something hot will do you a power of good. Make your chest a lot better, it will. I'll put some in a cup and leave them for you. Eat them when you feel like it. Come on, Your Lordship. . . . [*To* KLESHCH.] Oh, you devil, you! [*Goes into kitchen.*]

Anna [*coughing*]. Dear Lord. . . .

The Baron [*gently pushing down* NASTYA'S *head*]. Stop reading such trash, you silly fool!

Nastya [*muttering*]. Go away—I don't interfere with you, do I?

THE BARON *follows* KVASHNYA, *whistling.*

Satin [*sitting up in his bunk*]. Who gave me that awful beating yesterday?

Bubnov. Does it matter who?

Satin. I don't suppose it does, but I'd still like to know why they beat me.

Bubnov. Were you playing cards?

Satin. Yes.

Bubnov. Well, that's why they beat you.

Satin. The swine!

The Actor [*poking his head from the stove*]. One day they'll injure you fatally—kill you.

Satin. Injure fatally—kill you. . . . You are a blockhead.

The Actor. Why?

Satin. Because you can't kill a man twice.

The Actor [*after a short pause*]. I don't see that—why can't you?

Kleshch. You'd better climb down from the stove and start cleaning the place up. What are you lying about there for, like a regular lord?

The Actor. Mind your own business.

Kleshch. Wait till Vassilisa comes in—she'll show you whose business it is.

The Actor. To hell with Vassilisa! It's the Baron's turn to clean up today. Baron!

The Baron [*coming out of the kitchen*]. Sorry, I've no time for cleaning—just going off to market with Kvashnya.

The Actor. That's nothing to do with me. Go to Siberia for all I care, but today it's your turn to sweep the floor. I'm not going to do other people's work for them, damned if I am!

The Baron. Oh, go to hell! Darling Nastya will sweep up. Hey, you, ill-fated love, wake up! [*Takes the book away from* NASTYA.]

Nastya [*getting up*]. What do you want? Gimme it! The cheek! Calls himself a gentleman!

The Baron [*giving back the book*]. Please, Nastya, be a dear and sweep the floor for me, will you?

Nastya [*going to kitchen*]. Oh, no, I won't!

Kvashnya [*to* THE BARON *through kitchen door*]. Come on, you! They'll sweep up without you. Actor, he's asked you, so you'd better do it. It won't break your back, I'm sure. [THE BARON *goes into kitchen.*]

The Actor. Oh well—it's always me—I don't see why. . . .

The Baron [*comes out of kitchen, a yoke over his shoulders with baskets suspended from it on either side. In the baskets are pots covered with rags*]. Feels much heavier today—wonder why. . . .

Satin. Hasn't helped you much being born a baron, has it?

Kvashnya [*to* THE ACTOR]. Don't forget to sweep up, mind! [*Goes out into passage, letting* THE BARON *pass ahead of her.*]

The Actor [*climbing down from the stove*]. Inhaling dust is bad for me. [*With pride.*] My organism is poisoned with alcohol. [*Sits down on bunk, musing.*]

Satin. Organism—organon—

Anna. Andrey!

Kleshch. What now?

Anna. Kvashnya has left me some dumplings in the kitchen—you'd better have 'em.

Kleshch [*going up to her*]. And what about you? Won't you have any?

Anna. No, thank you. Don't want any. What do I want to eat for? You're a workingman—you need it.

Kleshch. You're not afraid, are you? Don't be. Who knows? You may still—

Anna. Go, eat! I feel awful—seems it won't be long now.

Kleshch [*walking away*]. You'll be all right, you'll see. You'll be getting up one of these days. I've seen it happen many a time. . . .

The Actor [*in a loud voice, as if he had suddenly awakened*]. In the hospital yesterday the doctor said to me: "Your organism," he said, "is completely poisoned with alcohol. . . ."

Satin [*smiling*]. Organon. . . .

The Actor [*insistently*]. Not organon—or-gan-ism!

Satin. Sikambre. . . .

The Actor [*waving his hand at him*]. What gibberish! I'm speaking seriously, I am. If my organism is poisoned, then it's bad for me to sweep the floor and—and inhale dust.

Satin. Microbiotics—ha! Damn good, that!

Bubnov. What are you muttering?

Satin. Words. . . . And here's another—trans-cen-den-tal. . . .

Bubnov. What's that?

Satin. Don't know. I've forgotten.

Bubnov. Then why say it?

Satin. Oh, I don't know. You see, my dear chap, I'm sick and tired of human words—all our words—sick and tired of 'em! Must have heard every one of them—oh, a thousand times, I suppose.

The Actor. Hamlet says: "Words, words, words!" Wonderful play, *Hamlet.* I played the gravedigger in it.

Kleshch [*coming in from the kitchen*]. And when will you start playing with the broom?

The Actor. Mind your own business. [*Beating his breast.*] "Ophelia, in thy orisons be all my sins remembered!"

Behind the scenes, somewhere far away, is heard a muffled noise, shouts, a policeman's whistle. KLESHCH *sits down to work, starts grinding away with his file.*

Satin. I love incomprehensible, rare words. When I was a boy I worked in a telegraph office and—and I used to read lots and lots of books. . . .

Bubnov. So you were a telegraphist, too, were you?

Satin. Yes, I was. [*Chuckling.*] There are some very excellent books and—er—lots of most curious words. . . . I was an educated man once—did you know that?

Bubnov. I've heard about it—a hundred times! Me—well, I was a furrier once. Had my own workshop. My hands and arms were all yellow from the dye. You see, I used to dye the fur. Yes, sir. So my hands and arms were yellow up to the elbow. Thought I'd never be able to wash it off—not to my dying day! I was afraid I'd die with yellow hands and arms. But now—look at 'em!—they're only dirty. Yes, sir!

Satin. So what?

Bubnov. Oh, nothing, nothing!

Satin. Why tell us about it then?

Bubnov. Well, you see, there's a moral to it. It shows that however much you paint yourself, it'll all come off in the end. Yes, sir, it will all come off.

Satin. Oh, my bones!

The Actor [*sits, with hands clasped around his knees*]. Education is all tommyrot; the main thing is talent. I knew an actor once who could scarcely read—used to read his lines syllable by syllable, but when he played the lead in a play, the theatre shook and rocked with applause. . . .

Satin. Bubnov, let me have five kopecks, please.

Bubnov. I've only got two myself.

The Actor. What I say is that all an actor needs to play leading parts is talent. And talent means faith in yourself, faith in your own powers. . . .

Satin. Give me five kopecks and I'll believe that you're a genius, a hero, a crocodile, a police inspector. . . . Kleshch, let me have five kopecks, there's a good fellow!

Kleshch. Go to hell! There are too many of your sort here.

Satin. What are you swearing for? Don't you think I know you haven't a bean?

Anna. Andrey, I feel awful. . . . I can't breathe. . . .

Kleshch. What can I do about it?

Bubnov. Open the door to the passage, can't you?

Kleshch. You're all right up there on the bunk, but I'm on the floor. Change places with me and try opening the door yourself. I've a cold as it is.

Bubnov [*calmly*]. Why should I open the door? It's your wife who's asking.

Kleshch [*sullenly*]. I don't care who's asking.

Satin. Oh, my head! Why do people have to bash each other over the head?

Bubnov. They bash you not only over the head, but over the rest of your body as well. [*Gets up.*] Must go and buy some thread. Not a sign of our landlord or landlady this morning. They haven't both pegged out, have they? [*Goes out.*]

ANNA *coughs.* SATIN, *his hands clasped behind his head, sits motionless.*

The Actor [*throws a disconsolate look around him and goes up to* ANNA]. Well, how are you? Feeling bad?

Anna. Can't breathe. . . .

The Actor. Want me to take you out into the passage? Well, then, get up. [*He helps the woman to get up, wraps some rags over her shoulders and, supporting her, leads her into the passage.*] Come on now—steady! I'm a very sick man myself, you know. Alcohol poisoning. . . .

Kostylyov [*in the doorway*]. Going out for a walk? Look at them—a couple of young lovers!

The Actor. Make way, you! Can't you see two sick people are trying to get past you?

Kostylyov. Pass along, by all means. . . . [*Humming some religious tune, looks around the doss house suspiciously, bending his head to the left as though listening to something in* PEPEL's *room.* KLESHCH *rattles his keys fiercely and scrapes with his file, looking askance at the landlord.*] Grinding away, eh?

Kleshch. Beg your pardon?

Kostylyov. Grinding away, I said. [*Pause.*] Mmmm—er—now what was it I was going to ask you? [*Quickly, in a low voice.*] My wife hasn't been here, has she?

Kleshch. I haven't seen her.

Kostylyov [*moving cautiously toward* PEPEL's *room*]. Taking up a lot of room in my house for two rubles a month, aren't you? A bed—yourself sitting on the floor—well, well! Five rubles' worth of space, so help me! I'll have to raise your rent, you know. Increase it by another half ruble at least.

Kleshch. Why not put a noose around my neck and strangle me? You'll be dead yourself soon and all you can think of is half rubles. . . .

Kostylyov. Why strangle you? Who'd be better off because of it? Why, man, you just carry on. Live and be merry. Meanwhile I'll put another half ruble on your rent, buy some icon lamp oil with it and—er—my offering will burn before the holy icon, burn there for me, to atone for my sins and for yours, too, my dear man. For yours, too. You never think of your sins yourself, do you? Well, then. . . . Oh, Andrey, Andrey, you're a wicked man! Your wife has gone into a decline because of your wickedness. No one likes you. No one respects you. Your work, too, is so noisy—gets on everybody's nerves. . . .

Kleshch [*shouts*]. What have you come here for—to plague me?

SATIN *grunts loudly.*

Kostylyov [*with a start*]. Good heavens, man!

The Actor [*comes in*]. I set the poor woman down in the passage and wrapped her up.

Kostylyov. What a kind fellow you are, to be sure! That's good—it will all be put down to your account.

The Actor. When?

Kostylyov. Why, my dear fellow, in the next world, of course! Everything we do is entered to our account there.

The Actor. Now, why shouldn't you reward me for my kindness here and now?

Kostylyov. How do you expect me to do that?

The Actor. Write off half my debt.

Kostylyov. Ha-ha! You will have your joke, my dear fellow. Always acting a part. Kindness and money aren't the same thing, are they? Kindness—why, it's the greatest blessing on earth, whereas the money you owe me is nothing but a debt! And that, of course, means that you have to pay it back. You must treat an old man like me with kindness without expecting to be paid for it.

The Actor. You're a dirty rogue, old man. [*Goes out into kitchen.*]

KLESHCH *gets up and goes out into passage.*

Kostylyov [*to* SATIN]. How do you like the grinder, eh? Ran off, ha-ha! Doesn't like me, does he?

Satin. Does anybody—except the devil?

Kostylyov [*chuckling*]. What a fellow you are for abusing people! Well, for my part, I love you all. Aye, I understand you, my poor, unhappy, good-for-nothing, worthless brothers in Christ. [*Suddenly, rapidly.*] What about Vassily? Is he in?

Satin. Go and look for yourself.

Kostylyov [*goes up to the door and knocks*]. Vassily!

THE ACTOR *appears at the kichen door. He is chewing something.*

Pepel. Who's there?

Kostylyov. It's me—me, Vassily.

Pepel. What do you want?

Kostylyov [*stepping aside*]. Open the door, there's a good fellow!

Satin [*without looking at* KOSTYLYOV]. He'll open the door and she'll be inside.

THE ACTOR *snorts.*

Kostylyov [*agitatedly, in a low voice*]. Eh? Who's there? What did you say?

Satin. Nothing at all. I was just talking to myself.

Kostylyov. Take care, my lad. You'll be cracking a joke too many one of these days—yes, sir! [*Knocks loudly at the door.*] Vassily!

Pepel [*opening the door*]. Well? What do you mean by disturbing me?

Kostylyov [*peering into the room*]. I—er—well, you see—er—

Pepel. Did you bring the money?

Kostylyov. I've some business to discuss with you.

Pepel. The money—did you bring it?

Kostylyov. What money? Wait—

Pepel. The money—the seven rubles for the watch—well?

Kostylyov. What watch, my dear fellow? Good heavens, man—

Pepel. You'd better look out! Yesterday, before witnesses, I sold you a watch for ten rubles. You gave me three, so let's have the other seven. What are you staring at me for? Don't you know what I am talking about? Hangs around here, disturbs people and doesn't know his own business.

Kostylyov. Sh-sh. . . . Don't be angry, my dear Vassily. The watch—it's—

Satin. —a stolen one.

Kostylyov [*sternly*]. I'm not a receiver of stolen goods! How can you—

Pepel [*seizing him by the shoulder*]. What do you mean by disturbing me? What do you want?

Kostylyov. Why, nothing. I—I want nothing. I'll go if—if you're in such a mood.

Pepel. Run along and bring me the money!

Kostylyov [*goes out*]. The ruffians! Good Lord. . . .

The Actor. A regular farce!

Satin. Excellent! I like that.

Pepel. What was he doing here?

Satin [*laughing*]. Don't you see? He's looking for his wife. Why don't you finish him off, Vassily?

Pepel. And ruin my life for trash like him?

Satin. Make a good job of it. Then marry Vassilisa and —you'll be our landlord.

Pepel. Something to look forward to, I must say! Why,

I shouldn't be surprised if you'd take advantage of my good nature, grab all I possess and me into the bargain and spend it all on drink in some pub. [*Sits down on bunk.*] The old devil—woke me up. And I had such a lovely dream. I dreamed I was fishing and caught a huge bream—the sort of bream you only see in dreams. I was playing him, playing him, every minute afraid that the line might snap, got my landing net ready—any moment now, I thought to myself—

Satin. That wasn't a bream, it was Vassilisa.

The Actor. He caught Vassilisa a long time ago.

Pepel [*crossly*]. Oh, go to hell and take Vassilisa along with you!

Kleshch [*comes in from the passage*]. Devilishly cold!

The Actor. Why didn't you bring Anna in? She'll freeze to death there.

Kleshch. Natasha took her into the kitchen.

The Actor. The old man's sure to throw her out.

Kleshch [*sitting down to his work*]. Well, then, Natasha will take her back.

Satin. Vassily, let's have five kopecks.

The Actor [*to* SATIN]. You idiot—five kopecks! Vassily, old chap, let's have twenty kopecks.

Pepel. I suppose I'd better give it to you quick—before you ask for a ruble. Here!

Satin. Gibraltar! Give me thieves every time: there are no better people in the world!

Kleshch [*morosely*]. It's all easy money with them. They haven't got to work for it.

Satin. Money comes easy to many people, but very few part with it easily. Work? Make work pleasant for me and maybe I'll work. Yes, sir, maybe! When work's a pleasure, life's good. When work's a duty, life's slavery. [*To* THE ACTOR.] Hey, there, Sardanapalus, let's go!

The Actor. Let's go, Nebuchadnezzar! I'm going to get as drunk as forty thousand lords!

They go out.

Pepel [*yawning*]. Well, how's your wife?

Kleshch. It won't be long now. . . .

Pause.

Pepel. Good Lord, man, grinding and filing away all day long—what a stupid waste of time!

Kleshch. What else do you think I ought to do?

Pepel. Nothing.

Kleshch. And how am I going to eat?

Pepel. Oh, people manage to live, you know.

Kleshch. The people here, you mean? What sort of people are they? Beggars, vagabonds, the scum of the earth —people indeed! I'm a workingman, I am. I'm ashamed to look at them. I've been working ever since I can remember. You don't think I'll be able to get out of here, do you? Well, I will—I'll crawl out of this cellar even if I tear the skin off my flesh. You wait—when my wife dies— I've lived six months here and it seems more like six years. . . .

Pepel. No one here is any worse than you—say what you like.

Kleshch. Not worse! They've neither honor nor conscience.

Pepel [*indifferently*]. And what's the good of honor and conscience? You can't put them on your feet instead of boots, can you? Honor, conscience is all right for people who have power, people on top.

Bubnov [*comes in*]. Oh-h, I'm frozen!

Pepel. Bubnov, have you a conscience?

Bubnov. What's that? A conscience?

Pepel. Yes.

Bubnov. What do I want a conscience for? I'm not rich.

Pepel. That's exactly what I said: honor and conscience is for the rich—yes, sir! And Kleshch here is abusing us because we have no conscience, he says.

Bubnov. Why? Did he want to borrow some of it?

Pepel. He's plenty of his own.

Bubnov. I see. He's selling it, is he? Well, he won't find any customers here. Now, if he had some bits of old cardboard, I'd buy them, and that, too, only on credit.

Pepel [*sententiously*]. You're a fool, Andrey, old fellow. You'd better listen to what Satin has to say about conscience—or the Baron.

Kleshch. I've nothing to talk to them about.

Pepel. They're much wiser than you, drunkards though they are.

Bubnov. And he who is both drunk and wise has got himself a double prize.

Pepel. Satin says every man expects his neighbor to have a conscience, but the trouble is, you see, nobody can afford to have one. And that's a fact.

NATASHA *comes in, followed by* LUKA *with a stick in his hand, a bundle on his back and a kettle and teapot slung from his belt.*

Luka. Good morning to you, honest people.

Pepel [*fingering his mustache*]. Ah, Natasha!

Bubnov [*to* LUKA]. Honest? Good Lord, no! We may have been—three summers ago.

Luka. Oh, it's all one to me. I respect crooks, too, for to my way of thinking there isn't such a thing as a bad flea: they're all black and they all jump about. Aye, that's how it is. Show me where I can settle down here, my dear.

Natasha [*pointing to the kitchen door*]. You can go in there, Granddad.

Luka. Thank you, my dear. I don't mind where I go. To an old man any place that's warm is home. [*Goes into kitchen.*]

Pepel. What an amusing old codger you've brought us, Natasha.

Natasha. More interesting than you. I say, Andrey, your wife is in our kitchen—come and fetch her after a little while, will you?

Kleshch. Oh, all right, I will.

Natasha. And, please, be a little more kind to her now —she won't last long, you know.

Kleshch. I know.

Natasha. You know, do you? It's not enough to know, you must understand. You see, it must be a terrible thing to die.

Pepel. Well, I'm not a bit afraid.

Natasha. You wouldn't! Such a brave man, aren't you?

Bubnov [*whistling*]. And the thread's rotten!

Pepel. Honestly, I'm not a bit afraid! I'm ready to die here and now! Take a knife, stab me to the heart, and

I'll die without uttering a sound! Why, I'd die gladly, for it'd be from such a pure hand that I'd receive the blow!

Natasha [*goes out*]. Tell that to someone else!

Bubnov [*in a drawn-out voice*]. And the dear old thread's rotten!

Natasha [*at the passage door*]. Don't forget about your wife, Andrey.

Kleshch. All right.

Pepel. A nice girl!

Bubnov. She's all right.

Pepel. Why is she like that with me? Won't have anything to do with me. She'll come to no good here, anyway.

Bubnov. She won't—through you.

Pepel. Why through me? I feel sorry for her.

Bubnov. Like a wolf for a lamb.

Pepel. Don't talk nonsense. I do feel sorry for her—very much so. She has a rotten life here. I realize that.

Kleshch. You wait till Vassilisa catches you talking to her.

Bubnov. Vassilisa? I should damned well think so. She won't give up what belongs to her without a fight. A real harpy, she is.

Pepel [*lies down on a bunk*]. You can go to hell, both of you—prophets!

Kleshch. You wait! You'll see!

Luka [*humming in the kitchen*]. In the dark of night, with no light to guide you. . . .

Kleshch [*going out into passage*]. Another one—howling!

Pepel. Oh, dear, I'm so bored! Why do I get so bored, I wonder? Everything's all right—couldn't be better—and, suddenly, you feel as though you're chilled to the marrow: you get so hellishly bored!

Bubnov. Bored, are you? Mmmmm. . . .

Pepel. Yes, I am. Bored to death!

Luka [*sings*]. Oh, with no light to guide you. . . .

Pepel. I say, old fellow!

Luka [*looking in from kitchen*]. You mean me?

Pepel. Yes, you. Stop singing, please.

Luka [*coming in*]. Don't you like it?

Pepel. I like it all right when people know how to sing.

Luka. And I don't know how to?

Pepel. You certainly don't.

Luka. Fancy that! And I thought that I was a good singer. It's always like that: a man thinks he's doing pretty well and all of a sudden he finds that others think different.

Pepel [*laughs*]. That's right!

Bubnov. First you say you're bored and now you're laughing.

Pepel. What's that to you, you big, black crow?

Luka. Who's bored?

Pepel. I am.

THE BARON *comes in.*

Luka. Are you now? And there in the kitchen a girl's reading a book and—crying! Aye, big tears rolling down her cheeks. I says to her: "What's the matter, my dear?" And she says: "I feel so sorry for her!" "Sorry for who?" I ask. "Why," she says, "for the girl in the book!" So that's how she spends her time. Funny, isn't it? Also out of boredom, I suppose.

The Baron. She's a silly girl.

Pepel. Have you had your tea, Baron?

The Baron. Yes—go on!

Pepel. Would you like me to stand you half a pint?

The Baron. Of course I would—go on!

Pepel. Go down on all fours and bark like a dog!

The Baron. Fool! Who are you—a Russian merchant? Or are you drunk?

Pepel. Come on, let's hear you bark! It'll amuse me. You're a gentleman, there was a time when you looked on a fellow like me as if I wasn't a human being at all and—all the rest of it!

The Baron. Well, go on!

Pepel. Well, then, and now I'll make you bark like a dog, and bark you will, won't you?

The Baron. All right, suppose I will. You fathead! What possible pleasure can you get out of it, if I realize myself that I've sunk almost as low as you? You should have made me crawl on all fours when you weren't my equal.

Bubnov. That's true!

Luka. Hear, hear!

Bubnov. What's gone is gone, what's left is just a bit

of trash. We've no gentlemen here. Everything's rubbed off. All that remains is naked man.

Luka. All are equal, then. And were you really a baron, my dear fellow?

The Baron. Now then, what's all this? Who are you, you scarecrow, you?

Luka [*laughs*]. I've seen counts and I've seen princes, but this is the first time I've ever seen a baron, and a damaged one, at that.

Pepel [*laughs uproariously*]. And it was you, Baron, who made me feel ashamed just now!

The Baron. It's time you used your brains a bit more, Vassily!

Luka. Dear, oh, dear, your life, I see, is not all beer and skittles, is it?

Bubnov. It's the sort of life that, as soon as you get up in the morning, you feel like howling.

The Baron. Well, I've seen better days—yes, indeed! Why, I remember I—er—used to wake up in the morning and—er—have a cup of coffee—in bed, mind you, in bed! Coffee with cream—yes, indeed!

Luka. But we're all human beings, for all that! Pretend as much as you like, twist and turn as much as you like, but men you were born and men you will die. And, you know, people are getting more and more intelligent and more and more interesting, and, though their lives may be getting worse, they always, mind you, want something better—a stubborn lot!

The Baron. Look here, old fellow, who are you? Where have you come from?

Luka. Me?

The Baron. A vagabond? A pilgrim?

Luka. We're all vagabonds on the face of the earth. Why, I've heard it said that even our earth itself is nothing but a vagabond in the sky.

The Baron [*sternly*]. That may be so, but—have you got any papers?

Luka [*not at once*]. Why? Who are you? A detective?

Pepel [*delightedly*]. Well said, old man! Well, Your Lordship, got it proper this time, didn't you?

Bubnov. Aye, the gentleman's caught it all right!

The Baron [*overcome with confusion*]. Oh, what's all this fuss about? I—er—I was only joking, old man! You see, my dear chap, I haven't got any papers myself.

Bubnov. Haven't you?

The Baron. What I meant was that I have papers, only they're no damned good.

Luka. They're all like that—papers, I mean—not one of them's any good.

Pepel. Baron, let's go to a pub.

The Baron. I don't mind, I'm sure. Well, so long, old man—you're a damned rogue, though!

Luka. That's as may be, my dear fellow.

Pepel [*at the passage door*]. Come on, for goodness' sake! [*Goes out, followed quickly by* THE BARON.]

Luka. Was that man really a baron once?

Bubnov. Who knows? He was a gentleman—that's true enough. Even now it shows sometimes. Can't get rid of his lordly habits, I suppose.

Luka. Aye, I expect gentility's just like smallpox. A man may get over it, but the pockmarks remain.

Bubnov. He isn't a bad fellow, really. Just kicks out now and again, as he did about your papers just now.

Alyoshka [*comes in whistling, with a concertina in his hands. He is a little tipsy*]. Hey, there, lodgers!

Bubnov. What are you hollering for?

Alyoshka. Sorry, I'm sure. I know my manners.

Bubnov. Been drinking again?

Alyoshka. Who, me? I'll say I have! Been chucked out of the police station by Inspector Medyakin just this minute. "Mind," he says to me, "I don't catch as much as a whiff of you in the street! Not another drop, see?" Well, I've got guts, I have, but that boss of mine just grumbles at me. But what's a boss, anyway? Ha! Just a silly mistake! He's a drunkard, my boss is. But I'm the sort of chap who—who wants nothing! I—I don't want nothing, and—and to hell with it! Here, take me for a ruble, take me for twenty—makes no difference to me. Because I want nothing—see? [NASTYA *comes out of the kitchen*.] Offer me a million—I d-don't want it! N-neither d-do I want a pal of mine, a drunkard, to order me about—a decent fellow like me! Don't want it!

NASTYA, *standing in the doorway, shakes her head as she watches* ALYOSHKA.

Luka [*good-humoredly*]. Good Lord, lad, you've got all muddled up, haven't you?

Bubnov. Human folly.

Alyoshka [*lies down on floor*]. There, eat me up, if you like! I don't care. I w-want nothing! I'm a desperate character! Show me any man worse'n me. Why am I worse'n others? Eh? Explain that to me. Now, take Medyakin. He says, if I catch you in the street again, I'll knock your block off! But I'll go out—I'll lie down in the middle of the street and let them run over me! I don't want nothing!

Nastya. Poor fellow! So young, and already giving himself such airs!

Alyoshka [*catching sight of her, kneels before her*]. Young lady—mamselle—*parlez français*—*Preiscourant!* I'm drunk. . . .

Nastya [*in a loud whisper*]. Vassilisa!

Vassilisa [*flinging the door open, to* ALYOSHKA]. You here again?

Alyoshka. How are you? Come right in, my lady!

Vassilisa. I've told you a hundred times, you young puppy, not to show your face here again, and now you're back, are you?

Alyoshka. Vassilisa, ma'am, want me to play you a new funeral march?

Vassilisa [*pushing him toward the door*]. Get out!

Alyoshka [*moving toward the door*]. Wait, you can't do that! Funeral march—just learned it! Fresh music. . . . Wait, you can't do that!

Vassilisa. Can't I? I'll show you whether I can do it or not. I'll set the whole street onto you, you—you damned scandalmonger, you! You're too young to go about telling all sorts of disgraceful tales about me.

Alyoshka [*running out*]. All right, I'm going. . . .

Vassilisa [*to* BUBNOV]. See he doesn't set foot in here again! D'you hear?

Bubnov. I'm not your watchman here.

Vassilisa. I don't care who you are. I'm letting you live here as a favor, don't you forget that! How much do you owe me?

Bubnov [*calmly*]. Haven't added it up.

Vassilisa. If you're not careful, I'm going to add it up for you!

Alyoshka [*opens door and shouts*]. Vassilisa, I'm not afraid of you—not a bit afraid of you! [*Hides himself.*]

LUKA *laughs.*

Vassilisa. And who are you?

Luka. A passer-by—a wayfarer.

Vassilisa. For one night, or to stay?

Luka. I'll see. . . .

Vassilisa. Your papers!

Luka. I'll get them.

Vassilisa. I want them now!

Luka. I'll bring them to you—take 'em to your lodgings.

Vassilisa. A passer-by, I don't think! If you'd said a bird of passage, it would've been more like it.

Luka [*with a sigh*]. Oh, you're a hard woman!

VASSILISA *goes to the door of* PEPEL's *room.*

Alyoshka [*peering out of kitchen, whispers*]. Has she gone?

Vassilisa [*turning around to him*]. You still here?

ALYOSHKA *disappears, whistling.* NASTYA *and* LUKA *laugh.*

Bubnov [*to* VASSILISA]. He's gone out.

Vassilisa. Who?

Bubnov. Vassily.

Vassilisa. Have I asked you about him?

Bubnov. I can see. You're looking around everywhere.

Vassilisa. I'm looking to see if everything's in order—understand? Why hasn't the floor been swept? How many times have I told you to keep the place clean?

Bubnov. It's the actor's turn to sweep.

Vassilisa. I don't care whose turn it is! But if the sanitary inspector comes and fines me, I'll—I'll throw the whole damned lot of you out!

Bubnov [*calmly*]. And how are you going to earn a living then?

Vassilisa. Don't let me see a speck of dirt here! [*Goes to kitchen, to* NASTYA.] What are you hanging about here for? Why's that stupid face of yours swollen? Don't stand

there like a dummy! Sweep the floor! Have you seen
Natasha? Has she been here?

Nastya. Don't know. Haven't seen her.

Vassilisa. Bubnov, has my sister been here?

Bubnov. Well, she brought him along.

Vassilisa. What about him—was he in?

Bubnov. Vassily? He was. She talked to Kleshch here—
Natasha, I mean.

Vassilisa. I'm not asking you who she talked to. Dirt
everywhere—filth! Oh, you pigs! See that this place is kept
clean—do you hear? [*Goes out quickly.*]

Bubnov. What a horrible beast of a woman!

Luka. Aye, not a very pleasant young woman, is she?

Nastya. Such a life would make anyone into a beast.
Tie anybody with some life in her to a husband like hers—

Bubnov. She isn't exactly tied to him, is she?

Luka. Does she always—explode like this?

Bubnov. Always. You see, she came to see her lover, and
he's out.

Luka. So she felt hurt, I suppose. Dear, oh, dear! The
number of people who try to order everybody about, to
intimidate each other with all sorts of threats, and all because there's no order in life, no purity. . . .

Bubnov. No order? We all want order, but we haven't
enough sense to avoid disorder. However, I suppose the
floor has to be swept. Nastya, won't you do it?

Nastya. Oh, of course! What do you think I am? Your
parlor maid? [*After a short pause.*] I'm going to get drunk
today—blind drunk!

Bubnov. Well, that's not such a bad idea.

Luka. Now, why should a young girl like you want to get
drunk? A moment ago you were crying, now you say you're
going to get drunk.

Nastya [*defiantly*]. And when I'm drunk, I'll cry again—
that's all there is to it!

Bubnov. That's not much, is it?

Luka. But what's the reason? Tell me. Even a pimple
doesn't come without a reason.

NASTYA *remains silent, shaking her head.*

Luka. I see. . . . Dear me, so that's the kind of people
you are. But what's going to happen to you? Oh, well,

I may as well sweep up here. Where do you keep your broom?

Bubnov. Behind the door, in the passage.

LUKA *goes out into passage.*

Bubnov. I say, Nastya.

Nastya. Yes?

Bubnov. Why did Vassilisa pounce on Alyoshka?

Nastya. He was going about saying that Vassily was tired of her and that he wanted to throw her over and— and take up with Natasha. I'm getting out of here— finding myself another place to live.

Bubnov. What for? Where?

Nastya. I'm sick of it. I'm not wanted here.

Bubnov [*calmly*]. You're not wanted anywhere, and, be- sides, nobody on earth is wanted. . . .

NASTYA *shakes her head. Gets up and goes slowly into passage.* MEDVEDEV *comes in, followed by* LUKA *with broom.*

Medvedev. I don't know you, do I?

Luka. And what about all the other people—do you know them all?

Medvedev. On my beat I have to know everybody. But I don't know you.

Luka. That's because, you see, there's not enough room on your beat for the whole earth—there's just a tiny little bit that can't fit into it. [*Goes out into kitchen.*]

Medvedev [*goes up to* BUBNOV]. It's quite true my beat isn't very large, though it's much worse than the largest one. Just a few minutes ago, before going off duty, I had to take Alyoshka the shoemaker to the station. There he was, lying down in the middle of the road, playing his con- certina and yelling: "I don't want nothing! I don't want nothing!" Carriages passing all the time and and—the traffic, you know. He could have been run over and there would have been a lot of—er—unnecessary trouble. A wild lad. . . . Well, so I arrested him for causing an obstruction. Very fond of creating a disturbance, he is.

Bubnov. Coming in for a game of draughts tonight?

Medvedev. Yes, I'll come. Ye-es. . . . And—er—how's Vassily?

Bubnov. All right. Same as ever.

Medvedev. You mean—still carrying on as usual?

Bubnov. Why shouldn't he? He can afford to.

Medvedev [*doubtfully*]. Can he? [LUKA *walks across into the passage carrying a pail.*] Ye-es. . . . There's been a lot of talk about Vassily—you haven't heard anything, have you?

Bubnov. I hear all sorts of talk.

Medvedev. About him and Vassilisa—you haven't noticed anything, have you?

Bubnov. What, exactly?

Medvedev. Oh, I don't know. I expect you do know and are telling lies. Everybody knows, you see. . . . [*Sternly.*] You'd better not lie to me!

Bubnov. Why should I lie?

Medvedev. Well, you'd better not, that's all! The dirty dogs! They say Vassily and Vassilisa are—you understand. . . . But why should I worry? I'm not her father. I'm only her uncle. Why should they laugh at me, I should like to know? [KVASHNYA *comes in.*] I don't know what people are coming to nowadays—they laugh at everything. Oh—ah—so—er—you're back, are you?

Kvashnya. I am, my handsome soldier boy! How do you like that, Bubnov? He's been pestering me at the market to marry him.

Bubnov. Go on—why not? He's got pots of money and —er—he's still young enough to make a great lover!

Medvedev. Me? Ho-ho!

Kvashnya. Oh, you numskull! No, sir, don't you dare touch this—this sore spot of mine! I've been through it all before, my dear man. For a woman to get married is just like jumping through a hole in the ice in midwinter: you do it once and you remember it for the rest of your life.

Medvedev. Don't you jump to conclusions—there are all sorts of husbands!

Kvashnya. There are and all; but, you see, I'm the same as ever. When that darling husband of mine kicked the bucket—may he roast in hell—I was so happy that I spent the whole day by myself. I just couldn't believe my luck!

Medvedev. Now, if your husband beat you without good cause, you should have complained to the police.

Kvashnya. I complained to God for seven years, and he never helped me!

Medvedev. Wife-beating is forbidden today—everything now must be done strictly according to the laws of the land—law and order everywhere. People must not be beaten without good cause. They are only to be beaten to preserve law and order.

Luka [*brings in* ANNA]. Well, we've managed it! You shouldn't have tried to walk alone. How can you—with a weak body like yours? Where's your place?

Anna [*indicating her bed*]. Thank you, Granddad.

Kvashnya. There's a married woman for you! Look at her!

Luka. The poor woman is very weak. Walks along the passage, holding on to the wall and moaning. Why do you let her walk by herself?

Kvashnya. Very sorry, sir, it's all our fault! I expect her maid must have gone out for a walk.

Luka. You may laugh, but you can't just cast off a human being like that, can you? Whatever he is, he's worth something. . . .

Medvedev. There ought to be supervision. For what if she should die suddenly? There's going to be trouble because of it. Must keep an eye on her.

Luka. That's right, Sergeant.

Medvedev. Yes, well—though I—I'm not quite a sergeant yet, sir.

Luka. Aren't you? Well, I must say you look every inch a sergeant!

The noise of stamping feet in the passage. Muffled cries can be heard.

Medvedev. Looks like they're having a row.

Bubnov. Looks like it.

Kvashnya. I'll go and see.

Medvedev. Afraid I must go, too. Duty's duty! Though why go to the trouble of separating people who're having a fight? Sooner or later they'd be bound to stop—fighting's such tiring work. Now I'd let them give each other a good drubbing and they'd think twice before fighting again—they'd remember their beating for a long time!

Bubnov [*climbing down from his bunk*]. You'd better talk to your superiors about that.

Kostylyov [*flinging the door open, shouts*]. Abram, come quick! Vassilisa's killing Natasha! Come quick!

KVASHNYA, MEDVEDEV, BUBNOV *rush into the passage.* LUKA *follows them with his eyes, shaking his head.*

Anna. Oh, God, poor dear Natasha!

Luka. Who's fighting out there?

Anna. Our landladies—they're sisters.

Luka [*going up to* ANNA]. What are they fighting over?

Anna. Nothing. They've both plenty to eat and they're both in good health.

Luka. What's your name?

Anna. Anna. You—you remind me of my dear father. You're just like him—gentle and soft. . . .

Luka. They pummeled me a lot, that's why I'm soft. . . . [*Laughs shakily.*]

Curtain.

ACT TWO

Same as Act One.

Evening. SATIN, THE BARON, KRIVOY ZOB *and* THE TARTAR *are playing cards on the bunk near the stove.* KLESHCH *and* THE ACTOR *are watching the game.* BUBNOV, *on his bunk, is playing draughts with* MEDVEDEV. LUKA *sits on a stool by* ANNA's *bed. The doss house is lighted by two lamps: one on the wall near the cardplayers, the other on* BUBNOV's *bunk.*

THE TARTAR. One more game, then no more game.

Bubnov. Zob, sing! [*Begins.*]

Day by day the sun comes up,

Zob [*joining in*].

But my prison is dark and drear.

The Tartar [*to* SATIN]. Shuffle card! Shuffle good! We know you—you big cheat!

Bubnov and Zob [*together*].

> Day and night the sentries—oh!
> Watch and pass my window near.

Anna. Blows—insults—that's all I ever got—I've had nothing else, all my life.

Luka. Don't fret, my dear, don't!

Medvedev. Look where you're moving, man!

Bubnov. Sorry! Yes, yes, yes. . . .

The Tartar [*shaking his fist at* SATIN]. Why you hide card, eh? I see you. . . . Oh, you cheat!

Zob. Stop it, Hassan! They'll cheat us, anyway. Bubnov, strike up!

Anna. Can't remember a day when I didn't go hungry. I grudged myself every piece of bread. All my life I've been terrified—worried that—that I might eat more than my share. . . . I've been going about in rags all my life— all my miserable, unhappy life. . . . And what for?

Luka. Oh, you poor child! Tired out, are you? Never mind.

The Actor [*to* ZOB]. Play the jack—the jack, damn you!

The Baron. We've got the king.

Kleshch. They'll always beat your card.

Satin. Such is our custom.

Medvedev. A king!

Bubnov. I've got one, too. . . . Well. . . .

Anna. And now I'm dying. . . .

Kleshch. Oh, so that's it! Stop play, Prince! Stop, I say!

The Actor. Don't you think he knows what to do without you?

The Baron. Take care, Andrey, or I'll chuck you out!

The Tartar. Deal again! The pot he goes to the water and gets broke—me, too!

KLESHCH *shakes his head and goes over to* BUBNOV.

Anna. All the time I keep thinking: dear Lord, shall I have to suffer in the next world, too? Not there, too!

Luka. Of course not. You just lie quietly and stop worrying. You'll have a rest there. We all have to put up with

it, my dear. Everyone has to put up with life in his own
way. . . . [*Gets up and goes quickly into kitchen.*]
  Bubnov [*sings*].

> Watch and guard me as you will,

  Zob.

> Escape I cannot, though I'd fain—

Both together.

> Freedom is my joy—but—oh!
> Chains my hands and feet restrain.

  The Tartar [*shouts*]. Aha! You push card up sleeve!
  The Baron [*embarrassed*]. Well, what do you want me
to do with it? Push it up your nose?
  The Actor [*emphatically*]. You're mistaken, Prince. No
one—ever—
  The Tartar. I saw it! Cheat! I no play.
  Satin [*gathering up the cards*]. Don't make such a fuss,
Hassan. You knew perfectly well we were cheats. Why,
then, did you play with us?
  The Baron. Loses forty kopecks and makes a noise as if
he'd lost three rubles—calls himself a prince, too!
  The Tartar [*warmly*]. You must play honest!
  Satin. Good Lord, what for?
  The Tartar. How you mean—what for?
  Satin. I mean what I say—what for?
  The Tartar. You not know?
  Satin. I not know. Do you?

The Tartar *spits in disgust; they all laugh at him.*

  Zob [*good-naturedly*]. You're a funny fellow, Hassan.
Don't you see? If they tried to live honestly, they'd starve
to death in three days.
  The Tartar. Me no care! You must live honest!
  Zob. There he goes again! Come, we'd better go out
and have some tea. Bubnov!
  Bubnov.

> Oh, you chains, my heavy chains. . . .
> My iron guards you are. . . .

Zob. Come on, Hassan, you stupid idiot! [*Goes out, humming.*]

I cannot break you, I cannot smash you. . . .

THE TARTAR *shakes a fist at* THE BARON *and follows his mate out of the room.*

Satin [*to* THE BARON, *laughing*]. Your Lordship has put your foot into it with a vengeance again. An educated man and doesn't even know how to cheat!

The Baron [*at a loss*]. I'm damned if I know how it—

The Actor. You've no talent—no faith in yourself, and without that—no one can do anything—ever!

Medvedev. I've one king—you've two—oh, well!

Bubnov. One's not bad if he's got a good head. Your move.

Kleshch. You've lost, Abram.

Medvedev. It's none of your business—understand? So shut up!

Satin. We've won fifty-three kopecks.

The Actor. Of which three kopecks are mine, though I'm hanged if I know what to do with three kopecks.

Luka [*coming out of kitchen*]. So you've cleaned out the Tartar, have you? I suppose you'll be going out for a drink now.

The Baron. Come along with us.

Satin. I'd love to see what you're like when drunk.

Luka. Same as sober, I expect.

The Actor. Come along, old man; I'll recite some satiric couplets to you.

Luka. What's that?

The Actor. Poems—understand?

Luka. Po-o-ems? What do I want poems for?

The Actor. You see, sometimes they're funny and sometimes sad.

Satin. Well, reciter of satiric couplets, are you coming? [*Goes out with* THE BARON.]

The Actor. Coming—I'll catch up with you. Now here, for instance, old man, is something from one poem. . . . Afraid I've forgotten how it begins—gone clean out of my head! [*Rubs his forehead.*]

Bubnov. Got you! You've lost your king. Your move.

Medvedev. Made the wrong move—damn and blast it!

The Actor. Before, when my organism was not poisoned with alcohol, I had an excellent memory. But now, you see, my dear chap, it's—er—all over. Yes, it's all over with me, I'm afraid! Take that poem—whenever I recited it in public, the audience went raving mad—the applause was terrific! You—er—I don't suppose you know what applause means to an actor, do you, old man? Well, you see, it's—er —it's like vodka! I used to come out on the stage, stand like this [*assumes a pose*]—stand—er— [*Pause.*] Afraid I can't remember a thing—not a word—can't remember! One of my favorite poems, too. It's a bad sign, old man, what do you think?

Luka. Aye, I don't think there can be anything worse than to forget what you loved best. Your whole soul is in what you love best.

The Actor. I've ruined my soul through drink, old man. I'm done for, my dear fellow. And why am I done for? Because I had no faith. . . . I'm finished. . . .

Luka. Why finished? You—you must get yourself cured! They treat people for drunkenness now—didn't you know that? Free of charge, too. Aye, there's a special hospital for alcoholics where they receive free treatment. You see, they've come to the conclusion that a drunkard is a human being, same as everybody else. And—they're glad, aye, glad, when a drunkard wants to be cured! Well, then, away with you! Be off!

The Actor [*thoughtfully*]. Go where? Where is it?

Luka. Oh—it's—er—in a town—now, what's it called? It's—er—a strange kind of name. . . . Don't worry, it'll come back to me presently! Only, you see, in the meantime you'd better prepare yourself. Keep away from drink. . . . Pull yourself together and—er—try to bear up! Later on you'll be cured and start your life all over again. Why, my dear fellow, what could be nicer than to start life all over again! Well, make up your mind, and—er—don't be too long about it.

The Actor [*smiling*]. All over again—start from scratch. . . . That's fine! I wonder, though. . . . All over again? [*Laughs.*] Why, yes! I could do it! I could, couldn't I?

Luka. Why not? A man can do anything, if he sets his mind to it!

The Actor [*suddenly, as if coming out of a trance*]. You're a funny old blighter! Well, so long! [*Whistles.*] Good-by, old man! [*Goes out.*]

Anna. Granddad!

Luka. What is it, my dear?

Anna. Come and talk to me.

Luka [*going up to her*]. Yes, let's have a chat by all means.

KLESHCH *looks around, goes up silently to his wife, gazes at her and makes some mysterious signs, as if wishing to say something.*

Luka. What is it, my dear fellow?

Kleshch [*softly*]. Nothing. [*Goes slowly to the door leading into the passage, stands still in front of it for a few seconds and—goes out.*]

Luka [*after following him with his eyes*]. Your husband seems very cut up.

Anna. I don't think about him any more.

Luka. Did he beat you?

Anna. Didn't he just! He alone is to blame for what I'm suffering now. . . .

Bubnov. My wife had a lover—a damned clever draughts player, he was, the rascal.

Medvedev. Mmmmm. . . .

Anna. Granddad, talk to me, please. . . . I feel sick. . . .

Luka. That's nothing, my dear. It's always like this before you die. It's nothing, nothing at all. You mustn't lose hope, my dear. You see, when you die you won't be worried any more—you won't want anything any more, and there will be nothing, nothing at all, to be afraid of! Peace and quiet—just lie quietly. Death sets everything at rest: it is kind to us. . . . When you die, you will rest, people say. And it's true, my dear. For, you see, how can anyone possibly find rest here?

PEPEL *comes in. He is slightly drunk, disheveled, gloomy. Sits down on a bunk near the door and remains silent and motionless.*

Anna. And what's it like there? More suffering?

Luka. There will be nothing of the kind there! Nothing! You must believe that. Peace—nothing but peace! They will summon you to the Lord and they will say: "Look, Lord, here's thy servant Anna. . . ."

Medvedev [*sternly*]. And how do you know what they will say there? Oh, you—

At the sound of MEDVEDEV's *voice* PEPEL *raises his head and listens.*

Luka. It just happens that I do know, Sergeant.

Medvedev [*conciliatorily*]. Do you now? Well, it's your business, I suppose. Though, mind, I ain't a sergeant yet.

Bubnov. I take two.

Medvedev. You do? Damn you!

Luka. And the Lord will look gently and tenderly at you, and He will say: "Why, I know this Anna! Well," He will say, "take her, Anna, straight to Paradise. Let her have peace. I know she's had a very hard life—she's very tired. . . . Let Anna have peace. . . ."

Anna [*choking*]. Granddad, you're a dear—oh, if it only was so! If only I could get some peace—if only I could feel nothing at all. . . .

Luka. You won't, I promise you. There will be nothing —nothing at all. You must believe that! Die with joy, without worrying about anything. Death, I'm telling you, is like a mother to us, like a mother to her little children. . . .

Anna. But I may still get better, mayn't I?

Luka [*with a pitying smile*]. What for? For more suffering?

Anna. Well—I'd like to live a little longer—just a little bit longer! If there'll be no suffering there, I could bear it here—yes, I could, I could!

Luka. There'll be nothing there! Just—

Pepel [*getting up*]. True—and, then again, maybe not!

Anna [*fearfully*]. Oh, Lord—

Luka. Oh, it's you, handsome. . . .

Medvedev. Who's that hollering?

Pepel [*going up to him*]. Me! What about it?

Medvedev. There's no cause for hollering—that's what! A man mustn't create a disturbance. . . .

Pepel. Oh, you damned fool! An uncle, too—ha!

Luka [*to* PEPEL, *in a low voice*]. Please, don't make a row. A woman's dying here—her lips are already dusted with earth—don't disturb her!

Pepel. I'll do it for you, Grandpa! You're a fine fellow, you are. Quite a first-class yarn spinner. Very good at telling fairy tales. Go on telling your tall stories—what does it matter? There's damned little that's pleasant in this world!

Bubnov. Is the woman really dying?

Luka. It don't look as if she was joking.

Bubnov. Ah, well, she'll stop coughing then. Her coughing was a damned nuisance. . . . I take two!

Medvedev. Oh, I'd like to put a bullet through your heart!

Pepel. Abram!

Medvedev. I'm no Abram to you!

Pepel. Tell me, you stupid fool, is Natasha ill?

Medvedev. What business is it of yours?

Pepel. Come on, tell—did Vassilisa beat her up very badly?

Medvedev. That's none of your business, either. It's a family affair. What have you got to do with it? Who are you?

Pepel. Never you mind who I am! I've only to say the word and you'll never see Natasha again!

Medvedev [*throwing up the game*]. What do you mean? Who are you talking about? Do you really think that a niece of mine would—oh, you thief!

Pepel. I may be a thief, but you never caught me, did you?

Medvedev. You wait! I'll catch you soon enough!

Pepel. If you catch me, it'll be so much the worse for your whole family. Do you really think I'll keep my mouth shut before the magistrate? He who keeps company with the wolf will learn to howl! Suppose they ask me who incited me to steal and showed me which house I could burgle? Why, Mishka Kostylyov and his wife! And who received the stolen goods? Why, Mishka Kostylyov and his wife!

Medvedev. You're lying! No one will believe you!

Pepel. They will, because it happens to be true! And I'll drag you into it, too—ha! I'll ruin the whole damned lot of you—you'll see!

Medvedev [*nervously*]. You are lying! You've made it all up! And, anyway, what harm did I ever do you, you mad dog?

Pepel. And what good have you ever done me?

Luka. Quite right!

Medvedev [*to* Luka]. You there! What are you croaking about? It's none of your business, is it? This is a family matter.

Bubnov [*to* Luka]. Leave 'em alone! They're not throwing a noose around our necks.

Luka [*meekly*]. I didn't mean anything. All I meant to say was that it was wrong for a man not to do a good turn to his neighbor!

Medvedev [*not understanding*]. That's different! We all know each other here, but you—who are you? [*Snorts angrily and goes out quickly.*]

Luka. Our gay cavalier is angry. . . . Dear me, your affairs, dear people, are certainly in a bit of—er—a tangle!

Pepel. Ran off to complain to Vassilisa.

Bubnov. You're behaving like a fool, Vassily. You seem to have become a little too brave these days. You'd better watch out! Bravery is all right for gathering mushrooms in the woods; it's no damned good here. . . . They'll wring your neck in no time.

Pepel. No, sir! They won't catch us Yaroslavl boys with bare hands as easily as that. If it's war, we're damned well going to fight!

Luka. Now, look here, lad, why don't you really get out of here?

Pepel. Where? Well, don't be afraid, out with it!

Luka. Go—to Siberia!

Pepel. Aha, I thought so! No, sir, I prefer to wait till they send me there at the government's expense.

Luka. You listen to me! Go to Siberia. You can make your own way there. They want fellows like you.

Pepel. My way has been marked out for me. My father spent all his life in prison and he placed an order for the same thing for me. You see, when I was a little boy I was already called a thief, the son of a thief!

Luka. A fine country, Siberia! A land of golden opportunities. A man who's got the strength and the good sense to use it will find it as congenial there as a cucumber in a hothouse!

Pepel. Why do you go on telling these tall stories, old man?

Luka. I beg your pardon?

Pepel. Gone deaf? Why do you go on telling lies, I said.

Luka. What sort of lies do you mean?

Pepel. All sorts. It's wonderful here, it's wonderful there—it's all lies, isn't it? Why do you do it?

Luka. Well, why not take my word for it and go and see for yourself? You'll thank me for it. What are you hanging about here for? Besides, why have you suddenly become such a seeker after truth? Just think for a moment: truth, for all you know, may strike you down like a blow from an ax.

Pepel. I don't care! If it's a blow from an ax—let it be!

Luka. You funny fellow! Why commit suicide?

Bubnov. What the heck are you two talking about? Can't understand a word of it. What sort of truth do you want, Vassily? And what do you want it for? You know the truth about yourself—and so does everybody else.

Pepel. Wait a moment, stop croaking! Let him tell me. Listen, old man, is there a God?

LUKA *smiles and is silent.*

Bubnov. People live like—like bits of driftwood carried down a stream. . . . A house is built and the bits of wood are thrown away.

Pepel. Well, is there? Speak!

Luka [*in a low voice*]. If you have faith, there is; if you haven't, there isn't. . . . Whatever you believe in, exists.

PEPEL *looks surprised and stares at the old man in silence.*

Bubnov. I'm going to have a cup of tea. Coming along, you two?

Luka [*to* PEPEL]. What are you staring at me for?

Pepel. So—wait—so it means that—

Bubnov. Well, I'll go by myself then. [*Goes toward door and runs into* VASSILISA.]

Pepel. So what it comes to is that—that you—

Vassilisa [to BUBNOV]. Is Nastya in?

Bubnov. No. . . . [*Goes out.*]

Pepel. Oh, so you've come, have you?

Vassilisa [*going up to* ANNA]. Still alive?

Luka. Don't disturb her.

Vassilisa. And what, pray, are you doing here?

Luka. I can go, if you like. . . .

Vassilisa [*walking toward door of* PEPEL'*s room*]. Vassily, there's something I'd like to talk to you about.

LUKA *walks up to the door leading to the passage, opens it and slams it to. Then climbs cautiously onto a bunk and from there onto the stove.*

Vassilisa [*from* PEPEL'*s room*]. Come here, darling.

Pepel. I won't. I don't want to.

Vassilisa. Why not? What are you so angry about?

Pepel. Oh, I'm fed up! I'm sick and tired of the whole silly business. . . .

Vassilisa. Are you sick and tired of me, too?

Pepel. Yes, of you, too. . . .

VASSILISA *draws her kerchief tightly around her shoulders, pressing her hands to her bosom. Crosses over to* ANNA'*s bed, peers cautiously behind the curtain and returns to* PEPEL.

Pepel. Well, say it!

Vassilisa. What do you want me to say? I can't force you to love me, can I? And—and it's not in my nature to beg for charity. . . . Thank you for telling me the truth.

Pepel. What truth?

Vassilisa. That you're tired of me—or isn't it true?

PEPEL *gazes at her in silence.*

Vassilisa [*moving toward him*]. What are you looking at? Don't you recognize me?

Pepel [*sighing*]. You're beautiful, Vassilisa. [*The woman puts her arm around his neck, but he shakes it off.*] But I never really cared for you. . . . I've lived with you and—all that, but I—I never really liked you.

Vassilisa [*softly*]. I see. Well—

Pepel. Well, there's nothing for us to discuss. Nothing. Stay away from me.

Vassilisa. Taken a fancy to someone else, have you?

Pepel. That's nothing to do with you. Even if I have taken a fancy to someone, I shan't ask you to be my match-maker.

Vassilisa [*meaningfully*]. That's a pity. . . . Perhaps I could arrange a match.

Pepel [*suspiciously*]. Oh? Who with?

Vassilisa. You know. . . . Why pretend? Vassily, I don't like beating about the bush. . . . [*Lowering her voice.*] I won't deny it—you've hurt me. For no reason at all—just as if you'd slashed me across the face with a whip. You said you loved me and now, suddenly. . . .

Pepel. Not so suddenly, either. I've felt like this for a long time. The trouble is, you've no soul. A woman must have a soul, for we are wild beasts and have to be trained— and what sort of training did you give me?

Vassilisa. No use crying over spilt milk, is there? I know very well that we can't help our feelings. You say you don't love me any more—all right! So be it. . . .

Pepel. Well, that's that, then! Parted quietly, no rows— what could be nicer?

Vassilisa. No, wait! You see, when I lived with you I—I was always hoping that you'd help me to get out of this dirty hole, free me from my husband, my uncle, from all this horrible life. . . . And for all I know, Vassily, it may not be you I loved, but this hope of mine, this idea of you as my deliverer. Do you understand? I was waiting for you to pull me out of here.

Pepel. You're not a nail and I'm not a pair of pincers. I thought myself that, being so clever, you would—you're clever, aren't you? You're a cunning she-devil, aren't you?

Vassilisa [*leaning closely toward him*]. Darling, come, let's help each other!

Pepel. How?

Vassilisa [*softly and forcefully*]. My sister—you're fond of her, aren't you?

Pepel. That's why you beat her so cruelly, isn't it? Take care, don't you touch her again!

Vassilisa. Wait! Don't get excited! Everything can be arranged quietly and without quarreling. Would you like to marry her? All right, I'm quite prepared to give you the money—three hundred rubles! Even more if I can manage to raise it.

Pepel [*moving away from her*]. Wait a moment! What's all this? What for?

Vassilisa. Help me to get rid of—my husband. Remove that noose from my neck. . . .

Pepel [*with a low whistle*]. Oh, so that's it! Oho-ho! You've thought it out very cleverly, haven't you? Your husband into the grave, your lover to Siberia and you—

Vassilisa. Darling, why, why Siberia? You needn't do it yourself—get some of your friends to do it! And even if you did do it yourself, who's to know? Natasha—think of her! You'll have money, you could go anywhere you like —you'll set me free forever and—and it will be a good thing for my sister, too, not to be near me. . . . I can't stand the sight of her. I'm furious with her because of you and—and I just can't control myself. I—I torture the poor girl, I beat her, I beat her so mercilessly that I can't help crying with pity for her myself. But I go on beating her and—I shall go on beating her!

Pepel. You brute! Boasting about your brutality, are you?

Vassilisa. I'm not boasting—what I say is true. Think it over, Vassily. You went to prison twice because of my husband, because of his greed. . . . He's sucking my blood like a bedbug—been sucking it for four years! And what sort of a husband is he to me? He bullies Natasha, jeers at her, calls her a beggar! He's poison to everybody. . . .

Pepel. You've thought it all out very cleverly, haven't you?

Vassilisa. It's obvious. Only a fool can fail to understand what I mean.

KOSTYLYOV *comes in cautiously and moves forward stealthily.*

Pepel [*to* VASSILISA]. All right, go!

Vassilisa. Think it over! [*Sees her husband.*] What brings you here? Looking for me?

PEPEL *jumps to his feet and stares wildly at* KOSTYLYOV.

Kostylyov. It's me—me! So the two of you were here alone, were you? I see. . . . Been having a chat, have you? [*Suddenly stamps his feet and screams.*] You dirty slut! You beggar! You harpy, you! [*Is frightened by his own screams, which are met by the others with silence and indifference.*] God forgive me, you've led me into sin again, Vassilisa. . . . Been looking everywhere for you. . . . [*Screams.*] Time to go to bed and you've forgotten to put oil in the icon lamp! Oh, you slut! Beggar! S-swine! [*Shakes his trembling hands at her.* VASSILISA *walks slowly toward the door, looking back at* PEPEL.]

Pepel [*to* KOSTYLYOV]. Hey, you! Get out—clear out of here!

Kostylyov [*shouts*]. I'm the landlord here! You clear out yourself, you thief!

Pepel [*thickly*]. Get out, you son-of-a-bitch!

Kostylyov. Don't you dare! I'll—I'll show you—I—

PEPEL *seizes him by the collar and shakes him. From the stove comes a loud noise and then the sound of yawning.* PEPEL *lets go of* KOSTYLYOV, *and the old man runs screaming into the passage.*

Pepel [*jumping onto the bunk*]. Who's that? Who's on the stove?

Luka [*thrusting out his head*]. Beg your pardon.

Pepel. You?!

Luka [*calmly*]. Yes, it's me. Oh, dear Jesus!

Pepel [*shuts passage door, looks for the bolt, but cannot find it*]. Oh, damn! Come down, old man!

Luka. One moment—I'm coming. . . .

Pepel [*gruffly*]. What made you climb on the stove?

Luka. Why? Shouldn't I?

Pepel. But—didn't you go out into the passage?

Luka. In the passage, my dear fellow, it's too cold for an old man like myself.

Pepel. You—heard?

Luka. Of course, I heard. Couldn't help hearing, could I? Well, lad, it seems you're in luck. Aye, you're lucky all right.

Pepel [*suspiciously*]. What sort of luck? How am I lucky?

Luka. Why, because I climbed on the stove.

Pepel. And—why did you start making such a hell of a din there?

Luka. Because, you see, I was getting too hot. That was a bit of luck for a poor orphan lad like you, wasn't it? And then again, you see, it crossed my mind—er—what if the poor lad should make a mistake and—er—strangle the poor old man?

Pepel. Ye-e-s. . . . I might have done it. . . . I hate him. . . .

Luka. Anyone might have done it! Nothing easier. . . . People often make such mistakes. . . .

Pepel [*smiling*]. Why? You haven't ever made such a mistake yourself, have you?

Luka. Now, listen to me, lad. Have nothing more to do with that woman! Keep away from her. Don't go near her. She'll get rid of her husband herself, and she'll do it much more cleverly than you. Yes, sir! Don't you listen to that she-devil. Look at me. Bald-headed, aren't I? Do you know why? Because of these same women. I knew more of them perhaps than there are hairs on my head. As for that Vassilisa—she's worse than a savage!

Pepel. I don't understand—I don't know whether to thank you or—whether you—too—

Luka. Not another word! You won't improve on what I said. Now listen to me: take the girl you're fond of here by the arm and get out quick—at the double! Get right out of here!

Pepel [*sullenly*]. Can't make people out. Which of 'em is good and which is bad. . . . Can't understand 'em at all!

Luka. What's there to understand? A man behaves in all sorts of ways. As his heart prompts him, so he behaves. Good today, bad tomorrow. And if you're serious about the girl, if you're really in love with her, take her away from here, and put an end to all this. If not, go away alone. You're young and you've got plenty of time to settle down with a woman.

Pepel [*taking him by the shoulder*]. Oh, no. You first tell me why you're saying all this.

Luka. Wait—let me go. . . . I must have a look at

Anna. She was breathing so heavily a moment ago. . . . [*Goes up to* ANNA's *bed, draws the curtains, looks, touches her with his hand.* PEPEL *watches him intently, looking perplexed.*] All-merciful Lord Jesus, give rest to the soul of thy newly departed servant Anna. . . .

Pepel [*softly*]. Is she dead? [*Without approaching, draws himself up to his full height and looks at the bed.*]

Luka. Aye, her suffering is over! Where's that husband of hers, I wonder?

Pepel. In the pub, I suppose.

Luka. He must be told.

Pepel [*with a shudder*]. I don't like dead people.

Luka [*going to the door*]. Why should one like them? It's the living one should like—the living.

Pepel. I'm coming with you.

Luka. Afraid?

Pepel. Don't like 'em.

They go out hurriedly. The stage is empty and silent for a few moments. A dull, uneven, incomprehensible noise is heard in the passage behind the door. Then THE ACTOR *comes in.*

The Actor [*stops on the threshold without shutting the door and, supporting himself against the jamb, shouts*]. Hey, old man, where are you? I've remembered—listen. [*Takes two staggering steps forward and, assuming a theatrical pose, recites.*]

> If the world, my friends, to Sacred Truth
> The craggy road cannot find,
> Glory to the madman who can bring
> A golden dream to oppressed mankind!

NATASHA *appears at the door behind* THE ACTOR.

The Actor. Old man!

> Though to our planet's diurnal course
> The sun forget to lend its fire,
> Some crazy madman's lofty thought
> Will illumine the world entire.

Natasha [*laughs*]. Scarecrow! You're plastered!

The Actor [*turning around to her*]. Oh, it's you, is it?

And where's the old man—the dear, dear old fellow? There seems to be no one here. Natasha, farewell! Fare thee well!

Natasha [coming in]. Saying good-by? You've never said good morning.

The Actor [barring her way]. I'm going away. Going away for good. When spring comes, I won't be here any more.

Natasha. Let me pass. Where are you off to?

The Actor. To look for a town where—where I can get proper treatment. You, too, must go away. Ophelia, get thee to a nunnery. You see, there's a hospital for organisms, I mean, for alcoholics. . . . Wonderful hospital. . . . Marble—marble floors! Plenty of light—everything spotless—good food—all for nothing! And a marble floor—yes! I'm going to find it, get cured and—and be a man again. . . . I'm on the way to be reborn again as—as—er—King Lear said. Natasha, my stage name is Sverchkov-Zavolzhsky—no one knows that, no one! I have no name here. Do you realize how awful it is to lose one's name? Even dogs have names. . . .

NATASHA *walks past* THE ACTOR *carefully, stops at* ANNA's *bed and looks.*

The Actor. Without a name you lose your personality.

Natasha. Look, my dear, she's dead.

The Actor [shaking his head]. It can't be.

Natasha [stepping back]. She is, I tell you. Look.

Bubnov [in the doorway]. Look at what?

Natasha. Anna—she's dead!

Bubnov. Oh well, she'll cough no more, then. [*Goes up to* ANNA's *bed, looks, then goes back to his place*]. Kleshch must be told. It's his affair.

The Actor. I'll go tell him. She's lost her name! [*Goes out.*]

Natasha [in the middle of the room]. I suppose one day I'll die like that, too—in a cellar—beaten black and blue. . . .

Bubnov [spreading out some rags on his bunk]. What's that? What are you muttering?

Natasha. Oh, nothing. I was talking to myself.

Bubnov. Waiting for Vassily? Mark my words, that

Vassily of yours will be the ruination of you one day.

Natasha. What does it matter who's my ruin? I'd much rather it was him.

Bubnov [*lying down*]. Oh well, it's your funeral. . . .

Natasha. I suppose it's a good thing she's died, but all the same, I can't help feeling sorry for her. . . . Dear Lord, what did she live for?

Bubnov. It's the same with everybody: they're born, they live and they die. I, too, will die—and you. . . . What's there to be sorry for?

Luka, The Tartar, Krivoy Zob, Kleshch *come in.* Kleshch, *hunched up, walks slowly behind the others.*

Natasha. Sh. . . . Anna!

Zob. We've heard. God rest her soul, if she's dead.

The Tartar [*to* Kleshch]. Must take her out. Take her into passage. Dead woman no place here. Living people sleeps here.

Kleshch [*in a low voice*]. We'll take her out. . . .

They all go up to the bed. Kleshch *looks at his wife over the shoulders of the others.*

Zob [*to* The Tartar]. Think there's going to be a bad smell? There won't be—she was all dried up while she lived.

Natasha. Dear Lord, if they'd only been sorry for her, if only someone had said a kind word! Oh, you!

Luka. Don't be upset, my dear. What does it matter? Why should they—why should we be sorry for the dead? Why, my dear child, we are not sorry for the living, we don't even know how to be sorry for ourselves. . . . So what can you expect?

Bubnov [*yawning*]. Besides, when you're dead no word can harm you no more. When you're ill it can, but not when you're dead!

The Tartar [*walking away*]. Must notify police.

Zob. Yes, the police must certainly be notified! Kleshch, have you informed the police?

Kleshch. No. Have to bury her, and all I've got is forty kopecks.

Zob. Well, in a case like that you must borrow, or else we'll take up a collection—five kopecks from one man and as much as he can spare from another. But you must notify the police—as soon as possible—else they'll think you killed the woman or something. . . . [*Goes to the bunk and is about to lie down beside* THE TARTAR.]

Natasha [*going up to* BUBNOV'*s bunk*]. I'm sure I'm going to dream about her now. . . . I always see dead people in my dreams. . . . I'm afraid to go back alone—it's dark in the passage.

Luka [*following her*]. It's the living you should be afraid of—that's what I think.

Natasha. See me across the passage, Granddad.

Luka. Come along, come along—I'll see you home.

They go out. Pause.

Zob. Dear me, Hassan, it will be spring soon, and it will be warm again. Yes, my friend, it will be warm. In the villages the peasants are already repairing their ploughs and harrows—getting ready for ploughing. . . . Ah, yes! And what about us, Hassan? Damned Mohammedan! Snoring already!

Bubnov. Tartars love to sleep.

Kleshch [*stands in the middle of the doss house, looking dully in front of him*]. What am I to do now?

Zob. Lie down and go to sleep—that's all.

Kleshch [*softly*]. And her—what about her?

No one answers him. SATIN *and* THE ACTOR *come in.*

The Actor [*shouts*]. Old man! Come hither, my faithful Kent!

Satin. The famous explorer Miklukha-Maklay is here—ha-ha!

The Actor. It's finally settled! Old man, where's the town? Where are you?

Satin. Fata-Morgana! The old man's told you a tall story. . . . There's nothing! No bloody towns, no bloody people—nothing!

The Actor. Don't talk nonsense!

The Tartar [*jumping up*]. Where is landlord? I go see landlord. No sleep—no rent. . . . Corpses. . . . Drunkards. . . . [*Goes out quickly.* SATIN *whistles after him.*]

Bubnov [*in a sleepy voice*]. Go to bed, fellows. Don't make a noise. A man must sleep at night!

The Actor. Yes, sir. Aha, there's a corpse here. A corpse. . . . "Our nets a corpse have caught"—a poem by B-béranger!

Satin [*shouts*]. Dead people don't hear! Dead people don't feel! Shout—scream as much as you like! Dead people don't hear!

LUKA *appears in the doorway.*

Curtain.

ACT THREE

"The Waste"—a plot of land strewn with rubbish and overgrown with weeds. In the background, a high, brick wall, which shuts out the sky. Beside it are elder bushes. To the right, a dark, timber wall of some outbuilding: a barn or stable. To the left, the peeling, gray wall of the building where KOSTYLYOV *has his doss house. It is built at a sharp angle so that its furthest corner reaches almost to the middle of the waste plot. Between it and the brick wall is a narrow alley. . . . In the gray wall with its peeling plaster are two windows: one on a level with the ground and the other about six feet higher and nearer to the brick wall. Beside this wall is a wide, low sledge turned upside down and a tree trunk about twelve feet long. To the right of the wall is a heap of old planks and girders.*

Evening. The sun is setting, throwing a crimson light on the brick wall. It is early spring, and the snow has melted only a short time ago. The black branches of the elder bushes are not yet in bud.

NATASHA *and* NASTYA *are sitting side by side on the tree trunk.* LUKA *and* THE BARON *are on the sledge.* KLESHCH *is lying on the heap of timber at the right wall.* BUBNOV's *face is at the ground-floor window.*

NASTYA [*with closed eyes and shaking her head in rhythm with her words, is telling a story in a singsong voice*]. And so at night he comes into the garden, as we've arranged, and goes straight into the summerhouse. I've been waiting for him for hours and I'm shaking with fear and grief. He, too, is trembling all over. White as chalk he is, and in his hand he has a revolver. . . .

Natasha [*chewing sunflower seeds*]. Goodness! No wonder they say these students are desperate characters. . . .

Nastya. And he says to me in a terrible voice: "My precious love. . . ."

Bubnov. Precious? Ha-ha!

The Baron. Look here, if you don't like it, don't listen, but do let her finish her story. Go on!

Nastya. "My one and only love," he says. "My parents," he says, "don't want to give their consent to our marriage, and—and threaten to disown me forever because of my love for you. And that's why," he says, "I must take my life." And his revolver was an enormous one and it was loaded with ten bullets. "Farewell," he says, "my heart's beloved! I've made up my mind and nothing in the world will make me change it. I can't live without you." And I says to him, I says: "Unforgettable friend of my bosom—Raoul. . . ."

Bubnov [*surprised*]. What did you say his name was? Crawl?

The Baron [*laughs uproariously*]. Nastya, you silly old thing, last time it was Gaston!

Nastya [*jumping up*]. Shut up, you poor wretches! Oh, you stray dogs! What do you know of love? True love? I know—I've experienced it—real, true love! [*To* THE BARON.] You good-for-nothing wastrel! Educated, you call yourself—used to drink coffee in bed, did you?

Luka. Wait, wait! Don't interrupt. Give her a chance, will you? It isn't what one says that matters, but why one says it. Yes, that's what matters! Go on with your story, lass. It's all right!

Bubnov. Show off your peacock's feathers, crow—carry on!

The Baron. Well, go on!

Natasha. Don't listen to them! Who are they, anyway?

They're just jealous. They've nothing to tell about themselves.

Nastya [*sits down again*]. I won't go on! I shan't say another word. If they don't believe me—if they go on laughing. . . . [*Suddenly interrupting her speech, remains silent for a few seconds and, closing her eyes again, continues in a loud and intense voice, waving her hand in rhythm with her speech, as though listening to the strains of far-off music.*] And so I says to him in reply: "Joy of my life, my beloved angel, I can't live without you, either, because I'm madly in love with you and I shall be in love with you as long as my heart beats in my bosom! But, please," I says, "don't take your young life! Please, darling, think of your dear parents and how necessary your life is to them, for you are their only happiness. Give me up, dear! I'd rather die longing for you, my only darling. I— I have no one in the world—I'm a bad one! Better that I should die—I don't matter! I'm no good at all and— and I've nothing—nothing. . . ." [*Buries her face in her hands and cries quietly.*]

Natasha [*turning away, in a low voice*]. Don't cry. Please, don't!

LUKA, *smiling, strokes* NASTYA's *head.*

Bubnov [*laughs loudly*]. Oh, you limb of Satan! Well, I never!

The Baron [*also laughs*]. Why, Grandpa, you don't think it's true, do you? It's all out of that book—*Ill-fated Love.* . . . It's all stuff and nonsense! Don't pay any attention to her!

Natasha. What has it got to do with you, you fool? You'd better shut up, if you haven't more sense than that.

Nastya [*furiously*]. God damn your soul! You're no damned good! Soul? You've no soul!

Luka [*takes* NASTYA's *hand*]. Let's go, my dear. Never mind—don't be angry! I know. I believe you. You are right, not they. If you believe you had a real love affair, then you had one! You did! As for him, don't be angry with him—don't be angry with someone you live with. . . . Perhaps he's jealous, and that's why he's laughing. Perhaps he's never had a real love—perhaps he's had nothing. . . . Come, let's go!

Nastya [pressing her hands tightly to her breast]. Granddad, I swear it happened! Everything happened just as I told you. He was a student—a Frenchman—Gaston his name was—he had a little black beard and patent leather shoes. . . . God strike me dead if I'm lying! And he loved me so passionately—so passionately!

Luka. Yes, I know. It's all right, I believe you! He wore patent leather shoes, you say? Well, well. . . . And did you love him, too? *[They disappear around the corner.]*

The Baron. Dear me, what a fool that girl is! She has a kind heart, mind, but she's such a damned fool, it's simply incredible!

Bubnov. And why, I wonder, are people so fond of lying? All the time! Just as if they were up before a magistrate. Honestly!

Natasha. Well, lying seems to be more fun than speaking the truth. . . . I, too—

The Baron. What? You, too. Go on!

Natasha. I like to imagine things. I imagine things and —wait. . . .

The Baron. For what?

Natasha [smiling embarrassedly]. Oh, I don't know. . . . For instance, tomorrow, I think, somebody will turn up— well, somebody special. . . . Or something will happen, something quite out of the ordinary. . . . Oh, I've been waiting for it to happen for ages. . . . I'm always waiting. But actually what is there to wait for?

A pause.

The Baron [with a grin]. It's no use waiting for anything. I don't expect anything. Everything has already happened. It's over and done with. Go on. . . .

Natasha. Or else I imagine that—that tomorrow I'll— I'll suddenly die. . . . And that gives me such a creepy feeling. Summer is a good time for thinking about death. . . . There are thunderstorms in summer—one might always be struck by lightning. . . .

The Baron. Life is not so easy for you here. That sister of yours—she's got the devil's own temper!

Natasha. But who finds life easy? It's damned hard for all of us—I can see that.

Kleshch [*until that moment indifferent and motionless— suddenly jumps to his feet*]. All of us! Oh, no. Not all of us! If it was for all, it wouldn't matter! Then it wouldn't hurt so much! No, sir!

Bubnov. What the hell's been biting you? Fancy, setting up such a howl!

KLESHCH *lies down on his old place again, muttering to himself.*

The Baron. I think I'd better go and make my peace with dear old Nastya. If I don't, she won't give me anything for a drink.

Bubnov. Mmmm. . . . Extraordinary how people like to tell lies! Well, Nastya—I'm not surprised at her! She's used to making up her silly face, so she naturally likes to make up her soul, too—add a bit of color to it. . . . But the others—why do they do it? Take Luka, for instance. He tells a lot of quite amazing lies and doesn't seem to get anything out of it, either. An old man, too. . . . What does he do it for?

The Baron [*smiling, walks away*]. People have such drab souls—they are all anxious to put some make-up on them.

Luka [*coming in from around the corner*]. You, sir, why do you upset the girl? Why don't you leave her alone? Let her have her cry if it makes her happy. You see, she weeps for her own pleasure—what harm does it do you?

The Baron. It's so silly, old man. One gets sick and tired of her. Today it's Raoul, tomorrow it's Gaston—and always the same old story! Still, I'm going to make it up with her. [*Goes out.*]

Luka. Go and be nice to her. It never comes amiss to be nice to people.

Natasha. You're such a kind man, Granddad. . . . Why are you so kind?

Luka. Kind, did you say? Well, I don't mind, I'm sure, if that's what I am. [*From behind the brick wall come the soft strains of a concertina and a song.*] You see, my dear, someone has to be kind—one must take pity on people! Christ took pity on everybody and he bade us do likewise. Let me tell you, showing sympathy for a man when he most needs it can do a lot of good. Now, for instance, I

used to be a watchman at the country house of an engineer
near Tomsk. Very well. The country house was in a forest,
a lonely place, it was, too. In winter I was left alone there,
in the country house, I mean. It was lovely there—aye,
real beautiful it was. Well, one night I hear someone trying to get into the house.

Natasha. Burglars?

Luka. Yes, burglars. So there they were, trying hard to get
in. Well, I picked up my gun and went outside. There
were two of them. I saw them at once. Trying to open
a window, they were, and so busy were they that they
didn't even notice me. I shouted at them: "Hey, you,
clear out of here!" So they rushed at me at once, with
an ax. I warned them: "Keep away or I shoot!" And I
kept covering them with my gun—first the one and then
the other. Well, so down on their knees they went, begging
me to let them go. But, by that time, you see, I was getting
pretty sore at them because of the ax, and I says to them:
"Why, you devils, when I told you to clear out, you
wouldn't do it, so now break off some branches from a tree,
one of you!" So they did. "And now," I says, "one of you
lie down and let the other flog him!" So they gave each
other a good flogging and, after they had done that, they
said to me: "Granddad, give us some bread, for Christ's
sake, we haven't had a bite for days." There's burglars for
you, my dear! [*Laughs.*] Aye, coming at you with an ax,
if you please! Yes. . . . Fine lads they were, both of them.
I says to them, "Why didn't you devils ask me for bread
straight away?" And they said, "We got tired of asking.
You keep asking people and nobody gives you anything—
it makes you feel pretty sore!" So they stayed with me all
that winter. One of 'em, Stepan, his name was, would
take my gun and disappear for days into the forest, and
the other, Yakov, his name was, was sick most of the time,
had a terrible cough, he had. And so the three of us kept
watch over the country house. When spring came,
"Good-by, Granddad," they said, and went back home to
Russia. . . .

Natasha. Were they on the run? Convicts?

Luka. Aye, that's what they were—on the run. Been sent

to some remote spot and escaped from there. Fine lads! Had I not felt sorry for them, they might have killed me or done me some injury. And then they would have been put on trial, sent to jail and afterwards to Siberia. It doesn't make sense, does it? Prison will not make a good man of you, neither will Siberia, but a man—can. Aye, a man can teach another man to be good. It's as simple as that.

Bubnov. Mmmm—yes! Now, I wouldn't know how to tell a lie. Why tell lies? What I say is—out with the unvarnished truth! The whole truth and nothing but. Why feel shy about it?

Kleshch [again jumps suddenly to his feet as though his clothes were on fire and shouts]. What truth? Where's truth? [*Pulling at his tattered clothes.*] Here's the truth! No work—no strength! That's the truth! No place to live! The only thing left is to die—like a dog—that's the truth! What the hell do I want truth for? Give me a chance to breathe freely! What have I done wrong? How am I to blame? What do I want truth for? The fact is, damn it, that I haven't a chance—not a chance—to live, that's the truth!

Bubnov. He's got it bad, hasn't he?

Luka. Good Lord, now listen to me, my dear fellow. You should—

Kleshch [trembling with excitement]. You talk about truth here. Truth! You, old man, keep comforting everybody. Let me tell you something—I hate everyone! This truth of yours included. The devil take it! Understand? I'll say it again: the devil take it! [*Rushes away around the corner, looking back as he runs.*]

Luka. Dear me, how agitated the man is! And where has he run off to?

Natasha. Just as if he'd gone out of his mind. . . .

Bubnov. Did his piece beautifully. Just like on the stage. It happens quite often to him. . . . Hasn't got used to life yet, he hasn't.

Pepel [comes in slowly from around the corner]. Peace to the honest company! Well, Luka, you crafty old geezer, still telling your tall stories?

Luka. You should have heard how that fellow carried on!

Pepel. Who? Kleshch? What's the matter with him? He was running like a scalded cat.

Luka. You'd run, too, if something like this tore at your heart.

Pepel [*sits down*]. I don't like him. He's too bitter and proud. [*Mimicking* KLESHCH.] I'm a workingman! And he thinks everyone's beneath him. Work, if you like, but what's there to be proud of? If people are to be valued by the amount of work they do, then a horse is a damned sight more valuable than any man: you drive it and—it doesn't utter a word. I say, Natasha, are your people at home?

Natasha. They've gone to the cemetery and they thought of going to evening Mass afterwards.

Pepel. Oh, I see. So that's why you're free! Quite unusual, isn't it?

Luka [*thoughtfully*, to BUBNOV]. Now, you say—truth. But truth, you see, is not a universal cure for human ills— you can't always cure a man by telling him the truth about himself. Now take a case like this, for instance. I knew a man who believed in a land of righteousness.

Bubnov. In wha-a-at?

Luka. In a land of righteousness. Somewhere on earth, he used to say, there must be a land of righteousness, in which some special kind of people live—good people! People who respect one another, who help one another without expecting anything in return and—and everything in that land is wonderful! And so this man was always about to set off in search of that land of righteousness. He was very poor and he had a hard life, but when things got so bad that there seemed nothing else for him to do except lie down and die, he never lost heart; he'd just smile and say: "Never mind! I can stand it! I'll wait a little longer and then say good-by to this life and go away to the land of righteousness. . . . There was only one thing that made him happy: the thought of that land. . . .

Pepel. Well? Did he go there?

Bubnov. Where? Ho-ho!

Luka. Now it so happened that a political exile, a very great scholar he was, came to that place—in Siberia, as a matter of fact. He came there with his books and maps and all sorts of things. So the man I was telling you about says to the scholar: "Do me a favor, sir, and show me where the land of righteousness is and how I can get there." Well, the scholar at once opened his books, spread out his maps, and looked and looked, but the land of righteousness was nowhere to be found! Everything is in order, all the lands are shown, but the land of righteousness isn't there! No sign of it!

Pepel [*in a low voice*]. Well? Doesn't it exist?

BUBNOV *roars with laughter.*

Natasha. Shut up, you! Well, Granddad?

Luka. The man wouldn't believe it. "It must exist," he says. "Look again! For," he says, "if there is no land of righteousness, your books and your maps are no damned use!" The scholar was offended. "My maps," he says, "are absolutely correct, but there is no land of righteousness anywhere." Well, of course, the man got angry. "What do you mean?" he says. "All my life I've put up with all sorts of hardships in the firm belief that such a land exists and, according to the maps, it doesn't exist at all. Why, it's sheer robbery!" So he says to the scholar, he says, "Oh, you dirty swine, you! You're a damned rogue and not a scholar at all!" And he punches him on the nose once, and then again! [*After a short pause.*] After that he went home and—hanged himself!

They are all silent, LUKA *looks at* PEPEL *and* NATASHA *with a smile.*

Pepel [*in a low voice*]. Damn you—not a very cheerful tale, is it?

Natasha. Couldn't stand the disappointment, I suppose.

Bubnov [*morosely*]. Oh, it's all fairy tales!

Pepel. Well, well—so there's the land of righteousness for you—not to be found, it seems.

Natasha. I'm sorry for the poor man.

Bubnov. Just another tall story! Not a hope! Ho-ho! A land of righteousness! What an idea! Ho-ho-ho! [*Disappears from the window.*]

Luka [*nodding in the direction of Bubnov's window*]. He laughs! Dear, oh dear. . . . [*Pause.*] Well, children, make the best of your life, I'll be leaving you soon.

Pepel. Where are you off to now?

Luka. To the Ukraine. I'm told they've discovered a new religion there, so I'd like to go and have a look. Aye, people are always looking for something better, they always want something better—may the Lord grant them patience!

Pepel. What do you think? Will they find it?

Luka. The people? They'll find it all right. He who seeks, will find. He who wants something badly, will find it.

Natasha. If they would only find something—think of something better.

Luka. They will! Only we must help them, lass, we must show that we appreciate their efforts.

Natasha. How can I help? I can't help myself.

Pepel [*determinedly*]. Look here, Natasha, let me say it to you again—here—before him—he knows everything. . . . Come away—with me!

Natasha. Where to? From one prison to another?

Pepel. I've told you—I'll go straight. I swear I will! If I say so, I'll do it. I can read and write—I'll work. Luka here has been saying I ought to go to Siberia of my own free will. Well, let's go there. Why not? Do you think I'm not disgusted with my life? Good Lord, Natasha, I know—I see it all! I console myself with the thought that other people are bigger thieves than I and yet are honored and respected. But that doesn't help much, does it? That has nothing to do with it! I—don't repent and—and I don't believe in conscience, but I do know one thing: this is not the way to live! I must live a better life! I must live so that—so that I can respect myself.

Luka. You're right, my dear fellow. May the Lord help you! It's true: a man must respect himself.

Pepel. I've been a thief ever since I can remember. Everyone always called me: Vasska the thief, Vasska, the son of a thief! Ah, so that's it! Very well, then, have it your way: I am a thief! Don't you see? Perhaps I'm a thief out of spite. I'm a thief because no one ever thought of calling me anything else. Won't you, Natasha, call me—something else? Well?

Natasha [*sadly*]. Somehow I don't believe you—whatever you may say. . . . And I feel so uneasy today—my heart's heavy, as if I were expecting something to happen. I'm sorry you started this conversation today, Vassily.

Pepel. When should I have started it? It isn't the first time I've talked to you about it.

Natasha. And why should I go away with you? You see, I'm not really in love with you. Sometimes I like you, but there are times when I hate the sight of you. When one is in love with a man, one doesn't find fault with him. But I do. . . .

Pepel. You'll love me in time, don't worry. I'll make you care for me. All you have to say is—yes. I've been watching you for over a year. . . . I can see that you're a good girl, that you wouldn't allow anyone to take liberties with you—a reliable person, and—and I'm very much in love with you!

VASSILISA, *smartly dressed, appears at the window and listens, standing at the side.*

Natasha. I see. You've fallen in love with me but with my sister you've—

Pepel [*embarrassed*]. Well, what about her? There are lots—like her. . . .

Luka. Don't worry about that, lass. Half a loaf is better than no bread.

Pepel [*gloomily*]. You—you must have pity on me! I lead a wretched sort of life—the life of a wolf—not much fun in it. . . . I feel as if I'm sinking in a bog; whatever I catch hold of is rotten—it breaks off in my hand. . . . I thought your sister might save me, but she's not that kind of woman. If she wasn't so greedy for money, I—I'd have done anything for her. Only she had to be all mine! But, well, she's after something else—she wants money and—and she wants freedom—freedom to sleep with any man she likes. She can't help me. . . . But you—you are like a young fir tree—prickly to the touch, but safe to hold on to. . . .

Luka. Why, yes, marry him, lass, do! He's a good lad. He won't let you down. Only don't forget to tell him now and then that he's a good lad, so that he doesn't forget it! He'll believe you. Just keep telling him: "Vassily, you're a good man—don't you forget it!" Just think, my dear, where else could you go? Your sister is a savage beast and her husband is worse—he's past praying for. And all this life here. . . . Where can you go? And he's a staunch, reliable fellow. . . .

Natasha. I've nowhere to go—I know—I've thought of it myself. Only you see, I've no faith in anybody. . . . But, of course, I've nowhere to go. . . . That's true enough. . . .

Pepel. There's one way for you here, but I won't let you go that way—I'd kill you first.

Natasha [*smiling*]. There, you see. . . . I'm not your wife yet, and already you're wanting to kill me.

Pepel [*embracing her*]. Chuck it, Natasha! I know you'll come with me whatever happens!

Natasha [*clinging to him*]. Anyway, one thing I will tell you, Vassily—and I swear I mean it!—the first time you strike me or—or wrong me in any way, I'll have no pity on myself—I'll either hang myself or—

Pepel. Strike you? Why, I'd cut off my right hand first!

Luka. Have no fear, my dear. He needs you more than you need him.

Vassilisa [*from the window*]. There, so now you're engaged! Congratulations!

Natasha. They've come back! Oh, Lord, they've seen us! Oh, Vassily!

Pepel. What are you afraid of? Nobody'll dare touch you now!

Vassilisa. Don't be afraid, Natasha. He won't beat you. He can neither beat nor love—I know!

Luka [*in a low voice*]. What a poisonous woman!

Vassilisa. He's a real terror—with words!

Kostylyov [*comes in*]. Natasha, you little good-for-nothing parasite, what are you doing here? Telling tales? Complaining about your family? Is the samovar ready? Has the table been laid?

Natasha [*going out*]. But you said you wanted to go to church. . . .

Kostylyov. Oh? We wanted to go to church, did we? What has it got to do with you? See that you do your work—do what you're told!

Pepel. Shut up—you! She isn't your servant any more. . . . Natasha, don't go—don't do anything for them!

Natasha. Don't you start ordering me about—it's a bit too soon! [*Goes out.*]

Pepel [*to* KOSTYLYOV]. Lay off her, will you? You've bullied her long enough! Now—she's mine!

Kostylyov. Yours? When did you buy her? How much did you pay for her?

VASSILISA *roars with laughter.*

Luka. Vassily, you'd better go. . . .

Pepel. Merry, are you? You wait—you'll be weeping soon!

Vassilisa. Oh, dear, I'm so afraid! Oh, dear, I'm so scared!

Luka. Go, Vassily, there's a good fellow! Don't you see she's trying to provoke you—egging you on?

Pepel. Is she now? Well, she's making a big mistake! Yes, you're making a big mistake! You won't get what you want!

Vassilisa. Neither will you get what I don't want!

Pepel [*shaking his fist at her*]. We'll see! [*Goes out.*]

Vassilisa [*disappearing from the window*]. I'll arrange a nice wedding for you, I don't think!

Kostylyov [*going up to* LUKA]. Well, how are things with you, old man?

Luka. Oh, all right, thank you, old man.

Kostylyov. I see. . . . I hear you're leaving.

Luka. It's time I was.

Kostylyov. Where are you going?

Luka. Oh, anywhere.

Kostylyov. Tramping, I suppose. You don't like staying long in one place, do you?

Luka. Well, you know, they say even water won't flow under a boulder.

Kostylyov. A boulder—yes, but a man must settle in one place. People can't live like cockroaches, crawling anywhere they like. They must stick to one place and not wander aimlessly all over the world.

Luka. And what about the man to whom any place in the world is home?

Kostylyov. Well, the man is a tramp, a vagabond, a useless fellow. A man must be useful, do a job of work. . . .

Luka. Must he now?

Kostylyov. Certainly. How else? What's a wanderer—a pilgrim? He's a stranger everywhere—or, in other words, a strange man, a man who is not like the rest of us. If he really is a pilgrim, he may know something, have found out something that's of no use to anybody or, again, he may have discovered the truth in his wanderings; but of course, not every truth can be useful—no, sir! So he'd do better to keep it to himself—shut up about it! Indeed, if he is a real pilgrim, he doesn't talk, or talks in a way that no one can understand. And, mind you, he wants nothing, interferes with no one and doesn't make trouble without good reason. How people live is none of his business. He has to lead a life of righteousness—he must live in the woods, in the thickets and—keep out of sight! He mustn't interfere with anybody or criticize anybody, but pray for everybody, for all worldly sins—for yours, for mine, for everything. For that's why he put worldly vanity behind him—so that he can pray. That's how it is. [*Pause.*] But you—what sort of pilgrim are you? You haven't any papers. An honest, respectable man has papers. All honest people have papers—yes, sir!

Luka. There are people *and* people!

Kostylyov. Don't try to be funny! Don't talk to me in riddles. I'm no stupider than you. What do you mean—there are people *and* people?

Luka. There's no riddle there. All I'm saying is that there is sterile land and there is fertile land—whatever you sow on it, grows, that's all.

Kostylyov. Well? What do you mean by that?

Luka. Now, take yourself, for instance. If the Lord God himself said to you: "Mikhail, be a man!" it wouldn't make any difference: you'd be the same as ever.

Kostylyov. Is that so? And—and you don't perhaps happen to know that my wife's uncle is a policeman, do you? And that if I—

Vassilisa [*comes in*]. Go and have your tea, Mikhail.

Kostylyov [*to* Luka]. Now look here, you—get out of my house! Beat it!

Vassilisa. Yes, indeed, be off with you, old man. You talk too much. Besides—for all we know you may be an escaped convict.

Kostylyov. Don't let me find you here again today—or else—

Luka. You'll call your uncle? Go on, call him. Tell him you've caught an escaped convict. He may get a reward—three kopecks. . . .

Bubnov [*at the window*]. What are you selling there? What are you asking three kopecks for?

Luka. They're threatening to sell me. . . .

Vassilisa [*to her husband*]. Come on.

Bubnov. For three kopecks? If you're not careful, old man, they'll sell you for one.

Kostylyov [*to* BUBNOV]. What are you glaring at us for like a house goblin from under the stove? [*Walks away with his wife.*]

Vassilisa. The world's full of suspicious characters and all sorts of crooks!

Luka. Have a good feed!

Vassilisa [*turning around*]. Hold your tongue, you dirty toadstool! [*Goes out with her husband.*]

Luka. I'll be off tonight.

Bubnov. That's right. It's always better to get away in time.

Luka. True enough.

Bubnov. I know. I probably escaped being sent to Siberia by getting away in time.

Luka. Oh?

Bubnov. It's quite true. What happened was that my wife had an affair with my foreman. Now, to be quite fair, my foreman was excellent at his job. Very clever at dying a dog's skin to look like raccoon, he was. Could also turn cat's skins into kangaroo, muskrat and all sorts of other furs. A very adroit fellow. Anyway, my wife fell for him and they became so crazy about each other that I was afraid they would poison me or get rid of me in some other way. I tried beating my wife, but the foreman retaliated by beating me—packed a wicked punch, the rascal! Once he broke one of my ribs and pulled half my beard out. So, of course, I flew into a rage, too, and one day I bashed my wife over the head with an iron measuring rod —in short, a regular war broke out between us! However, I soon realized that there was nothing in it for me, for they were certainly getting the better of me. It was then that I made up my mind to murder my wife, and I meant to do it, too! But I checked myself in time and—got away.

Luka. Best thing you could have done. Let them go on turning dogs into raccoons.

Bubnov. There was a snag in it, though. My workshop was in my wife's name and I was left as you see me now! But, to tell the truth, I shouldn't have kept my workshop very long. I'm a hard drinker, you see.

Luka. A hard drinker? Ah!

Bubnov. Drink like a fish! The moment I start, I can't stop—spend everything I possess on drink. All I'm left with is my skin and bones. And another thing—I'm lazy. I just hate work!

SATIN *and* THE ACTOR *come in, arguing.*

Satin. Nonsense! You won't go anywhere. It's sheer lunacy. Old man, what have you dinned into the ears of this hooligan here?

The Actor. It's you who're talking nonsense! Grandpa, tell him that he doesn't know what he's talking about. I'm going away. I did some work today—swept the streets and haven't had a drop of vodka. Not a drop. What do you think of that? Here are the two fifteen-kopeck bits and I'm as sober as a judge!

Satin. The whole thing's too absurd! Give me the money —I'll spend it on drink or lose it at cards.

The Actor. Go away! It's for my trip.

Luka [*to* SATIN]. And why do you lead him astray?

Satin. Tell me, O soothsayer, beloved of the gods, what life doth hold in store for me! I'm broke, my dear fellow, lost everything! But everything isn't lost yet, Grandpa— there are cardsharpers much cleverer than I!

Luka. What a merry fellow you are, to be sure!

Bubnov. I say, actor, come over here!

THE ACTOR *crosses over to the window and squats in front of it. They talk together in an undertone.*

Satin. When I was young, my dear fellow, I was the life and soul of the party. Does me good to think of it. Hail-fellow-well-met sort of man. An excellent dancer, good amateur actor, liked to make people laugh—had a glorious time!

Luka. What made you stray from your path of glory?

Satin. What a damned curious old man you are! You want to know everything—don't you? What for?

Luka. I'd like to understand the ways of men. Now I look at you and I can't make you out. You're such a fine figure of a man—no fool, either, and suddenly—

Satin. Prison, Grandpa. I spent four years and seven months in prison, and after that I found every way barred to me.

Luka. Aha! And what were you sent to prison for?

Satin. For a dirty rotter! Killed him in a fit of rage and exasperation. . . . It was in prison I learned to play cards.

Luka. Did you kill him because of a woman?

Satin. Because of my sister. But—do leave me alone, please. I don't like being cross-examined. Besides, all this happened a long time ago. . . . It's nine years since my sister died. Oh, she was a wonderful girl, that sister of mine!

Luka. You certainly take life lightly! That locksmith now —he raised such a clamor a short while ago—oh, dear!

Satin. Kleshch?

Luka. Yes. "There's no work," he shouted, "there's nothing."

Satin. He'll get used to it. What is he going to do now, I wonder?

Luka [*softly*]. Look—here he comes.

KLESHCH *walks in slowly, his head bent low.*

Satin. Hey, widower! What are you so damned miserable about? A penny for your thoughts.

Kleshch. I'm trying to think what to do now. I have no tools—the funeral took everything I had.

Satin. Let me give you a word of advice—don't do anything! Just burden the earth with your presence.

Kleshch. Go on—talk. . . . Me—I'd die of shame before people.

Satin. Stop talking rubbish! People aren't ashamed because they let you live worse than a dog, are they? Just think —you won't do any work, I won't do any work, and hundreds, thousands of others won't do any work—everybody'll stop working, nobody will do a damned thing—what'll happen then?

Kleshch. They'll all starve to death, I suppose.

Luka [*to* SATIN]. If that's what you really think, then you'd better join the runners. There is such a sect, you know, who refuse to work and wander about from place to place and die nameless and are buried in secret.

Satin. I know. They're no fools, Grandpa.

From the window of KOSTYLYOV's *room* NATASHA *can be heard screaming* "What for? Stop! What've I done?"

Luka [*agitatedly*]. Natasha! It was her voice! Oh, dear!

A noise, scurrying feet, breaking of crockery can be heard from KOSTYLYOV's *rooms, and* KOSTYLYOV's *shrill cry:* "Oh, you damned heathen! You dirty slut!"

Vassilisa's Voice. Stop. . . . Wait. . . . Let me get at her. . . . Take that—and that. . . .

Natasha's Voice. Help! They're beating me! They're killing me!

Satin [*shouts through the window*]. Hey—you there!

Luka [*bustling about*]. Vassily, we must call Vassily—oh, Lord—you there, do something. . . .

The Actor [*running off*]. I'll get him at once. . . .

Bubnov. They've been beating her rather a lot lately.

Satin. Come on, old man—we shall be witnesses! [*Goes out.*]

Luka [*following* SATIN]. What sort of witness am I? What's the use of it, anyway? If only Vassily would come at once—oh, dear, oh, dear!

Natasha's Voice. Sister—dear sister—ah-h-h. . . .

Bubnov. They've gagged her. . . . I'd better go and have a look. . . . [*Goes out.*]

The noise in KOSTYLYOV's *room dies down, getting fainter and fainter, probably because they had gone into the passage. The old man's cry:* "Stop!" *is heard. A door is slammed to with a bang, and this sound cuts off the other noises abruptly. Quiet on the stage. Twilight.*

Kleshch [*sits impassively on the sledge, rubbing his hands vigorously. Then he begins to mutter something, at first indistinctly, then.*] Why, of course . . . One must live. [*Louder.*] Must get some kind of shelter. Without a roof over your head there's nothing! Only man by himself— alone. . . . All alone. . . . No help. . . .

Goes out slowly, bending low. A few moments of ominous silence. Then, somewhere in the passage, a confused noise arises, a chaos of sounds. It grows, getting nearer and nearer. Individual voices are heard.

Vassilisa's Voice. I'm her sister! Let go of me!

Kostylyov's Voice. What right have you—?

Vassilisa's Voice. Jailbird!

Satin's Voice. Call Vassily—quick! Zob—hit him!

A police whistle.

The Tartar [*runs out, his right hand in a sling*]. What law is it? Kill people in daytime?

Zob [*followed by* MEDVEDEV]. Oh, I let him have a real smasher!

Medvedev. You there! What right have you to fight?

The Tartar: And you? What's your duty?

Medvedev [*running after the porter*]. Stop! Give me back my whistle!

Kostylyov [*runs in*]. Abram, catch him! Hold him! He attacked me!

From behind the corner KVASHNYA *and* NASTYA *come in, supporting* NATASHA *who is disheveled.* SATIN *follows them, walking backward and pushing away* VASSILISA, *who is waving her arms and is trying to attack her sister.* ALYOSHKA *jumps up and down like a madman beside her.* ALYOSHKA *whistles into her ear, shouts, howls. They are followed by a few more ragged figures of men and women.*

Satin [*to* VASSILISA]. Keep away, you fiend. . . .

Vassilisa. Get out of my way, jailbird! I'll tear her limb from limb even if I have to pay for it with my own life.

Kvashnya [*leading* NATASHA *aside*]. Calm down, Vassilisa, will you? Shame on you! What are you rampaging for?

Medvedev [*seizes* SATIN]. Aha! Caught you!

Satin. Zob, pitch into them! Vassily! Vassily!

They all struggle in a heap near the alley by the brick wall. NATASHA *is led away to the right and made to sit down on*

a pile of wood. Pepel jumping out of the alley, silently
brushes them aside with powerful movements.

Kostylyov [hiding behind the corner]. Abram, get Vassily! All of you, help him to catch Vassily—the thief—the
robber!

Pepel. Oh, you—old lecher! [*Aims a terrific blow at*
Kostylyov, *who falls to the ground so that only the upper*
part of his body can be seen from behind the corner.
Pepel *rushes up to* Natasha.]

Vassilisa. Beat him—please, please, beat the thief!

Medvedev [shouts to Satin]. Keep out of this—this is a
family affair! They're relatives—and who are you?

Pepel. How—how did she attack you? With a knife?

Kvashnya. Look what those beasts have done! Scalded
the girl's feet with boiling water.

Nastya. Overturned the samovar on her!

The Tartar. Maybe it was an accident. Must find out
for sure. Mustn't talk like that. . . .

Natasha [almost in a faint]. Vassily—take me away—
hide me!

Vassilisa. Oh, Lord! Look, all of you! He's dead! Murdered!

All crowd near the passage around Kostylyov. Bubnov
emerges from the crowd and goes up to Vassily.

Bubnov [in a low voice]. Vassily! The old man—he's
dead!

Pepel [looks at him as though he doesn't understand].
Go—get some help—she must be taken to the hospital.
. . . Oh, I'll get even with them!

Bubnov. Somebody has killed the old man, I'm telling
you.

The noise on the stage dies down like a campfire on which
water has been thrown. Single exclamations can be heard
uttered in an undertone: "Not really?" "Well, well!"
"We'd better get out of here!" "The devil!" "He'd better
look out now!" "Let's get away before the police come!"
The crowd dwindles. Bubnov *goes out.* The Tartar,
Nastya *and* Kvashnya *rush up to* Kostylyov's *body.*

Vassilisa [rising from the ground, shouts in a triumphant

voice]. Murdered! There's his murderer! Vassily murdered him. I saw it. I saw it! Well, Vassily? Police!

Pepel [*moving away from* NATASHA]. Let go of me— go away! [*Looks at the old man. To* VASSILISA.] Well? Are you glad? [*Touches the corpse with his foot.*] Dead—the old bastard! You've got what you wanted. . . . Why not? May as well settle you, too! [*Rushes at* VASSILISA: SATIN *and* ZOB *catch hold of him quickly.* VASSILISA *disappears in the alley.*]

Satin. Come to your senses, man!

Zob. Whoa-a! Not so fast!

Vassilisa [*appearing*]. Well, Vassily, my dear? You won't escape your fate now, will you? Police! Abram, whistle!

Medvedev. They've torn off my whistle, the devils!

Alyoshka. Here it is! [*Whistles.* MEDVEDEV *runs after him.*]

Satin [*taking* PEPEL *to* NATASHA]. Vassily, old boy, there's nothing to be afraid of! Killed in a fight—it's manslaughter. You'll get off cheap.

Vassilisa. Hold Vassily! He killed him—I saw it!

Satin. I, too, hit him three times. . . . He didn't need much, did he? Call me as witness, Vassily.

Pepel. There's no need for me to—to justify myself. All I want is to drag Vassilisa into it—and I will drag her into it! She wanted it all along. . . . She tried to persuade me to kill her husband—yes, she urged me to do it.

Natasha [*suddenly, in a loud voice*]. Oh, now I understand! So that's it, Vassily? Listen to me, all of you— they're in it together! My sister and—and he—they're in it together! They had it all planned! Isn't that so, Vassily? You—you said all that to me a little while ago so that she should overhear it, didn't you? Listen, all, she's his mistress —you know it—you all know it—they're in it together! It was she—it was she who incited him to kill her husband —he was in their way and I—I was in their way, too. . . . So now they've crippled me. . . .

Pepel. Natasha, what's the matter with you? What are you saying?

Satin. Good Lord!

Vassilisa. It's a damned lie! She's lying! I—he, Vassily, killed him.

Natasha. They're both in it! God damn you both!

Satin. Well, what a mix-up! Look out, Vassily, they'll ruin you between them!

Zob. It's beyond me! Goodness, what a mess!

Pepel. Natasha, you can't be serious! You can't possibly believe that I—with her. . . .

Satin. Honestly, Natasha, think what you're saying!

Vassilisa [*in the alley*]. They've killed my husband, sir. Vassily Pepel, the thief, killed him, Inspector. I saw it—everybody saw it. . . .

Natasha [*tossing about in agony, almost on the point of fainting*]. All of you, listen, please, listen to me: my sister and Vassily killed him! Officer, officer, listen, this sister of mine has incited—persuaded her lover—there he is, damn him! They killed him! Arrest them—put them on trial. . . . Take me to jail, too! Take me to jail, for Christ's sake!

Curtain.

ACT FOUR

Same as Act One. But PEPEL's *room is no longer there, the partitions having been removed. There is no anvil where Kleshch used to sit.* THE TARTAR *is lying in the corner where* PEPEL's *room used to be. He is tossing about and groaning from time to time.* KLESHCH *is sitting at one end of the table, repairing a concertina and at times testing the stops.* SATIN, THE BARON *and* NASTYA *sit at the other end of the table. In front of them they have a bottle of vodka, three bottles of beer and a large hunk of black bread.* THE ACTOR *is moving about restlessly and coughing on the stove.*

It is night. The stage is lit by a lamp in the middle of the table. The wind can be heard howling outside.

KLESHCH. Aye, he disappeared during the confusion.

The Baron. Vanished under the very noses of the police like unto smoke from the face of the fire.

Satin. So flee the sinners from the face of the righteous.

Nastya. He was a good old man, and you—you're not men, you're just rust!

The Baron [drinks]. Your health, my lady!

Satin. An interesting old codger—yes, indeed! Nastya here fell in love with him.

Nastya. Yes, I did. I got to like him very much. Quite true. He saw everything and understood everything.

Satin [laughing]. And, generally speaking, he was to many of us like soft bread to the toothless.

The Baron [laughing]. Like a plaster on a boil.

Kleshch. He was compassionate. The trouble with you is you have no compassion.

Satin. What good will it do you if I show compassion for you?

Kleshch. You needn't show compassion, but you needn't hurt people's feelings, either.

The Tartar [sits up on his bunk, rocking his wounded arm as if it were a baby]. Old man was good. He had law in soul. Man who has law in soul is good. If man lose law, he's finished.

The Baron. What law, Prince?

The Tartar. Oh, such a one—different one—you know which. . . .

The Baron. Go on.

The Tartar. Don't hurt man—that's the law.

Satin. You mean the code relating to misdemeanors, their repression and punishment, don't you?

The Baron. And don't forget the code of penalties imposed by justices of the peace.

The Tartar. I mean Koran. Your Koran must be law. Soul must be Koran—yes, sir!

Kleshch [testing the concertina]. It wheezes, damn it. The Prince is right: one must live according to the law, according to the Gospels.

Satin. Go on, do it.

The Baron. Just try it.

The Tartar. Mahomet gave Koran. He said: this is law.

Do as written there. Then time come when Koran not enough. Time will give own law. Different time give different law.

Satin. You're damned right. The time came and gave us the code relating to criminal misdemeanors. It's a strong law. Won't wear out for a long time.

Nastya [*bangs her glass on the table*]. Why, oh why, do I go on living with you here, I don't know. I'll go away. Anywhere. To the end of the world.

The Baron. Without shoes, my lady?

Nastya. Stark naked. Crawl on all fours.

The Baron. That will certainly make a lovely picture, my lady. If you do it on all fours!

Nastya. Yes, I will. So long as I don't have to see your ugly face any more. Oh, I'm sick to death of it all! Of all this life. All these people.

Satin. Please take the actor with you when you go. He's going there, too. He has just learned that only half a mile from the world's end there's a hospital for organons.

The Actor [*poking his head out from the top of the stove*]. Or-ga-nisms, you fool!

Satin. For organons poisoned with alcohol.

The Actor. Yes, sir! He will go. He will. You'll see.

The Baron. Who is he, Your Highness?

The Actor. I!

The Baron. Thank you, servant of the goddess—what's her name? The goddess of drama, of tragedy—what was she called?

The Actor. The Muse, you blockhead. The Muse, not the goddess.

Satin. Lachesis—Hera—Aphrodite—Atropos, damned if I know which! It's all the old man's doing: he got the actor worked up. See what I mean, Baron?

The Baron. The old man's a fool.

The Actor. Ignoramuses! Savages! Mean men without hearts! Mel-po-me-ne! You will see. He will go away. "Guzzle your fill, ye gloomy Intelligences!"—a poem by Béranger. Yes, sir, he will find himself a place where there's no—no—

The Baron. Where there's nothing, Your Highness?

The Actor. Yes, nothing. This hole will be my grave, weak and infirm I die! Why do you live—why?

The Baron. You there, Edmund Kean or the Debauched Genius, don't yell so loud!

The Actor. I'll yell if I want to!

Nastya [raising her head from the table, flings out her arms]. Yell as much as you please! Let them all hear!

The Baron. What's the sense of it, my lady?

Satin. Leave them alone, Baron. To hell with them! Let them shout. Let them smash their heads in, if they like. There is some sense in it. Don't interfere with people, as the old man used to say. Yes, it's he, that piece of old yeast, who's soured our dear fellow lodgers.

Kleshch. Beckoned them to go somewhere, but didn't show them the way.

The Baron. The old man's a charlatan.

Nastya. You're wrong. You're a charlatan yourself.

The Baron. Shurrup, my lady!

Kleshch. He didn't like truth, the old man didn't. Aye, he was very much against it—and rightly so! For what's the use of truth here? Even without it we can hardly breathe. Take the Prince there—had his arm crushed at work. He'll have to have it amputated, I expect. There's the truth for you!

Satin [striking the table with his fist]. Shut up, you brutes! You fools! Not another word about the old man! [*More calmly.*] You, Baron, are the worst of all. You don't understand a thing and—you talk a lot of nonsense. The old man is not a charlatan. What is truth? Man—that is truth! He understood this. You don't. You've as much intelligence as a brick wall. I understand the old man. He told you lies, but that was out of pity for you, damn and blast your guts! There are lots of people who tell lies out of pity for their fellow men. I know. I've read about it. They lie beautifully, excitingly, with a sort of inspiration. There is such a thing as a lie that comforts and reconciles you to your lot. A lie that justifies the heavy piece of iron that crushes a workman's hand and—and condemns those who are starving. I know what a lie means. Those who are weak in spirit and those who live on what others produce by the sweat of their brows—they need lies, the weak as a support and the others as a screen. But he who is his own master, who is independent, who does not batten on his neighbors—he has no use for lies. A lie is the creed of slaves and masters—truth is the god of the free man!

The Baron. Bravo! Well put! I agree with you entirely. You speak like a decent man.

Satin. Why shouldn't a cardsharper sometimes speak well if honest men speak like cardsharpers? Ah, yes, I've forgotten a lot, but there's still something I do know. The old man? He's an intelligent fellow. He had the same effect on me as acid on an old dirty coin. Let's drink to his health! Fill the glasses!

NASTYA *pours out a glass of beer and hands it to* SATIN.

Satin [*with a smile*]. Whatever the old man does or says is part of his own experience of life. He looks upon everything with his own eyes. Once I asked him, "Grandpa, what do people live for?" [*Tries to imitate* LUKA's *voice and mannerisms.*] "Why, my dear fellow, people live in the hope of something better. Now, let's say, there are carpenters in the world and all of them are just trash. Then one day a carpenter is born among them the like of whom has never been seen on earth. He surpasses them all and there is no equal to him. He leaves his unmistakable imprint on all his trade and advances it twenty years at one go. In the same way all the rest—locksmiths, shoemakers and other workmen as well as peasants and even the gentry live in the hope of a better life. Everyone thinks that he's living for himself alone but, as a matter of fact, he lives in the hope of something better. For a hundred years and perhaps even longer they live for a happier mankind."

NASTYA *stares intently at* SATIN's *face.* KLESHCH *stops working on the concertina and also listens.* THE BARON, *his head bowed low, drums quietly on the table with his fingers.* THE ACTOR, *leaning over from the stove, tries to lower himself cautiously onto the bunk.*

Satin. "Everyone, my dear fellow, everyone in the world lives in the hope of something better. And that is why, you see, we must show consideration to every human being.

We must respect every human being. For how do we know who he really is, why he was born and what he could do? Perhaps he was born to bring us happiness, for our greater benefit. And more especially we must show consideration to children, to little children. Children need a lot of elbowroom. Never interfere with their lives. Be considerate to little children!" [*Laughs softly. Pause.*]

The Baron [*thoughtfully*]. Mmmm . . . yes. In the hope of something better? That—er—reminds me of my family. An old family, going back to the time of Catherine the Great. Noblemen, swashbucklers, French emigrés, they served in the Russian army and civil service, kept rising higher and higher. In the reign of Nicholas the First my grandfather, Gustave de Bille, held a high post. Rich as Croesus he was, hundreds of serfs, horses, cooks. . . .

Nastya. You're just making it up. It isn't true.

The Baron [*jumping up*]. I beg your pardon! Well, go on.

Nastya. It isn't true!

The Baron [*shouts*]. A house in Moscow! A house in Petersburg! Carriages—carriages with—coats of arms!

KLESHCH *takes his concertina and withdraws to a corner from where he watches the scene.*

Nastya. Not true!

The Baron. Shurrup! I say—dozens of footmen!

Nastya [*with relish*]. N-not true!

The Baron. I'll kill you!

Nastya [*getting ready to run off*]. There were no carriages!

Satin. Stop it, Nastya. Don't tease him.

The Baron. One moment, you trash! My grandfather—

Nastya. You had no grandfather! There was nothing!

SATIN *bursts out laughing.*

The Baron [*exhausted by his outburst, sits down on the bench*]. Satin, will you please tell that whore—I see, you're laughing, too, are you? You—you don't believe me, either? [*Screams in despair, banging the table with his fists.*] It is true, damnation take you!

Nastya [*triumphantly*]. Oh, so you're howling now, are

354 MAXIM GORKY [ACT IV

you? Understand now what it feels like when nobody believes you?

Kleshch [going back to the table]. I was afraid there was going to be a fight.

The Tartar. Oh, people big fools. Very bad.

The Baron. I won't allow anyone to make a fool of me! I have proofs, documents, damn you!

Satin. Throw them away. And forget all about your grandfather's carriages. You won't go far in a carriage of the past.

The Baron. All the same, how dare she!

Nastya. Well, I never! How dare I, indeed!

Satin. You see, she does dare. How is she any worse than you? Although in her past she had neither carriages nor a grandfather and not even a father and mother. . . .

The Baron [calming down]. Damn you, you can reason calmly. I'm afraid I—I haven't enough will power.

Satin. Get some. It's a useful commodity. [*Pause.*] Nastya, have you been visiting the hospital?

Nastya. What for?

Satin. To see Natasha.

Nastya. You're too late, I'm afraid. She left hospital ages ago. Left it and—disappeared. Can't be found anywhere.

Satin. Well, that means she's gone for good.

Kleshch. It will be interesting to see who's going to get the better of whom—Vassily of Vassilisa or the other way around.

Nastya. Vassilisa will wriggle out of it. She's shrewd. And Vassily will be sent to Siberia.

Satin. For killing a man in a fight? He'll just get a prison sentence.

Nastya. A pity. Siberia would be much better. I wish you'd all be packed off to Siberia or swept like dirt into some hole!

Satin [surprised]. What's the matter with you? Gone off your head?

The Baron. I'll box her ears for being so impertinent!

Nastya. Just you try to touch me!

The Baron. I shall!

Satin. Leave her alone. Don't touch her. Don't hurt

any man's feelings. Can't get that old man out of my head! [*Laughs.*] Don't hurt a man's feelings! And what if my feelings had been hurt once and so deeply, too, that I couldn't forget it for the rest of my life? What then? Forgive? Never! I wouldn't forgive anyone!

The Baron [*to* Nastya]. Please understand once and for all that you're not to put yourself on the same footing as me. You're trash!

Nastya. Oh, you wretch! Why, you're living off me like a worm off an apple!

Unanimous outburst of laughter by the men.

Kleshch. Oh, what a fool! An apple!

The Baron. You just can't be angry with her. She's an idiot!

Nastya. You're laughing, are you? Oh, no, you're not amused. You're only pretending.

The Actor [*gloomily*]. Let them have it!

Nastya [*picks up a cup from the table and throws it on the floor*]. If I could, I'd smash you all like that!

The Tartar. Why break crockery? Oh, you silly chump!

The Baron [*getting up*]. That's enough. I'm going to teach her manners now!

Nastya [*running away*]. Go to hell, all of you!

Satin [*calling after her*]. Don't be silly! Who are you trying to scare? What is it all about, anyway?

Nastya. Wolves! I hope you'll all die in a ditch! Wolves! [*Goes out.*]

The Actor [*gloomily*]. Amen!

The Tartar. Ugh, bad woman—Russian woman! Impudent—does what she damn like! Tartar woman—no! Tartar woman knows law.

Kleshch. What she wants is a good hiding.

The Baron. The b-bitch!

Kleshch [*testing the concertina*]. It's ready, but no sign of its owner. The lad's having a high time, I suppose.

Satin. Have a drink.

Kleshch. I don't mind if I do. Time to turn in, too.

Satin. Getting used to us?

Kleshch [*drinks, then goes to his bunk*]. I suppose so. There are decent folks everywhere. At first you don't notice it, but after a while you realize that folks are decent on the whole. They're all right.

THE TARTAR *spreads out some rags over his bunk, kneels and prays.*

The Baron [*to* SATIN, *pointing at* THE TARTAR]. Look!

Satin. Leave him alone. He's a good fellow. Don't interfere with him. [*Laughs.*] I'm feeling very benevolent today. Damned if I know why.

The Baron. You're always benevolent when you're drunk. And intelligent.

Satin. When I'm drunk I like everything. Yes, sir. He's praying? That's fine! A man may believe or not believe— that's his own affair. Man's free—he pays for everything himself: for his belief, for his unbelief, for his love, for his intelligence—he pays for everything himself and that is why he's free! Man, that's the truth! What is man? It's not you or I or they—no, sir! It's you, I, they, Napoleon, Mahomet—all in one! [*Traces a man's figure in the air.*] Understand? It's tremendous. In this is the beginning and the end of everything. . . . Everything is in man and everything is for man. Only man exists—the rest is merely the work of his hands and his brain! Man! why, it's—magnificent! It sounds so—so noble! M-man! Man must be respected. He mustn't be pitied. He mustn't be humiliated by being pitied—he must be respected! Let's drink to man, Baron! [*Rises.*] It's good to feel that you're a man. I'm a convict, a murderer, a cardsharper— granted! When I walk down the street people look upon me as a crook, they get out of my way and look back over their shoulders at me and—and often say to me, "Scoundrel! Charlatan! Why don't you work?" Work? What for? To fill my belly? [*Laughs.*] I always despised people whose main concern is filling their bellies. . . . That's not what matters, Baron! That's not what matters! Man is above that. Man is above the desire to have a square meal!

The Baron [*shaking his head*]. You can reason things out. That's fine. I suppose it makes you feel good. I'm afraid I'm incapable of it—don't know how to. [*Looks around and then, softly, guardedly.*] You see, my dear fel-

low, sometimes I—I'm frightened. Understand? I get into
a panic because—well—what next? It can't go on like
this, can it?

Satin [*pacing up and down*]. Nonsense! What's a man
to be afraid of?

The Baron. You see, as far as I can remember, there's
always been a sort of fog in my head. I've never been able
to understand anything. I—I always feel sort of embarrassed. I have an odd feeling that all my life I've done
nothing but change clothes. Why? Why? I can't understand. I studied—wore the uniform of the Noblemen's
Institute—but what exactly was I studying? Can't remember. Got married, put on a frock coat, then changed
into a dressing gown—but the woman I married was no
good. Why? Can't understand. Squandered everything I
possessed—went about in an old gray jacket and a pair of
faded trousers, but how I went broke I never noticed.
Served in the Inland Revenue Department—wore a uniform, a cap with a cockade—embezzled government funds
—they put a convict's clothes on me and—now I'm wearing this. . . . And it all happened as in a dream. . . .
Funny, isn't it?

Satin. Not very. Stupid, rather, I'd say.

The Baron. Yes, I think so, too. But, look here, I must
have been born for some purpose, mustn't I?

Satin [*laughing*]. I suppose so. A man is born in the
hope of something better! [*Nodding.*] Yes—that's right!

The Baron. That little slut Nastya! Ran away! Where
could she be, do you think? I'd better go and see. After
all, she is— [*Goes out. Pause.*]

The Actor. I say, Tartar! [*Pause.*] Prince!

THE TARTAR *turns his head.*

The Actor. Pray—for me. . . .

The Tartar. What?

The Actor [*lowering his voice*]. Pray—for me!

The Tartar [*after a short pause*]. Pray yourself. . . .

The Actor [*climbs down the stove hurriedly, goes up to
the table, pours himself out a drink with a shaking hand,
drinks and almost runs to the passage*]. I'm off!

Satin. Hey you, sikambre, where are you off to? [*Whistles.*]

MEDVEDEV, *dressed in a quilted woman's jacket, comes in, followed by* BUBNOV; *both are a little tipsy.* BUBNOV *carries a bunch of twisted buns in one hand and in the other a couple of smoked fish, a bottle of vodka under one arm and another in his coat pocket.*

Medvedev. A camel is a kind of donkey—only without ears.

Bubnov. Don't be silly! You're a kind of donkey yourself.

Medvedev. A camel has no ears at all—he—er—hears with his nostrils.

Bubnov [*to* SATIN]. My friend, I've been looking for you in all the pubs and pothouses. Take a bottle—my hands are full.

Satin. Put the buns on the table, and then you'll have a hand free.

Bubnov. Thanks—thanks a lot. Never thought of that myself. Look, copper, look! See him? A clever fellow, ain't he?

Medvedev. Crooks are all clever—I know. They can't do without brains. An honest man is all right even if he's a fool, but a dishonest one must have brains. But you're wrong about the camel. He's a beast of burden. He has no horns. No teeth, either, for that matter.

Bubnov. Where are they all? Why isn't there anyone here? Hey, come out, all of you! The drinks are on me! Who's over there in the corner?

Satin. How much longer will your money last, do you think? Spending it all on drink as you do. Scarecrow!

Bubnov. Not very much longer. This time I've only saved up a little bit. Zob! Where's Zob?

Kleshch [*walking up to the table*]. He isn't here.

Bubnov. Rrrrh. . . . Rover! Gobble-gobble-gobble! Turkey-cock! Don't bark and don't gobble. Drink, make merry and don't look so glum. Everything's on me, I like treating people. If I was rich, I—I'd open a free-for-all pub! Damned if I wouldn't! With a band and a choir, a big choir. Come, everyone, drink, eat, listen to the music—cast away care! You're poor? You're a beggar? Well, come right in—into my free-for-all pub! Satin, I'd like—I'd rather. . . . Here, take half of my cash!

Satin. You'd better give me all you have now.

Bubnov. My entire capital? Now? Here, take it. One ruble—here's a twenty-kopeck piece, a few odd coppers—that's all!

Satin. Splendid! It'll be safer with me. I'll gamble with it. . . .

Medvedev. I'm the witness—the money's been given for safekeeping—how much in all?

Bubnov. You? You're a camel. We don't want no witnesses.

Alyoshka [comes in barefoot]. Fellows, I've got my feet wet.

Bubnov. Come and wet your whistle. That's enough! My dear lad, you sing and you play—that's lovely! But drink—no! It's no good. Drink's bad for a man.

Alyoshka. I can tell that by looking at you! It's only when you're drunk that you look like a human being. Kleshch, have you mended my concertina? [Sings and dances.]

> Oh, if my stupid face
> Hadn't been so handsome,
> You'd have jilted me, my love,
> And I'd have been so lonesome!

Oh, I'm frozen stiff, fellows! It's so c-cold!

Medvedev. Mmmm. . . . And may I ask who your love is?

Bubnov. Leave him alone. Don't forget, my dear fellow, that you've been sacked. No longer a copper—finished! Neither a copper nor an uncle.

Alyoshka. Just Auntie's husband!

Bubnov. One of your nieces is in jail and the other's dying. . . .

Medvedev [haughtily]. Nonsense! She's not dying, she's missing!

SATIN *bursts out laughing.*

Bubnov. Makes no difference. A man without nieces is no uncle.

Alyoshka. Your Excellency, drummer of the retired goats' brigade!

My sweetheart has money,
Not a penny have I,
But my heart's gay and merry,
Oh, a cheerful lad am I!

C-cold!

*ZOB comes in; from now on until the final curtain a few
more men and women drift in, undress and lie down on
the bunks, muttering.*

Zob. Bubnov, what did you run off for?

Bubnov. Come here, sit down. Let's have a singsong,
fellow-me-lad. My favorite song, ah?

The Tartar. Night—must sleep. Sing song daytime.

Satin. Never mind, Prince. You'd better come over here.

Tartar. Never mind, you say? There's going be noise.
When people sing there's noise.

Bubnov [*crossing over to* THE TARTAR]. How's your
hand, Prince? They haven't cut it off yet, have they?

The Tartar. What for? Plenty time. Perhaps never cut
off. Hand's not iron—cut off quick enough.

Zob. You're in a bad way, Hassan. You're no damned
good for anything without a hand. It's by having hands
and backs that the likes of us are of any value. Lose your
hand and you're no longer a man. You're in a proper mess,
pal! Come and have a drink—and to hell with it all!

Kvashnya [*comes in*]. Good evening, dear lodgers! Oh,
isn't it just perishing outside? Snow, slush. . . . Is my
policeman here? Copper!

Medvedev. Here!

Kvashnya. Wearing my jacket again? And you're a bit
—er—merry, ain't you? What's the idea?

Medvedev. We're celebrating Bubnov's birthday, my
dear. And, besides, it's cold—snow, slush. . . .

Kvashnya. You'd better look out—slush, indeed! None
of that nonsense, d'you hear? Off to bed with you!

Medvedev [*goes into kitchen*]. Well, I'm rather sleepy,
I admit. Aye, time to turn in.

Satin. You're a bit strict with him, aren't you?

Kvashnya. That's the only way, love. You must be strict
with a man like him. I've married him because I thought
he'd be of some use to me, seeing as how he's a military

man and you're such a rough lot, and me only a woman. And now he starts drinking! That's not of much use to me, is it?

Satin. You've got yourself a bad partner, I'm afraid.

Kvashnya. Couldn't get a better one, love. You wouldn't live with me, would you? Too much of a gentleman! And even if you did, it wouldn't last more than a week—you'd gamble me away at cards, me and all my tripe. . . .

Satin [*laughs*]. Most certainly would gamble you away. . . . Yes, true enough, landlady!

Kvashnya. There you are! Alyoshka!

Alyoshka. Here! That's me!

Kvashnya. What sort of tales are you spreading about me?

Alyoshka. Me? All sorts. Honestly. There's a marvelous woman for you. Meat, fat, bones—fourteen stone of it, but not an ounce of brains.

Kvashnya. You're exaggerating a bit there, I'm afraid. I've got a lot of brains—enough and to spare! What I mean is—why do you go about saying that I beat my policeman?

Alyoshka. I'm sorry, I thought you did when you pulled him by the hair.

Kvashnya [*laughing*]. Fool! You ought to pretend not to see. We mustn't wash our dirty linen in public, must we? And, besides, it hurts his feelings and that's why he's taken to drink.

Alyoshka. So it's true what they say! Even a hen likes vodka.

SATIN *and* KLESHCH *roar with laughter.*

Kvashnya. Oh, you whippersnapper! What sort of a man are you anyway, Alyoshka?

Alyoshka. A first-rate man, ma'am! A Jack of all trades! What I sees, I wants!

Bubnov [*beside* THE TARTAR's *bunk*]. Come on, we won't let you sleep, anyway! We'll be singing all night. Zob!

Zob. Sing? All right.

Alyoshka. And I'll accompany you.

Satin. Let's hear how good you are!

The Tartar [*smiling*]. Well, Bubnov, old devil, bring the vodka! We'll drink, we'll be merry, when death come, we'll die.

Bubnov. Fill his glass, Satin. Zob, sit down. Well, my dear fellows, a man doesn't need much, does he? I've had a drink and I'm happy! Zob, start my favorite one! I'll sing and I'll weep. . . .

Zob [*begins to sing*].

　　　　　Day by day the sun comes up—

Bubnov [*joining in*].

　　　　　But my prison is dark and drear . . .

　　　　　The front door opens quickly.

The Baron [*in the doorway, shouts*]. I say, come here, come here, quick! There—in the back yard—the actor— he has hanged himself!

Silence. They all stare at The Baron. Nastya *appears behind his back and slowly, her eyes wide open, walks to the table.*

Satin [*in an undertone*]. Damn—ruined the song—the fool!!

Curtain.

THE MERMAID SERIES

THE MERMAID SERIES of English dramatists was the brain-child of a twenty-six year old medical student, later a famous sexologist. "At that time," Havelock Ellis writes in his autobiography,* speaking of the year 1886, "it happened that a London publisher, Henry Vizetelly, was conspicuous by the way in which he had published fairly literal translations of the chief contemporary French novelists. My friend Eleanor Marx Aveling [daughter of Karl Marx] had translated *Madame Bovary* for him, and he had issued translations—it is true by no means always literal—of a large number of Zola's novels. He had himself been a distinguished journalist in earlier days, he was familiar with France, and he was really engaged in a quite honorable and useful work. It occurred to me that a series of volumes of the best plays, unexpurgated, of the Elizabethan dramatists—for which I devised at the suggestion of Beaumont's poem the name Mermaid Series—would be an excellent scheme for Vizetelly to undertake. I had no idea of proposing myself for editor, and indeed could hardly feel competent for the post. I wrote to Vizetelly putting the scheme before him, and almost by return of post he replied accepting it, asking me to undertake the work of general editor, and inquiring what remuneration I would wish to receive. Such a proposal seemed too tempting for a young unknown man to put aside, whatever his disabilities, and even though he was in the midst of training for an arduous profession. I accepted with alacrity, and speedily repaired, so far as I could, my incompetence. I knew nothing as to what fees a general editor was entitled, and the sum I asked (three guineas per volume) was, no doubt, too small . . . I selected the dramatists, the space to be devoted to each, and I chose the editors [though Vizetelly told Ellis that he needed 'one or two names of mark' to launch the project] cooperating in their work, besides myself editing Marlowe, Middleton, Ford and Porter. . . ." Ellis goes on to describe the bowdlerizing of the Baines note at the hands of his publisher and assorted associates—including, surprisingly enough, Swinburne and Symonds.†

Ellis then relates how Vizetelly was sent to jail as the publisher of that famous pornographer, Emile Zola; and how, soon afterwards, he died. At this point, Ellis continues, "the Mermaid Series was taken over [by T. Fisher Unwin, a publisher], without any word of explanation or apology to me, or any word of protest from me, though I do not flatter myself he [Unwin] knew that my silence was contempt. I was well aware that for a publisher the editor of a series is an insignificant figure even though he may be altogether responsible for its conception, mainly responsible for its production, and largely responsible for its success. I had, of course, arranged for volumes ahead, many of them nearly ready for publication; the editors of these were equally disregarded by the new publisher. . . . The Mermaid Series swiftly passed away so far as I was concerned, and languished to death after it was taken out of my hands. But it was not superseded. I am pleased to be assured—as I revise these lines some forty years later, a paper on 'Havelock Ellis and the English Drama' comes to

* *My Life*, by Havelock Ellis. Quoted by permission of the publisher, Houghton Mifflin Co.

† Instigated, as Houston Peterson tells in his life of Ellis, by the protest of "a well-meaning woman" but put through with rather hysterical despatch by Vizetelly.

hand, written by a devoted student of the drama, Montague Summers
—that 'the Mermaid Series remains a magnificent service rendered to
the English drama, a pioneer work, a work that demanded courage,
scholarship, and enthusiasm.' "

In 1917, the firm of T. Fisher Unwin arranged for publication of
the Mermaid Series in the United States by Charles Scribner's Sons.
In 1926 Unwin was absorbed by Ernest Benn Limited who continued
supplying Scribner's with the Mermaid volumes until 1945. After the
Second World War some 12 of the Mermaid volumes were re-issued
in London by Ernest Benn Limited and A. A. Wyn Incorporated in
New York. On this occasion, the Curator of the Brander Matthews
Dramatic Museum at Columbia University (Henry W. Wells) wrote:
"If a class of students in our century was to know the Elizabethan
drama through any more attractive medium than an anthology, this
series provided the almost certain means. Earlier editions . . . were
directed to . . . British gentlemen. The new library . . . was addressed to a very much larger and democratic public. It always sold
well in America. Yet one by one these books went out of print. . . .
The gradual strangulation of the Mermaid Series seemed a mark of
doom upon the popular success of Elizabethan studies themselves. . . .
But lovers of the most humane movement in all English literature
have at present cause for congratulation . . . the Mermaid Series is
being re-issued." But the price of this 1948-49 hard-back edition was
beyond the means of the academic and democratic public Mr. Wells
speaks about. The necessary next step was to issue the books—completely reset—in paper-back form at little more than one dollar each.

It also seemed high time to continue the work itself where Ellis, so
long ago, had left off. In 1887 were issued the Marlowe, the Dekker,
the Congreve, Middleton Volume I, and Massinger Volume I. In 1888
followed Heywood, Ford, Shirley, Wycherley, Otway, Webster and
Tourneur, and an anthology entitled *Nero and Other Plays;* in 1889-90,
the second volumes of Middleton and Massinger, respectively. In the
nineties came Steele, Chapman, Vanbrugh, and three volumes of Jonson.
In the nineteen-hundreds, Shadwell, Farquhar, Greene, and two volumes each of Dryden and Beaumont & Fletcher. The rest was silence.*

In addition to reprinting the original Mermaids, Hill and Wang Inc.
is issuing several new Mermaids a year.

As published by Hill and Wang Inc., the Mermaid Series is a section
of a still larger series, *Dramabooks,* which also includes books old and
new *about* theatre and drama. The Advisory Editor of Dramabooks as
a whole is Eric Bentley.

The Publishers

---

* Ellis's editors—aside from those whose work never appeared—were Alexander
C. Ewald, H. P. Horne, Edmund Gosse, Roden Noel, Ernest Rhys, A. C. Swin-
burne, John Addington Symonds, Arthur Symons, A. W. Verity, and W. C. Ward.
The choice of editors after 1890 was presumably made by T. Fisher Unwin. Those
chosen were: G. A. Aitken, William Archer, T. H. Dickinson, C. H. Herford,
Brinsley Nicholson, William Lyon Phelps, George Saintsbury, J. St. Loe Strachey,
A. E. H. Swaen.

DRAMABOOKS

Hill and Wang has established DRAMABOOKS as a permanent library of the great classics of the theatre of all countries, in an attractive, low-priced format.

PLAYS

MD 1   *Christopher Marlowe* edited by Havelock Ellis. Introduction by John Addington Symonds
(Tamburlaine the Great, Parts I & II, Doctor Faustus, The Jew of Malta, Edward the Second)

MD 2   *William Congreve* edited by Alexander Charles Ewald. Introduction by Macaulay (Complete Plays)

MD 3   *Webster and Tourneur* Introduction by John Addington Symonds
(The White Devil, The Duchess of Malfi, The Atheist's Tragedy, The Revenger's Tragedy)

MD 4   *John Ford* edited by Havelock Ellis
(The Lover's Melancholy, 'Tis Pity She's a Whore, The Broken Heart, Love's Sacrifice, Perkin Warbeck)

MD 5   *Richard Brinsley Sheridan* edited with an Introduction by Louis Kronenberger
(The Rivals, St. Patrick's Day, The Duenna, A Trip to Scarborough, The School for Scandal, The Critic)

MD 6   *Camille and Other Plays* edited, with an Introduction to the well-made play by Stephen S. Stanton
(Scribe: A Peculiar Position, and The Glass of Water; Sardou: A Scrap of Paper; Dumas, *fils*: Camille; Augier: Olympe's Marriage)

MD 7   *John Dryden* edited, and with an Introduction by George Saintsbury
(The Conquest of Granada, Parts I & II, Marriage à la Mode, Aureng-Zebe)

MD 8   *Ben Jonson* edited, with an Introduction and Notes, by Brinsley Nicholson and C. H. Herford
(Volpone, Epicoene, The Alchemist)

MD 9   *Oliver Goldsmith* edited by George Pierce Baker with an Introduction by Austin Dobson
(The Good Natur'd Man, She Stoops to Conquer, An Essay on the Theatre, A Register of Scotch Marriages)

MD 10   *Jean Anouilh* Volume 1
(Antigone, Eurydice, The Rehearsal, Romeo and Jeannette, The Ermine)

MD 11   *Let's Get a Divorce! and Other Plays,* edited, and with an Introduction on The Psychology of Farce by Eric Bentley
(Labiche: A Trip Abroad, and Célimare; Sardou: Let's Get a Divorce!; Courteline, These Cornfields; Feydeau: Keep an Eye on Amélie; Prévert: A United Family; Achard: essay on Feydeau)